NF

UNIVERSAL BANKING IN THE TWENTIETH CENTURY

Universal Banking in the Twentieth Century

Finance, Industry and the State in North and Central Europe

Edited by

Alice Teichova
Emeritus Professor of Economic History
University of East Anglia
and Honorary Fellow
Girton College, Cambridge, UK

Terry Gourvish
Director, Business History Unit
The London School of Economics and Political Science, UK

Agnes Pogány
Economics University of Budapest
Hungary

Edward Elgar

332,1094
U58

Published by
Edward Elgar Publishing Limited
Gower House
Croft Road
Aldershot
Hants GU11 3HR
England

Edward Elgar Publishing Company
Old Post Road
Brookfield
Vermont 05036
USA

British Library Cataloguing in Publication Data
Universal Banking in the Twentieth
Century: Finance, Industry and the State
in North and Central Europe
   I. Teichova, Alice
   332.1094

Library of Congress Cataloguing in Publication Data
Universal banking in the twentieth century: finance, industry and
   the state in north and central Europe / edited by Alice Teichova, Terry
   Gourvish, Agnes Pogány; [contributors, Philip L. Cottrell ... et
   al.].
      p.   cm.
      1. Banks and banking—Europe. 2. Finance—Europe. 3. Europe–
   Industries. 4. Banks and banking—Europe—Government policy.
   I. Teichova, Alice. II. Gourvish, T.R. (Terence Richard)
   III. Pogány, Agnes. IV. Cottrell, P.L.
   HO2974.U64   1994
   332.1'094—dc20   94–12101

ISBN 1 85278 977 8
Printed and Bound in Great Britain by
Hartnolls Limited, Bodmin, Cornwall.

Contents

PART IV   BANKERS AND BANK–INDUSTRY NETWORKS

Tables and figures

Contributors

Philip L. Cottrell, PhD, Professor of Economic History, University of Leicester, UK

Margarita Dritsas, PhD, Associate Professor of Economic History, University of Crete, Greece

Peter Eigner, Mag, Lecturer, University of Vienna, Austria

Gertrude Enderle-Burcel, PhD, Senior Research Associate, Austrian State Archives, Vienna, Austria

Jozef Faltus, PhD, Ing, CSc, Professor of Economic History, Economics University, Bratislava, Slovak Republic

Terry Gourvish, PhD, FRHistS, Director, Business History Unit, The London School of Economics and Political Science, London, UK

Jan Hájek, PhD, CSc, Research Fellow, Institute of History, Czech Academy of Sciences, Prague, Czech Republic

Per H. Hansen, PhD, Lecturer, Odense University, Denmark

Sverre Knutsen, PhD, Lecturer, Norwegian School of Management, Sandvika, Norway

Vlastislav Lacina, PhD, CSc, Research Fellow, Historical Institute, Czech Academy of Sciences, Prague, Czech Republic

Even Lange, PhD, Professor of Economic History, Norwegian School of Management, Sandvika, Norway

Ragnhild Lundström, PhD, Professor of Economic History, University of Uppsala, Sweden

Alois Mosser, PhD, Professor of Economic History, Economics University, Vienna, Austria

Charlotte Natmeßnig, Research Student, University of Vienna, Austria

Jan Ottosson, PhD, Research Associate, Department of Economic History, Uppsala University, Sweden

Agnes Pogány, PhD, Lecturer, Economics University of Budapest, Hungary

Franjo Štiblar, PhD, Professor of Economics, University of Ljubljana, Ljubljana, Slovenia

Dieter Stiefel, PhD (Economics University Vienna) and PhD (University of Vienna), Professor of Economic History, University of Vienna, Austria

Zoltán Szász, PhD, Research Fellow, Institute of History, Hungarian Academy of Sciences, Budapest, Hungary

Alice Teichova, PhD, CSc, Dr.h.c., Em. Professor of Economic History, University of East Anglia, Honorary Fellow, Girton College, Cambridge, and Visiting Research Associate, Business History Unit, The London School of Economics and Political Science, London, UK

Désirée D. Verdonk, PhD, Research Associate, Economics University, Vienna, Austria

Introduction

A. Teichova
T. Gourvish
A. Pagány

The studies presented in this volume deal with the many facets of banking as an integral part of the operation of European capitalist market economies in the twentieth century. Scandinavian and Central European countries were selected for study because of the high degree of comparability and quantifiability both in terms of the level of industrialization and the pace of economic growth.

While each of the economies studied exhibited unique characteristics, there were also striking similarities in the way bank–industry relations developed in the several countries of Central Europe and Scandinavia from the turn of the century. These similarities can be found in the activity of commercial and savings banks in financial markets, bank shareholdings, and the conversion of short-term advances by repeated renewals into long-term loans. Above all, they can be found in the remarkable continuity of ties between banks and the industrial companies clustering around them, a process which created *Konzern*, or banking industrial groups, as well as long-term and unbroken personal relationships between bankers and industrialists.

The authors of this volume produce evidence that the historical role of the banks in utilizing domestic and foreign financial resources was in the main a function of the relatively slow penetration of financial markets in the business activities of the regions studied. With the exception of the UK and France, this type of banking became prevalent in continental Europe from the 1880s and a close relationship between industrial companies and the banks was established everywhere, although there were differences in the evolving relationship in each country. Indeed, these relationships have survived and they continue to influence the credit-financing of industry.

The geographical diffusion of universal banking across Europe both accompanied and furthered the rapid parallel rise of large-scale enterprise, of national and international cartels and of other monopolistic and oligopolistic organizations. In this process commercial banks, as an integral part of the capital market in Sweden and in Central Europe, played a crucial role in financing industry (Lundström, Lange, Hájek, Chapters 1–3). In both areas the symbiotic relationship between banks and industry which was inherited from the pre-1914 period had a decisive impact on the inflation and crisis-prone interwar years (Hansen, Knutsen, Lacina, Chapters 6, 7 and 10).

However, empirical results revealed marked differences. A hitherto neglected but politically and economically powerful factor in the financing of industry by banks in Central Europe was the 'national question'. Sources for Czech, Slovak and Slovenian banks show that in their competition with the leading Vienna and Budapest banks they employed the tactics of the 'national' approach to recruit clients, while in Budapest in particular, legal measures were considered by the government to contain the growth of Slav financial institutions (Hájek, Szász, Štiblar, Faltus, Chapters 3, 4, 5 and 11).

Competition, backed up by state intervention to strengthen the Czech financial element in the new Czechoslovak Republic, was carried into the post-1918 period through 'nostrification', i.e. by severing ownership links with Vienna and Budapest banking and business enterprise and replacing them with Czechoslovak or West European allied finance and business (Lacina, Faltus, Chapters 10 and 11).

In Sweden the banks' sphere of influence in industry, which had crystallized during the 1910s, weathered both the crisis of the early 1920s and the impact of the world economic crisis in the 1930s. They also showed comparative stability during the intensive merger movement of the interwar period (Lundström, Chapter 1), in contrast to the situation in Norway (Lange, Knutsen, Chapters 2 and 7).

Yet the opposite was the case in Austria and Hungary. In the context of Central Europe economic conditions were powerfully influenced by the dissolution of the Austro-Hungarian Empire and the postwar hyperinflation (Natmeßnig, Cottrell, Pogány, Chapters 8, 13 and 16).

The banks, and above all the big Viennese institutions, had acquired large amounts of shares during the inflation of the early 1920s and when prices collapsed in the wake of the excessive speculation of the mid-1920s (Cottrell, Chapter 13) and the world economic crisis in the 1930s their illiquidity led to insolvency and mergers. In Austria the most spectacular banking crash of the interwar period occurred with the insolvency of the Österreichische Creditanstalt für Handel und Gewerbe in 1931 which was followed by the tightest state-aided bank mergers which forced the economy into a shrinking process – known as 'austrification' – and practically into a one-bank system (Stiefel, Chapter 13).

Empirical studies in this volume address a largely neglected aspect which nevertheless has affected the path bank–industry relations have taken in different countries where the state has intervened through legislation. The role of company and banking laws in modern times is not merely a legislative but a highly political one. There exist great differences in this sphere between individual countries.

In Scandinavian countries banking legislation was introduced which was often regarded as a model for legislation elsewhere. To a large extent it focused on the elimination of unsound banking practices (Lundström, Hansen, Knutsen, Chapters 1, 6 and 7). Indeed speculation in financial markets could not be fully controlled even by Swedish legislation (the Kreuger crash is an example of this) because financiers readily adapted formally to legal requirements. Also Swedish banks attempted to circumvent the prohibition of share ownership by banks, yet the existence of legislation and control imposed a certain self-discipline on the activity of bankers. Therefore, the effect of legislation on bank behaviour and on stock exchange dealings was found to be relevant to the Austrian case where no effective legislation existed in spite of moves to introduce proposals for banking laws in parliament. Even after the big bank crash in 1931 and the state's role as the lender of last resort to the one big remaining bank – the Creditanstalt – the depleted Austrian banking system survived on public money without granting any control or influence to the state (Enderle-Burcel, Chapter 9).

A quantitative approach is applied to bank–industry relations by Verdonk (Chapter 14) and Pogány (Chapter 16) using a computer program to analyse the credits granted to the customers of universal banks. They present an empirically based picture of the volume and distribution of credits by selected Austrian and Hungarian banks in the interwar years. In this way it has been possible to revise certain widely held assumptions. For instance results showing the geographical distribution of the number and amount of loans to foreign industrial companies in comparison with loans to domestic firms confirm the Southeast European direction of credit flows from Viennese commercial banks. However, they disprove the hypothesis that Viennese banks were too heavily involved in advancing credits to foreign industrial companies and thus adversely affected economic growth in Austria. Further empirical tests, in which credit flows from banks to industry were compared with investment statistics in interwar Austria, point to the historical reality that low investment and a slack reinvestment of profits by industrial firms were of more significance in determining the business climate rather than a lack of bank credit (Mosser, Chapter 15). This qualifies the widely held view that there existed a constant credit squeeze imposed by Austrian banks on the ailing economy.

A further quantifiable aspect is presented in this volume by the incidence of interlocking directorships. While Dritsas (Chapter 17) shows the beginnings of networks between businessmen and banks in industrializing Greece, Ottosson for Sweden (Chapter 18) and Eigner for Austria (Chapter 19) establish that the number of seats which bank directors held on the boards of industrial joint-stock companies or vice versa is not decisive by itself. The application of network programs in both the Swedish and Austrian cases, with special reference to longitudinal development, produces substantial results. Networks of directors in Sweden and Austria reveal great similarities which can be summarized as follows: interlocking directorates increased markedly in the period from before the First World War to the eve of the Second World War; in both countries these networks showed a high degree of stability which remained unbroken over two to three decades; Austrian banks maintained strong links with banks and leading enterprises in the successor states of the former Austro-Hungarian Empire. In this volume the quantitative findings of the network analysis for Sweden and Austria are presented in a coordinated form for the first time.

Evidence produced in this volume establishes that bank mergers were influenced more by competition among commercial banks for 'good' industrial customers rather than by competition among banks for depositors. During the interwar period crisis-induced and state-aided mergers in all the economies discussed in this book led to a decrease in the number of universal banks but at the same time the size of the industrial *Konzerne* (net of dependent companies) of the surviving banks increased as they absorbed the dependent subsidiary companies (i.e. the *Konzern*) of the banks which were taken over.

In conclusion, the editors wish to express their thanks to the funding organizations which supported the research projects, above all, to the Economic and Social Research Council in the UK, the Austrian Ministry of Science and Research, and the Bank of Sweden Tercentenary Foundation. First drafts of the papers in this volume were read at conferences at the Business History Unit, London School of Economics, in September 1991, and at the Budapest School of Economic Sciences, in September 1992. Warm thanks are due to the sponsors of the conferences: in London, the British Academy, British Council, Baring Foundation, Nuffield Foundation and Sir Jeremy Morse; in Budapest, the Hungarian General Credit Bank and the National Bank of Hungary. The editors are also indebted to Mrs Sonia Copeland, who acted as organizer to both conferences.

A. Teichova
T. Gourvish
A. Pogány
Vienna, London and Budapest

PART I

CONTINUITY AND DISCONTINUITY IN HISTORICAL PERSPECTIVE

1 Continuity and change in Swedish banking
Ragnhild Lundström

Sweden
N24
N64
621

Industry

From aggregate figures of industrial production in Sweden one might conclude – as is often done – that the First World War was only a parenthesis in long-run economic development. Structural changes and trends in industrial production visible in the 1920s could be traced back to the decade immediately before the war (see Table 1.1). Thus the war years and the postwar depression might be excluded as a temporary break in those trends and ascribed to the extraordinary conditions that prevailed.

From the middle of the 1920s, Swedish manufacturing developed along the path it had already taken before the war. The mining, metal and engineering industries continued to increase their share of total production – mainly due to the growth of the engineering industry – although at a slower pace than before the war. The structural change of the forest industries which had begun around the turn of the century continued, with a relative stagnation of sawmills (included under Wood industry in Table 1.l) and an increase in pulp and paper production.

Table 1.1   Production in Swedish mining and manufacturing (million SEK at constant 1910–12 prices)

	Mining, metals and engineering	Wood ind.	Pulp & paper	Food ind.	Textiles	All ind.
1911	560	288	205	729	258	2 414
1913	779	209	247	762	309	2 804
1916	1 010	321	278	870	309	3 334
1921	557	187	209	807	193	2 772
1925	942	281	392	857	335	3 419

Source: L. Schön, *Historiska nationalräkenskaper för Sverige. Industri och hantverk 1800–1980* (Lund, 1988).

In the 1920s around 20 per cent of Swedish industrial production was exported, as was the case also before the war. In 1925 half the production in the pulp and paper industry was exported as was 30 per cent of the production in the mining, metal and engineering industries, and similar figures were recorded in the prewar years. As in pre-war years, the Russian market was again the most expansive and promising one for exports of Swedish engineering products.

Although it is true that by the mid-1920s conditions had returned to normal, the war cannot be considered as a mere parenthesis in Swedish industrial development, not even in the long run. On the contrary, the war produced such great changes in the circumstances of Swedish industry – and Swedish business leaders reacted to these changes accordingly – that the effects were to last for a very long time. In certain respects wartime developments established the industrial structure and the enterprise and ownership patterns in Sweden for the remainder of the twentieth century.

During the war, and due to the war, the nascent Swedish engineering industry achieved its real breakthrough. For the new engineering works with specialized production it was no doubt a great advantage that competition from the German engineering industry disappeared, however temporarily. The Swedish engineering industry had at least six years – in some cases longer – to expand both at home and abroad. Even in its home market, the Swedish electrical engineering industry, for example, had earlier had to withstand fierce competition from older, larger and more advanced German firms like Siemens and AEG; during the war they got their much needed breathing space. It is significant that the quotations of ASEA shares fell as soon as there were rumours about peace, and they were rather frequent during the first years of the war.[1] The war also gave a great impetus to SKF. However excellent the SKF ball and roller bearings might have been thought, the company's great expansion in France, the UK and, not least, the United States to a large extent must be attributed to wartime conditions. On the one hand, the competition from the large German ball-bearing industry vanished in these markets; on the other hand, demand increased immensely due to war production. If there had been no war, it is hardly likely that SKF would have had the strength and potential to acquire the whole German ball-bearing industry during the 1920s and to achieve the strong position in the international market that it did later.

During the war years, many Swedish engineering firms experienced vigorous growth. At the beginning of the interwar period, the foundation of their further growth was already laid, and their position in the market already secured.

The war also had long-term effects on economic life in Sweden in many other respects, although perhaps in a more indirect way. The record profits during the war and the sanguine way in which most businessmen and financiers acted during the war boom – admitted that many lacked both experience and foresight – were to cause great problems to Swedish industry and Swedish banks in the early 1920s. Practically all Swedish firms faced problems when prices fell so sharply owing to postwar depression. The situation was aggravated by measures taken by the government and the central bank in order to bring Sweden back to the gold standard at the prewar exchange rate. This meant an appreciation of the Swedish currency and thus rising prices of Swedish export products. To this can be added more specific problems for certain firms and even whole branches of industry, problems that stemmed from conditions caused by the war. This is true of both the Swedish iron and the sawmill industries. Increased demand and rising prices during the war had halted a much needed modernization and structural reorganization, respectively, of activities which were both pillars of early Swedish industrialization. All through the 1920s, in some cases much longer, these industries had to struggle with problems which were actually the result of over optimism during the war.

Industry and banks

From 1911 Sweden was self-supporting with regard to capital, after having been a net capital importer for almost 50 years. Its industrialization was well under way and it already had a fairly well diversified industry, about half capital goods and half consumer goods. The further development of the country's industry and infrastructure could be financed within its own borders. (This fact, however, was not acknowledged and hardly known until the early 1920s when official balance of payments statistics were introduced. Thus the Swedish state placed some fairly large loans on the international capital market as late as 1913.) Exports and imports were nearly in balance and the fast growth of the merchant marine had begun to result in a net income from shipping, which was to increase in subsequent years.

During the war Sweden became a net exporter of capital of rather sizeable amounts, when measured by Swedish standards. There is hardly a school child in Sweden who does not know that during the First World War Sweden could repurchase all its debts to other countries, debts that had been accumulated over half a century. The strongly positive balance of payments during the war was due both to increased exports and net revenue from shipping on the one hand and decreased imports on the other.

In 1915 exports doubled. Many firms that were not used to exporting did so, e.g. woollen and shoe manufacturers who received large orders from the German and Austrian armies. Even pig iron was exported. The largest increases in exports, however, were recorded by firms manufacturing engineering products, and more than half of those exports went to Russia.

In 1915 and 1916 industrial production increased by 20 per cent at constant prices. Some firms, especially within the engineering industry, increased their volume of production much more than this. Many firms reached their maximum production capacity and felt a need to expand. New investments in fixed assets increased considerably in 1917 and continued to increase also in 1918 (see Table 1.2), although at that time the volume of production was already stagnating. If measured at constant prices, exports now decreased, due both to difficulties in shipping because of the war and to the default of the Russian market after the revolution.[2]

Table 1.2   Visible capital formation and financing in joint-stock companies (million SEK)

	1915	1916	1917	1918	1921
Investments	84	338	682	853	−200
Fixed assets	29	81	218	354	104
Stocks	35	177	346	247	−290
Shares	20	80	118	252	−14
Self-financing (profits minus dividends for preceding year)	104	265	250	29	−470
Issuing of new shares	41	123	320	609	79
Existing firms	34	86	255	382	34
New firms	7	37	65	227	45
Increase in Commercial banks'					
Lending	153	420	866	1412	−507
Deposits	204	499	723	1282	−241

Source: Svenska aktiebolags balansräkningar åren 1911–1925 (SOU Statens Offentliga Utredmingar 1929:4); SOS (Sveriges Officiela Statistisk), Uppgifter om bankerna, respective years.

When expanding, industry first turned to the stock market, where at this time it was easy to raise capital. Share prices had started to rise in 1915 and continued to rise at an accelerating speed.

The banks participated in the issuing of new shares in at least two ways. First, they lent money to the purchasers of shares. Lending against shares as collateral increased from around 30 per cent of bank lending in the prewar years to 45 per cent at the end of the war. Second, most banks had also founded issuing houses or investment companies and thus benefited from the profits that were made on the stock market. (Eventually they had to take their share of the losses too.) These new investment companies implied that the share syndicates with close ties to the banks which had prevailed earlier were now institutionalized as joint-stock companies, a development that was made possible by the bank law of 1911 permitting banks to own shares.

It is difficult to say to what extent banks led or followed the expansion in share capital and share loans. From monthly bank statistics it appears, though, as if demand from borrowers preceded the increase in bank deposits during much of 1917. From late autumn in 1917 and until the summer of 1918, however, deposits led the way and lending lagged behind. In order to solve the energy problem the state fuel commission, a wartime institution, bought large quantities of wood from farmers owning forests, and this led to a large increase in bank deposits. With such a sizeable increase in deposits banks were encouraged to initiate new issues of shares in their client firms, or indirectly so through the medium of their issuing houses.

The issuing of new shares increased almost twofold in 1918 (see Table 1.2), at a time when both exports and productive of industrial goods decreased; thus, no imminent need of new production capacity seems to have existed. The merger movement which had begun earlier continued, and this was a kind of business in which the issuing houses were experts. Mergers practically always resulted in an increase of equity and, thus, there was a strong tendency to over-capitalization. The financial assets of joint-stock companies also increased in the form of ownership of shares in other firms (see Table 1.2).

There were already signs of crisis in 1919. Share prices fell and the turnover on the stock exchange decreased to one-third of what it had been the year before. The first effects were felt by the issuing houses and the stockbrokers, whose main assets were shares and whose profits came from trading in shares. Several such firms recorded losses for 1919.

The banks were also affected. Through their close cooperation with issuing houses and because of their large amount of lending to these houses against share collateral, they were in a rather delicate position which hampered their actions when share prices fell. If loans were not renewed, share prices would fall even more. In the Autumn of 1919 some 100 people connected to banks, in most cases as owners of bank shares, founded a firm, the sole purpose of which was to halt the decline in share prices. Large purchases were made of shares in the largest corporations.

At this very time, liquidity in the hitherto very expansive capital goods sector started to deteriorate. Profits had fallen after a peak in 1917, but they were still fairly high. The increase in share capital, through both new and bonus issues, indirectly resulted in lower internal savings (see Table 1.2); although the dividend as such was not raised, the sum total that had to be paid out increased considerably. On the other hand, there was great hesitation about reducing dividends, since such a move was expected to cause further falls in share prices.

During 1920 the liquidity problem for many of the capital goods industries became acute. Large dividends for 1919 had to be paid out from still diminishing profits, and although the companies' stocks in trade were decreased (see Table 1.2) as were their short-term deposits on cheque accounts with banks, they were in need of credit. Since deposits were withdrawn and lending had to be increased lest client firms were to run out of liquid funds, the liquidity of the banks also deteriorated.

Thus, even before the depression of 1921, there were considerable problems in both Swedish business firms and the banks. In 1921, when prices fell by 50 per cent, as did exports, and share prices dwindled to a fraction of their wartime boom level, problems that had been latent ever since 1918 became visible. Firms could not meet their loans and private persons could not put up more collateral when shares lost up to 90 per cent of their value. It was more or less up to the banks to decide who would have to go bankrupt and who would be saved at least from that calamity. To generalize, private borrowers who defaulted were saved from bankruptcy in most cases, their debts being written off against the banks' taking over their shares. There were also other deals, dependent on the future prospects of the person in question. The judgement, however, was made by the banks. Most industrial firms were saved, for several reasons. Some had mortgaged property as collateral, and these were no times to try to sell a factory building. Some were old clients of the bank, and it was considered a loss of prestige on the part of the bank if such firms were forced to liquidate. In many cases the bank exchanged its credit to the firm for shares, placed someone from the bank on the board and set out to 'reconstruct' the firm. Such reconstructions could imply almost any changes except the change of the firm's name. In many other cases, the problems of the firm were considered to be only temporary, and they were solved by permitting it to pay lower interest rates or no interest rates at all for a while, or by granting some years free of loan amortization. In all cases, it meant a closer relationship between the bank and the industrial firm and usually a greater dependence on the bank by the firm in question.

The situation of the early 1920s was not a new one for the banks, though their memories were short. It had been like this after every boom and speculation, at least since the late 1850s: in 1858, in 1878, in 1901, in 1908, and lastly in 1912. In that sense there was a continuity. And it was said in the banks that it usually took around 30 years to get a firm on its feet so that the bank could part from its engagement and sell the shares of the firm on the stock market. This was also to be true this time.

Thus developments during the war laid the foundation of the links between banks and industry in the interwar years, which have been the main theme of the Uppsala project as part of a large-scale international research cooperation.

Banks
Swedish commercial banks have always existed in symbiosis with Swedish manufacturing industry. (The direct translation of the Swedish word for this type of bank is 'business bank'.) From 1860 onwards there has been a high correlation between industrial production and bank lending (or vice versa; this is another chicken and egg question). I tend to regard the Swedish commercial banks as

a type of service or money-transport institute that best served the conditions of Swedish industry, implying lower transactions costs, and thus out-competing other forms of financial intermediaries, at least for some time. This does not mean that at all times banks were followers, with no great influence on the shaping of Swedish industry. Banks were of particular importance for Swedish engineering industry. The iron and sawmill industries could often rely on mortgageable assets, such as forests, when they needed to borrow and had a wider choice of financiers, e.g. mortgage institutions and the central bank. In earlier times their need for trade credit was supplied by importers in other countries and later this need was met by the Swedish commercial banks when they had been established and proved their efficiency. The conditions for the new engineering industry were different. Engineering firms needed share capital to create fixed assets and initially had no connections in foreign markets. The commercial banks helped with both, by lending to the shareholders with shares as collateral, and by supplying trade credit and arranging contacts with foreign markets.

In the latter part of the 1890s, when total bank lending doubled, lending against shares increased threefold, and a peak of 33 per cent of all commercial bank lending was recorded for 1898. As mentioned above, this portion increased to 45 per cent at the end of the First World War.[3] It is impossible to estimate how much of this kind of lending was made against the collateral of shares in engineering firms. Considering the great increase in the share capital of the engineering industry during the war (see Table 1.3), one might perhaps dare to assume that the owners of firms within this industry also took a large part of the new share lending.

Table 1.3   Nominal share capital in selected industries (million SEK)

	1911	1919	1925
Mines	92	95	102
Iron and metal manufacturing	55	164	147
Engineering industry	121	686	510
Sawmills	56	104	101
Pulp industry	134	274	288
Paper industry	25	74	75
Combined iron and wood	84	211	230
Chemical industry	33	187	276
Food industry	206	250	276
Textile industry	67	155	176
Shipping	46	173	179
Issuing houses and stockbrokers	64	287	154

Source: Svenska aktiebolags balansräkningar åren 1911–1925 (SOU 1929:4).

Bank lending against shares as collateral fell during the 1920s, both in absolute terms and as a percentage. At the end of the decade it was around 30 per cent of total bank lending on average. After the new crisis in the early 1930s, it further decreased to around 10 per cent at the time of the Second World War. In the interwar years turnover on the Stockholm stock exchange fell, and it was not until the 1970s that the peak of the First World War was reached, and not until the booming and speculative 1980s that it was considerably exceeded.

New banks were founded in periods of expansion in Swedish manufacturing. In 1860 there were 12 commercial banks in Sweden. In the 1860s their number increased to 27, in the 1870s to 44. That number remained constant until the latter part of the 1890s when 22 new banks were founded. Another large increase occurred around 1905 until the maximum figure of 83 banks was reached in 1909. In 1917 six new banks were founded, in 1918 another six, and in 1919 three. At that time, however, the merger movement of Swedish banks had already begun, and the total number of banks continued to fall. It is interesting to note that bank mergers seem to follow the same pattern as that of the development in industry and stock market quotations. In the first decade of the century there were 19 bank mergers with 11 of those taking place during a sharp rise in share prices. During the war there were 42 mergers, 30 of which occurred during 1917–19. The 12 bank mergers that took place in the first half of the 1920s, however, cannot be ascribed to rising share prices or easy bank lending. Six banks defaulted in 1922 and for that reason were taken over by other banks, in a rescue operation jointly administered and financed by the Swedish state and the larger banks.

At the end of the 1920s there existed some 30 banks. Some of them had changed completely in character since 1910, when the large merger movement got under way. From regional or even local banks, as they were still in the early 1910s, they had turned into country-wide banks, with branch offices from north to south. This, of course, had strengthened them in many ways. Seasonal differences between the supply of deposits and the demand for credit could be coped with more easily. And when a new kind of depositor emerged with the growth of the share of wages in national income, these banks were ready.

The commercial banks in Sweden had their breakthrough at the same time as the manufacturing industry. In the middle of the 1870s the commercial banks surpassed the mortgage institutions as lenders, when they accounted for 40 per cent of total institutional lending in Sweden. The period from the mid-1890s till the early 1920s was the hey-day of commercial banks. In 1910 their lending accounted for about 55 per cent of total lending by financial institutions; at around 1920 they reached their peak of about 66 per cent. Starting at the time of the crisis of 1921, the commercial banks lost in importance, if measured by their share of total assets of financial institutions and of total lending. In the interwar years their lending also decreased in absolute figures (although this is a product of a decrease in the 1920s and an increase in the 1930s). In the years immediately preceding the Second World War, the commercial banks' share of total lending in the Swedish society was somewhat above 30 per cent, a figure that decreased to slightly above 20 per cent in the 1950s and 1960s.[4]

In the interwar period new financial institutions emerged and some of the old ones were able to compete better with the commercial banks: savings banks, mortgage institutions, insurance companies and state and other pension funds. In the 1970s and 1980s several of the firms that were saved and helped by the commercial banks in the crisis of the early 1920s had grown and became so liquid that they not only arranged for their own lending but could themselves act as direct lenders.

In many ways, the 1980s resembled the turbulent years during the First World War, especially as regards the events on the stock market and the large increase in bank lending. In the interim Sweden has not witnessed any such pronounced speculation. Thus it will be most interesting to see the outcome this time, both for firms and banks. Will there be another 30 to 40 years before the banks can again sell the shares that they have had to accept against forfeited debts? In the 1870s, it was a question of shares and bonds in railroads; in the 1920s, of shares in engineering firms. In the 1990s, it is a question of shares in and loans to building and real estate firms. Economic historians can perhaps express the hope that the subject will be studied more by bankers and industrialists.

Notes
1. This appears from the weekly business magazine *Affärsvärlden*, which includes share quotations and analyses of the Stockholm Stock Exchange from 1901 onwards.
2. The account is based on A. Östlind, *Svensk samhällsekonomi 1914–1922* (Stockholm, 1945).
3. Figures based on SOS (Sveriges Officiela Statistisk), *Uppgifter om bankerna* for respective years.
4. Figures from I. Nygren, *From Stockholms Banco till Citibank*, Stockholm, 1985 and H. Lindgren, *Bank, investmentbolag, bankirfirma*, Stockholm, 1988.

2   The Norwegian banking system before and after the interwar crises
Even Lange

During the interwar years the Norwegian system of financial institutions nearly broke down. Three successive crises in the 1920s and early 1930s brought a large number of banks to the brink of collapse. More than 150 of the 750 banking institutions operating in 1920 actually went into liquidation or were taken over by others. A working banking system was restored only through extensive support from the government and the Bank of Norway. The assistance provided could not, however, prevent central parts of the system from crumbling. The private commercial banks were particularly exposed to the crises, and roughly half of them ceased to operate between 1920 and 1935. Only one of the five biggest commercial banks survived without intervention from the authorities; two went bankrupt, two muddled through by means of moratoriums supervised by the central bank. No other banking system in a neutral country seems to have been as badly shaken by the depression of the 1920s.[1]

Why was this so? The explanation is of course a complex one. Part of it is related to the simple fact that the Norwegian economy as a whole suffered more heavily than others from a prolonged setback after the First World War. An ill-advised monetary and general economic policy aggravated the problems. The Bank of Norway, supported by the political establishment and most economists, pursued a policy of return to gold from a level of roughly half the prewar parity. This policy was pursued in a stop–go manner for nearly eight years, depressing the economy for a much longer period than elsewhere in Western Europe.

International developments and domestic policies cannot, however, fully explain the very severe problems in the financial sector. Weaknesses inherent in the banking system itself must also be taken into account. The extensive government support deemed necessary to prop up the vacillating banks in fact prolonged the deflationary period by several years, thereby increasing the economic difficulties.[2] To understand the deep trouble experienced by Norwegian banks in the interwar years, the particular nature of the banking system must be considered. The first purpose of this chapter is to survey the Norwegian system of banking institutions as it developed during the nineteenth century, giving a background for the important weaknesses that were exposed during the interwar period.

The traumatic experiences of the interwar crises on the other hand profoundly influenced the financial system in Norway for the following 50 years. Some

12

remarks on the consequences for the further development of the institutional structure and role of banking conclude the chapter, underlining the long-term continuity in important features of the Norwegian banking system.

Nineteenth-century development

The main characteristics of the Norwegian banking system at the end of the nineteenth century can be summed up as follows: strong public sector involvement; weak private institutions; and considerable dependence on foreign sources of capital.[3] Norwegian banking was formed as a consequence of the necessity to develop a national financial system and institutions from scratch as the country gained independence from Denmark in 1814. The Bank of Norway, founded in 1816 as a semi-public central bank, quickly established itself in a pre-eminent position in the organized credit market. It enjoyed from the start a note-issuing monopoly. The public sector also, until the end of the nineteenth century, held the exclusive right to issue bearer bonds. State monopolies thus barred two important ways of funding private banks in the formative period. Unlike banks in Sweden and continental Europe, Norwegian banks from the start had to rely exclusively on deposits, which seems to have seriously hampered their development. In addition, parallel systems of public finance institutions were established. First among them were the so-called discounting commissions. Originally set up to distribute government loans during the credit crises occurring at intervals between the 1820s and the 1850s, the commissons in some urban areas developed into a kind of substitute for commercial banks, discounting commercial paper on a regular basis. In the rural areas the Norwegian State Mortgage Bank, established in 1851, took care of a large part of the long-term lending, financing the modernization of Norwegian agriculture.

The Bank of Norway also engaged in direct long- and short-term lending to private citizens and businesses through a network of branch offices in the main cities, established throughout the nineteenth and well into the twentieth century. These activities, normally left to private banks, were initially legitimized by the lack of such national institutions to cater for the needs of Norwegian businesses. In the long run, however, the effect was to stultify the growth of the private banks by leaving less room for them in the market. Until the end of the century, the central bank acted more as a competitor than as a lender of last resort for the private banks. Particularly during the depression of the 1880s, the Bank of Norway failed to provide necessary support to banks in difficulty, thereby contributing to a first wave of bank failures.[4] The Norwegian savings banks, established in a few towns as early as the 1820s and in larger numbers in the countryside from the 1840s onwards, were community institutions, rather than private banks. Their purpose was originally a philanthropic one: later on, they developed into instruments of local community development. Many were founded on capital from the old municipal grain stores or stocks. Their boards regularly consisted of municipal leaders.[5]

Until well beyond the middle of the nineteenth century, then, public sector banks virtually monopolized the organized credit market for business customers. The state banks, including the Bank of Norway, preserved their position as the most important institutional sources of business credit in Norway for two-thirds of the century. Moreover, infrastructure investments like the development of railways and the telegraph networks were financed almost entirely through the public sector.[6] One reason for the predominance of public sector banking institutions was their superior ability to mobilize foreign capital for domestic purposes. Both the discounting commissions and the Mortgage Bank were funded through bonds placed on the European market by the Norwegian state. The same applied to important parts of the infrastructure development, such as the railways and the telegraph. From the 1880s onwards an increasing volume of bonds guaranteed by the Norwegian state was placed in London and Paris. This way of channelling badly needed foreign capital to Norway was open only to the public sector. Private agents had no comparable credit standing abroad.

Foreign funding under national control was one important legacy of the public banking system. Another one was the lack of a professional financial community of any importance until the end of the nineteenth century. The officials of the public sector banks regarded themselves as civil servants, not as bankers, and did not build a culture of financial skills and know-how transferable to the Norwegian business community. One of the directors of the Bank of Norway in the 1830s remarked that he might as well have been appointed emperor of Morocco as bank director.[7] No profession of experienced bankers gained a foothold in the formative years. This proved to be a long-term handicap and a very difficult one to overcome.

Decentralization

The dominant position of public sector institutions for most of the nineteenth century reflects the largely underdeveloped structure of Norwegian banking in general. Public sector banks mostly engaged in long-term lending based on mortgages, leaving other needs of the business community unattended. The few merchant houses that had survived the post-Napoleonic depression were unable to handle banking business outside a limited circle of family and friends.

Important credit flows had to be maintained informally, and on very unsatisfactory conditions outside the banking system. A vulnerable credit system based on bills of exchange was operated through a few merchants able to draw on large trading houses in Hamburg and London. So-called 'blanco bills', disassociated from the trade transactions usually covering a bill, fuelled a large system of commercial credit. This credit system necessitated complicated networks of endorsements between individuals that entered into business relations as well as extensive mutual discounting of their respective bills. The system lacked stability and was unable to withstand even small setbacks, as the misfortune of one participant in an 'endorsement consortium' spread through the network.[8]

The first commercial banks were established by the mercantile communities in Christiania (Oslo) and Bergen by the middle of the century, as a remedy for this increasingly unacceptable situation. Christiania Kreditkasse, founded by the local trade association in 1848, explicitly aimed at bringing the expanding commercial class out of its previous dependence on the vulnerable credit based on bills of exchange.[9] Similar disenchantment with the bill credit system motivated the establishment of a commercial bank by Bergen traders seven years later. Through the 1860s and 1870s about ten commercial banks were founded in larger towns in response to identical needs.

In this way, the Norwegian system of private banks was founded by the customers, directly motivated by their need for better organized commercial credit, and funded through deposits. From the start this system was also almost exclusively trade-oriented and geared towards financing circulating capital. Contrary to the situation in other Scandinavian and central European countries at the time, there was no room for merchant banking in Norway. As funding by issuing banknotes or bonds was prohibited, the private banks had to rely almost exclusively on deposits from the business community. Their ability to enter into long-term investments in industry was strictly limited. Thus Norwegian banks of the nineteenth century never established themselves as business coordinators or industrial developers. They were servants, not masters, of the business community. As a consequence, the system of private banks developed into a highly decentralized structure. Early attempts by the Christiania Kreditasse to set up branch offices outside the capital had to be abandoned when confronted with the chauvinism of local business circles at both ends. Plans for a branch office in Trondheim triggered the establishment of a local bank, whereas business interests in Christiania were afraid that branch offices would drain the city of much-needed working capital.[10] As a result, no branch-based organization could be developed. The rule that each urban community needed its own independent private bank prevailed into the interwar years.

The important role played by the savings bank sector in the second half of the century further accentuated the decentralized structure of Norwegian banking. The original purpose of savings banks was to accumulate deposits from the public and buy low-risk bonds. They were not supposed to lend. During the 1840s, however, Norwegian savings banks were turned into more conventional banking institutions serving local business needs. The Aker Savings Bank founded in 1843 stated that it aimed at 'supporting thrifty citizens by discounting their bills and providing businesses with working capital'.[11] Following the Aker example, the activity of the many savings banks established in the period 1850–80 to a large extent overlapped with that of the far less numerous commercial banks.

Through the last decades of the century the savings banks, like the commercial banks, predominantly used their working capital to discount bills and bond-bills, the preferred paper for short- and medium-term debt in Norway. This instrument was based on personal collateral, requiring an intimate knowledge of the customers. Only the larger savings banks located in towns placed important parts of their funds in mortgages.[12]

There were obvious business reasons for this policy. Discounting short- and medium-term bills gave more flexibility and a higher yield than mortgages. Until 1888 mortgage interests were regulated by law, whereas the discount rates for bills were left to the market. But savings banks had to face sharp public criticism during the 1870s and 1880s. They were accused of pursuing a far too expansive lending policy. And Norwegian savings banks lent a far higher proportion of their working capital than similar institutions in other countries. They also grew much faster in relation to the commercial banks than elsewhere in Europe. As late as 1890 the savings banks held 44 per cent of the Norwegian institutional loan market, a share more than twice as large as that of the commercial banks (Table 2.1).

Table 2.1   Shares of Norwegian loan market, 1850–90 (per cent)

	1850	1870	1890
Public sector banks	60	36	30
Savings banks	32	41	44
Commercial banks	2	19	21

Source: NOS Central Bureau of Statistics.

The loan customers of savings banks in urban areas seem not to have differed much from those of commercial banks. Although most of the savings banks were located in the countryside, the urban savings banks in 1880 held nearly two thirds of the working capital in their sector, clearly outdistancing the commercial banks in number as well as in capital.[13] The normal division of functions between savings and commercial banks was blurred, as the savings banks to a great extent acted as substitutes for commercial banks.

The strong position of the savings banks in the late nineteenth century was an important influence on the Norwegian banking system. While acting as agents of investment, the savings banks restricted their operations to the local environment. Moreover, most of these banks were not run by professionals, and tended to stay away from high-risk projects. Although they ventured into the fields of commercial banking and were criticized for their expansive lending policy, the savings banks could not fully compensate for the lack of private banks.

On the whole they failed to provide sufficient backing for industrial development or satisfying the credit needs of commerce in a modern economy.

To summarize the main structural features of the Norwegian banking system after this brief sketch of its development towards the end of the nineteenth century, three points can be made:

1. The public sector covered important parts of long-term credit, through the Bank of Norway, the Mortgage Bank and government agencies.
2. The savings banks, with the status of local community institutions, handled the lion's share of short- and medium-term business loans.
3. Private banks played a subordinate role in the credit system, mostly providing circulating capital for larger business firms.

Economic growth
A central theme of discussion regarding the formative period of the banking system concerns the implications of these features for Norwegian economic development. The question is whether the structure of banking institutions held back modernization and economic growth, or whether it was the other way round, that is, whether the banking structure just reflected an underdeveloped economy. In other words: did the customers get the banking they needed? Two interpretations confront each other in this matter. One maintains that the development of credit institutions is subordinated to economic development in general. The other assigns a more independent role to the banking system. This of course reflects well known positions in the international debate on the relationship between banking institutions and economic growth in the nineteenth century.[14]

In the Norwegian case, the insights gained from research so far indicate that institutional shortcomings in the credit sector did not matter much for economic development before the 1870s. From 1830 to 1875 GNP seems to have risen by an impressive 3 per cent per year, based on growth in agriculture, fishing, timber and shipping. Modernization of these traditional sectors seems to have been possible within the framework of the rudimentary Norwegian credit institutions. The later transition to industrialism, however, required backing from financial institutions that had not been developed through the early modernization phase. From the late 1870s onwards Norwegian economic development seems to have suffered from the absence of an adequate banking system. Growth rates fell dramatically and the insufficient supply of capital needed for the transformation of business structures at some point between 1880 and 1890 became an important limitation.

As a response to the perceived need for a more active and powerful structure of banking institutions a new wave of private banks was founded in the 1890s. Commercial banks also embarked on the financing of new manufacturing industries and modern shipping to an extent previously unknown. This announced a phase in the development of the Norwegian banking system that might be called 'the rise and fall of commercial banking'.

As we have already emphasized, Norwegian commercial banks in 1890 were at a great disadvantage compared to the position held by commercial banks in neighbouring countries. During the 30 years that followed, their role in the Norwegian financial system changed dramatically. First of all the number of commercial banks increased from a little over 30 to 192. Their working capital, which in 1890 had represented about 20 per cent of the total in banking, less than half of that handled by the savings banks, increased fourfold in real terms between 1900 and 1916. This brought their share of the loan market to nearly 40 per cent in 1900 and 60 per cent in 1920, which was more than twice as much as the savings banks. In the same period the public sector banks reduced their share of the market from 30 to 12 per cent (Table 2.2).

Table 2.2   Shares of Norwegian loan market 1890–1920 (per cent)

	1890	1900	1920
Public sector banks	30	22	12
Savings banks	44	34	26
Commercial banks	21	39	60

Source: NOS Central Bureau of Statistics.

The rise of the commercial banks occurred in two separate spurts – the first from 1895 to 1900, the next from 1910 to 1920. They established a leading position in the Norwegian financial system as a result of sudden booms and much of the expansion turned out to be ill-founded. A banking crisis involving the collapse of several newly founded banks at the turn of the century halted growth for about ten years, but had no other significant long-term effects. The new boom before and throughout the First World War continued along roughly the same lines as the previous one, followed by the interwar disasters.[15]

Research into the character of commercial bank lending has barely begun, and much of what we know is based on the material of committees investigating the banks which failed. All the same it seems fair to say that flaws inherent in the banking structure as it developed before 1890 were emphasized by the commercial bank expansion. Quantitative growth was not followed by significant qualitative changes increasing the strength of banking in general.

The decentralized structure of the banking system was maintained. New banks as well as old continued to serve local communities, and only one of them, the Trade Bank of Norway, developed some sort of branch banking. As the funding remained almost exclusively based on deposits, no fundamental change took place regarding the banks' ability to carry long-term industrial responsibilities either. Instead of transforming and invigorating the banking system, the rise of the commercial banks from 1890 to 1920 essentially seems to have exposed the system to greater risks.[16] Trying to satisfy the needs for banking services in a booming modern economy, the commercial banks heavily overstretched themselves, partly because they had to rely on the defective traditions developed in a subordinate position through the nineteenth century. A financial culture, able to draw on experience from varied circumstances and integrated in the international banking community, had not been established. It was not easy to compensate for the absence of a well entrenched banking expertise.

Government measures did not provide much guidance for commercial banks to assume their new and dominant role. Although the business environment of the expansion period after 1895 differed sharply from conditions in the preceding century, political attitudes towards banking did not reflect the change. When the public sector banks and well regulated savings banks retreated from their dominant position in the loan market, no new regime of regulation outside the Bank of Norway was established to assist the expanding private commercial banks. The banks were largely left to themselves, without any specific banking legislation or effective inspection agency to control them before the end of the First World War.[17] In the guise of a new institutional mix, old weaknesses survived.

The calamities of the 1920s and early 1930s in a way restored the old institutional balance, cutting the commercial banks down to size, strengthening the position of savings banks and public sector institutions (see Table 2.3)

Table 2.3   Shares of Norwegian loan market, 1920–80 (per cent)

	1920	1935	1970	1980
Public sector banks	12	28	29	38
Savings banks	26	32	19	17
Commercial banks	60	25	24	22
Insurance and others	2	15	27	23

Source: NOS Central Bureau of Statistics.

The savings banks profited during the crises from their more sheltered position and limited exposure to industry and shipping, and increased their working capital through transfer of accounts from the vacillating commercial bank system. Their position of relative strength in the interwar years revived their habit from the period before 1890 of catering for the needs of the business community at large. The Bank of Norway as a result of the crises had to handle directly large business loans taken over for commercial banks in difficulty or default, and thus also reverted to the old ways of the nineteenth century. Under the Labour government in power from 1935, moreover, new public sector funds and banks were given the responsibility of handling important parts of the long-term credit for economic development, as had been the case in the 1800s.[18]

The division of labour between different institutions in the Norwegian credit market until the late 1970s was heavily influenced by the interwar commercial bank disaster. Norwegian commercial banks retreated to financing short-term loans for circulating capital. Insurance companies and other private institutions handled part of the long-term credit for industry. But most of the strategic capital investment was taken care of by public sector institutions, periodically relying on important transfers of capital from abroad, a feature also replicating the nineteenth century situation.

The interwar banking crises, then, seem largely to have restored the pattern of credit institutions that existed before the rise of the commercial banks in the 1890s. The private banks made no further attempts to break away from that basic pattern until the deregulation of Norwegian financial markets in the 1980s. A new banking crisis has followed, with an unmistakable flavour of the interwar years.

Notes

1. K. Petersen, *Bankkriser og valutauro*, Oslo, 1982; F. Hodne, *The Norwegian Economy 1920–1980*, London: Croom Helm, 1983, ch. 3.
2. F. Sejersted, *Ideal, teori og virkelighet, Nicolay Rygg og Pengepolitikken i 1920-årene*, Oslo, 1972.
3. E. Lange, 'Kapitaltilgangen til norsk næringsliv, hva kan vi lære av historien', *Research on Banking, Capital and Society*, report no. 1, The Norwegian Research Council for Applied Social Science, NORAS 1989.
4. S. Knutsen, 'Bank, samfunn og økonomisk vekst', *Research on Banking, Capital and Society*, report no. 10, NORAS 1990.
5. B.R. Rønning, 'Norsk sparebankvesen inntil 1850', *Studier i sparing og sparebankvesen*, Oslo, 1972.
6. H. Skånland, *Det norske kredittmarked siden 1900*, Oslo, 1967, tab 11.
7. E. Engebretsen, *Norsk Bankvesen*, Oslo, 1939, p. 34.
8. E. Hoffstad, *Det norske privatbankvæsens historie*, Oslo, 1928.
9. E. Engebretsen, *Christiania Bank og Kreditkasse 1848–1948*, Oslo, 1948, p. 14ff.
10. E. Hoffstad, op. cit., note 8, p. 125f.
11. B.R. Rønning, op. cit., note 5, p.16f.
12. Å. Egge, 'Trekk ved sparebankenes utvikling 1850–1920', *Studier i sparing og sparebankvesen*, Oslo, 1972.
13. Ibid., p. 235.
14. H.W. Nordvik and S. Knutsen, '*Bankenes rolle i norsk industriell utvikling 1850–1914*', *Research on Banking, Capital and Society*, report no 10, NORAS 1990.
15. H. Skånland, op. cit., note 6, ch. V.
16. S. Knutsen, *Bank, samfunn og økonomisk vekst*, mimeo, Department of History, University of Oslo, 1990.
17. E. Hoffstad, op. cit., note 8.
18. T.J. Hanisch and E. Lange, *Veien til velstand*, Oslo, 1939.

Further reading
Asmund Egge, 'Kredittvesenet i Norge under industrikapitalismens gjennombrudd', i G.A. Blom (ed.) *Utviklingen av kredit og kredittinstitusjoner i de nordiske land ca 1850–1914*, Trondheim, 1978.
Erling Engebretsen, *Norsk bankvesen*, Oslo, 1939.
Tore J. Hanisch og Even Lange, *Veien til velstand*, Oslo, 1986.
E. Hoffstad, *Det norske privatbankvæsens historie*, Oslo, 1928.
Gunnar Jahn et al., *Norges Bank gjennom 150 år*, Oslo, 1966.
Arne Jensen et al. (ed.), *Studier i sparing og sparebankvesen i Norge 1822–1972*, Oslo, 1972.
Sverre Knutsen, *Bank, samfunn og økonomisk vekst* (Hovedoppgave i historie, Universitetet i Oslo, 1990).
Helge W. Nordvik et al., *Penger spart, penger tjent. Sparebanker og økonomisk utvikling på Sør-Vestlandet fra 1839–1989*, Stavanger, 1989.
Kaare Petersen, *Forretningsbankenes historie*, Oslo, 1986; *Studier i sparing og sparebankvesen*, Oslo, 1972.
Francis Sejersted, *Ideal, teori og virkelighet*, Oslo, 1972; (ed.), *En storbank i blandingsøkonomien*, Oslo, 1982.
Hermod Skånland, *Det norske kredittmarked siden 1900*, Oslo, 1967.

3 Origins of the banking system in interwar Czechoslovakia

Jan Hájek

Banking in the Czech Lands experienced considerable changes in the decade before the First World War. The only comparable period in terms of banking development was the late 1860s to early 1870s. It is no coincidence, then, that the years before the war are sometimes called – in relation to overall economic development – the second 'Gründerzeit', or period of rapid growth in joint-stock company formation in the 1870s.[1] It can be stated that the events in these two periods of dynamic development not only established the banking system before the First World War, but also decisively influenced its character in Czechoslovakia between the wars.[2] If we want to deal with this system in greater detail and understand some of its specificities it is essential to refer back to its roots, i.e. to the period before 1914.[3]

Shortly after the turn of the century the development of the credit system in the Czech Lands went through important changes. These not only reflected external factors but also the consequences of the Great Depression of the last quarter of the nineteenth century.

Unlike other regions of Austria–Hungary or even of neighbouring Germany, finance in the Czech Lands was much less drastically affected by the economic decline of the early years of the new century. Nevertheless, it experienced certain crisis conditions, which led to a re-evaluation of the existing credit system and to its substantial reorganization.

Because of the chronic lack of resources for the advancement of free enterprise in the previous economic development of the Czech Lands the popular savings institutions played a very important role in financial and credit relations in the second half of the nineteenth century. First among them were the independent credit cooperatives established on the model devised by the German economist H. Schultze-Delitzsch, which spread from the end of the 1850s. At the end of the 1860s these cooperative credit societies or *záložny* (savings banks; in Germany *Vorschussverein*) preceded many important banking institutions, such as the Živnostenská banka (Trade Bank) in Prague or the Záložní úvěrový ústav (savings institution) in Hradec Králové. In the national Czech environment the credit cooperatives constituted a significant economic influence. They also asserted themselves in the national German (German-speaking) regions of the Czech Lands, especially in the credit-financing of small- and medium-sized enterprises.[4] At the beginning of the twentieth century the traditional cooperative banking movement went through a severe internal crisis. This manifested itself for example in the bankruptcy of several important Czech savings banks (for instance in Třeboň, Mělník, etc.) The greatest attention was attracted by the default of the 'Svatováclavská' savings bank in Prague in Autumn 1902. The Czech and partly also the German press published extensive discussions on the economic importance and function of savings and credit banks even earlier. One of the main questions was whether the savings banks should only provide credits secured by appropriate collateral or whether they should participate in broader financial or industrial enterprise. The effort to re-evaluate the existing function of savings and credit institutions can be gleaned from the following statement published in the Czech press at that time: '... the increasing effort to establish a powerful economic organization of our nation is manifested not only by the search for new ways, which would set the seal on our effort, but also by the *criticism of the existing forms.*'[5]

At this time significant changes also took place in the organization of another type of small savers' finance in the Czech Lands – the savings bank.[6] In 1901 the Centralbank der deutschen Sparkassen was founded, and in 1903 the Ústřední banka českých spořitelen (Central Bank of Czech Savings Banks). The establishment of these central institutions led to the concentration of the dispersed funds of many local savings banks. Thus the traditional savings bank system was incorporated into the new, relatively modern type of financial enterprise.

The above changes, as well as those caused by the establishment of both German and Czech head offices for the small but very numerous agricultural credit cooperatives, founded under the Raiffeisen system[7] (in the Czech Lands called *kampeličky*), provided the possibility for incorporating the older types of small savings institutions into the new conditions of economic development. This transformation was one of the necessary preconditions for the people's savings and credit banks maintaining their importance in the Czech Lands' economy. The extraordinarily widespread forms of gathering people's small savings created a broad basis for the expansion of the activity of practically all the large financial institutions. This feature was then fully integrated into the financial system of Czechoslovakia between the wars.

However, the head offices of the savings banks were not the only new banking institutions established in the Czech Lands at the turn of the century. At that time an important centre of national Czech banking capital was established in Prague.[8] Besides the older Živnostenská banka, the Úvěrní banka v Kolíně (Credit Bank in Kolín) brought its head office to Prague in 1900 and changed its name to Pražská úvěrní banka (Prague Credit Bank). Shortly before this (in 1898) the Česká průmyslová banka (Czech Industrial Bank) was established there. Together with the Central Bank of the Czech Savings Banks these financial institutions represented a nucleus of Czech banking before the First World War.

Though the majority of such banks were to pursue only certain special financial transactions at the time of their establishment, they extended the scale of their business interests very quickly and soon operated as mixed (universal) banks. Such a transformation of business orientation was a common feature of the development of Cisleithanian (the Austrian part of the Austro-Hungarian Empire) banking.

A further increase in the number of Czech banking institutions occurred a decade later. In particular, the first banks established during this foundation wave – the Česká banka (Czech Bank) in Prague (1907), Moravská agrární a průmyslová banka (Moravian Agrarian and Industrial Bank) in Brno (1908) and also the Moravsko-slezská banka (Moravia-Silesian Bank) in Brno (1910) – conducted business as universal banks. Increasing competition in financial markets forced the newly founded institutions to search for a role in the banking system.[9] Consequently they specialized in defined areas of business. In the years 1909–13 the Pozemková banka (Land Bank, 1909), Banka pro průmysl pivovarský (Brewing Industry Bank, 1910), Akciová banka Bohemie (Joint-Stock Bank Bohemie, 1910), Agrární banka (Agrarian Bank, 1911), Deutsche Agrarbank für Österreich (1912), and the Banka stavebních živností a průmyslu (Building Trade and Industry Bank, 1913) were all founded in Prague. The specialization of banking institutions proceeded to such an extent that several small (occupational) banks were also established, for example for beekeepers, butchers and tinsmiths. These somewhat weird efforts played only a marginal role, however. More important was the fact that in some of the provincial centres (e.g. in Plzeň and Olomouc) societies originally established with limited liability were turned into small joint-stock banks.

Immediately before the First World War this extensive increase in the number of Czech banks provoked a correspondingly critical response, as more and more voices demanded fewer banks with a strong capital base rather than numerous small ones. Some reduction in the excessive number of small and medium banks came after the war. However, in spite of these changes, Czech banking retained its fragmented character for a considerable period.

One of the main features at the turn of the century was the increasing introduction of nationalistic conflict into business activity.[10] This phenomenon did not manifest itself only in banking; it can be observed in many other spheres of the economy of the Czech Lands. In essence, the Czech–German language conflict at the end of the nineteenth century gradually spilled over into economic activity. On the one hand these increasing manifestations of economic nationalism among the German-speaking population proved that its economic strength relative to the Czechs was deteriorating. This quite understandably induced anxiety and even malice in German speakers. The result was an unceasing challenge to the economic positions of both nationalities in practically all economic spheres accompanied by equally dramatic complaints from both sides.

A striking example of this nationalism was the massive withdrawal of deposits in spring 1903 initiated by Czech depositors who turned against the German national Böhmische Sparkassa – the oldest public financial institution in Bohemia. In the space of a month, from 10 February to 19 March 1903 some 28 600 depositors withdrew more than 41 million crowns, a large part of which was transferred to accounts with national Czech financial institutions. Evidence of this transfer can be seen in Table 3.1, which provides data for the two largest savings banks in Prague, the Böhmische Sparkasse and the Městská Spořitelna Pražská (Prague City Savings Bank).[11]

Table 3.1 *Deposits of Böhmische Sparkasse and Městská Spořitelna Pražská, 1901–4*

	Böhmische Sparkasse				Městská Spořitelna Pražská			
End of the year	Deposits ('000s)	Change, %	Deposit volume (m crowns)	Change, %	Deposits ('000s)	Change, %	Deposit volume (m crowns)	Change, %
1901	139.5		218.6		100.9		113.5	
		+5.5		+11.8		+9.0		+13.6
1902	145.0		230.4		109.9		127.1	
		−22.4		−27.0		+19.4		+24.7
1903	122.6		203.4		129.3		151.8	
		+1.1		+3.0		+5.5		+4.6
1904	123.7		206.4		134.8		156.4	

The Czech press made triumphant comments on this 'run' on the Böhmische Sparkasse in a series of sharply worded articles (some of which became the subject of court actions). It was noted that the money withdrawn by Czech depositors did not stay 'in the stockings', as pessimists and enemies had predicted, but quite the reverse: 'the Czech deposits withdrawn from the Bohemian Savings Bank watered all the land of national Czech credits in this blessed spring of Czech economic revival.'[12]

In Cisleithanian capital relations Vienna's financial institutions unambiguously played the most important role. The Czech Lands' banking obviously occupied an inferior position but the balance did shift to the disadvantage of the Vienna centre. The gradual increase in the importance of Czech banking and especially the Czech national banks in the context of the Cisleithanian region can be proven by comparing the joint-stock capital of national Czech banks with the national German ones in the Czech Lands and with the banks in the Monarchy's financial centre, i.e. with the joint-stock capital of the Viennese banks (see Table 3.2).

Table 3.2   Joint-stock capital of Czech and German commercial banks in the
Czech Lands and of commercial banks in Vienna, 1890–1913

	1890		1900		1910		1913	
Banks	Capital (m Crowns)	In %	Capital (m Crowns)	In %	Capital (m Crowns)	In %	Capital (m Crowns)	In %
Czech	7.8	2.0	29.1	5.5	169.0	16.7	225.0	18.0
German	24.0	6.2	49.9	9.5	102.7	10.1	135.7	10.9
In Vienna	358.2	91.8	447.5	85.5	742.4	73.2	888.7	71.1
Total	390.0	100.0	526.5	100.0	1014.1	100.0	1249.4	100.0

Source: Österreichische Statistik (ÖS), Bd XXXVI, Heft 3, LXVII, Heft 3, ÖS-Neue Folge, 13d.X, Heft 2, Bd XV, Heft 2.

The relationship between Czech and German banks was not the only thing to change. Certain shifts could be observed even inside the Czech financial system. At the turn of the century the Zemská banka království českého (Bohemian Kingdom Land Bank), a public institution, was regarded as the most important Czech bank. It was the largest issuing house in Cisleithania at that time (it kept this pre-eminence in central Europe until the interwar period), and it was an unofficial sponsor of Czech finance in many regards, often complementing the insufficient services of the central Austro-Hungarian Bank. However, from the turn of the century the exclusively commercially oriented Živnostenská banka gradually usurped its role. A second challenger in the battle for pre-eminence of the prewar period was the Ústřední banka českých spořitelen (Central Bank of Czech Savings Banks), a very aggressive financial institution and in many areas showing even more initiative than the Živnostenká banka.

The transfer of prestige from the Bohemian Kingdom Land Bank to the Živnostenská banka can easily be demonstrated by changes in the social influence of their officials. Dr K. Mattuš, the chief director of the Land Bank, who necessarily participated in every important social event of the 1890s, slipped out of social life gradually after the turn of the century, and the representatives of commercial banks came more and more to the fore, notably the future chief director of the Živnostenská banka, Dr Jaroslav Preiss.

The network of Czech and domestic German banks in the Czech Lands was completed by the branch offices of the great Viennese financial institutions. Practically all the large Vienna banks had their branch offices in Prague. Their high repute, their broad coverage over the whole of Austria and abroad and, last but not least, the extent of their capital, were greatly respected in the Czech Lands. Thus they acquired many customers, particularly from the strata of medium and large entrepreneurs both from the national Czech and national German communities. The large Viennese banks did not limit their activity to Prague when they established branch offices in the Czech Lands. They founded branches in every important economic centre. Almost half (i.e. 227 or 45 per cent) of the 516 branch offices belonging to the Cisleithanian joint-stock banks were situated in the Czech Lands. The extraordinarily dense network of bank branch offices proves the economic significance of this territory as the most important industrial part of the Monarchy.

Of course, the domestic banks also had a considerable share in the large number of branch offices in the Czech Lands. The national German banks – especially the Böhmische Union-Bank, the Böhmische Eskompte-Bank, and also the national bilingual Hospodářská úvěrní banka (Landwirtschaftliche Kreditbank-Agricultural Credit Bank) – established their branch offices first of all in the border regions of the Czech Lands. In contrast, the interests of the national Czech banks were concentrated in the interior. The reason for this was not only the banal fact of the different ethnic affiliations of the population in these areas. The older and more developed German banks began to extend their influence in the Czech Lands at a relatively early stage in the most attractive regions of Bohemia. The later-established, or rather later-enlarged national Czech banks wanted – in consequence of this time-lag – to assert themselves not in the economically stagnating border regions but in the dynamically developing inland areas where the centre of a developing Bohemian industrial production was located.[13] This situation was closely connected with the fact that the national Czech banks decided to establish numerous branch offices in the Czech Lands relatively late. While in the period 1900–1910 they opened only one branch a year, in the years 1911 and 1912 they established more than 30 offices.[14]

The general principle of establishing bank branch offices in the territory of a state can in most cases be expressed by the 'metropolis–province' model. In the case of the Czech banks there is, however, a clear effort to penetrate the exposed financial market in Vienna. Many of them succeeded. Thus the Živnostenská banka had a total of 13 small branch offices (so-called *'expozitur'*) in various quarters in Vienna before the war in addition to its main branch office. The efforts of the Czech banks to penetrate the centre of the Monarchy, in accordance with the specific position of Bohemia, changes the basic model of the establishment of branch offices into the opposite form, i.e. 'province–metropolis'. In addition, the establishment of the branch offices of country banks from the Czech Lands in Prague is evidence of the real existence of this 'inside-out principle', albeit at a lower level. Since the Czech Lands' financial market was dominated by older and more developed German banking capital, either in the large Vienna banks or the domestic German ones, the growing Czech banks had to assert themselves abroad.[15] Attempting to generalize a schematic framework shows how the Czech banks proceeded with their expansion within the frontiers of the Czech Lands and created a model of changes arising from this expansion.[16]

This first period includes the end of the nineteenth and the beginning of the twentieth centuries. It may be called 'the period of search', where the gradually expanding Czech banks searched not only for forms but also for directions for their business activity outside the Czech Lands. At that time the Czech banks had not yet decided the direction of their activity; thus one meets with rather unusual financial operations in the Prague milieu that have their roots further afield.

New business contacts were established as a result of official journeys by directors or other representatives of Czech banks to neighbouring countries. In this way Czech banking institutions eventually found profitable directions for their range of operations in the Slav Eastern and Southern regions of the Monarchy, and they entered into relatively extensive credit contacts with these areas. This business began to develop at the turn of the century (in the years 1900–1901) but was more prominent in 1904–6 and after. There was then an urgent need to transform these increasing banking contacts into more durable ones. To this end a network of Czech banks' branch offices was gradually established in these areas. The process of establishing branch offices in the Southern and Eastern regions of the Monarchy took place between about 1906 and 1908. After 1908 this form of capital expansion was gradually replaced – or rather completed – by an even higher type of capital penetration, i.e. the establishment of local, seemingly independent, bank branches. This occurred in 1909–11, the period of the greatest development of Czech banking before the First World War. Shortly after this expansion a change took place in the orientation of the expanding Czech banking system. This change, together with new interests in the domestic financial market, were reflected in an impressive increase in the number of domestic branches and a sharp increase in the competition for deposits. At the time, Czech banks made very few attempts to establish branches outside the Czech Lands, and only the branch and exchange offices of Czech banks in Vienna expanded.

The Czech banks did not return to their programme of foreign expansion until the wave of establishing branch offices in the Czech Lands diminished. Newly established branch offices outside the Czech Lands were rather sporadic in the immediate postwar years, and no dependent banking branches were established. This development was connected with certain difficulties which affected Czech banking as a result of its earlier, excessive growth. The years before the First World War saw a certain slowing down in development. Some institutions experienced considerable problems at that time: first of all, the Záložní úvěrní ústav in Hradec Králové, then the Ústřední banka českých spořitelen and Akciová banka Bohemia.

Banking in independent Czechoslovakia
This outline of Czech banking development up to the First World War has emphasized important factors which were directly or indirectly reflected in the

organization of the Czechoslovak financial system between the wars. The present section will examine the position of the banking system in the first years of independent Czechoslovakia, and some of the common features derived from the development of individual commercial bank groups will be discussed.

The largest group in interwar Czechoslovakia in terms of numbers and capital size was the national Czech banks. The majority of them were small- or medium-sized banks which as individual enterprises had no economic influence. Most of them were established either in the years immediately before the war or in the period of the postwar boom. The larger Czech banks had more varied origins, however. They included institutions founded at the end of the 1860s (i.e. Živnostenská banka, Pražská úvěrní banka) and those founded at the turn of the century (e.g. Česká průmyslová banka and Ústřední banka českých spořitelen), those founded shortly before the war (e.g. Agrární banka) and a bank established after the foundation of the Czechoslovak Republic, the Banka československých legií (Bank of the Czechoslovak Legions).

The Živnostenská banka kept its leading position among the Czech banks. However, its greatest rival had been replaced by a comparative newcomer, the Agrární banka, which grew rapidly during the war, and overtook the Ústřední banka českých spořitelen which was weakened by difficulties during the prewar years.[17]

It is significant for Czech finance that the Živnostenská banka was originally established as a financial centre of the Czech savings and credit institutions. The Ústřední banka českých spořitelen concentrated, above all, on collecting the funds of local savings banks. The Agrární banka concentrated upon and utilized the resources of small agrarian financial institutions, especially those of the local agricultural credit companies and the credit cooperatives of the Raiffeisen type. This is also evidence of the important role played by the mobilization of savings in the economic conditions prevailing in the Czech Lands and in independent Czechoslovakia.

The second group backed by strong capital was represented by the so-called bilingual, i.e. Czech–German banks. Practically all of them were established under the nostrification law in the early years of the new state in 1919–22. They took over the business of the branch offices of the large Viennese banks. The Banka pro obchod a průmysl, dříve Länderbanka (Bank for Trade and Industry, formerly Länderbank) took over the business of the Vienna Länderbank's branches in the territory of the new Czechoslovak state. The Anglo-československá banka (Anglo-Czechoslovak Bank) was established with the takeover of the branches and clientele of the Anglo-Austrian Bank; the Česká komerční banka (Czech Commercial Bank) took over the branch offices of the Vienna bank Merkur; and the Všeobecná česká bankovní jednota (Universal Czech Bank Association) took over the business and branches of the Wiener Bankverein. The only exception seems to have been the Česká eskomptní banka a úvěrní ústav

(Czech Discount Bank and Credit Institution), which had been founded in 1863 as an individual domestic bank. However, a large part of its stock fell into the hands of the Niederösterreichische Eskomptegesellschaft in 1901 so that the Česká eskomptní banka was in essence a branch of this bank from that time.

The position of the bilingual banks in the banking system in interwar Czechoslovakia corresponded fully with their origins. The majority of them were banks with extraordinarily strong capital resources, and though small in number they accounted for roughly one-third of the total joint-stock capital of all the Czechoslovak commercial banks, a sum which was comparable with the capitalization of the far more numerous national Czech banks. And thanks to the contacts they enjoyed in Vienna with European financial markets, they also handled inflows of foreign capital into the Czechoslovak economy.

The third and comparatively weakest group was represented by the domestic German banks, which had been established as individual enterprises in the territory of the future Czechoslovakia. These institutions made up about 15 per cent of the bank capital of the Czechoslovak Republic. The Böhmische Union-Bank, the most important of them, had been founded in 1872 when the Prague branch office of the Vienna Union-Bank became independent. There was also the Deutsche Agrar- und Industriebank, established in 1912. This institution may be compared with the similarly oriented Agrární banka (see above). Established only a year earlier, it became much more successful in its subsequent development.

All these important banks in interwar Czechoslovakia were, with one exception, already established before the First World War, and only two of them were unable to assert themselves until the war. Thus it can be seen that in spite of certain changes and modifications brought about by economic and political developments, the credit system in interwar Czechoslovakia was already in place in all its essentials before the creation of an independent Czechoslovakia. The residues of the prewar state necessarily influenced the form of the banking system under the new political conditions. The character and the functioning of this system cannot be fully understood without a knowledge of its development and historical roots.

Notes

  1. E. März, *Österreichische Industrie- und Bankpolitik in der Zeit Franz Joseph I*, Wien, 1968; *Die Habsburgermonarchie 1848–1918, Band 1. Wirtschaftliche Entwicklung*, Wien, 1973; H. Matis, *Österreichs Wirtschaft 1848–1913. Konjunkturelle Dynamik und gesellschaftlicher Wandel im Zeitalter Franz Josephs I*, Berlin, 1972; O. Urban, *Československé dějiny 1848–1914. Hospodářský a sociální vývoj* (Czechoslovak history 1848–1914. Economic and Social Development), Praha ,1978; J. Komlos, The Habsburg Monarchy as a Customs Union, Economic Development in Austria–Hungary in the Nineteenth Century, New Jersey, 1983; V. Lacina, *Hospodářství českých zemí 1880–1914*, (Economy of the Czech Lands 1880–1914), Praha, 1990.
  2. O. Růžička, *Banky, jejich vývoj, funkce a politika* (Banks, their Development, function and policy), Praha, 1924; A Pimper, *České obchodní banky za války a po válce. Nástin vývoje z*

let 1914–1928 (Czech Commercial Banks in and after First World War. Outline of the Development in the Years 1914–1929), Praha, 1929; M. Ubiria-V. Kadlec-J. Matas, *Peněžní a úvěrová soustava Československa za kapitalismu* (Finance and Credit System of Czechoslovakia in the Time of Capitalism), Praha, 1958.

3. B. Michel, *Banques et banquiers en Autriche an debut du 20e siecle*, Paris, 1976; R.L. Rudolph, *Banking and Industralization in Austria–Hungary. The Role of Banks in the Industralization of the Czech Crownlands 1873–1914*, Cambridge, 1976; J. Purš, 'Banks and the Industralization of the Czech Lands: Evolution of the Structure of the Financial System and the Function of Banks until 1880,' *Hospodářské dějiny* (Economic History), 10, Praha, 1982.

4. J. Hájek, 'Počátky a rozmach českého záloženského hnutí ve třetí čtvrtině 19. století' (The Beginnings and the Advancement of the Czech Credit Cooperative Movement in the Third Quarter of the 19th Century), *Hospodářské dějiny* (Economic History), 12, Praha, 1984.

5. *Národní listy* (National Paper) no. 25 from 25 January 1901, p. 5.

6. I. Plecháček, *K dějinám spořitelnictví v Československu* (To the History of the Saving-bank Movement in Czechoslovakia), Praha, 1983.

7. I. Plecháček, '*Zdroje zemědělského úvěru v Českých zemích ve druhé polovině 19. století*' (Sources of Agrarian Credit in the Czech Lands in the Second Half of the 19th Century), *Hospodářské dějiny* (Economic History), 12, Praha, 1984.

8. J. Horák, *Přehled vývoje českých obchodních bank* (Outline of the Development of the Czech Commercial Banks), Praha, 1913; Z. Jindra, 'K rozvoji českého bankovního kapitálu před 1. světovou válkou' (To the Development of the Czech Banking Capital before the First World War), *Československý časopis historický*, 5, l957.

9. J. Hájek, *Rozvoi národnostně českých bank od konce 19. století do roku 1914* (The Advancement of the National Czech Banks from the End of the 19th Century to the Year 1914), Praha, 1986.

10. D.F. Good, 'National Bias in the Austrian Capital Market before World War l', *Exploration in Economic History* 14, 1977.

11. *Compass. Finanzielles Jahrbuch für Österreich-Ungarn*, Jhrg XLI – 1908, Wien, 1907, I. Bd, pp. 839–40.

12. *Národní listy* (National Paper) no. 92 from 3 April 1903, p. 1.

13. O. Urban, *Kapitalismus a česká společnost* (Capitalism and Czech Society), Praha, 1978.

14. J. Hájek, Development of the Czech Banking Capital in Bohemia before 1914, *Hospodářské dějiny* (Economic History), 18, Praha, 1990.

15. C. Nečas, *Na prahu české kapitálové expanze* (On the Threshold of the Czech Capital Expansion), Brno, 1987.

16. Hájek, op. cit., note 9.

17. V. Lacina, '*Živnostenská banka před a během první světové války (1907–1918)*', (Bank of Trade before and in the First World War, 1907–1918), *Český časopis historický*, 88, Praha, 1990; V. Lacina, '*Živnobanka a její koncern v letech velké hospodářské krize (1929–1934)*' (Bank of Trade and its Concern in the Years of Great Economic Crisis, 1929–1934), *Československý časopis historický* 31, Praha, 1983; J. Novotný, '*Agrární banka v letech 1911–1929*' (Agrarian Bank in the Years 1911–1929), diss., Praha, 1978.

4 Banking and nationality in Hungary, 1867–1914

Zoltán Szász

Modernization and capitalist development have exerted their influence on the various regions and ethnic groups of Hungary in differing degrees. Owing to the historical traditions and the inherited differences of development, the central and western parts of the country were already more developed in the mid-nineteenth century, while in the eastern area only the South Transylvanian *Királyföld* (King's Land), i.e. the Saxon (German-speaking) territory, was economically in advance of the other regions. After 1867, accelerating capitalist development in the Habsburg Monarchy favoured the bourgeoisie of the two strongest ethnic groups, the two 'ruling nations', i.e. the German and the Hungarian elements, but it also created favourable conditions for the social and economic development of all the nationalities of Hungary.[1]

The nationalities were primarily agricultural communities over the entire period, much more so than Hungarian society. Apart from a few craftsmen and merchants, their middle classes consisted mainly of clerics, teachers and a handful of clerks, lawyers and other professional persons of either noble or non-noble birth. The growth of this middle class was delayed compared with that of the Hungarians and occurred especially and most effectively through involvement in the financial life which characterized the last third of the nineteenth century. Besides the big banks and smaller credit institutions working according to classical methods of finance, a slightly different network of banks was established by the nationalities, and this was shaped by local, national and political factors. This network in the peripheries owed its existence first to the pooling of small capital, a general factor in economic growth, and second to the social development of the nationalities, if one can consider them separate societies at this time.

The Slovak savings bank at Turócszentmárton (Turčansky Sv. Martin) and the Romanian bank at Resinár, both founded in 1868, were the first such banks. The 1880s saw the acceleration of the process. The Slovak Tátra Bank had a capital of 800000 crowns in 1900 and deposits of 6 million crowns. At that time there were eleven Slovak banks with 1.5 million crowns of registered capital, while the other 25 banks of the region not belonging to the nationalities had a total capital of 2.7 million crowns. It was the Romanian banks in particular which developed quickly. They were all founded after 1871, and by 1900 there were over 80 of them with nearly 35 million crowns in deposits.[2] The Hungarian Serbs accumulated their capital mainly in the Serbian banks of Croatia, while in their homeland, the Vajdaság (Voivodina), they had mostly credit societies. The Saxon banking institutions occupied a special position. This ethnic group of 200000 persons had organized credit facilities as early as 1840. Their institutions, which had considerable reserve funds, dominated the money market of Transylvania for a long time and provided half of the bank loans of a region with two million inhabitants. The deposits of the Hermanstädter Allg. Sparkasse alone amounted to 13 million crowns in 1900. Figures for the nationalities' banking institutions are given in Table 4.1.

The ever more numerous banks of the nationalities placed the money entrusted to them as discounts and bills of exchange, but primarily as mortgage loans. The predominance of these loans was at the same time a guarantee of uninterrupted development, for the financial crises not only left these banking institutions untouched but even contributed to their charging higher interest rates in some areas.

The credit policy of the nationalities' banks in Hungary revealed local characteristics which varied with the prevailing economic situation. The Slovak banks tried to make their way into industry through the help of Bohemian and Moravian banking institutions and gave credit to small-scale Slovak industry. The Saxon banks aimed at relatively modest profits and took part also in the development of town and villages. The Romanian and Serbian banks specialized in financing merchants and well-to-do peasants. Their common feature was thus a strong orientation towards agriculture.

With their greater flexibility, the banks of the nationalities were able to compete quite successfully with the more rigid Hungarian credit institutions which were developed centrally from Budapest. The Saxon banks of Nagyszeben (Sibiu, Hermannstadt), for example, could be a match even for the large central banks. This was primarily due to the fact that there had been a strong concentration of capital among the banks of the nationalities from the very beginning. The Bodencreditanstalt alone had a share of more than 30 million of the 75 million crowns in mortgage loans placed by the Saxon banks in 1900, just as the Albina held 2.5 million of the 7.5 million crowns in loans of the Romanian banks. The share of the Tatra Bank was 1.16 million crowns in mortgage loans out of the total of 2.26 million of the three big Slovak banks at that time.

The development of these banks coincided with the coming of a new generation in the leadership of the political movements of the nationalities. The old intellectuals gave way to members of the bourgeoisie rallying round the banking institutions and the members of the intelligentsia in close connection with them. The members or supporters of the new political movements were mostly active banking directors who often sat on the boards of several banks. The social and economic significance of the credit banks as main sources of capitalist profit was fully appreciated by contemporaries. Besides the autonomy of their Churches

Table 4.1   The banking institutions of the nationalities in Hungary, 1890–1912[3]

Year	Romanian banking institutions in Hungary		
	Number	Registered capital, thousand crowns	Net profit
1890	26	1 264	232
1900	82	8 871	1 303
1904	–	11 184	1 811
1908	159	20 776	2 839
1912	202	36 415	4 007[+]

Year	Saxon banking institutions in Hungary		
	Number	Registered capital, thousand crowns	Net profit
1890	23	1 423[*]	343[*]
1900	32	3 089[**]	1 155[**]
1904	–	–	–
1908	–	–	–
1912	42	10 666	2 352

Year	Serbian banking institutions in Hungary		
	Number	Registered capital, thousand crowns	Net profit
1890	8	1 109	129
1900	12	–	–
1904	–	–	–
1908	49	6 179	784
1912	–	–	–

Year	Slovak banking institutions in Hungary[++]		
	Number	Registered capital, thousand crowns	Net profit
1890	5	1 080	44
1900	9	1 730	258
1904	16	2 456	355
1908	29	5 012	628
1912	41	13 061	–

[*] Data for the 15 largest banks only.   [+] Data for 1911.
[**] Data for the 23 largest banks only.   [++] Data for joint-stock banks only.

(as far as the Serbian, Romanian and Saxon Churches were concerned), it was the network of their own banks that was meant to compensate the nationalities for their lack of independent state life. The banks granted significant financial support to their political and cultural activities and traditions, the precise extent of which cannot be assessed.[4]

The banks of the nationalities were at the same time important links in the Hungarian banking system, destined to provide the regions inhabited by nationalities with loans and to connect their bourgeoisie organically with the economic life of the country. They also served as bridges between the capital and the tendencies manifesting themselves in Hungarian financial life on the one hand, and the demand for loans in the peripheries on the other. So the banking institutions of the nationalities were – with all their national characteristics and independence – organic parts of the economic structure of the Habsburg Monarchy and, at the same time, reflected one of its most obvious features, namely that the bourgeoisie of the various nations competed with one another for a developing market of their own throughout the whole period from 1867 to 1914.

The Budapest banks could not supply the entire country evenly with credit. In the peripheries not even the medium-sized landowners could be satisfied. So the banking institutions of the nationalities could make use of their advantage on the spot and draw part of this social group into their sphere of interest. They could not, however, provide them with loans to the necessary extent and even refrained from granting excessive credits for fear they would collapse like some of the Hungarian banks before them. It was the lack of sufficient credit for the Hungarian landowners that provoked the first conflict between the Hungarian elite and the banks of the nationalities.[5]

With the gradual growth of capitalism in the 1870s and 1880s, the economic decline of the medium-sized landowners became more and more conspicuous. This was the beginning of a process which contemporaries called 'the transfer of Hungarian land into the hands of foreigners'. The slogan 'let us save the Hungarian medium-sized estates' reflects the new agrarian and anti-capitalist approach combining the idea of the 'unpatriotic' nature of large capital and the concept of 'the national calling of the landed classes'.[6] It is a distinguishing feature of contemporary Hungary how nationalist political elites treated this formerly purely economic, but now strongly political, problem.

State intervention

The Hungarian governments of 1867 to 1914 were fully aware of the political significance of the establishment and growth of the nationalities' banking institutions. They also realized that these banks did not constitute a direct threat to the Hungarian ethnic group. Economic liberalism prevented them from getting involved directly in the market and in financial life, anyway. At the same time, they could not avoid observing the ruling political atmosphere and its consequences. The government dealt from time to time with the 'problems of banking institutions in nationality areas'. In 1894, the Minister of the Interior pressed for the setting-up of Hungarian banks to counter the activities of the local banks. In 1895 Prime Minister Bánffy suggested that unlimited partnerships should be more rigorously controlled, but the idea received no support from ministers.[7]

The primary reason for increasing press attacks on the nationalities' banks was not so much the political fear of the Hungarians but rather the lack of sufficient capital for the mainly Hungarian medium-sized landowners of these regions. This attitude fitted in very well with the idea of counterbalancing the nationalities' banks by strengthening the Hungarian ones, an idea stressed from time to time either in the press or in the petitions of the counties in the ensuing decades. This aim might have been achieved by the establishment of state-supported rival banks in the peripheries which could counterbalance the local ones by offering lower rates of interest. Although the official economic policy of the state was basically liberal, a welfare programme was now advocated to save the gentry. (When the foundation of the Transylvanian branch of the Mortgage Bank was urged, the main argument was that the delay had 'provided the Albina and other similar banking institutions with plenty of opportunities for their anti-national and destructive activities'.)[8] One of those most closely concerned, a director of the Romanian Albina, once asked the politician Ugron Gábor why he had declared the activity of the nationalities' banks to be harmful, since he himself had been helped to establish a sound business by the Albina alone. The politician answered that he had not been agitating against the Romanian banks as such, but he was obliged to keep the Hungarian society mollified by referring constantly to the 'national threat' in order to support the case of the landowners.[9] This must have been the idea behind the suggestion of establishing rival banks in the non-Magyar territories: 'Let us found an Albina of our own at last!'[10] The responsible ministers also thought in terms of a competitive situation promoted by the state. The Hungarian banks saw only one means of counterbalancing 'the generally useful but from the Hungarian, i.e. national, point of view harmful' development of the banks in the peripheries: 'the honest competition of Hungarian capital and nothing else'.[11]

The economic life of the nationalities was, however, not controlled by the state before the turn of the century. The first attempt at state intervention took place in 1902–4, when the government had observed the close connections between the Alldeutscher Verband and the German national movement in Hungary. It was, however, impossible to launch a complaint in diplomatic channels against the Alldeutscher Verband in Germany without some evidence. Prime Minister Széll Kálmán wished to have the correspondence of the German newspaper editors in Southern Hungary watched, but his efforts appear to have been in vain. The economic relationship of the Saxons of Transylvania and the German ethnic group of Southern Hungary was, however, gathering momentum at that time, and this did not pass unobserved, because the Saxons of Transylvania controlled the Swabian press of Southern Hungary through their banks. From then on, investigations proceeded along the following line: if the Saxons were connected with the Alldeutscher Verband and some of their leaders received money from Germany, it was their cash remittances that could be monitored.[12]

Parallel with the measures aimed at suppressing the German national movement in Southern Hungary and the diplomatic steps taken in this direction it was the problem of emigration from Upper Hungary that directed the attention of the Széll government to the banking institutions of the nationalities.[13] The Hungarian government was not at all indifferent to the fact that the political ideas of the mainly Slovak newcomers to the New World inevitably affected the thinking of those remaining at home. The Slovak immigrants of America now earned much more than they had earned before and could save and send home considerable sums of money that reached their families mainly through the Slovak Bank of Pittsburgh and the Tátra Felsömagyarországi Bank Rt (Tátra Banking Co. of Upper Hungary) at Turócszentmárton.[14] The owners of the Pittsburgh Bank were considered to be 'pan-Slav agitators', i.e. fighters for Czechoslovak and all-Slav unity, and the Tátrabank was in turn a fully Slovak institution. So the movement of the Slovak bourgeoisie, which was gathering momentum around the turn of the century, and its growing financial basis obviously supported the supposition that the impact of 'pan-Slav propaganda' among the Slovaks in America was the main cause of the growing activity of the Slovaks at home. It was a generally accepted assumption, therefore, that part of the money coming from America was spent on promoting the political aims of the Slovak nationalists.[15]

When the election of a new president became due at the Tátrabank in 1902, the government reacted immediately. The Minister of Commerce began to negotiate with the leaders of the public administration of the region and suggested that the Hungarian banks should take action against the nationalities in Upper Hungary. The report of the local authorities revealed little evidence of suspicious business dealings, however. The only thing that the bank could be accused of was investing the profit gained from the money sent home from America for the purposes of national politics: 'Part of the interim interest, presumably representing a large sum every year, is the financial basis of propaganda for the Slovaks'.[16]

The Prime Minister's Office considered the German relations of the Saxon banks and the American connections of the Tátrabank as problems which had the same origins. This idea gave birth to a third strategy: plans were to be worked out for the 'regulation of the political machinations of the banking institutions of the nationalities' and information for that purpose was to be acquired.

In his letter to the Minister of Commerce written in connection with the German national movement, the Prime Minister asked 'if it was not necessary to initiate a legislative measure to authorize the government to liquidate the companies involved in nationality politics, just as it had the right to dissolve associations representing a danger to the state'. At the same time he asked if the existing regulations 'made it possible for a state authority to look into the books and correspondence of the Saxon banks in order to throw light on their national machinations'.[17]

Parallel with the settlement of the pan-German problem in the autumn of 1902, the Minister of Commerce ordered the heads of the counties of Turóc, Trencsén, Nyitra and Árva to find out the causes of the rapid growth of the Tátrabank. He also wished to know if the Hungarian banks could be used to counterbalance their Slovak counterparts.[18]

The replies he received revealed that the causes of the strengthening of the Slovak network of banks lay in their low rates of interest, low dividends and their 'network of agents standing in close contact with the public', to say nothing of their firm policy concerning landed property. The leaders of the counties concerned suggested state intervention in the form of economic compensation which they considered sufficient to settle the problem. They maintained that the further expansion of the Slovak banking institutions could be restricted by the establishment of a central Hungarian bank at Turócszentmárton with branch establishments in Upper Hungary, and by the promotion of the local activity of the National Credit Society of Smallholders (Kisbirtokosok Országos Hitelszövetkezete) and the National Land Mortgage Bank (Országos Földhitelintézet) by means of state concessions.

Early in 1903 the Minister of Commerce prepared his scheme for counterbalancing the banking institutions of the nationalities including a concrete proposal for the general settlement of credit operations in Upper Hungary. He attributed the strengthening of the Slovak banks to the growing demand for credit under the conditions of recession, and to the cheap credit and flexibility which they offered. Starting from the supposition that the source of capital for the Slovak banks was the Industrial Bank of Prague and the remittances in cash flowing in from America alone meant a turnover of 6 to 8 million crowns, while 'the endangered territory was poor and in need of credit', the Minister thought the problem could be settled by concessions to the Magyar Földhitelintézet (Hungarian Land Mortgage Bank). The final sentences of the document are really characteristic of the circumstances of the time, as it turns out that the much quoted 'growth of the nationalities' in Upper Hungary was far from being as intense as had been imagined. 'We must not refrain from considerable sacrifices, but even less from measures demanding only little sacrifice, if any. Should these measures succeed, cheaper credit will certainly bring economic advantages for the region besides salutary political achievements'.[19]

The Prime Minister was, however, thinking of less liberal solutions. In his reply to the Minister of Commerce he explained at great length that increasing emigration was due to the relative overpopulation of the mountainous region, which was in turn caused by the insufficient development of industry there. This was why emigration mainly affected the homeland of the nationalities. He greatly regretted the situation, but noted that to encourage the activities of rival banks would only depress interest rates in Upper Hungary. In this way the state would add substantially to the money supply and stimulate an economic growth which 'would appear to reward the nationalities'. More important still, he noted that

> we cannot set any ideological weapon against the national feeling of the common people who are hardly able to appreciate great historical traditions ... The Slovaks of this country would not go for loans to the 'patriotic' banking institutions even if they offered lower rates of credit than those run by non-Magyars where they are drawn by their national feelings. Merchants and perhaps medium-sized landowners may have feelings like that but we must not commit the error of considering the economic motivation predominant.[20]

The prime ministership of Khuen-Héderváry opened a new phase in Hungary's policy towards the nationalities owing to the crisis in domestic policy. The above problems, side issues as they were even from the point of view of the policy towards the nationalities at that moment, were removed from the Prime Minister's sphere of interest. Control over the banks on the peripheries became the official duty of the Minister of Commerce. The responsible ministers had always been against all administrative interventions and only thought of stimulating competition to a certain degree. The Minister of Commerce, however, suggested an overall reorganization and extended his earlier propositions regarding Upper Hungary also as a region 'where other national propaganda prevailed, such as the eastern and southern parts of the country, where the economy was equally stagnating, emigration was equally high and the soil for anti-state activities of German and Romanian banking institutions was equally well prepared'.

However, this presented a by no means negligible problem since the state's intentions to free the banks of the nationalities from politics were in contrast with the provisions of the Nationalities Act, according to which all nationalities had the right to establish state-controlled associations, raise funds and invest them to promote their own schools, their language, art, science, literature, economic life, industry and commerce. The Commerce Act, however, did not make it possible for any institutions other than the law courts to look into the correspondence and business books of the banks. So the Minister of Commerce did not go beyond his ideas of a basically liberal control of economic life and endeavoured to take liberal legal measures against the nationalities' banks.[21]

In 1903 the Ministry of Agriculture also dealt with the problem: first, in connection with the increasing loans of the Albina Bank of Nagyszeben in the Székely district; then with reference to the plans to suppress usury in Upper Hungary. Towards the end of the same year, the Tisza government even entrusted the Minister of Agriculture with preparing measures against the banks of the nationalities.[22] The Minister of Agriculture Tallián Béla treated the problem as one of property relations. He addressed government ministers in a circular saying that he 'found it necessary to prepare and steadfastly realize a programme that would improve credit conditions and, at the same time, counter the efforts of the banking institutions of the nationalities'. In the spring of 1904 he convened a meeting of his fellow ministers, the Országos Központi Hitelszövetkezet (National Central Credit Society), the Kirbirtokosok Országos Földhitelin-tézete (National Mortgage Bank of Smallholders), the Magyar Földhitelintezet (Hungarian Land Mortgage Institute) and the responsible leaders of the counties. He also asked for the published accounts of each of the nationalities' banks to be submitted by the Statistical Office. Owing to lack of time, he could not carry out the suggestion that a report be made of the distribution of land, the stage of landownership and the demand for mortgage loans and personal credit in the territories inhabited by national minorities.

The minutes of this meeting, which was planned and convened in the strictest confidence, have unfortunately been lost. But the preliminary papers and ensuing developments make it possible for us to reconstruct some of the questions raised and the suggestions made. One of the draft copies of a document written by the Minister of Agriculture states, for example, that 'national incitement in Southern Hungary, Upper Hungary and Transylvania has shifted in the last two decades to the economic sphere'. Over and above influencing free competition by means of rival banks, he suggests buying up the shares of the non-Magyar banks: 'the whole sum being not too high and the influence gained thereby could force these banking institutions to remain strictly within the limits of their economic functions'. As far as Upper Hungary was concerned, the Agriculture Minister suggested that the Minister of Commerce find a way of preventing 'the cash remittances of the Slovak emigrants to America from promoting national propaganda' in Slovakia, through the large banks of Hungary. It is also suggested in the report that should the Romanian banks contact those banks of Budapest which offered cheaper credit than the Austro-Hungarian Bank then the government should stop them. If the Hungarian banks influenced by the government withdrew capital from the Romanian ones, they could shake the Romanian organization of credit to its foundations. A more modest suggestion hinted at the withdrawal from the Romanian banks of the considerable funds of the highest Romanian Church authorities and other local authorities, and their investment instead in state bonds.[23] It is quite clear that no resolution was passed at the meeting. The Minister of Agriculture was charged with the preparation of a detailed proposal by the autumn of 1904, but he was prevented from doing so by the ensuing large-scale political conflict between the government and the opposition and finally by the fall of the government.[24]

At the time of the coalition government of 1906–9 the nationality question was approached differently. More spectacular solutions such as libel cases came to the fore and there is no trace of the measures initiated by the former Minister of Agriculture. When a liberal government returned to power in 1910, the Minister of Religion and Public Instruction returned to the subject early that year. It was at his suggestion that the Under-Secretary of State for the Minister of Finance prepared a scheme aimed at 'strengthening the Hungarian ethnic element along the linguistic borders by means of a reasonable policy concerning landed property', at concentrating the rival Hungarian banks on the peripheries, and at 'including the banks of the nationalities with the large centres of the Hungarian economy'. However, the question was obviously not put on the agenda of the day. Referring to the meeting of 1904, the Under-Secretary remarked that

> the question itself was not suitable to be discussed publicly and the talks themselves proved that it could not be solved in that manner. Such talks can even result in an increased activity on the part of the credit institutions of the nationalities as actually happened at that time. Having been informed of the talks at once, they started to work at high pressure to make themselves secure against the prospective countermeasures of the Hungarian banks.[25]

We are not in a position to check if the banking institutions of the nationalities were actually informed of the talks of March 1904, though we have no reason to doubt the information. This is, however, unimportant. The non-Magyar banks could guess from the attacks in the Hungarian press at the turn of the century that sooner or later they would suffer restrictions imposed by the Hungarian state: the more so, since as early as 1902 the Financial Committee of the Parliament had spoken of the need for general state control of banking institutions. Prime Minister Széll replied to a parliamentary question that he would do whatever his sphere of authority permitted him to do.

The Saxon and Slovak banks, being stronger and relying more on foreign sources of credit, would have been endangered less by state intervention than the Romanian ones which could draw on only a minimum of foreign credit resources. They had therefore to build a defence system for themselves against financial crises and any possible state measures. As early as 1901 they contemplated steps to be taken should the Hungarian big banks withdraw their credit 'owing to hostile propaganda or political pressure'. Disaster could then be avoided only by mobilizing assets to the maximum degree even at the price of reducing profits. The Albina, the only Romanian bank issuing securities, undertook in 1903 to buy back mortgage loans, thereby securing the profit-earning capacity of the allied Romanian banks in face of all kinds of intervention coming from above.[26]

So the various campaigns in the press and the threat of state intervention totally missed the point. Instead of throwing obstacles in the way of the centralization of the non-Magyar credit service, it even promoted it, especially that of the Romanians. New banks were founded the existence of which was accepted and considered natural by their Hungarian counterparts, though not without jealousy.

The reason why the large banks did not want to take steps against the non-Magyar banks lay in the fact that the latter hardly showed tendencies going beyond their complementary economic role in the Monarchy, so they were not considered as rivals. The big banks controlling the market within the country competed primarily with one another. The rival of the Credit Bank (Hitelbank) was the Commercial Bank (Kereskedelmi Bank) and vice versa, and the non-Magyar banks were involved in this rivalry only indirectly.[27]

The leading politicians in Hungarian government circles realized the force inherent in the rapid economic, and especially financial, development of the nationalities. They even intended to put restraints on it. However, given the structure of the economy and the liberal principles of the government, as well as the lack of inner stability and the conflicts within the ruling classes, it was impossible for them to apply measures taken in political and cultural life to effectively oppress the economy of the nationalities.

Notes

1. Among the literature on the problem see L. Katus, 'Über die wirtschaftlichen und gesellschaftlichen Grundlagen der Nationalitätenfrage in Ungarn vor dem ersten Weltkrieg', in P. Hanák (ed.), *Die nationale Frage in der Österreichisch–Ungarischen Monarchie 1900–1918*, Budapest, 1966, pp. 149–216; *Die Agrarfrage in der Österreichisch–Ungarischen Monarchie 1900–1918*, Bucharest, 1965, pp. 79–172; C. Göllner (ed.), *Die Siebenbürger Sachsen in den Jahren 1848–1918*, Köln–Wien, 1988, pp. 66–103; B. Köpeczi (ed.), *Kurze Geschichte Siebenbürgens,* Budapest, 1990, pp. 551–78.

   A comprehensive picture of the development of the Hungarian economy and society can be found in E. Kovács and L. Katus (eds), *Magyarország története* (History of Hungary) 1848–1890, vol. 6, Budapest, 1979, and P. Hanák and F. Mucsi (eds), *Magyarország története* (History of Hungary) 1890–1918, vol. 7, Budapest, 1978, pp. 263–516, 1003–18.

2. Hungarian National Archives, The presidential documents of the Ministry of Agriculture (hereafter FM eln) 1915, no. 65651; 1903, no. 7538. N.N. Petra, *Băncile românești din Ardeal, și Banat* (Romanian banks in Transylvania & Banat), Sibiu, 1936, pp. 39–40. *Magyar Compass* (Hungarian Compass) *1890–91*, vol. I, p. 335; ibid., *1900–1901*, vol. I, pp. 533, 754–5; ibid., *1904–1905*, vol. I, p. 852. J. Vučkovic, *Srpski Kompas* (Serbian Compass) *1909*, Zemun, 1909, pp. 238–46.

3. R. Rösler, *Die Kreditorganisation der Sachsen in Siebenbürgen,* Hermannstadt, 1914, Supplement no. 2. N.N. Petra, op. cit., note 2, pp. 31, 34–5. *Revista Economica* 21 Sept. 1901. *Magyar Compass* (Hungarian Compass) *1890–1891, 1900–1901, 1903–1904.* A. Pachány, A *magyarországi tótok* (The Slovaks in Hungary), Budapest, 1913, p.173. *Slovenski Peaznîk,* 15 Dec. 1909. Veridicus, *Die Nationalitätenfrage in Ungarn als Geschäft*, Budapest, 1909, p. 26. J. Vučkovic, *Srpski Kompas* (Serbian Compass) *1909,* Zemun, 1909, pp. 238–46.

4. Rösler, op. cit., note 3, p. 59. I. Russu-Siriaviu, *Români din statul ungar* (Romanians in the Hungarian state), Bucharest, 1904, p. 296.

5. 'The big banks do not start a conversation with the medium-sized estate owner in Transylvania, the savings bank lends money at 9–10 per cent interest.' M. Bartha, 'Uj csapás (New disaster)' in *Ellenzék*, 3 August 1888.

6. B. Köpeczi (gen. ed.) and Z. Szász (ed.), *Erdély története (History of Transylvania)* vol. III, Budapest, 1986, pp. 1568–91.

7. Hungarian National Archives FM eln, 1895, no. 1014. 'A note of the Vll. Department of the Ministry of Agriculture on 27th August 1895'. See also G.G. Kemény, *Iratok a nemzetiségi kérdés történetéhez Magyarországon a dualizmus korában 1867–1919* (Documents on the history of the nationality question in Hungary in the dualistic era, 1867–1918), vol. II, Budapest, 1956, pp. 144–5, 395–8.

8. *'Erdélyiek bolondítása (The fooling of Transylvanians)'* in *Ellenzék*, 18 August l888.

9. C. Parteniu, 'Secuii şi "Albina" (The Székely and "Albina")' in *Revista Economica*, 1901, no. 47.

10. 'Nemzeti feladatok (National tasks)' in *Budapesti Hírlap*, 9 January l900.

11. Hungarian National Archives, Documents of the Commercial Bank, Projects. 'A memorandum of the Transylvanian Hungarian Mortgage Bank in 1894'. *Pénzintézeti Szemle*, 25 February 1906.

12. Hungarian National Archives, Documents of Prime Minister's Office (hereafter ME) 1905 XIV, no. 1274 (1902 XXI, no. 1943–3168, no. 1943–2137). For details see Z. Szász, '*A magyar kormámy tervei a nemzetiségi pénzintézetek állami ellenőrzésére* (The plans of the Hungarian Government for the control of the nationality banks by the state) *1902–1904*' in *Századok* 100 (1966) no. 1118–37.

13. The political reaction to emigration first emerges as an official problem in 1899. (Hungarian National Archives, ME 1910 XIV, no. 2164–899, XXXI, no. 8129.)

14. Hungarian National Archives, ME 1904 XIV, no. 741–1902; XXI, no. 4673.

15. Hungarian National Archives, ME 1902 XXIII, no. 4446. 'A note of Lord Lieutenant of the county Nyitra' on 2 December 1902.

16. Hungarian National Archives, ME 1904 XIV, no. 741–1902; XXI, no. 4673. The government planned to establish a Hungarian–American Bank in order to take the emigrants' remittances in cash, but it gave up the idea because of a crisis in domestic politics (Hungarian National Archives, ME 1910 XIV, no. 2164).

17. Hungarian National Archives, ME 1909 XIV, no. 1274–1902; XXI, no. 1943–3168, 2137.

18. Hungarian National Archives, FM eln, 1915 no. 65651 (presidential doc. 1903 no. 7538).

19. Hungarian National Archives, FM eln, 1915 no. 65651 (presidential doc. 1903 no. 7538). Gy. Rácz, *A magyar földbirtokosság pusztulaśa* (The deterioration of the Hungarian landowning class), Budapest, l904, p. 72.

20. Hungarian National Archives, ME 1903 XV/a, no. 2570, a note of 31 July 1903.

21. Hungarian National Archives, ME 1903 XV/a, no. 3166.

22. Hungarian National Archives, FM eln, 1915 no. 65651 (presidential doc. 1903 no. 7538).

23. 'It is not only a financial question to weaken the Romanian banks, since these agitate the clergymen, the teachers and these all three the thousands and thousands of the Romanian voters.' Hungarian National Archives, ME 1904 XIV, no. 741 (VKM eln 13314/1904).

24. The Minister of Finance asserted in the financial commission of the Parliament on 14 June 1904 (!) that the government would not want to be concerned with this question. See *Magyar Pénzügy*, 16 June 1904, Hungarian National Archives, ME 1904 XIV, no. 741–3924.

25. Hungarian National Archives, PM eln. res. 1911. 35. Documents of the Ministry of Finance, Draft, 26 January 1912.

26. Hungarian National Archives, ME 1904 XIV, no. 152 (3384) '*The third conference of Romanian banks' managers*', *Magyar Pénzügy*, 16 June 1904.

27. *Pénzintézeti Szemle*, 25 February 1906. See the report of the bank agent of the Hungarian Commercial Bank of Pest in Braşov, 4 February 1911. Hungarian National Archives Documents of the Commercial Bank.

5   Universal banking in the Slovene region, 1900–1945

Franjo Štiblar

The study of the history of banking in Slovenia is neither systematic nor institutionalized. Occasional studies in the past were the result of individual initiatives. With the establishment of Slovenia as an independent country in 1991, the interest in studying its past has increased and banking history is no exception. The aim of this chapter is twofold: first, to discover the historic roots of a newly established country, and second, on the basis of past experience to promote a better understanding of current events, since many of the present dilemmas were already known in the past.

This study has very modest intentions. It aims to describe the historic development of Slovenian banking at the same time as showing the relevance of banking to the emergence of the Slovenian state. The history of twentieth century universal banking in the Slovene region is identical to the history of Slovene corporate banking from its very beginning.

While universal banking was developed on Austro-German lines in what is contemporary Slovenia, it did not emerge before corporate banking was introduced in 1900. Although financial intermediating was present in Slovenia from the early nineteenth century in the non-incorporated form of private bankers, and even more through credit cooperatives in the countryside as well as the regulatory or self-managed savings institutions in urban areas, their activity was limited to short-term transactions. After financial institutions were incorporated as joint-stock banks they diversified their business activity by adding long-term investment banking. They then became directly involved in the ownership and management of industry. Even in the provinces of Austria with a prevailing Slovene population German-speaking entrepreneurs dominated the economy, although they did not establish their own banks. Instead, financial intermediation was managed by branches of the banks from Vienna. Their appearance was provoked by the early success of corporate banks established in the region by Slovenes. Thus, there were no German-language banks with a central office in Slovenia before the First World War. However, after the war, the newly established state of the South Slavs did not permit the incorporation of foreign banks.

Only a year after the establishment of the first savings bank in Vienna in 1820 the first savings institution, Krainische Sparkasse, was established in Ljubljana, capital of Carniola.[1] Carniola was one of those provinces in the Austrian part of the Austro-Hungarian Empire with a majority of Slovene speakers. It was controlled by the economically dominant German population in the region, where the linguistic duality (German versus Slovene) played an important role in economic and socio-political life. Following the Empire's Law on the Regulation of Savings Institutions (1844) and the Law on Cooperatives (1873), unincorporated financial institutions (both German and Slovene) began to emerge in the Slovene region.

The German-language financial intermediaries, however, failed to attract the Slovene population, both rural and urban, which started to become a more and more significant economic force with the successful industrialization of the region in the second half of the nineteenth century. They confined their activities to accumulating and exporting savings (through their investment in securities outside the region) while non-domiciled financial institutions (from Vienna and Berlin) were responsible for the capital investment by financing the expansion of predominantly German-owned industries in the area (paper, iron, railways).

The response of the Slovenes was to introduce their own financial intermediaries: the self-governing or regulatory savings institution in the cities as well as the credit cooperatives in the countryside. Here they replaced the individual bankers and local lenders in a highly fragmented market. Larger risk distribution, better communication in the domestic Slovene language and a 'solidarity' spirit were among the advantages of these intermediaries. They helped to widen the network of Slovene unincorporated financial institutions very quickly. By 1900 they numbered over 200 and by 1912 there were over 500. With strictly short-term financing, usually supported by a strong collateral, these lending cooperatives and savings 'banks', functioning as a system through their associations, brought about the integration of primary capital supply, an indispensable part of overall economic development and modernization. They first accumulated financial savings, then directed them (especially the Slovene financial intermediaries) to a large extent into the financing of local housing, school and public utilities.

The attempts to develop corporate banking in what is now Slovenia in the nineteenth century emerged from the German-speaking financial institutions and from the initiative of cooperative loan associations. These attempts were short-lived, however. Thus, for example, on the German side a branch of the Austrian National Bank was opened in Ljubljana in 1856, but had a short lifespan; the Laibacher Gewerbebank was established in 1867, then merged with the branch of the Steierische Eskomptebank, and survived until 1878; the Krainische Eskomptegesellschaft functioned in Ljubljana between 1876 and 1885. On the Slovene side, besides the Zavarovalna Banka (1871–76), mentioned later, a plan to open the Slovenska Obća Banka in 1872–73 was also a failure.[2]

The Development of universal banking

1900–1912

Within Austria, the Cisleithanian portion of the dual Monarchy, the generally prosperous years between 1900 and 1912 (second 'Gründerzeit') were marked in banking by two opposing developments. On the one hand, there was a tendency for the concentration of financial capital in the hands of the large Viennese banks. On the other, there was a rapid growth of corporate banking within the non-German territories of Austria, including in the Slovene regions.[3]

Linguistic specialization seems to have been a significant element in the early success of Slovene joint-stock banks. They served a Slovene-speaking clientele which had been largely bypassed by German–Austrian intermediaries. In time, German–Austrian banks (Krainische Sparkasse) accepted a modicum of Slovene in their dealings with the public, after they had experienced losses when deposits were transferred to Slovene financial institutions.

In the provinces of Austria (and Slovene regions were no exception to this) the process of concentration of capital made itself felt by the acquisition of non-corporate private banks and their transformation into branches and by the absorption of joint-stock provincial banks into so-called communities of interest (Interessengemeinschaften), dominated by the Viennese banks. The evolution of corporate banking in Slovenia ran counter to these tendencies by extending its services to an ethnic market which German–Austrian banks had failed to develop. It began with the establishment of the Ljubljanska Kreditna Banka (LKB, founded in Ljubljana in 1900), the Jadranska Banka (JB, Trieste, 1905) and the Ilirska Banka (Ljubljana, 1916).[4] All three were joint-stock banks and at the same time universal banks. They provided both short-term commercial credit and facilities for long-term corporate financing.

The LKB was incorporated in Ljubljana on the initiative of the city's mayor Ivan Hribar and private banker Maks Vršec. In the initial stock offering of the LKB, the Živnostenská Banka (Prague, Vienna branch) took 50 per cent (and supplied the majority of its managing directors), individual subscribers took 36 per cent, while the remaining shares were subscribed for by cooperatives. It was not until 1916 that a corporate bank was founded by credit cooperatives, namely, the Ilirska Banka of Ljubljana.[5] By this time credit cooperatives, operating under statutory restrictions, could no longer provide the entire range of financial services demanded by the evolving cooperative sector, hence the tendency to increase the activities of joint-stock banking.

From Ljubljana the Slovene banking initiative spread to Trieste, where the Jadranska Banka (JB) was founded in 1905. Individual investors (from Trieste, Slovene interior and Dalmatia) subscribed 60 per cent of the initial stock; the LKB held 16 per cent, a number of Croatian banks took up 20 per cent, while credit cooperatives accounted for the remaining 4 per cent. Both the LKB (initial capital: 0.5 million crowns) and the JB (1 million crowns) grew rapidly, so that by 1912 their capital stock amounted to 8 million crowns each. The branch network of the LKB included Klagenfurt, Split, Trieste, Sarajevo, Gorica and Celje. The JB was concentrated in Dalmatia, for which Trieste served as the main economic link with the rest of Austria. Besides Ljubljana, it had branches in Dubrovnik, Split, Šibenik, Zadar, Kotor, Metković and Opatija. The charters of both banks provided for a full range of banking services. In addition to commercial lending, following German traditions, both banks soon began to organize new joint-stock companies and underwrite stock issues. Corporate ventures in which they participated included medium-size enterprises in the food industry (breweries, sugar refining), metalworking (manufacturing of shotguns), a brick kiln, brokerage firms and steamship companies.[6]

The Viennese banks may have perceived the potential significance of the Slovene regional market only after the LKB got off to a successful start. Two Viennese banks established branches in Ljubljana: the Creditanstalt, by buying out the local private bank of L.C. Luckmann in 1906; and the Verkehrsbank, by acquiring that of E. Mayer in 1908. In addition to Carniola, in Carinthia too Viennese capital moved in on the heels of the LKB, which was the first corporate bank to establish a branch in Klagenfurt. Soon afterwards the Creditanstalt transformed the private bank Suppan into its Klagenfurt branch.[7]

A comparison of the asset structure of Slovene banks with that of the Vienna and Prague banks in 1912 shows the evolution of bank credit from the initial stages (Slovene banks) to a higher stage (Czech banks) and to a mature stage (Vienna banks). Advances on securities and goods represented 32 per cent of the assets of the Slovene banks, but only 7 per cent and 6 per cent respectively of the other two groups of banks. At the same time, the order is reversed in the proportion of debtors on current account (Vienna banks having 65 per cent, Czechs 50 per cent, while Slovene banks had only 33 per cent), where substantial economies of scale and more advanced borrowing on a continuous basis were possible. Among liabilities the Viennese banks relied more heavily on transferable deposits (demand deposits) with 57 per cent than the Czechs (43 per cent) or the Slovene banks (23 per cent). On the other hand, time deposits to the banks represented 23 per cent of liabilities in the Slovene banks, compared with 19 per cent in the Czechs and only 10 per cent in the Viennese banks.[8]

After twelve years, Slovene banking represented 3.5 per cent of the capital stock in Austria outside Vienna in 1912. Although this is lower than its 4.5 per cent share of the total population, Slovene corporate banking was supported by the proportionally more important credit cooperatives and public savings institutions (banks). Their combined assets were over 400 million crowns (the corresponding value for corporate banks 63 million crowns) representing over 5 per cent of assets of such institutions in Austria. The shares of the LKB and the JB were traded on the Vienna stock exchange, and both banks participated in inter-bank consortia for underwriting securities. Apparently, linguistic specialization enhanced financial integration rather than causing financial isolation.

1912–18

With the start of the Balkan Wars in 1912 and subsequently the First World War, conditions for financial intermediation deteriorated in all Austrian provinces. The financial power of banks declined, but apparently for the Slovene banks less than for the Austrian banks. While the cost of living increased by more than twelve times, the total balances of the LKB increased six times and that of the JB eight times. At the same time the Viennese banks increased their balances by less than three times. Among the reasons for the smaller financial contractions of Slovene banks were the vicinity of the war (with increased payment transfers related to it) and the concentration of the Slovene banks on small-scale industry (consumer goods) which was relatively more prosperous during the war. The establishment of a new Slovene bank, the Ilirska banka of Ljubljana, in 1916, is a sign of a relatively positive financial climate in this region during the war.

The war strongly influenced the structure of banking assets in the Slovene banks. Among liabilities the share of savings deposits was decreasing (due to the hoarding of coins and falling real incomes), as was in real terms the share of current accounts. The real value of the capital stock fell substantially and had to be increased after the war. On the assets side there was an increase of the share of cash. As the supply of goods lagged behind demand during the war years, it was not necessary to give buyers credit; therefore bills of exchange practically disappeared from the banks' asset balances.

1919–30

The period 1919–25 could be called a 'Gründerzeit' of the Slovene economy, including its financial sector (about 50 years after the Austrian 'Gründerzeit' period 1867–73 and a decade after its second period at the beginning of the twentieth century). The majority of Slovene provinces were united under a new South Slavic state, the Kingdom of Serbs, Croats and Slovenes, in 1918. The negative effect of the lost markets of the previous Austro-Hungarian Empire was more than offset by the positive effects of 'nationalization' of the economy (firms and banks in the Slovene region were taken over by Slovenes, not without compensation), by the opening of the large Yugoslav market and by an expansive monetary policy until 1923. During that period 80 new Slovene joint-stock companies were added to the stock of only eleven existing before. In the financial sector, the number of corporate banks in Ljubljana (the only remaining Slovene financial centre after Trieste was lost to Italy) increased from three to nine, and their branches from eight to 31, while non-Ljubljana banks maintained six branches in Ljubljana. The stock exchange was established in Ljubljana in

1924, trading first only in commodities and securities, with foreign exchange added in 1927. In 1920 the Društvo Bančnih Zavodov (Society of Banking Institutions) was established in Ljubljana with the aim of providing common business rules and a common banking policy (for instance, the fixing of a maximum 5 per cent interest rate on deposits). Nevertheless, competition from other Yugoslav banks and from the non-incorporated credit cooperatives and savings institutions prevented them from having monopolistic control of the financial market.

After the war the LKB increased its nominal share capital fivefold, thus obtaining a majority domestic holding and retaining its position as the largest Slovenian financial institution. The JB was decentralized into three units during the war (Adriatische Bank in Vienna, Banco Adriatico in Trieste and Jadranska Banka with its central office in Belgrade). The first two branches got into difficulties due to outside pressures and mismanagement and were liquidated in 1925, while the third branch was absorbed later. Thus the strongest Slovene bank before the First World War disappeared from the scene in the 1920s. In 1920, the Ljubljana branch of Vienna's Creditanstalt (CA) was transformed into a Slovenian institution – the Kreditni Zavod za Trgovino in Industrijo (KZTI, Credit Institution for Trade and Industry), in which the CA retained a substantial 30 per cent share in its capital. As explained in detail in Tosti,[9] this financial institution of the universal type played an important role in the Slovene economy in the 1920s, was hit by the crisis of the 1930s as were other Slovene financial institutions, but survived even through the Second World War. A similar process of reorganization due to 'nostrification'[10] occurred in the case of the establishment of the Hipotekarna Banka Jugoslovanskih Hranilnic in Ljubljana (1921–30), Mariborska Eskomptna Banka (1918–22) and some smaller corporate banks in Prekmurje.

Besides reorganization, some new banks were incorporated in Slovenia after the First World War. The most important among them was the Zadružna Gospodarska Banka (Cooperative Economic Bank). It was established in 1920 on the initiative of cooperative circles, as were the Zadružna Banka (Cooperative Bank) in Ljubljana in 1920 and the Celjska Posojilnica (Celje's Credit Institutions) in Celje in 1922. At the same time, a growing number of Slovene entrepreneurs established several new smaller corporate banks, suitable for their specific needs. Such were the Obrtna Banka (Craftsmen Bank, 1920), Slavenska Banka (1920), Prometna Banka (Traffic Bank, 1921), Trgovska Banka (Trade Bank, 1922), all in Ljubljana, the Merkantilna Banka (1922) in Kočevje and the Kreditna Banka in Murska Sobota.

By 1923, the number of Slovene corporate banks and their branches reached a peak. An end to the 'founding euphoria' was caused by the deflationary monetary policy of the Yugoslav government (which successfully stabilized the domestic dinar by 1925) and the difficulties of the Slavenska Banka Zagreb connected with it. This bank had a Slovene manager and close business connections with several Slovene banks. When the Slavenska Banka became bankrupt owing to unsuccessful postwar speculations, several Slovene banks were liquidated, and some others reduced their total assets by clearing bad debts. Among the disappearing banks (not all, however, in connection with the fall of the Slavenska Banka) were the Mariborska Eskomptna Banka (leaving the industrial centre Maribor without its own financial support), Hipotekarna Banka, Ilirska Banka, Trgovska Banka, Merkantilna Banka Kočevje and some smaller banks. Surprising as it may seem, this liquidation of some banks and some bad debts of other banks contributed to the consolidation of the Slovene banking sector, which established solid foundations at the start of the world economic crisis in 1930.

1930–41

In 1930, the Slovene banking capital was concentrated in Ljubljana and within Ljubljana the three largest financial institutions (the LKB, the KZTI and the Zadružna Gospodarska Banka Ljubljana) accounted for over 88 per cent of total banking assets. In that year total banking assets reached a peak. In 1931 the Yugoslav government adopted the gold standard, which lasted for only a few months. The collapse of the Creditanstalt in Vienna (with strong financial ties with Slovenia), the outflow of capital from Austria and Germany, and Hoover's moratorium on reparation payments (Yugoslavia should have received payments) contributed to the contraction of Slovene banking in the period 1931–34.

Related to the work of Jonker and van Zanden,[11] the Slovene banking sector, closely connected with Austrian and German banking sectors, the big losers in the world crisis, suffered enormously. Although the financial contraction in Slovene banking was halted after 1935, the years to the Second World War brought little more than a stagnation of banking assets. According to Hočevar's calculations, Slovene banks cut their total assets by 10–20 per cent per annum in the period 1931–34, thus reducing them by half in nominal terms by 1935.[12] At the same time, the amount of outstanding bank credits decreased at a lower rate, while the amount of saving deposits fell faster. In the period 1935–40 the total banking assets of the Slovene banks increased by approximately 10 per cent, cash holdings in banks more than doubled, the amount of outstanding bank credits increased by 10 per cent, basic capital stock increased 20 per cent and profits increased steadily from year to year. The profit rate increased from 8 per cent in 1935 to close to 10 per cent in 1940. In nominal terms the total banking assets of Slovene banks were in 1940 80 per cent lower than in 1930. This indicates a substantial contraction of Slovene banking activities, even if one takes into account deflationary movements during the 1930s.

1941–45

After the axis powers attacked Yugoslavia in 1941, the Slovene territory was divided among three occupiers: Germany, Italy and Hungary. This involved in effect the liquidation of Slovene banking, since a previously unified economic area was divided disproportionately. While in the period 1941–43 almost two-thirds (and after 1943 even more) of the Slovene territory was occupied by the Germans, taking into account inhabitants, workers and firms, only 5 per cent of Slovenia's total banking assets were under German control. Most of the trans-actions were made by the newly established branches of the large Viennese banks (Creditanstalt-Bankverein, Laenderbank). They had a majority of their assets invested in Viennese central offices or in the Reichsbank in Berlin. At the same time, industrial investments (war industry) in the Slovene territory under German occupation were financed from outside.

By occupying the region of Prekmurje Hungary controlled about 8 per cent of inhabitants, 3 per cent of firms, 2 per cent of workers and 3 per cent of Slovene banks.[13] These banks, located in Murska Sobota, were put under the direct control of the financial centre in Budapest thus losing most of their independence. The Ljubljana region, which was under Italian occupation in the period 1941–43, included less than one-third of the earlier Slovene economy (inhabitants, firms and workers), but dealt with over 90 per cent of Slovene financial intermedi-aries. This disproportion led to the contraction of personnel and closing of several Slovene banks and offices, while most of the financial intermediation was undertaken by branches of the Italian banks opened in Ljubljana (Banco Com-merciale, Banco di Roma, Banco Triestina). The situation did not improve for the Slovene banks after the Germans occupied the Ljubljana region in 1943.

On the other hand, under territories liberated by the Slovene partisans towards the end of the Second World War, a new independent monetary system and banking system started to emerge.[14] Thus in the period 1944–45 for the first time in history a Slovene issuing bank was established (Denarni Zavod Slovenije). At the same time, financial intermediation within a simple institutional arrange-ment was flourishing (payment systems, credits for liberation, financial instruments used for compensation for confiscated commodities, etc.). When the Second World War ended in 1945 and a new Yugoslavia was established all these elements of Slovene financial independence were eliminated. They have reappeared only now, after the proclamation of the independent state of Slovenia in 1991.

Conclusion

The historical development of universal banking in the territory of Slovenia (in fact Slovene corporate banking) in the first half of the twentieth century can be summed up as follows. First, institutional financial intermediation appeared early in the nineteenth century in this region in a non-corporate form and from the 1900s in a corporate form, leading to universal banking. Although lagging behind the Austrian financial centre, the Slovenes developed their own financial sector. It played an important role in somewhat late industrial development and modernization, similar to experience elsewhere.

Second, at the start of the Balkan Wars and the First World War the financial power of Slovene banks decreased less than in the Austrian banks (reasons being the vicinity of war transfers and the concentration of Slovene banking on small-scale consumer goods industries, which were relatively prosperous during the war).

Third, the war influenced the structure of banking assets in Slovene banks, reducing the share of savings deposits and the real value of capital stock among liabilities, and at the same time increasing the share of cash on the asset side.

Fourth, the period 1919–25 was a 'Gründerzeit' of Slovene banking (50 years after Austria). It was true that through nostrification the power of branches of foreign banks decreased after the war, but at the same time Slovene banks obtained an enlarged Yugoslav economic space enabling them to achieve rapid development. The expansion ended with the introduction of a restrictive monetary policy. The establishment of the Society of Banking Institutions in 1927 was not a sign of monopoly because competition from branches of banks from other Yugoslav territories and from non-incorporate financial institutions remained.

Fifth, the great economic and financial crises in the 1930s did not avoid the Slovene territories, due to the strong financial ties not only of German but also of Slovene financial intermediaries with the financial centres in Austria and Germany, which were both strongly affected by the banking crisis. The financial power of the banking sector was more than halved during the first half of the 1930s, and later on merely stagnated in the second half of the 1930s.

Sixth, a new crisis hit Slovene banking during the occupation in the Second World War, when the Slovene domestic banks were practically put out of business. Branches of Viennese banks and newly established Italian banks controlled most of the financial transactions pushing Slovene banks into a corner.

Finally, an independent Slovene banking sector started to emerge among partisans in 1944, but was dissolved after the New (Second) Yugoslavia was established in 1945. Its development was restored after the independence of Slovenia in 1991.

The role of banking and banking policy was adapted to conditions in the territory of Slovenia. First, foreign personnel played a major role not only in branches of foreign banks, but also in the first Slovene bank (Czechs and Slovaks), owing to lack of domestic expertise. Second, domestic Slovene banking was 'relation banking' (having closer ties with domestic enterprises), while foreign banking was predominantly 'transaction banking' (transferring deposits to the main branches out of the region, and bringing back some of the financial assets as investments through different channels).

Banks performed all types of traditional financial operations. On the active side, they started with short-term credits for financing variable capital and later continued with long-term credits and buying shares, thus becoming universal banks. On the passive side they collected deposits, where the share of time deposits was higher than in Austria.

In the bilingual territory of Slovenia language differences determined the parallel emergence of Slovene and German banking. The economic strength of the two differed significantly. The first was smaller in its scale, but closely connected with local interests. Within Slovene banking further divisions of the financial intermediaries appeared along political lines. However, the Germans opened only bank branches in the Slovene territory with their centres in Vienna and in Berlin. Thus they induced an outflow of capital (savings deposits were channelled into central offices) and at the same time an inflow of capital (financing investments in German-dominated industries). This German approach was especially evident before the emergence of domestic corporate banking in the year 1900 and during the occupation in the Second World War.

For comparison, the available data show that Slovene corporate banking was only at its initial stage of development in comparison with the higher stage of Czech banks and the mature stage of Austrian banks in 1912. The Slovenes' share in Austrian banking was less than proportional with regard to the shares in the population and economic power of the Slovene territory in the first decade of the twentieth century, as was the share of Slovene financial intermediation in the interwar years of the 1930s. Both sub-proportional shares of the Slovene corporate banking in Austria and subsequently in Yugoslavia were more than offset by the over-proportional shares of Slovene non-corporate financial intermediaries (lending cooperatives, saving institutions) in the related countries.

The role of government and state measures in banking was important even before the crisis, when the restrictive monetary policy of the central government in Belgrade caused financial contraction, but at the same time a consolidation of the banking sector. During the crisis, additional government regulation did not have as severe an impact on the financial centre except during the unsuccessful short-term introduction of the gold standard in 1931.

The question of a correlation between universal banking and nationalism has a specific answer in the case of Slovenia as a less developed region which wished to become independent. To counter the economic dominance of foreigners (Austrians and Germans) and to establish an economic foundation for the desired political autonomy, independent Slovene universal banking was one of the prerequisites. This was not to be nationalistic but simply to show that independent banking was a means to preserve a national identity and to prevent economic and political subordination to major powers outside the region. As an illustration, in the first Yugoslavia, between the wars, foreign capital had a 70–80 per cent share in the banking sector. Commercial banking without closer

54   Universal banking in the twentieth century

ties to the Slovene economy could not play such an important role. The analysis shows that the history of Slovene banking can be rightly observed as a relevant part of the history of the Slovene nation, because of its important contribution to the economic foundations of a rising Slovene consciousness.

Implications from historical experience for present banking in Slovenia are quite strong. Many questions and problems relevant for today's development of the Slovene banking sector were raised as early as the beginning of the century. We have a similar situation with regard to the entry of the Austrian banks, the indirect presence of German banks and the less successful entry of Italian banks, while other countries, at present, have not shown a special interest in establishing branches of their main banks or even a new bank in Slovenia. At the same time, as before, foreign ownership of real property (land, housing, firms) is high on the political agenda again today.

Notes

1. A Slovene population was also significantly present in other Austro-Hungarian provinces, such as Styria, Carinthia, Pomurje, Dolenjsko, Primorsko and the city of Trieste.
2. S. Granda, 'Poskus organiziranja slovenske Ljubljanske obče banke, 1872' (An Attempt to Establish a Slovene Ljubljana General Bank, 1872), in *Zgodovina denarstva in bančništva na Slovenskem*, Zgodovinski časopis Ljubljana, 1987, pp. 47–52.
3. T. Hočevar, 'Financial Intermediation in a Multilingual State: The Case of Slovene Corporate Banking in Austria, 1900–1912' *Slovene Studies*, 8:1, University of New Orleans, pp. 45–56.
4. There was no previous German corporate financial venture in Slovene territory, while the only Slovene attempt, Prva Obča Zavarovalna Banka Slovenije (1871–76) was a failure, partly due to the Viennese financial crash of 1873 and partly to mismanagement. This failure left a bitter aftertaste among Slovene investors and weakened confidence in joint-stock companies.
5. Thus, the Ljudska Posojilnica as an important cooperative held 40 per cent of the capital in the Ilirska banka.
6. The large industries in Slovene territory, even when started by local entrepreneurs, were under control or absorbed by firms located outside the region. Thus, for instance, coal mining and the paper industry were under the control of Vienna-based firms, while the steel complex was controlled by the Berlin bank. The inflow of capital for expansion of these firms was at least in part offset by exports of capital by a few existing German local intermediaries, the largest of which was the Krainische Sparkasse of Ljubljana.
7. B. Michel, *Banque et banquiers en Autriche au debut du 20e siècle,* Presses de la Fondation nationale des sciences politiques, Paris, 1976, p. 108.
8. T. Hočevar, 'Financial Intermediation in a Multilingual State: The Case of Slovene Corporate Banking in Austria, 1900–1912', in *Slovene Studies,* 8:1, University of New Orleans, p. 53.
9. A. Tosti, 'Denarni zavodi v Sloveniji po prvi svetovni vojni', [Monetary Institutions in Slovenia After World War I], *Bančni Vestnik,* Ljubljana, 1989, pp. 1–158.
10. Nostrification after the First World War should be distinguished from the post-Second World War nationalization in Slovenia. While in the first case it meant a transfer of ownership from foreign to Slovene (private) hands, in the second case it was a transfer from Slovene private to state and later social ownership. In relation to the current discussion about ownership transformation in Slovenia, it could be observed that the policy towards foreign ownership of Slovene firms and banks was relatively restrictive immediately after the First World War.
11. J. Jonker and J.L. Zanden, 'Method in the Madness? Banking Crises Between the Wars, An International Comparison', in *Report from the International Conference on 20th Century Universal Banking, International Comparisons,* Budapest, 1992, pp. 1–16.
12. T. Hočevar, 'Slovensko poslovno bančništvo, 1913–1941' (Slovene Business Banking, 1913–41), in *Bančni Vestnik 33,* Ljubljana, 1984, pp. 9, 271.

13. Ibid., p. 272.
14. See Z. Čepič, 'Prispevek k proučevanju valutarne reforme leta 1945' (Contribution to the Study of Currency Reform in 1945), in *Zgodovina denarstva in bančništva na Slovenskem*, Zgodovinski časopis Ljubljana, 1989, pp. 105–19; D. Guštin, 'Finančni viri in denarništvo NOB na Slovenskem, 1941–1945' (Financial Sources and Monetary Matters in the National Independence Struggle in Slovenia, 1941–1945), in *Zgodovina denarstva in bančništva na Slovenskem*, Zgodovinski časop Ljubljana, 1987, pp. 81–104.

PART II

CENTRAL BANKS, THE STATE AND UNIVERSAL BANKS

6 Production versus currency: the Danish Central Bank in the 1920s

Per H. Hansen

In recent years, research into central banking and bank regulation has attracted considerable interest. Numerous studies on historical banking crises and cases of lender of last resort operations have been inspired by an increase in financial instability in the Western world. Thus, an old and sometimes controversial theme has come back into prominence. The issue is important, because a better understanding of the evolution of the micro functions of central banks will increase our understanding of alternatives when faced with the challenges or threats to the financial systems of today. The lender of last resort activities of the Danish Central Bank, the Nationalbanken (the Bank), are the subject of this chapter.

The first section summarizes the 'theory' of the lender of last resort. This is followed by some brief comments on the general features of the banking system, the legal setting and the attitude of the Nationalbanken towards troubled banks before the 1920s. The third section traces the role of the Nationalbanken as a lender of last resort during the banking crisis of the 1920s, and then the principles and motives for support to distressed banks are considered. The chapter concludes with a summary of the experience of the banking crisis of the 1920s.

The 'theory' of the lender of last resort

Walter Bagehot's description of the functions of the Bank of England remains the starting point for research on the lender of last resort. In times of crisis, the central bank is supposed to support illiquid but solvent banks by lending and rediscounting on adequate collateral and against a penalty rate. The purpose of this assistance is not to support the individual bank, but to avoid a general run on the banking system due to information asymmetries (Bagehot, 1873; Baltensperger and Dermine, 1987; Bordo, 1989; Goodhart, 1988; Guttentag and Herring, 1987; Kindleberger, 1989, pp. 172–200; Rockoff, 1986; Solow, 1982; Laffargue, 1982).

There is general consensus that the lender of last resort shall be the central bank,[1] because of its status as a non-competitive and non-profit institution (Goodhart, 1988), and because it can issue legal tender[2] (Laffargue, 1982; Bordo, 1989; Guttentag and Herring, 1987; Kindleberger 1989). Thus, as a Weberian ideal type, lender of last resort assistance has to come from the central bank to illiquid but solvent banks.[3] In order to avoid a run, the assistance should be given immediately and in sufficient amounts. Insolvent banks would be allowed to fail, or else merged with another bank (Minsky, 1982a; Guttentag and Herring, 1987; Rockoff, 1986; Bagehot, 1873; Eichengreen and Portes, 1987; Kindleberger, 1989; Solow, 1982, p. 241). However, as some writers have pointed out, central banks have often had to provide assistance to insolvent banks and against inadequate collateral (Guttentag and Herring, 1987, Kindleberger, 1988).

The setting
The Nationalbanken was established in 1818 as a private joint-stock bank with the primary purpose of stabilizing the value of the krone at par. A few years before, in 1813, the monetary system had broken down due to the hyperinflation caused by the financing of Denmark's participation in the Napoleonic wars. The Nationalbanken was granted a monopoly of note issue and independence from the state. Besides its issuing function the bank could also operate as a commercial bank by discounting bills of exchange, lombarding securities, etc. (lombarding means lending against securities – bonds or shares – as collateral). Until 1875 Denmark was on a silver standard, and from 1845 – parity with silver being re-established in 1838 – notes were redeemable into silver on demand. The reserve requirements, also introduced in 1845, were revised several times during the period due to an increased transaction demand for money (see Table 6.1).

The changing reserve requirements influenced the opportunities of the Nationalbanken for assisting the commercial banks during financial distress. It was only in 1908 and again in 1914 and 1915, that these were improved considerably.

The bank was, at least formally, independent of the government, the parliament and the shareholders (Hansen, 1968, pp. 131–4 and 364–7; Rubow, 1918), but until 1936 it was organized and functioned as a joint-stock company and therefore a private profit-maximizing unit. Even though the private business operations formed a decreasing part of the operations of the bank, this was potentially in conflict with the macro and micro functions of a central bank (Goodhart, 1988 and Tilly, 1989).

The banking system
The Danish banking system developed as a universal banking system from the mid-nineteenth century with joint-stock banks spread all over the country and the largest banks located in Copenhagen (Hansen, 1991b; 1992). Two of the main banks, all of which were located in Copenhagen, had already established branches in some provincial towns from the 1870s, either by taking over local banks or by founding new ones (Hansen, 1991b, pp. 25–7), but the banking system remained basically decentralized during the first half of the twentieth century. The savings banks held a far more important position within the credit market than in most countries outside Scandinavia (see Table 6.2)

Table 6.1 *Metal reserve requirements against the note issue of the Nationalbanken (amounts in million kroner)*

	1845	1847	1854	1859	1873	1877	1897	1901	1908	1914	1915	1927
Maximum note issue	33	40	48	–	–	–	–	–	–	–	–	–
Reserve (%)	50	50	50	50 < 48 m. 100 > 48 m.	100	100	100	100	50	40	33	50
Maximum fiat issue	–	–	–	–	27	30	33	38	–	–	–	–

Source: Rubow, 1918, pp. 436–46; Rubow, 1920, pp. 266–9; Olsen, 1968 and Hansen, 1968.

Table 6.2   Deposits of commercial and savings banks (million kroner)

Year	Commercial banks' deposits	Commercial banks' capital	Commercial banks' number[a]	Savings banks' deposits[b]	Savings banks' number
1870	27	17	18	118	168
1880	78	54	41	254	443
1890	176	71	46	454	516
1900	310	101	86	582	512
1905	509	148	104	711	514
1910	701	235	135	811	521
1915	1077	264	141	995	513
1920	4037	587	208	1459	505
1925	2357	360	193	1872	526
1930	2344	445	180	2097	532
1935	2197	452	168	2190	526
1940	2898	519	162	2158	516

Notes:
[a]   From 1920 to 1924 there are some differences between Banktilsynet, 1945 and Johansen, 1985. The number of banks before 1920 is probably underestimated.
[b]   From 1924 the savings banks from 'Sønderjylland', the Southern part of Denmark that before 1920 belonged to Germany, are included in the deposits as well as the number columns.

Source: Johansen, 1985 and Banktilsynet, 1945.

Before 1930, the three main banks' share of total bank assets declined from 70 to 50 per cent, but many banks in the provinces remained very small and operated on a much smaller scale than the large banks, and with a different composition of assets and liabilities. Most provincial banks were not universal banks; instead they restricted their business to discounting bills of exchange and lending to local merchants, artisans and farmers on a short-term basis. The main banks and, to a lesser degree, the big provincial ones were engaged in a variety of operations, including investment banking. Furthermore, the main banks acted as correspondents to many provincial banks, and thus as a buffer between these and the Nationalbanken.

The figures in Table 6.3 suggest that Danish banks, on average, had sufficient capital to be universal banks. However, capital's share of total liabilities declined over time, while deposits increased until about 1910 when they stabilized at about 75 per cent of total liabilities.

The main characteristic of bank assets is the decline in bills of exchange and the corresponding rise in advances. Securities accounted for a comparatively stable part of the assets, although with higher shares during the years 1890–99 and 1910–19 when activity in the issuing business was intense (Table 6.4).

Table 6.3   Liabilities of Danish banks, 1870–1939 (%)

Year	Capital	Deposits	Foreign liabilities	Other liabilities	Total
1870–79	38	50	–	12	100
1880–89	30	63	–	7	100
1890–99	25	68	–	7	100
1900–09	22	70	–	8	100
1910–19	17	76	–	7	100
1920–29	13	77	3	7	100
1930–39	15	76	2	7	100

Source: Hansen, 1991b, p. 28.

Table 6.4   Assets of Danish banks, 1870–1939 (%)

Year	Bills	Advances	Foreign assets	Securities	Other assets	Cash	Total
1870–79	33	34	7	13	9	4	100
1880–89	26	31	9	16	13	5	100
1890–99	22	35	7	18	14	4	100
1900–09	20	44	5	15	13	3	100
1910–19	15	46	5	16	15	3	100
1920–29	14	54	3	13	13	3	100
1930–39	13	52	3	14	12	6	100

Source: Hansen, 1991b, p. 27.

Bank regulation

Until 1919 Danish banks were unregulated except for the note issue monopoly of the Nationalbanken. This very liberal economic environment contributed to the industrial development of Denmark, but also to the problems of the banking industry in the 1920s (Hansen, 1970; Nyboe Andersen, 1947, pp. 177–8). As a result of the depression of 1876–78, when financial institutions came under great pressure, a savings bank act was passed (in 1880), while the commercial banks that were hit most severely by the crisis, remained unregulated. However, following the banking crisis of 1907–8, the government took action, and appointed a board that was to prepare a bill on banking, and finally, in 1919, the first Bank Act was a reality. The main principle of this Act was, as had already been indicated in the Savings Bank Act of 1880, to consider the public interest (Hansen, 1991a). In future banks were to publish a standardized set of accounts and quarterly balance sheets. The Act contained some limitations on competition, including a minimum share capital requirement and some formal demands concerning the articles of the individual banks. Furthermore, it introduced requirements with regard to solidity, liquidity, the banks' holding of own shares etc. However, in general, competition between banks was maintained. The most important element in the Act was the establishment of bank supervision headed by a bank inspector. His duty was to ensure bank observance of the Act and to investigate the solidity and liquidity of individual banks.

Banking crises before the 1920s
In 1857, in the first serious banking crisis in Denmark, the Nationalbanken failed to act as a lender of last resort. The resources of the bank were insufficient, and in addition there was some animosity between the government and the bank. Eventually the state provided the funds to lend to commercial firms and banks. Furthermore, since the money advanced from the government was in Sterling bills, the problem of exchange became crucial. This operation was performed by the newly established commercial bank, the Privatbanken, which offered to deliver the money in Danish currency faster than the Nationalbanken. From the viewpoint of the Nationalbanken, the problem was that reserve requirements were too rigid during emergencies, and, since the bank did not accept deposits, it was unable to increase liquidity. From the outside, the bank was considered too conservative and unable to perform the tasks of a note-issuing bank during times of crisis. A new manager of the bank was appointed in 1859, and over the next 20 to 30 years he turned it into a fully developed central bank, concentrating on the macro as well as the micro functions of a central bank. During the depression of 1876–78 and the crisis of 1885, the bank acted as a mature lender of last resort, by supporting the commercial banks as well as the savings banks. The bank's ability to support the commercial banking system in these crises was better than in 1857 because the reserves of the bank in this period were never threatened.

From the mid-1890s Denmark experienced an industrial 'take off', supported primarily by the three main banks. About 1895 these banks acquired such strength that the ability of the Nationalbanken to manage the monetary matters of Denmark was impaired (Hansen, 1968, pp. 353–64).

In 1907–8 the banking system was in trouble again. This time a construction boom, one that had been financed uncritically by three medium-sized, rapidly expanding banks in Copenhagen, formed the background. When the international crisis reached Denmark, the banking system was hit hard. Since the distressed banks had been supported financially by the main banks, the ability of the Nationalbanken to control the banking system was reduced (Hansen, 1968, p. 363). Furthermore, the main banks had borrowed foreign short-term money that was now called in, thus straining the monetary and financial system even further. Emergency assistance was supplied to the three Copenhagen banks and a few provincial banks by the state, the Nationalbanken and the three main banks, who formed a committee which guaranteed the liabilities of the troubled banks. The committee believed the banks to be only illiquid, but it soon turned out that they were insolvent as well and had to be liquidated. The expenses were heavy, and the lion's share was paid by the state.

This rescue operation by the state, the central bank and the main banks is important, because it created a precedent. The combination of forces between the Nationalbanken and one or more of the main banks, and in the case of large banks, the state, was to become a common feature of lender of last resort operations during the 1920s. This tradition was founded in the banking crisis of 1907–8.

The banking crisis of the 1920s.
In 1913, on the eve of the First World War, the public liabilities of the Danish commercial banks, for the first time ever, exceeded those of the savings banks. During the war and until 1921, bank deposits and capital soared, mainly due to a positive balance of payments and idle money during the years of war. Many new banks were founded, while the number of savings banks decreased a little. Since deposits in savings banks almost stagnated from 1916–17, the relative importance of banks during this period increased. A considerable part of bank money was canalized into industrial and commercial capital, and many firms became over capitalized (Johansen, 1988). When the decline in the price level set in the second half of 1920, many firms (especially in trade) got into financial distress because they had built up their stocks at prices at which they were now unable to sell. The problems hit the banks too and in the following years the banking system went through a crisis that brought the savings banks back into prominence, as deposits were held in cash, invested in securities or switched from the banks to the savings banks. Tables 6.4 and 6.5 demonstrate some of the effects of the banking crisis.

From 1920 to 1932 35 banks were liquidated, 19 were merged with other banks and 17 were reconstructed and continued their operations with new capital. During the same period, the aggregate share capital in the Danish banks was reduced through write-offs, liquidations and takeovers by 359 million kr., while new capital paid in amounted to 204 million kr.

The severity of the crisis was emphasized by the crash of the largest bank in Scandinavia with total assets of 1.482 billion kr. (31 December 1920).[4] The Land-mandsbanken had to be reconstructed in July 1922 due to heavy losses, but the total failure of the bank was only gradually realized by the government, the Nation-albanken and the public. The bank passed through three reconstructions and anxiety about its situation was not removed until the state in 1923 guaranteed all claims on the bank. Finally, in 1928, the state paid in new share capital, thus becoming the sole owner of the bank. The total losses of the bank were estimated to be about 500 million kr.

Table 6.5   Deposits, note issue (million kroner) and index of bank share prices (1914 = 100), 1918–32

Year	Index of share prices 1914 = 100	Bank deposits	Savings bank deposits	Note issue	Metal reserve (as % of note issue)
1918	129.1	2.669	1.472	450	43.8
1919	130.8	3.550	1.480	489	47.1
1920	110.5	4.037	1.459	557	41.4
1921	104.4	4.168	1.517	471	49.2
1922	94.4	3.326	1.620	459	50.7
1923	96.0	3.179	1.785	473	45.7
1924	91.1	2.639	1.823	478	48.1
1925	85.7	2.357	1.872	438	50.9
1926	79.9	2.196	1.913	386	58.0
1927	84.2	2.270	1.949	354	55.3
1928	86.6	2.172	1.970	360	50.2
1929	86.6	2.248	2.018	367	50.8
1930	83.9	2.344	2.097	360	51.8
1931	77.5	2.245	2.179	346	43.5
1932	65.1	2.108	2.169	332	42.6

Note: From 1918 to 1926 the legal requirements to the metal reserve were 33%, from 1927 to 13 October 1931 they were 50%, and thereafter they were 33%.

Source: Statistisk Årbog 1929, 1932, 1933 and Johansen, 1985 and Nationalbankens regnskaber, 1918–33.

Table 6.6   Total write-offs in Danish banks, 1921–32 (million kroner)

Year	Total assets	Losses on loans	Losses on securities	Total losses	Losses as % of assets
1921	4921	64.2	3.9	69.6	1.41
1922	4423	240.1	24.2	265.3	6.00
1923	4213	62.6	5.5	68.7	1.63
1924	3859	19.0	29.3	49.0	1.27
1925	3398	141.8	55.5	202.9	5.97
1926	3085	14.5	5.7	21.1	0.68
1927	2956	29.3	0.4	31.5	1.07
1928	2887	75.1	1.3	77.5	2.68
1929	2969	12.4	0.2	13.5	0.45
1930	3059	16.2	0.2	17.4	0.57
1931	2874	11.2	40.7	52.7	1.83
1932	2777	15.5	1.5	18.7	0.67

Source: Hansen, 1991b, p. 37.

Other big banks too came under pressure during the 1920s. The Disconto-og Revisionsbank, with total assets of 418 million kr. (31 December 1920), failed in 1924 and was closed. Total losses exceeded 100 million kr., including 23 per cent of the deposits. The Andelsbanken, with total assets of 171 million (31 December 1920), was liquidated in 1925 with a loss of all its capital and 9 per cent of its deposits. Finally, the Privatbanken was close to failure when it suspended payments for four days in September 1928. When it re-opened, it was reconstructed with capital from the Nationalbanken and a syndicate led by the Swedish banker, Jacob Wallenberg. The Privatbanken wrote off all reserves and 80 per cent of its share capital – about 80 million kr.

From 1920 to 1930, 57 banks had to write down their share capital. Some of them were reconstructed with support from the Nationalbanken, the state or the main banks, some were taken over and some were allowed to liquidate. No banks were permitted to fail merely because of liquidity problems, but most of the banks in trouble were illiquid. Excessive loan arrangements with single customers as well as lombarding of shares were among the most common immediate causes of banking difficulties (Banktilsynet, 1945; Mordhorst, 1968).

Section 16 of the 1919 Bank Act stated that if a bank had lost more than 50 per cent of its share capital, it had to call a general assembly in order to restore the capital to 50 per cent of the registered capital. If this proved impossible, the bank had to be liquidated. Right from the beginning the Nationalbanken had criticized this regulation as it was feared that the calling of a general assembly of a bank in order to restore its capital would expose the bank to a run (Ussing, 1926, pp. 235–9). Indeed, when a bank got into this position, the first thing the bank inspector did was to refer the bank to the Nationalbanken or a main bank in order to seek support (Bestyrelsesprotokol, vol. 3, supplement 2338).

From 1920 to 1932 a total of 40 banks applied for assistance from the Nationalbanken (Bestyrelsesprotokol, vols 3 and 4), while 30 other banks were reconstructed or liquidated without contacting the bank (Mordhorst, 1968, pp. 114–55). Some of the banks that turned to the Nationalbanken only applied for temporary loans due to settling days, while others applied for loans of up to 60 million kr. for several years. The Nationalbanken's various ways of helping troubled banks were: the provision of loans or rediscounting bills of exchange or both; assistance in arranging a merger with a healthy bank; supporting the bank's share price; renunciation of a claim on the troubled bank; paying in new preference share capital or long-term deposits; and taking over a dubious loan arrangement. Some of these actions by the bank clearly went beyond the ideal type of lender of last resort assistance.

In two cases the bank provided capital to support the establishment of a new bank in a region, where an old one had failed. Although the management of the bank declared that it was not one of the objects of the bank to establish new banks, it helped the new banks with share capital on the condition that they supported the depositors of the failed ones by lombarding their claims (Bestyrelsesprotokol vol. 3, pp. 203 and 205). Consideration for depositors of liquidating banks was also the reason why the bank, in four cases, lombarded passbooks until a final dividend could be paid out. Among these cases were the two large banks, the Andelsbanken and the Disconto- og Revisionsbank (Bestyrelsesprotokol vols 3 and 4; Mordhorst, 1968, pp. 114–55). Only in six cases was the fear of a run explicitly stated as the reason why the banks in question applied for help from the Nationalbanken. Loss of share capital was the most frequently cited motivation.

Share-price support was carried out by the bank for the first time in February 1921, when the chairman of the Disconto- og Revisionsbank expressed his fear that anxiety about the bank's condition would result in falling share prices, ulti-matively leading to a run on the bank. In cooperation with the three main banks, the Nationalbanken decided to back the share price with 10 million kr. (Bestyrelsesprotokol vol. 3, p. 183). Late in 1921, two other banks requested similar support, as they feared that the depreciating share prices would initiate a run, and the Nationalbanken agreed to support the shares. One of these banks was the Landmandsbanken, whose manager was afraid that a run on the Land-mandsbanken would lead to a run on the entire banking system. Consequently, the Nationalbanken agreed to lombard shares in the Landmandsbanken with a limit of 30 million kr. The shares were to be bought by a group of 'friends' of the bank, but the major participant in this group turned out to be the Land-mandsbanken itself. In 1931, the Nationalbanken once more had to allocate resources (2 million kr.) to back share prices, this time in another main bank, the Handelsbanken.

The more traditional methods of lender of last resort assistance, i.e. loans against securities and the rediscounting of bills of exchange were employed by the Nation-albanken as well. Normally, the bank only advanced money to troubled banks against adequate collateral, but in a few cases this rule was violated. In 1921, the bank advanced 30 million kr. on securities and 38 million kr. in rediscounts to the Disconto- og Revisionsbank. The other big bank that failed, the Andels-banken, borrowed 6 million kr. in November 1924 in order to get through settlement day. However, this was only the beginning; in January 1925 the manager of the Andelsbanken wrote a letter to the Nationalbanken, asking for new capital. Before this request was settled, however, the bank had to advance 25 million kr. to the Andelsbanken. When the Arbejdernes Landsbank (the Workers' Bank) applied for help in March 1923 because trade unions were expected to withdraw their deposits due to a strike and a lock-out on the labour market, the Nationalbanken declined and suggested the bank sell some of its bond portfolio. Later, when it was realized that the Arbejdernes Landsbank had lost not only the profits of the year, but also its reserves and some of its share capital, the Nationalbanken advanced about 2 million kr. and offered to take part in the reconstruction of the bank. Nevertheless, the Nationalbanken declined to participate in a reconstruction plan designed by the bank inspector and, instead, the trade unions guaranteed the bank against losses on its biggest debtor, a cooperative fuel-trading company, which also owned a large part of the bank's stock.[5] The Nationalbanken also granted credits to some minor banks and, of course, to the main banks, the Landmandsbanken (from 1922), the Privatbanken (from 1925) and the Landelsbanken (from 1931). All three banks were granted credits in excess of 40 million kr., and at times the amount was significantly higher, at least when it came to the Landmandsbanken.

The kind of financial support most frequently in the minutes of the Nationalbanken is a contribution of capital, which does not fall within the micro function of a central bank. From 1920 to 1932, the bank paid in 64.1 million kr. of new capital in eighteen banks, two of which were entirely new. The main banks contributed 5.4 million kr.,[6] but received more than 50 million kr. In most cases when the bank paid in new capital, this occurred in cooperation with at least one of the main banks, usually the correspondent bank to the failed bank. Frequently, the bank inspector was involved in the evaluation of the possibilities of reconstructing the troubled bank (Bestyrelsesprotokol vols 3 and 4; Mordhorst, 1968, pp. 114–55).

Principles and motives

The Nationalbanken thus accepted responsibilities which went far beyond what the ideal type of lender of last resort operations implies. Why did the bank do this? In 1920 it was a well-established tradition that the Nationalbanken was responsible not only for monetary aggregates, but also for individual market participants. It was realized that bank failures might have a contagious effect, and thus affect the real economy. By assisting banks in trouble the Nationalbanken had several alternatives depending on the type of the problem. Furthermore, there was the possibility of refusing to assist a bank, a fate that hit eleven banks out of 40. Of these, again, six were liquidated with losses for depositors and one with losses for shareholders. Only four banks managed to continue operations without help from the Nationalbanken.

Not much is known about the reasons why the Nationalbanken turned down the requests for assistance from some banks. However, from what is known, it would seem that the Nationalbanken distinguished between banks which were considered solvent and those considered insolvent. Thus, in cases where an insolvent bank sought lender of last resort assistance, it was refused. However, in at least one case, that of Landmandsbanken, it was argued that the bank was too large to fail and it was rescued despite its insolvency.

The managers of the bank rarely engaged in discussions about the principles concerning assistance to banks, but some information is known. In February

1923 the government introduced a bill to support the depositors of seven failed banks. The Minister of Commerce feared that the banking crisis might restrain people's willingness to save (Forslag, 1923). In March the Minister invited the Nationalbanken, the main banks, the Association of the Provincial Banks and the bank inspector to a meeting in which he asked the Nationalbanken and the main banks to indemnify depositors of the failed banks. The main banks and the Nationalbanken refused to take part in the operation, which was estimated to cost 5.5 million kr., and one of the managers of the Nationalbanken declared that 'the proposed help was in direct contradiction to those principles according to which the Nationalbanken had worked until then. In cases where the bank had provided help to depositors of failed banks, the principle had been to assure continuation of operations, while in this situation it would be a present to the depositors' (Bestyrelsesprotokol vol. 3, pp. 209–10).

In early 1922, the Nationalbanken and the main banks had contributed preference share capital to two small insolvent banks. The reasons stated were, in the first case, that the bank in question was the only bank in that region and that the local society strongly wanted it to continue; whereas in the second case this measure would secure the depositors. In other words, the bank went beyond what it itself had found sensible. The management felt a certain responsibility for the maintenance of an integrated capital market in Denmark, and therefore had to violate its own principles regarding lender of last resort assistance.

These principles have been outlined by a prominent manager of the Nationalbanken, Carl Ussing, who retired in 1924. In his book on the history of the bank from 1914 to 1924, published in 1926, Ussing distinguishes three different groups of troubled banks. Illiquid banks belonged to the first group and it was the duty of the bank to advance money freely to these. If they had been left to the market, as some observers insisted, they would have failed. To let the banks fail would cause a decline in the money supply and affect the real economy. This could not be allowed to take place (Ussing, 1926, pp. 207 and 227–9). In the second group Ussing placed banks with losses of more than 50 per cent of their share capital. These banks needed new capital, and Ussing conceded that this, accomplished by an increased note issue, would create inflation. However, he noted that: 'It is possible that at other times you would have done things differently and chosen bank failures and deflation, but it was a period of unstable production and banking, and major bank failures would have caused even more interruptions in production, and consequently an enormous unemployment which would lead to communism and the spread of panic to other banks.' (Ussing, 1926, pp. 229–30). Although slightly paranoid, this statement expressed Ussing's 'protection of production' view as opposed to the 'protection of the currency' view held by some contemporary economists. Ussing felt that lender of last resort operations could not be carried out regardless of the political and economic situations. Insolvent banks belonged to the third group. These banks were to be allowed to fail, since it was beyond the duties of the Nationalbanken to make gifts. A principle of indemnification would be destructive to the conduct of banking (Ussing, 1926, pp. 230–31).

In principle, then, the Nationalbanken adhered to the 'theory' of the lender of last resort, but in practice other considerations became relevant as well. As a consequence the bank supported distressed banks with new capital in the early 1920s, although it might not have supported them in another political and economic context. The attitude of the Nationalbanken towards big banks may illustrate this point. When a major bank was troubled, the bank, the main banks and the government participated in the negotiations. In these cases it was the policy of the bank to get the state to guarantee the advances to the troubled bank and thereby accept responsibility.

Four of the five major banks were in serious trouble in the period 1922–8. The first was the Disconto- og Revisionsbank in January 1922. Following a meeting of the Nationalbanken, the liberal prime minister and the main banks, the bank sent a letter to the prime minister in which it was agreed that a bank failure of such a magnitude would cause serious disturbances in business life affecting a considerable number of provincial banks and their customers. The failure would be a national disaster with consequences for the credit standing of Denmark abroad. Consequently, the bank paid in new capital and put credit at its disposal, but wanted the state to guarantee its advances to the failed bank (Bestyrelsesprotokol vol. 3, supplement no. 2322).

In the case of the Landmandsbanken, the bank once again tried to involve the State in order to avoid a national disaster which would 'affect thousands of businesses and individuals all over the country, and reduce the credit standing abroad' (Bestyrelsesprotokol vol. 3, supplement no. 2338). In a letter to the prime minister of 10 July 1922 the bank wrote:

> It is not necessary to describe what disaster a bank failure means to the affected region and the business community dependent on the failed bank. It is a disaster, not only to the firms whose continuation is dependent on bank credit and for the firms and individuals cut off from their deposits, but also to the countless number of businessmen and workers, whose very existence is dependent on the ability to deliver or pay of those directly hit.
>
> In each situation it is important that the assistance is provided immediately and before any public discussion about the standing of the bank is allowed to take place. If assistance is provided after anxiety and loss of confidence in the bank have arisen, it will usually be too late and often too expensive. (Bestyrelsesprotokol vol. 3, supplement no. 2338)

In 1922, it was agreed that closure of the Disconto- og Revisionsbank as well as the Landmandsbanken had to be avoided in order to protect the payment system and the economy. However, when the Disconto- og Revisionsbank was again faced with failure in 1924, it was allowed to fail, although the foreign claims on the banks were secured in order to preserve Denmark's credit abroad (Bestyrelsesprotokol vol. 3, pp. 229–32). What was declared a national disaster in 1922 was not so in 1924. When the Andelsbanken, the bank with the largest and most widespread number of branches, came under pressure in 1925, it was also allowed to fail.

The case of the Privatbanken is not quite so unambiguous. In late 1925 the bank was in serious distress for the first time, and the Nationalbanken, the bank inspector and the government agreed that a closure of the Privatbanken would be a national disaster and that the anxiety might spread to other banks (Bestyrelsesprotokol vol. 3, p. 330). Therefore the Nationalbanken decided to support the Privatbanken with credit of 50 million kr. against adequate collateral (p. 334). However, the bank would not guarantee all claims against the Privatbanken, at least not publicly, so there must have been some doubt in the management as to how far it ought to go with respect to the rescue operation. It was only when the Bank of England inquired about the standing of the Privatbanken that the management voted in favour of a guarantee, should this prove necessary (pp. 335–6).

Perhaps this ambiguity is also part of the explanation why the Privatbanken got into trouble again in 1928, since the hesitation of the Nationalbanken in 1925 may have contributed to the fact that the Privatbanken had not been adequately reconstructed. In 1928 monetary conditions were eased, and the Nationalbanken went some way to avoid liquidation, even though the state did not wish to participate. The bank did not accept the principle that 'the rescue of a major bank is a national concern, and therefore a concern of the State' (Ussing, 1926, p. 233).

Altogether there is some evidence, though not conclusive, that the attitude of the Nationalbanken depended on the targets of monetary policy. The monetary targets during the period from the end of the war to around 1928 can be split up into clearly distinguishable types, which may have influenced the willingness of the bank to be the ultimate reserve of the banking system. Immediately after the war it was being argued that the international value of the krone should be restored, and that the Nationalbanken should tighten monetary policy in order to raise the gold value of the krone. However, the management of the Nationalbanken strongly disagreed that this was the most important issue. The Russian revolution and social unrest in Denmark meant that the bank chose 'protection of production' rather than 'protection of the currency'.[7] Furthermore, the lender of last resort assistance to the Landmandsbanken in 1922 increased the money supply and stimulated economic activity.[8] At the beginning of 1924, however, the bank embarked upon a deflationary policy giving first priority to the international value of the krone. The new policy was implemented in March 1924, when the Nationalbanken introduced a credit-rationing policy and instructed the banks to reduce lending (Olsen, 1968, pp. 96–7). As a result, the krone reached parity in 1926, and Denmark was back on gold from January 1927. The attitude of the Nationalbanken towards commercial banks in crisis suggests that it was not only the bank's macro policy that was changed in 1924, but also its micro policy. One of the banks to pay the price of this change was the Disconto- og Revisionsbank.

Conclusion

This study of the lender of last resort operations of the Danish central bank has considered whether the Nationalbanken acted as an ideal type of last resort lender. The motives for the emergency assistance rendered to banks in crisis have also been studied. The results may be expressed as a hypothesis, which needs a much more thorough investigation before it is possible to arrive at a deeper understanding of the Nationalbanken's operations.

Since the last quarter of the nineteenth century, the Nationalbanken acted consciously as a lender of last resort, and it was able to do this in spite of rigid reserve requirements, because the reserves were never threatened during this period. In the crisis of 1907–8, a tradition of cooperation was established between the Nationalbanken, the main banks of Copenhagen and the state in lender of last resort operations. This tradition became a common element during the severe banking crisis of the 1920s. The involvement of the main banks should probably be seen in the light of their self-interest, since they were often correspondent banks to the banks they helped to support. In other words, they had large amounts at stake, advanced to the bank in question, and this, in combination with their wish to preserve confidence in the banking system, made them participate in rescue operations even though their own financial situation was not healthy either.

In contemplating rescue operations for banks in distress, the Nationalbanken made some distinctions. The most important one was between illiquid but solvent banks on the one hand and insolvent banks on the other. Liquid banks, whether small or large, were always helped through their crisis in order to maintain the credit market and the economic activity in the affected region. In the case of major banks, other considerations were involved as well. They received massive support in order to rescue the payment system, Denmark's credit standing abroad and the economy. When it came to major banks, a 'too big to fail' doctrine was used, even though the concept had not yet been formulated. Thus, the Landmandsbanken, the largest bank in Scandinavia, went bust in 1922 and was definitely insolvent, but was helped through the crisis regardless of costs. In principle, the bank seemed to adhere to the 'theory' of lender of last resort, but, in quite a few cases, it went beyond what the ideal type of a lender of last resort suggests. It paid in new capital in insolvent banks and it lombarded depositors' claims on failed banks.

Some evidence indicates that external considerations affected the attitude of the Nationalbanken as a lender of last resort. The targets of monetary policy influenced the willingness of the central bank to supply liquidity to troubled banks. In 1924, when monetary targets were changed and a policy of credit rationing was introduced, the Nationalbanken allowed a major bank to fail, which had been considered too big to fail in early 1922.

The Nationalbanken had to experience more than once that being a lender of last resort was no easy task, and the bank learned it the hard way. The most difficult problem seemed to be the correct assessment of a bank's standing in a very short time. In some cases it seems that the bank misjudged the situation of a distressed bank, and on some occasions this may have increased the costs of the rescue operation. 'Too little, too slowly' is not the most appropriate lender of last resort policy. But the management did benefit from the experience of the banking crisis of the 1920s. In late 1931, when the last of the major banks, the Handelsbanken, was subject to a run and therefore asked for emergency liquidity assistance, the Nationalbanken guaranteed publicly that it would support the Handelsbanken to such an extent that the bank thought necessary. Thus, the run was stopped. This lender of last resort operation was much more mature and self-conscious than the majority of the ones in the preceding decade. No doubt, this was due to the dearly bought experience of the 1920s, although it is tempting to see some kind of symbolism in the fact that the copy of Walter Bagehot's *Lombard Street* in the library of the Nationalbanken is a 1931 edition.

The Nationalbanken was not the only one to draw experience from the banking troubles of the 1920s. The public and the politicians demanded a revision of the Bank Act of 1919, and finally in 1930 a new bank act was passed. The main new prescription of the Bank Act of 1930 was an upper limit on a bank's lending to a single customer (a maximum of 35 per cent of the bank's capital). Rules about liquidity and capital requirements were made more rigorous and limitations to the banks' right to own shares in companies other than banks and to own real estate were established (Olsen, 1968, pp. 154–5, Hansen, 1991a).

The banking community also learned from the crisis. The banks experienced an image problem, manifested in increased deposits in the savings banks and a corresponding decline in the deposits of the banks. The banks became more cautious in the 1930s and 1940s because of the experience of the 1920s, and business had to rely on other forms of financing, including self-financing (Nyboe Andersen, 1947, pp. 210–11). Thus the banking crisis of the 1920s had serious repercussions in Danish society and profoundly influenced the conduct of central banking, banking and almost every kind of business operation.

Notes
1. Anna Schwartz, 1986, pp. 24–5, does not agree on this point.
2. During the gold standard period, however, reserve requirements limited the fiduciary issue.

3. Lender of last resort assistance can also, in principle, be provided by a general increase of liquidity in the market, by open market operations, but there is some disagreement as to whether the market is capable of allocating the liquidity to banks in need. This doubt is raised because there is a tendency to introduce credit rationing in times of crisis and consequently no money can be borrowed by troubled banks (Guttentag and Herring, 1984, 1987; Kindleberger, 1989, pp. 153–5; Saunders, 1987, pp. 208–11).
4. This information and the following for two other banks are from *Statistiske Undersøgelser* no. 24 (1968).
5. Arbejderbevægelsens Bibliotek og Arkiv: Staunings Privatarkiv, kasse 115.
6. Capital was also paid into troubled banks from the state and large companies.
7. The managing director also expressed it in this way: 'What it was all about, was to get the people occupied with work, rather than with revolution' (Ussing, 1926, p. 174).
8. This is an example of lender of last resort operations leading to inflation. Cf. Minsky, 1982a, p. 33; 1982b, p. 68.

Sources
Arbejderbevægelsens Bibliotek og Arkiv, *Staunings Privatarkiv*.
Danmarks Nationalbank, *Bestyrelsesprotokol (Minutes) of the Nationalbanken*, vols 3 and 4 with supplement.
'Forslag til lov om statsstøtte til forskellige bankers sparere', *Rigsdagstidende 1922/23, Tillæg A*, Column 5247–54.
Nationalbankens regnskaber (Accounts) 1918–33.

References
Bagehot, Walter (1873), *Lombard Street. A Description of the Money Market*, new ed., London, 1873, 1915.
Baltensperger, Ernst and Jean Dermine (1987), 'The Role of Public Policy in Ensuring Financial Stability: A Cross Country, Comparative Perspective', in Richard Portes and Alexander K. Swoboda (eds), *Threats to International Financial Stability*, Cambridge, pp. 67–90.
Banktilsynet (1945) 1920–1945, Copenhagen.
Bordo, Michael D. (1989), 'The Lender of Last Resort: Some Historical Insights', Summary of Paper, Cliometrics Sessions at the ASSA Meetings in Atlanta, pp. 35–7.
Eichengreen, Barry and Richard Portes (1987), 'The Anatomy of Financial Crises', in Richard Portes and Alexander K. Swoboda (eds), *Threats to International Financial Stability*, Cambridge, pp. 10–58.
Goodhart, Charles (1988), *The Evolution of Central Banks*, Cambridge, Massachusetts.
Guttentag, Jack and Richard Herring (1984), 'Credit Rationing and Financial Disorder', *Journal of Finance*, 39, 1984, pp. 1359–82.
Guttentag, Jack and Richard Herring (1987), 'Emergency Liquidity Assistance for International Banks' in Portes and Swoboda (eds), *Threats to International Financial Stability*, Cambridge, pp. 150–86.
Hansen, Per H. (1991a), 'Bank Regulation in Denmark up to 1930', Paper presented at the First European Economic History Conference, Copenhagen, July 1991.
Hansen, Per H. (1991b), 'From Growth to Crisis. The Danish Banking System from 1850 to the Interwar Years, *Scandinavian Economic History Review*, vol. 39, no. 3, 1991, pp. 20–40.
Hansen, Per H. (1992), 'The Evolution of Universal Banking and Banking Crises: The Danish Case', *20th Century Universal Banking: International Comparisons. Report from the International Conference*, vol. II, pp. 1–29, Budapest University of Economic Sciences. Department of Economic History, Budapest, 1992.
Hansen, Sv. Aage and Knud Erik Svendsen (1968), *Dansk pengehistorie, vol. I, 1700–1914*, Copenhagen.
Hansen, Svend Aage (1970), *Early Industrialization in Denmark*, Copenhagen.
Johansen, Hans Chr. (1985), *Dansk økonomisk statistik 1814–1980*, Copenhagen.

Johansen, Hans Chr. (1988), 'De private banker under den første verdenskrig', *Om Danmarks Historie 1900–1920*, Festskrift til Tage Kaarsted, pp. 165–79, Odense.

Kindleberger, Charles P. (1988), 'Bank Failures: The 1930s and the 1980s', *The International Economic Order. Essays on Financial Crisis and International Public Goods*, New York.

Kindleberger, Charles P. (1989), *Manias Panics and Crashes. A History of Financial Crises*, 2nd ed., London.

Laffargue, Jean Pierre (1982), 'Comment', in Charles P. Kindleberger and Jean Pierre Laffargue (eds), *Financial Crises: Theory, History and Policy*, Cambridge, pp. 248–50.

Minsky, Hyman (1982a), 'The Financial-Instability Hypothesis. Capitalist Processes and the Behavior of the Economy', in Charles P. Kindleberger and Jean Pierre Laffargue (eds), *Financial Crises: Theory, History and Policy*, Cambridge, pp. 13–39.

Minsky, Hyman (1982b), 'The Financial Instability Hypothesis: An Interpretation of Keynes and an Alternative to "Standard" Theory' in Hyman Minsky, *Inflation, Recession and Economic Policy*, Armonk, New York, pp. 59–70.

Mordhorst, Kirsten (1968), *Dansk Pengehistorie*, vol. 3, Copenhagen.

Nyboe Andersen, P. (1947), *Laanerenten*, Copenhagen.

Olsen, Erling and Erik Hoffmeyer (1968), *Dansk Pengehistorie*, vol. 2, 1914–1960, Copenhagen.

Rockoff, Hugh (1986), 'Walter Bagehot and the Theory of Central Banking' in Forrest Capie and Geoffrey E. Wood (eds), *Financial Crises and the World Banking System*, London, pp. 160–80.

Rubow, Axel (1918), *Nationalbankens historie 1818–1878*, Copenhagen.

Rubow, Axel (1920), *Nationalbankens historie 1878–1908*, Copenhagen.

Schwartz, Anna J. (1986), 'Real and Pseudo-Financial Crises' in Forrest Capie and Geoffrey E. Wood (eds), *Financial Crises and the World Banking System*, London, pp. 11–31.

Solow, Robert M. (1982), 'On the Lender of Last Resort' in Charles P. Kindleberger and Jean Pierre Laffargue (eds), *Financial Crises: Theory, History and Policy*, Cambridge, pp. 37–48.

Statistisk Årbog 1929, 1932 and 1933.

Statistiske undersøgelser no. 24. *Kreditmarkedsstatistik*, Copenhagen.

Tilly, Richard H. (1989), 'Banking Institutions in Historical and Comparative Perspective: Germany, Great Britain and the United States in the Nineteenth and Early Twentieth Century', *Journal of Institutional and Theoretical Economics*, vol. 145, 1989, pp. 189–209.

7   Norwegian banks and the legacy of the interwar years

Sverre Knutsen

Norway
N24
621
628

> *... the ideas of economists and political philosophers, both when they are right*
> *and when they are wrong, are more powerful than is commonly understood.*
> J.M. Keynes, *The General Theory of Employment, Interest and Money*

The regulation of financial institutions and markets in Norway underwent radical changes after 1945. During the postwar period, these changes led to increased state intervention in the financial system and to increased government control of financial institutions and the flows of capital and credit. The changes were mainly concentrated in two periods. The first was the early 1950s, when a corporative system for determining and monitoring monetary and credit policies was established. The second can be dated to the mid-1960s, when a new, radical and comprehensive law on money and credit was passed. However, the origin of the transformation process that led up to this change in the regulatory regime can be traced back to the 1930s. In fact, the 1930s may be regarded as the seedbed of the change from an unstable, market-based financial system to a credit-based and state-led system in Norway.[1] These changes dramatically altered the framework for both banking and other financial institutions. This chapter focuses on some of the main features of Norwegian financial history between 1935 and 1955 in an attempt to analyse the processes which led to the postwar financial changes.

One possible explanation for the change in regulatory policies and practice after 1945 is that central decision makers in the Labour Party and the Labour Government that came to power in the Autumn of 1945 found it necessary, during the early 1950s, to reshape the financial system as a means to achieve important strategic goals in economic policy: economic growth; modernization through industrialization and redistribution. In the labour leadership the conviction gradually emerged that the management and direction of financial flows was a necessary condition for achieving its strategic objectives. The alteration of the financial system was thus a result of deliberate changes in the financial regulatory regime. The object of this chapter is to discuss whether a hypothesis like the one presented above can shed new light on a neglected part of Norway's financial history. The first section discusses banking legislation in the interwar period, following the banking crisis of the 1920s. The second tries to answer the question: what kind of financial system prevailed in Norway during the period from 1900 to the 1940s? In the third section we deal with the economic situation in Norway in the late 1940s and the breakthrough of Keynesianism, followed by the rise of a new financial regulatory regime during the early l950s with its consequences for banking. The final section provides a tentative conclusion.

Banking crisis and bank legislation in Norway in the 1920s

Social and economic life in Norway was characterized by great turbulence during the interwar period. The 1920–21 slump was followed by a protracted deflationary crisis, endless currency instability, severe business problems and a huge and protracted banking crisis. A deflationary monetary policy was implemented, which had a serious and damaging impact on the Norwegian economy during the 1920s. The banking crisis of the 1920s became very extensive, and a large number of banks collapsed. As many as 129 commercial banks disappeared and only a limited number of new banks were established to replace them. The banking crisis represented a heavy blow to the Norwegian banking system, and affected the Norwegian economy and financial system for decades to come.[2] Weakened by the numerous bank failures, the commercial banks played a more modest role in the economy during the interwar years than before. Increasing dissatisfaction with the ability of the banking system to serve industry adequately became widespread both in industrial and political circles. This discontent gave an impetus to changes in the financial system in the 1930s.

There was no banking crisis of similar dimensions in the 1930s. However, during the years of severe depression, 1931–32, two out of the three largest Norwegian commercial banks got into difficulties. Both the Bergens Privatbank and Den norske Creditbank encountered liquidity problems and depositor-runs during the autumn of 1931, and had to ask the authorities to sanction a moratorium. This was accepted. The Bank of Norway and the political authorities declared full support for the two banks, and they were successfully refinanced during the moratorium period. Contrary to what happened during the 1920s, the support from the Bank of Norway and the authorities at this time was without ambiguity or hesitation.[3]

Until 1918 there was no particular legislation to regulate the activities of the commercial banks. Legislation for savings banks, however, was enacted in 1824. A new law on savings banks was enacted in 1887, partly as a response to savings bank failures during the depression of the 1880s. Its first priority was to protect depositors.[4] As a consequence of the almost uncontrolled establishment of new independent banks during the wartime boom, the Storting (parliament) adopted a preliminary law on commercial banking in April 1918. Before this anyone was free to establish a joint-stock bank in Norway. According to the preliminary law, however, a concession was now necessary to operate a bank, and it was even strictly prohibited to set up a local branch without a concession from the authorities. This was done to prevent the largest banks in the capital from establishing local branches, since the majority of the Storting (parliament) was in favour of local independent banks, and thus opposed to large banks as well as branch banking.[5]

At the same time the Storting established a commission to prepare the first permanent legislation on commercial banking. Legislation followed in 1924 when the Norwegian banking system was hit by a severe banking crisis. Its main points were as follows:

- Commercial banks could only be organized as joint-stock companies with limited liability.
- The commercial banks were, together with savings banks, given the exclusive right to accept deposits from an indefinite circle of depositors.
- Protection of depositors was given first priority. The minimum equity was to be 10 per cent of bank commitments.
- Bank share capital was not to be less than NOK 400 000.
- Guarantees for loans were limited to 75 per cent of equity.
- Loans provided to a single client were not to exceed 25 per cent of the bank equity.
- Strict rules were imposed on the banks concerning their investments. Investments in real estate were limited to the buildings that the banks needed for their own operations, and were not to exceed 10 per cent of the bank equity.
- The right to acquire shares in other companies was limited to an amount equivalent to 20 per cent of the bank equity.
- Concerning liquidity the law demanded a cash-reserve equivalent to a minimum of 20 per cent of the bank's short-term obligations, and a minimum of 5 per cent of total obligations.

According to para. 11 of the new law, it was prohibited for the manager of the bank or managers of local branches to be engaged in commerce, shipping or manufacturing industry or any company engaged in such activities. At the same time all members of the board were excluded from membership of the boards of companies which were borrowers in the bank. These prohibitions related to practices which had been quite customary in the banks before the new Act. New legislation on savings banks was also enacted in 1924, as well as a separate law on the establishment of a bank inspectorate for both commercial and savings banks.

During 1923 when the collapse of the commercial banks started in earnest, the Bank of Norway realized that the developing banking crisis was so severe and so widespread that some form of intervention was necessary. To prevent a collapse of the banking system as a whole, Governor Rygg of the central bank proposed that the Storting (parliament) should pass a temporary 'Bank Administration Act', which it did in March 1923. Until then, the Bank of Norway had acted as a lender of last resort, providing banks in distress with liquidity. The bank-support policies by the authorities included financial assistance from the government made available by loan guarantees issued by the Storting. But the monetary authorities were increasingly reluctant to continue these rescue operations in their original form, and to contribute to the massive support loans that were needed. One important motive for Governor Rygg of The Bank of Norway was probably that he considered a continuous and increasing supply of liquidity from the central bank to the commercial banks as incompatible with the goal of returning to gold at the prewar parity, which necessitated a restrictive monetary policy. The Bank Administration Act stipulated that banks facing a crisis could apply for public administration under the supervision of the Bank of Norway in order to avoid bankruptcy. A new board of directors would be appointed and old deposits and other debts would be frozen. The bank could receive new deposits, however, which would be given priority over the old. The aim was to protect banks which had assets exceeding their debts, but were experiencing temporary liquidity problems. The ultimate goal was to reconstruct the banks under public administration or in the worst case liquidate them in an organized way.

However, the public guarantee for new deposits in banks under administration caused depositors to move their deposits from 'free' banks to those under administration, and this in turn caused liquidity strains in banks not under public administration. The Act also created several other unforeseen problems and complications. The Bank Administration Act was in force until July 1928. After this date '[...] no banks were allowed the special protection afforded by the act, and had to be liquidated if they were unable to reach an accommodation with their creditors under the ordinary bankruptcy legislation'. [6]

The Norwegian financial system from 1900 to the 1940s
The period 1895–1920 was one of expansion for the banking system in Norway, in particular for the commercial banks.[7] In 1895 there were 48 commercial banks with 220 million kroner in total assets. By 1920 the number of banks had risen to 192 and their total assets amounted to 5461 million kroner. The savings banks formed a very important part of the Norwegian banking system also. In 1895 there were 373 savings banks with 257 million kroner in total assets. In 1920 their number had increased to 562 and their total assets amounted to 2253 million kroner. As the figures indicate Norway had developed an extremely decentralized banking system by 1920, consisting of a large number of small, local and independent commercial and savings banks. A network of branch offices did not exist. During the whole period under consideration, almost all the customers of the commercial banks were business clients. Personal loans were

the exception rather than the rule. Even in the savings banks the majority of customers were business clients, although these banks to a certain extent served a personal loan-market.

Table 7.1 presents data on the loans provided by Norwegian commercial and savings banks. These show that the credit provided by the commercial banks over the entire period 1900–1935 was mainly in the form of short-term loans. The data also show that credit on current drawing accounts rose substantially as a percentage of total loans, in particular until 1920, when such loans amounted to almost 75 per cent of total lending. But the savings banks show a somewhat different pattern. Long-term loans, mainly mortgages, represented a larger share of their loan portfolio. However, the distribution of loans to categories of clients has to be taken into consideration. In 1930, 36 per cent of total loans provided by savings banks were to the primary sector and only 8 per cent were lent to manufacturing industry/handicraft businesses. As Table 7.1A in the Appendix shows, 23 per cent of the loans provided by the savings banks went to housing, real estate and personal loans. By comparison, 41 per cent of the commercial banks' loans in 1927 went to manufacturing industry, 35 per cent to the service sector and only 0.5 per cent to the category housing, real estate and personal loans.

Finally, we have to emphasize that the Norwegian commercial banks did not develop into 'universal' banks during the formative years to 1914. Their lending was typically short-term. Investment banking was not an integral part of commercial banking practices. The commercial banks did not engage in underwriting activities, neither did they take equity holdings in industrial firms. Certainly, these practices saw some changes during the interwar period and some banks took part in the financial reorganization of firms. But this was primarily caused by the efforts of the banks to save what could be saved of their nonperforming loans in industrial companies. In this way, they became 'universal banks' by default.

A stock market in the modern sense had its first breakthrough in Norway during the 1890s. The increase in share capital was significantly more important as a capital source for manufacturing industry in 1900–1920 than it had been previously. This was partly a result of considerable foreign portfolio investments in Norwegian energy-intensive industrial enterprises in this period. But the issue of shares was also an important source of risk capital for small and medium-sized companies. Issuing of shares was one of the most important ways for industry to obtain capital.[8] Until 1920, investment in shares became almost as attractive for the public as savings in bank deposits.[9] Table 7.2 indicates that stock market issues played an important role in financing corporate growth during the two first decades of the twentieth century. During the interwar period and after the Second World War we observe that this role was severely reduced.

Table 7.1   Distribution of credit provided by Norwegian commercial and savings banks on short- and long-term loans (%)

Commercial banks	1900	1914	1920	1935
Mortgages	12.8	9.2	1.4	8.7
Short-term loans	87.2	90.8	98.6	91.3
Of which: current-drawing accounts	30.5	46.3	73.7	57.3
Total loans (million kr.)	321	752	4034	1069
Savings banks	1900	1914	1920	1935
Mortgages	28.4	33.8	20.4	43.7
Short-term loans	71.6	60.4	79.6	56.3
Of which: current-drawing accounts	–	5.8	37.8	11.3
Total loans (million kr.)	278	598	1732	1347

Source: Historical Statistics, 1968.

Table 7.2   Supply of capital from the stock market as a percentage of the financing of net fixed capital in Norwegian companies

	1900–14	1915–20	1921–26	1927–30	1931–39	1946–51
Share capital	37	37	54	–	4	5

Source: Skånland, 1967, op. cit.

A huge expansion of the stock market and an extensive formation of new joint-stock companies occurred during the First World War and the postwar boom. However, this surge was not soundly based. It depended on the extraordinary profit possibilities of the war, and a considerable financial bubble developed. After a panic and crash in the Autumn of 1920, the stock market encountered substantial long-term problems. The banking crisis triggered a much broader financial crisis, including dramatic changes in the capital markets. The stock market collapsed completely between 1920 and 1922, and during the remainder of the interwar years the stock market played a minor role in the supply of risk capital to industrial enterprises.

While the figures presented in Table 7.2 confirm that the stock market was an important source of financing corporate growth until 1920, the decreased importance of the stock market during the interwar period also may indicate a considerable shift in the relationship between external and internal financing of investments in these years. Table 7.3 presents data showing this relationship.

Table 7.3   External and internal financing as a percentage of the financing of net fixed capital formation in Norwegian enterprises

	1900–14	1915–20	1921–26	1927–30	1931–39	1946–51
External financing	75	71	68	56	38	62
Internal financing	25	29	32	44	62	38
Total net fixed capital formation	100	100	100	100	100	100

Source: Skånland, 1967.

The fall in the share of external financing in the 1920s and 1930s (and the corresponding increase in internal financing) was primarily a consequence of paying off loans under deflationary conditions.[10] But after the Second World War the stock market still played a marginal role in financing industry. At the same time the importance of internal finance decreased considerably. Consequently the significance of the loan market increased, and manufacturing firms had to place more and more reliance on loans.

The banking crisis and the partial collapse of the banking system during the 1920s led to considerable shifts in financial market structure during the remainder of the interwar period. The market share of the commercial banks in the loan market fell by 40 percentage points from 1920 to 1940, to a total of only 24 per cent. The fact that the total assets of the commercial and savings banks were halved during the interwar years implies that the role of the banking system was substantially reduced in this period. At the same time life insurance companies and pension funds grew in importance as suppliers of credit. The most important change, however, was the remarkable increase in the market share of the state banks, from 12 per cent in 1920 to 26 per cent in 1940.

The bond market also declined substantially in importance from 1921 to 1923 and remained unstable until 1932. During the 1930s, however, the value of bond issues increased continuously from 100 million NOK in 1932 to almost 800 million in 1938. The state and the state banks were the major issuers in the bond market. In 1920 approximately 10 per cent of bearer bonds were issued by private enterprises, but their share grew to almost 18 per cent of the floated bond loans in 1939.[11] This suggests the increased importance of the bond market in Norwegian corporate finance during the 1930s. To a certain extent this development compensated for the failure of the banking system during this period, as well as the much reduced importance of the stock market as a capital source for industrial enterprises.

We have noted that the state banks expanded their share of the credit market during the interwar period. The first state-owned bank in Norway was Kongeriket Norges Hypothekbank (The Mortgage Bank of the Kingdom of Norway), established in 1851. This bank soon became a very important institution in the Norwegian financial system, and supplied agriculture with long-term credit. Its main source of funding was the foreign bond market. By 1945 there were eight Norwegian state banks in operation. The basis for the development of a state bank system was the efforts to secure the supply of credit to particular sectors of the economy according to regional, industrial or social criteria. In 1935, a Labour Party government with J. Nygaardsvold as prime minister came to power, and remained as a minority government until the German occupation in 1940.[12] The inability of the non-socialist parties to deal with the depression of the 1930s and to form a coalition government encouraged this development, as did the Labour Party's drive against unemployment and their programme to fight the crisis through state intervention. The Labour Party reached a compromise with the Agrarian Party, which secured a majority for the Nygaardsvold government in the Storting. The government's commitment to carry out a pro-farming policy was essential to this compromise.

After the turn of the century there were no serious controversies at the political level in connection with the founding of the state banks. However, when the new Labour government proposed the foundation of a new state-owned bank with the task of supplying credit to the manufacturing industry, both the Conservative, the Liberal and Agrarian Parties opposed the proposal, mainly on ideological grounds. The Conservative Party considered the plan to be a step in the direction of 'state socialism', although the Labour Party had retreated from orthodox socialism since the early 1930s. This process was strengthened after the formation of a Labour government in 1935. The new state bank was first and foremost considered an important tool in the drive for industrialization and as a measure to underpin government plans for the creation of new jobs in manufacturing industries. However, the Agrarian Party suggested the founding of a semi-public bank, a compromise which the Labour Party accepted. In July 1936, a law establishing the Manufacturing Bank of Norway Ltd was passed. The state retained 51 per cent of the share capital, and offered the remaining 49 per cent to the private banks.

Both the governments[13] and the majority of the Storting accepted the deflationary initiatives, as well as the bank-support policies of the Bank of Norway. It was only during the latter part of the decade that the monetary policy of the central bank was subject to sustained criticism from academics, some sections of the press, the Agrarian Party and many farmers, as well as from the Labour Party.

The discount rate, which was fixed by the Bank of Norway, was the main instrument used in monetary and credit policy during the interwar years. The Labour Party demanded that the discount rate should be determined by the government. In 1926, after the discount rate had been raised by the central bank, the parliamentary leader of the Labour Party attacked the decision in the Storting. The reply from the Minister of Finance of the Liberal Party government illustrates how the majority viewed the relationship between the authorities and the central bank: 'I will not form a judgement of whether the central bank has made a correct decision. However, the government is unanimous that it neither should give any advice, nor try to instruct the Bank of Norway in matters like this'.[14]

The banking crises in the 1920s brought the central bank initiatives into the searchlight of public opinion, and the policies of the Bank of Norway were discussed regularly in the Storting. The Labour Party opposition several times demanded that the banking system and even the Bank of Norway should be placed under more rigid government control. The new bank legislation of 1924 and the establishment of the Bank Inspectorate were regarded as insufficient measures by the Labour Party. In 1932 the party even alleged that the management of the banks 'was responsible for the wretched condition of Norwegian economic life' during the depression.[15] During the 1920s the Labour Party representatives proposed time and again in the Storting that the banking system, including the Bank of Norway, should be placed under the supervision of a public 'bank council'. In 1932 the Labour Party presented a similar proposal, as a part of a political programme to 'fight the crisis'. According to this plan all financial institutions should be placed under the direct control of such a 'bank council'. The party proposed that the institution mainly should consist of 'peasants and smallholders, fishermen, workers and white-collar workers', and that its members should be appointed by the Storting.[16] However, these proposals were not implemented when the Labour Party minority government came to power in 1935.

Both the Agrarian and the Labour Parties were concerned about the high price of credit during the late 1920s and the 1930s, and presented several proposals to regulate interest rates by legislation. The most far-reaching of these initiatives was a proposal from the Labour Party, demanding an interest rate ceiling on loans. There was considerable disagreement about this proposal in the Storting. But several MPs across party boundaries argued in favour of interest rate reductions. As a result of the parliamentary debate on this issue, a new temporary law gave the government the right to fix the interest rate on loans provided by commercial and savings banks, as well as on deposits. This legislation was not used by the government before the Second World War, but undoubtedly the threat that it might be used served as a mechanism for disciplining the banks.

The growing pressure on the banks from market competition as well as from politics stimulated defensive measures by bank managers. They tried to strengthen the coordination of the banks' activities through price cartels and other forms of association (in order to achieve price- and market-share stability), as well as to establish control within the social and political environments of the banks.

The concept of a market-based financial system fits Norwegian conditions during the period 1900–1940. Several points may be summarized to substantiate this point of view. First, from the 1890s to 1920, the stock market was a major source of financing industrial firms and projects. The bond market became increasingly important during the interwar period, when the stock market collapsed.

Second, the commercial banks provided their customers with short-term credit. They were not engaged in investment banking, did not engage in underwriting activities and equity issues and did not supply industry with long-term capital. Commercial banks did not own or control industrial firms. The banks were generally not involved in mergers, acquisitions or reconstructions. When they did undertake such activities this was primarily in order to save what could be saved of non-performing loans to faltering industrial companies.

However, we have to admit that there are some deviations relative to the ideal-type of a market-based system. The Norwegian capital market was limited and quite dependent on the supply of foreign capital. This made the Norwegian capital market unstable and volatile. A considerable part of the supply of risk capital from the stock market until 1914 went to the development of large-scale, energy-intensive industrial enterprises based on hydro-electric power. The vast majority of Norwegian firms, which were small and medium-sized, had to rely on short-term credits provided by the banks, even for long-term investments. During the nineteenth century, manufacturing industry to a large extent had to rely on credit provided by public sector banks and savings banks. This strong public sector influence on the financial system before the turn of the century was partly a consequence of market failure and partly a result of institutional constraints. As our analysis has shown, the public sector banks or state banks increased their market shares of the loan market during the 1930s, as a consequence of the banking crisis of the 1920s. Thus the loan market became increasingly important as a source for industrial finance. In this perspective the period 1890–1920 may look like a liberal and market oriented intermezzo of the long-term development of the Norwegian financial system. However, in spite of such objections, a model separating market-based from credit-based financial systems has proved to be very helpful in analysing the financial system.

Towards a new financial regulatory regime
In 1945 the standard of living in Norway was 20–30 per cent below its prewar level. The German occupying power drained considerable resources from

Norwegian society to feed and supply up to 400 000 soldiers stationed on Norwegian soil. Approximately 35 per cent of GNP was used to pay this bill, and the German occupation authorities financed occupation costs by the printing press. The war losses were also substantial, but the destruction did not reach the levels to be found in many other occupied countries, for example in Eastern Europe.

We shall not discuss the occupation period in further detail here. But from the point of view of financial history, there are points of particular interest, especially the following:

- Notes in circulation increased almost six times during the war.
- The liquidity of the banks increased substantially. At the same time the amount of loans provided by the banks decreased.
- Unemployment and debt problems disappeared.
- A considerable system of wartime controls and regulations was created.

All these factors played an important role in the postwar economy.

A coalition government headed by the Labour Party led the country until a Labour government came to power in the Autumn of 1945. The main objectives of the government and the party behind it were economic growth and development, modernization through industrialization, full employment and redistribution. Growth as a central part of postwar economic policies was an objective in common with most of the governments in the West. The opinion among the Labour leadership was that redistribution to raise the standard of living for the common man had to be achieved on the basis of increased production. Because of the experiences with the depressions and dissatisfaction with economic policies during the interwar period, the Labour leadership did not believe that market forces and the prescriptions of orthodox liberal economics would bring about growth: 'The size of the pie had to be substantially increased, and market forces would not achieve that feat by themselves. Government planning and intervention would be necessary to insure economic growth. It was not a question of suppressing the market, but of supplementing it by political and economic intervention'.[17]

Together with planning and state intervention, the Labour leadership was convinced about the necessity to develop a new institutional framework to bring about economic growth: '[...] parliamentary democracy alone constituted an insufficient institutional base for large-scale economic growth and modernization. It would have to be supplemented by a democratically organized corporative structure'.[18]

The main economic task confronting the authorities after the war was reconstruction and recovery from the economic consequences of the war. Several problems and obstacles had to be respectively solved and removed. There was a considerable lack of capital goods for reconstruction as well as a shortage of consumer goods. At the same time the over-liquid banks and a huge pent-up demand for consumer goods represented a strong inflationary threat. There was cross-political agreement on the necessity for controls and regulations during the immediate reconstruction period. But from 1946–47 divergences on economic policies came to the fore, in particular the question of how to fight against postwar inflation. The majority of non-socialist parliamentary representatives advocated measures to curb prices by a drastic reduction of money supply and restore market forces in the economy as fast as possible.

During the immediate postwar years the Labour government rejected any kind of deflationary policies. Instead it implemented an interventionist policy of price controls, subsidies, and continued rationing. This system prevailed for a long period in Norway. Temporary laws voted by the Labour majority in the Storting were interpreted by the opposition as efforts to accomplish radical changes in the Norwegian economic structure. The temporary price and regulation law of 1947, known as 'Lex Brofoss' was

> the most far-reaching enabling law enacted in peacetime in Norway. The law trans-
> ferred to the Directorate of Prices wide discretionary powers not only to set prices
> but also to decide on matters of production and distribution in considerable detail, to
> close down existing businesses or to establish new ones, and to increase production
> or change production patterns entirely.[19]

As long as the lack of commodities prevailed, strict rationing could curb prices in a satisfactory way. But as a consequence of the Norwegian acceptance of aid under the Marshall Plan and membership of OEEC, trade was gradually liber-alized.[20] At the same time the rationing of consumer goods was gradually removed. Subsidies increased substantially, as well as demand for foreign currency. This development undermined the efficiency of the price stabiliza-tion policy based on extensive price and import controls. The collapse of these policies occurred in 1950. The steep rise in prices initiated by the Korean War increased the need for subsidies to a prohibitive level. During the period from April to August that year subsidies were drastically reduced and commodity prices increased correspondingly.

The system of direct regulation was gradually dismantled during the early 1950s. But the government did not give up its ambitions to modernize through planned, large-scale industrialization. The system of direct regulation gave scope for micro-level regulations, and a dirigiste version of planning. When the system was partly dismantled, a shift to the use of more indirect measures in economic policy was necessary. Direct state ownership of the means of production was never a serious option to achieve the objectives of the industrialization drive. In fact the Labour Party changed its policy from detailed regulation towards a system characterized by macroeconomic management of the economy. One of the leading contemporary historians of the Norwegian labour movement in the postwar period states that 'The Norwegian Labour Party changed with surprising speed from a seemingly extreme dirigiste version of planning to an indicative, market-oriented strategy of macroeconomic planning'.[21] This assertion seems correct, but should be qualified. The Labour Party did not limit itself to macro-economic management. The politicians were seeking new ways to conduct *microeconomic planning*. To be able to influence allocation of resources, the government had to find a way to manage financial flows to ensure that particular activities, projects and enterprises given priority by the government received the desired funding. To obtain this goal the Labour Party leadership, and in particular Erik Brofoss, moved the banking system to centre stage in policy making.[22]

The financing of the planned modernization through large-scale industrial-ization was soon considered to be crucial, and a strategy was based on the development of export industries utilizing Norwegian resources and compara-tive advantages. The construction of hydro-electric power plants and electrochemical and metallurgical enterprises was given the highest priority. It was a central element in the Labour Party's economic policy to keep the interest rate low, if necessary by regulation, to ensure sufficient funding to selected high-priority projects and enterprises. In January 1946 the government declared that its goal was to keep the interest rate low at the actual 2.5 per cent level. During the very first postwar years with overliquidity in the banking system and a system with rationing and direct regulations, the interest rate was indeed low. But when the system was dismantled and the price level rose during the early 1950s, even interest rates started to rise along with an increase in the demand for credit.

However the government was determined to maintain a low interest-rate policy, if necessary by administrative means. During the war, the so called 'Adminis-tration Council'[23] passed resolutions in May 1940, which set an interest rate ceiling on almost every type of loan, as well as on deposits.[24] In the political programme for the four-year period subsequent to the elections in the Autumn of 1945, the Labour Party stated: 'A low-level interest rate has to be secured, and the interest rate will be lowered, if necessary by law'.[25] In November 1945 the Ministry of Finance declared its firm intention to keep a low interest-rate level with regard to the 'reconstruction policy'. But the policy to maintain low interest rates through administrative measures was not confirmed to the immediate postwar reconstruction period. The Labour Party government continued this policy, with its legal basis in a temporary Act on the regulation of interest rates, passed in December 1947. A new temporary law on interest rates was enacted in 1953.[26] The Act even contained new regulations on bond-market entry. According to this legislation anybody who wished to issue bonds was obliged to apply to the authorities for a permission. The interest rate and all other conditions connected with the proposed issue had to be examined and approved by the authorities.

This policy and legislation introduced a protracted *credit rationing* system in Norway. Credit rationing was considered to be a precondition to ensure low-priced credit to selected projects and firms given priority by the government. But at the same time a precondition for the system to work was the ability of the government to direct financial flows to such projects, and thus allocate resources in accordance with the goals of economic policy.

The role of the banking system and the policy towards financial institutions were elaborated in a committee report submitted to the Labour leadership in October 1948.[27] Among the members of the committee were Anders Frihagen[28] and Erik Brofoss. The latter was the main architect of Labour economic policies at this time. In the report the socialization of the financial institutions was described as a 'long-term goal', but in reality this policy was abandoned. Even the policy from the election programme of 1945. demanding public represen-tatives on the Boards of Directors of the commercial banks, was firmly rejected by the report. The essence of the policy proposed by the report was the following: 'The influence of society on the banking system must be strengthened by developing the state banks, and by a more efficient control with the bank and credit institutions'.[29]

The government chose a corporative solution, based on voluntary coopera-tion between the banks and the authorities in order to carry out these new monetary and credit policies. The cooperation took place within the framework of the so-called Cooperation Committee, which was established in 1951. This committee was composed of representatives from the Bank of Norway, the Ministry of Finance, the Bank Inspectorate and the commercial and savings banks. In 1955 they were joined by representatives from the life-insurance industry.

The state banks increased their loans substantially after the war. Two new public banks were established: one to finance housing (Statens husbank, 1946) and one to finance education (Statens lånekasse for studerende ungdom, 1947). During 1951 the financing of the state banks met with great obstacles, because it became impossible to sell state bank bonds at the low interest-rate level fixed by the authorities. The government then had to transfer funds from the Treasury to the state banks. Thus it became very important for the state to get the banks, as well as the life-insurance companies, to buy more government securities. This was the government's main motive in having representatives of the life insurance companies on the Cooperation Committee. At the beginning 'The Norwegian Life-insurance Companies' Association' was very reluctant to become a member, because it wished to avoid increased pressure to buy low interest-rate bonds. After a while, however, the Association was forced to take part in the Cooper-ation Committee, since the Ministry of Finance and the Bank of Norway expressed the view that 'the life-insurance companies have a substantial impact on the development of the monetary and credit market'.[30]

The government asked the 'Penge- og Finansrådet', which was a consultative committee on monetary and financial matters, to draw up a report on monetary and credit policy based on a precondition to keep the interest rate low, in spite of upward pressures. The report was presented to the government in January 1952.[31] Subsequently the government informed the Storting about its new guidelines for monetary and credit policy, based on this report.[32] The main objectives were as follows:

1. Secure stabilization of prices.
2. Prevent an increase in the interest-rate level.
3. Secure the funding of the state banks.
4. Restrain the credit supplies from the private banks.
6. Secure an efficient distribution and allocation of credit according to the goals of economic policy.

The temporary law on interest rates, issue control etc. mentioned above, was an outcome of this debate in the Storting on the reorientation of the monetary and credit policies. To fulfil these objectives, the government also stated that they wished to find a 'satisfactory solution through cooperation between the authorities and the private financial institutions'.[33] The Cooperation Committee was considered well suited to meet this purpose.

During the first four years of its existence, the Cooperation Committee passed resolutions, laying down general guidelines for the lending and investment policies of the banks. In principle the banks were 'free' to follow these instructions. From 1955, however, a system with one-year binding agreements was adopted. These annual agreements laid down the rules for the lending policies the banks were obliged to carry through the following year, the amount of government securities the financial institutions were obliged to buy, and so on. Hence the financial institutions and markets during the early 1950s were in effect subject to a new regulatory regime. Why did the commercial banks, as well as the other financial institutions, accept this development? The main reason seems to be that the authorities, as a 'return service' for the voluntary cooperation of the banks and the other financial institutions, desisted from the enactment of a new, extensive regulatory legislation.[34]

Governments in the industrialized West made growth and development central objectives for economic policies in the postwar period, and to a large extent this had its origins in the disillusion of the previous decades. The old paradigm of orthodox neoclassical economics, with its stress on the 'self-regulating' ability of the liberal market economy, had failed to provide a recipe for coping with the crises and depressions of the interwar period.

The Great Depression of the 1930s opened the way to Keynesianism in Norway as well as several other countries.[35] Ragnar Frisch initiated a renewal of Norwegian economics in the early 1930s, and he developed certain central ideas which later came to be known as Keynesian macroeconomics. As a teacher at the University of Oslo, Frisch created the so-called Oslo school. During the interwar years Frisch and his pupils exerted relatively limited influence on the policies of the Labour Party government in power from 1935. After 1945, however, their influence on policy making became important:

> The Keynesians returning from exile in 1945 and the economists who had spent the war years analyzing the Norwegian economy and planning for the post-war period at the Bureau of Statistics and the Department of Economics (at the University of Oslo) were well prepared to influence the Norwegian economy. Powerful planning tools were developed in the form of econometric models and the National Budget.[36]

Keynesian ideas became very important for Norwegian policy making as well as for the ideological and political development of the Labour Party after 1945. As has already been pointed out, the sources for this new economic ideology were manifold. Both experiences with the interwar crisis and wartime experiences have to be taken into consideration.

Conclusion

The developments described above put the Norwegian banking system under a new regulatory regime. But our analysis has also pointed out a fundamental and essential change in the Norwegian financial system as a whole, from a largely market-based financial system before the Second World War to a state-led and credit-based system, which emerged during the early 1950s. During the 1960s and 1970s the new regulatory regime was considerably reinforced. This strengthened the system of credit rationing, and thus furthered the change of the financial system. The financing of industrial development became entirely dependent on loans. In order to keep the price for capital low, interest rates were set administratively by the authorities. The allocation of credit and capital flows was thus largely in the hands of the government and subject to discretionary criteria.

During the immediate postwar years monetary and credit policies were not the focus of public interest. But when the reconstruction period was completed and the dirigiste version of planning abandoned, there was a shift in the focus of attention. Central figures in the Labour Party leadership and government circles found it necessary to reshape the financial system as a means to achieve major strategic goals in economic policy such as economic growth, modernization through industrialization and redistribution. The conviction gradually emerged that the direction of financial flows was a condition to ensure the accomplishment of these strategic objectives. Erik Brofoss probably was one of the major forces behind this reorientation.[37]

Appendix

Table 7.1A Distribution of loans from savings and commercial banks, 1927 and 1930 (million kroner)

	Savings banks				Commercial banks			
	1927: mill. kr.	%	1930: mill. kr.	%	1927: mill. kr.	%	1930: mill. kr.	%
Public institutions	10	0.6	10	0.7	45	2.4	9	0.8
Municipalities	259	15.5	177	12.1	58	3.1	33	2.9
Agriculture	580	34.6	492	33.7	107	5.7	134	11.7
Fisheries	36	2.1	35	2.4	80	4.3	31	2.7
Mining	1	0.1	1	0.1	34	1.8	5	0.4
Manufacturing industries	149	9.0	115	7.9	757	40.5	340	29.8
Shipping	32	1.9	30	2.1	258	13.8	114	10.0
Commerce	161	9.6	117	8.0	391	20.9	265	23.2
Transport	8	0.5	8.0	0.5	3	0.2	12	1.1
Housing, real estate	378	22.7	337	23.1	9	0.5	66	5.8
Misc	56	3.4	137	9.4	128	6.8	133	11.6
Total, mill. kr./ Per cent	1670	100	1459	100	1870	100	1142	100

Source: NOS VIII. 191. *Undersøkelse om enkelte bankforhold, 1932.*

Table 7.2A Market shares in the Norwegian loan market, 1900–1955, selected years (million kroner)

	1900	1910	1920	1930	1940	1945	1950	1955
State banks	183	263	816	1014	1197	809	1958	4892
Saving banks	278	449	1732	1491	1258	754	2245	3760
Commercial banks	349	524	4034	1295	1104	910	3287	5006
Credit associations		6	23	79	290	334	808	1322
Insurance, pension funds	42	70	126	308	797	760	1201	2266
Total	852	1312	6731	4187	4646	3567	9499	17246

Percentage:

	1900	1910	1920	1930	1940	1945	1950	1955
State banks	21%	20%	12%	24%	26%	23%	21%	28%
Saving banks	33%	34%	26%	36%	27%	21%	24%	22%
Commercial banks	41%	40%	60%	31%	24%	26%	35%	29%
Credit associations	0%	0%	0%	2%	6%	9%	9%	8%
Insurance, pension funds	5%	5%	2%	7%	17%	21%	13%	13%
Total	100%	100%	100%	100%	100%	100%	100%	100%

Source: Skånland, 1967, op. cit.

Notes

1. Such a taxonomy has been put forward by various authors, e.g. J. Zysman, *Governments, Markets and Growth*, N.Y., 1983, G. Dosi, 'Finance, innovation and industrial change' in *Journal of Economic Behaviour and Organization*, no. 3, 1990, and T.M. Rybczynski, 'Industrial finance system in Europe, US and Japan' in *Journal of Economic Behaviour and Organization*, 3–4, 1984.
2. For a more detailed and comprehensive presentation and analysis of the banking crisis, see H.W. Nordvik, 'Den norske bankkrisen i mellomkrigstiden- En sammenligning med dagens bankkrise', in *SNF-Bulletin Nr. 1/1992*; and S. Knutsen, 'From Expansion to Panic and Crash. The Norwegian Banking System and Its Customers 1913–1924' in *Scandinavian Economic History Review*, no. 3, 1991, pp. 41–71.
3. H.W. Nordvik, 'Penge- og valutapolitikk, Bank og Kredittvesen og krisen i Norsk økonomi på 1930-tallet' in E. Hovland, E. Lange and S. Rysslad (eds), *Det som svarte seg best. Studier i økonomisk historie og politikk*, Oslo, 1990.
4. Å. Egge, 'Trekk ved sparebankvesenet og sparebanklovgivningen i slutten av forrige århundre' in A. Jensen et al. (eds), *Sparing og sparebankvesen i Norge 1822–1972*, Oslo, 1972.
5. Knutsen, 1991, op. cit., note 2.
6. H.W. Nordvik, 'Banks and customers in times of crisis: Norwegian experiences in the 1920s', unpublished paper presented to international conference on universal banking at LSE, September 1991.
7. A more detailed and comprehensive analysis of the development during this period is found in Knutsen, op. cit., note 2.
8. H. Skånland, *The Norwegian Credit Market Since 1900*, Central Bureau of Statistics of Norway, Oslo, 1967.
9. Ibid.
10. H. Skånland, op. cit., note 8, p. 117.
11. H. Skånland, op. cit., note 8, table 22.
12. During the years of exile in London, the government was extended to a coalition government. A new Labour Party government came to power in the Autumn of 1945, and kept this position for 20 years to come.
13. During the 1920s there were nine different minority governments in Norway. Four of them were Conservative, four Liberal and one Labour. The latter lasted for only two weeks, from 28 January to 15 February 1928.
14. Minister of Finance Holmboe, *Stortingsforhandlinger 1926*, no. 7a, p. 90 (My translation/S.K.).
15. *Det Arbeidende Folks Krisekrav*, Oslo, 1932. (My translation/S.K.).
16. Ibid.

17. E. Lange and H. Pharo, 'Planning and Economic Policy in Norway, 1945–1960' in *Scandinavian Journal of History*, no. 3, 1991.
18. Ibid.
19. Ibid.
20. The Labour government was reluctant to accept Marshall Aid in the beginning, as well as joining the OEEC, which was a precondition to receive such aid.
21. T. Bergh, 'Pragmatic and Democratic Socialism. Ideological and Political Trends in the Norwegian Labour Party during the 1940s and 1950s', in *Scandinavian Journal of History*, no. 3, 1991. (T. Bergh is author of the standard work on Labour Party history after the Second World War: *A history of the Labour movement in Norway*, vol. V, Oslo, 1987).
22. E. Brofoss, Minister of Finance 1945–47, Minister of Trade 1947–54, governor of the Bank of Norway 1954–70.
23. Established 14 April 1940 in order to administer the occupied parts of Norway in 'co-operation' with the German occupation authorities. The German 'Reichskommisar' dissolved the 'Administration Council' on 25 September 1940.
24. H. Kofoed, *Den norske bankforening 1915–1940*, Oslo, 1940, p. 184 f. In fact this introduced a 45-year regime of administratively fixed interest rates in Norway.
25. *Det norske Arbeiderpartis arbeidsprogram*, Oslo, 1945.
26. This 'temporary' legislation was in force until 1965, when it was included in an extensive 'law on money and credit'.
27. Bankvesenet i Norge. Innstilling fra en av Sentralstyret nedsatt komité', document til Landsstyret 22–24 October 1948, Sak 3 a.
28. A. Frihagen, Managing Director of Den Norskc Industribank (The Manufacturing Bank of Norway Ltd), member of the Nygaardsvold government 1939–45 (in exile in London, 1940–45) and Managing Director in Bank Inspectorate from 1951.
29. 'Bankvesenet i Norge. Innstilling fra en av Sentralstyret nedsatt komité', document til Landsstyret 22–24 October 1948, Sak 3 a.
30. Archive of the Bank of Norway: Letter from the governor of the Bank of Norway, E. Brofoss, to 'The Norwegian Life-insurance Companies' Association', 28 September 1955.
31. 'Innstilling fra Penge- og Finansrådet', 13 januar 1952, appendix to St. meld. no. 75, 1952.
32. 'Retningslinjer for penge- og kredittpolitikken', St. meld. no. 75, 1952.
33. Ibid., p. 23 (My translation from Norwegian/S.K.).
34. *Norges Banks skriftserie* no. 9, Oslo, 1980, p. 40.
35. When we analyse the breakthrough of the Keynesian paradigm, we want to emphasize that we in this context define the notion 'Keynesian ideas' as a more general set of symbolic ideas, and thus as more than Keynes's own ideas. On Keynesianism in Norway, see also T. Berg and T.J. Hanisch, *Vitenskap og politikk*, Oslo, 1984; J. Chr. Andvig, *Ragnar Frisch and the Great Depression*, Oslo, 1986; H.W. Nordvik, 'Krisepolitikken og den økonomiske politikken i Norge i 1930-årene' in *Historisk tidsskrift*, no. 3, 1977.
36. Lange and Pharo, op. cit., note 17.
37. I have recently started work on an extensive research project called 'Financial system, industrial policy and industrial development in Norway 1950–1985'. The role of Mr Brofoss will be investigated more thoroughly in connection with this work, based on material from the Bank of Norway Archives and the private archive of E. Brofoss.

8   The establishment of the Anglo-Czechoslovak Bank: conflicting interests*
Charlotte Natmeßnig

The establishment of the Anglo-Czechoslovak Bank provides a perfect example of the problems and difficulties the big Viennese banks had to face as a result of the break-up of the Austro-Hungarian Empire after the First World War. It also clearly demonstrates the differences between the points of view and interests of Czechoslovakia, a newly founded successor state and those of Britain, despite the fact that Czechoslovakia was an associated state of the victorious allies, of which Great Britain was one.[1]

From the very beginning, the central aim of the Czechoslovak government was to establish an efficient national economy in the new state, which should be entirely independent of the complex network of financial and economic relations in the former Habsburg Monarchy. British interests, on the other hand, shifted towards Central Europe after the First World War, seeking opportunities to make new investments and to expand former commercial links to make up for the loss of the Russian market. Financial and economic interests – in this case the Bank of England's interests – were based on the assumption that the economic entity represented by the former Habsburg Empire would survive, and that Vienna would regain its former position as the financial and commercial centre of the region despite the drastic political changes that had culminated in the founding of the national successor states after the dissolution of the Habsburg Monarchy.[2] When the Governor of the Bank of England, Montagu Norman, launched the project for the reconstruction of the Anglo-Austrian Bank in order to secure the payment of the prewar debts of its London branch, he made it clear that he would support the project only if the management of the bank retained its former structure and continued to operate as it had done in the past. He insisted on taking over a company in full working order with its head office in Vienna operating a network of branches connected with the industrial companies of its concern throughout the former monarchy. The 30 branches of the Anglo-Austrian Bank operating in the territory of the new Czechslovak state were to play a key role. Most of them had been founded after the turn of the century and together they represented the bank's main assets. Their connections with all the important branches of industry were most valuable for the industrial concern of the Anglo-Austrian Bank.[3]

* The author expresses her gratitude to Professor Alice Teichova without whose constant support and encouragement this chapter would not have been written and thanks Mrs Barbara Wilson for reading the manuscript.

The Anglo-Austrian Bank was founded in 1863 and started business in January 1864. The initiative had come from British financiers under the leadership of Grenfell & Glyn who wanted to establish an institution which would transfer capital to the Continent and check the dominant influence in the Habsburg Monarchy of the French *crédit mobilier* type. The bank was supposed to operate as a *crédit mobilier* and also as an English foreign bank mediating between the financial centres of Vienna and London. It was established with two offices, one in Vienna and one in London, with equal management status.[4]

The Anglo-Austrian Bank followed the path of development typical of a universal bank and especially in the boom years before the First World War extended its relations with various industrial enterprises. By financing and controlling them it built up an industrial concern comprising more than 70 joint-stock companies. At the end of the war it was among the biggest Viennese banks in whose companies a large amount of the total industrial and banking capital was concentrated.[5] Up to the beginning of the First World War the main business of the London branch remained to grant and mediate acceptance credits and in 1914 its balance sheet amounted to 100 million crowns, about one-seventh of the bank's total balance sheet.[6]

When the First World War broke out, the London office was a debtor in sterling to various companies in Great Britain. Like all London branches of enemy banks, the London branch of the Anglo-Austrian Bank was sequestered and forbidden, under the Enemy Trading Act, to conduct any business. Acceptors whose clients were unable to meet maturing bills because of the dislocation of the exchanges were enabled by the Treasury Act of September 1914 to apply to the Bank of England for the necessary funds to meet the payment of pre-moratorium acceptances. The Anglo-Austrian Bank applied for heavy advances under this scheme and by the end of the war they amounted to more than £2 million net. Part of the principal had been repaid, leaving a net balance of £1 073 000 outstanding. The rate of interest charged was 2 per cent above the bank rate and the total interest paid back in respect of the loan was £131 303. Under the agreed scheme for repayment of the debt, the interest rate was recalculated at 5 per cent simple interest as from October 1914.[7] Statements on the advances drawn up by the Bank of England at the end of 1920 and 1921 show that these reached £1 339 000 including 5 per cent interest thus making the Bank of England the main creditor of the London branch of the Anglo-Austrian Bank.[8]

Montagu Norman wanted to secure repayment of the debts of the London branch on similar terms to those agreed with the Länderbank, which meant a change in the bank's nationality and the transformation of its debts accrued in allied countries into shares in a new company. The Anglo-Austrian Bank and the Länderbank had been the only Viennese banks operating branches in former enemy countries and their branches in Paris and London had accumulated debts to the respective governments.[9] In view of the creditors' interest there is no doubt that securing these debts had been underlying Norman's commitment to the reconstruction and transformation of the Anglo-Austrian Bank. However, there was another factor in his engagement which can hardly be overlooked: the bank was to become a means of channelling money from Britain to Central and South-Eastern Europe and thus establishing a sphere of influence in this region.[10] Norman based his commitment to the reconstruction of the Anglo-Austrian Bank on his belief that Austria, despite the break-up of the Habsburg Empire, would remain the financial centre of Central and South-Eastern Europe.[11]

In Britain, as in other allied states, leading political and economic institutions regarded the successor states as a *cordon sanitaire* against Bolshevism and they also hoped to check Germany's possible resurgence by penetrating into markets formerly dominated by her.[12] Thus the Viennese banks, with their extensive network of branches and diversified industrial concerns, seemed to offer the best possibility of gaining a financial foothold in the very centre of Central and South-Eastern Europe. The sphere of interest could then easily be expanded through the existing instruments of the banks and markets for British exports opened up at the same time. Apart from gaining a hold on a Viennese bank it would even be more advantageous to establish a Vienna branch of a London bank as 'British financial operations would be conducted with greater secrecy'.[13] However, the complexity of the economic and political situation was to cause unforseen difficulties for the British in their endeavour to realize this plan. Some of these are discussed below.

All the successor states, on the other hand, were eager to attract foreign capital – especially French and British – not only to secure their own economic position after the collapse of the Habsburg Empire but also to underpin their efforts to break off the intertwined economic and financial links binding them to Vienna which had played the dominant role as the centre of the Habsburg Monarchy.[14] In Austria the participation of foreign capital in certain industries also served as a means to circumvent socialization. This policy was pursued by entrepreneurs on the assumption that once foreign capital had gained a share in business enterprises government would refrain from enforcing the sociopolitical measures demanded by the socialist movement.[15]

After the Habsburg Empire had collapsed and the newly founded successor states had established their own currencies, the big Viennese banks suddenly found themselves heading multinational enterprises, but their main assets and spheres of influence were threatened by legal measures taken by the new states. They faced the alternative of either reducing and adjusting their business to the shrunken Austrian home market or trying to hold on to their sphere of interest in the former Habsburg Empire. In general they opted for the latter, as they were convinced that in the long run these temporary difficulties could be overcome and that Vienna would remain the dominant financial centre of Central and South-Eastern Europe.[16] Inflation rose drastically after the end of the war and the need to meet the financial demands of their industrial concerns and the stipulations of the Treaty of St Germain, fixing the repayment of prewar debts at prewar parity, made the Viennese banks eager to attract foreign capital participation. Furthermore, they had to face the fact that their share capital was steadily dwindling as a result of the inflationary process and that, by international standards, they were no longer the big institutions of the prewar period because the real value of their share capital had shrunk to that of comparatively small banks.[17]

The financial and monetary policy of severing all economic and financial links with Vienna, which the Czechoslovak government had pursued from the outset,[18] was initially intended to prevent the Czechoslovak economy from being drawn into the maelstrom of Austria's inflation. The main aim of the Czechoslovak Finance Minister, Alois Rašin, was to get control of the currency in the Czechoslovak territory and to ensure that the circulation of banknotes was adjusted to the needs of the national economy and the credit of the state to be restored.[19] At the same time Czechoslovakia's policy was to cut the big Viennese banks off from their sphere of interest by preventing them from controlling and financing their branches and the subsidiaries of their industrial concerns in the territory of the new state. Moreover, these measures were to accelerate the process of 'Czechoslovakization' – nationalization of foreign property – in Czechoslovakia, thus offering a further means of breaking the hold of the big Viennese banks on the Czechoslovak economy.[20]

In November 1918 Alois Rašin introduced the first measures which were to pave the way for the actual separation of the currency. These decrees were designed to protect the Czechoslovak money supply against the influx of banknotes from countries of the former currency union. Thus, Austrian banks were virtually cut off from their subsidiary enterprises operating in the new state of Czechoslovakia. Above all, the Austro-Hungarian Bank was forbidden to discount war bonds in the state of Czechoslovakia and to transfer any payments to banks except for wages. The transfer of deposits in crowns and the discount of Treasury Bills of the Austro-Hungarian Bank had to be authorized by the Czechoslovak Ministry of Finance.

Even so, the influx of paper money and coins continued because the purchasing power of the crown in the Czechoslovak state was higher than in the other successor states and it was quoted at a higher rate on the Zurich exchange. Czechoslovakia therefore took the further step of passing the Currency Separation Act of February 1919, to avoid being drawn into the whirlwind of Austrian inflation. The stamping of the banknotes was accompanied by the withdrawal of 50 per cent of privately held banknotes and their conversion into a 1 per cent compulsory public loan as well as by freezing savings accounts. Complete separation and administration of currency was achieved by taking over the office of the Austro-Hungarian Bank in Prague and setting up the Banking Office which was to become the Czechoslovak National Bank in 1926.[21]

Currency separation was one step towards establishing an independent national economy; the second, which was to sever the widespread financial and business links concentrated in Vienna, was nationalization and nostrification. At the end of 1919 the Czechoslovak government passed a law which required the head offices of companies and industrial enterprises situated in Vienna but with undertakings operating in Czechoslovak territory, to be transferred to Czechoslovakia. The economic variant of nostrification dominated by nationalism – in the case of Czechoslovakia, 'Czechoslovakization' – was carried out in all successor states and strongly favoured by the respective governments. The stipulations of the peace treaties and respective laws and decrees of the successor states provided the legal framework for the transformation and restructuring of property on such a large scale. At the same time Czechoslovak enterprises and banks supported by the Czechoslovak government bought some of the shares Austrian citizens held in companies which fell under nostrification in Czechoslovakia. Inflation in Austria, and accompanied as it was by continuing depreciation in the value of the Austrian crown, made it easier for Czechoslovak nationals to acquire these shares.[22]

It was this political and economic policy, implemented in the first two years of the Czechoslovak Republic, that caused difficulties for the management of the Anglo-Austrian Bank and consequently forced the Bank of England to alter its first intentions. As a result of economic changes which he had not taken into account when launching the project of reconstructing the Anglo-Austrian Bank, Montagu Norman had to adjust his interest to political reality so as not to risk the whole project. However, the root of the difficulties lay in the particular way all Viennese banks had done business up to the end of the First World War. The structure of their administration had been highly centralized and, in the long run, had contributed to Vienna's dominance of finance and commerce in the Habsburg Monarchy. Head offices in Vienna ran a whole network of branches and industrial subsidiaries throughout the territory of the Austro-Hungarian Empire. It was the head offices and not their branches which administered funds on current and deposit account and allocated the necessary sums to their branches.[23]

Like all big Viennese banks the Anglo-Austrian Bank had run its business on these lines. When the first rumours of the Czechoslovak government's intention of creating its own currency spread, the head office in Vienna decided to retransfer the greater part of the sums originally deposited with its branches in Czechoslovakia. On the advice of and in agreement with the Austro-Hungarian Bank, as the former bank of issue of the monarchy, 166 million crowns were transferred to the branches of the Austro-Hungarian Bank in Czechoslovakia in the form of 4 per cent Treasury notes. They were to be discounted at the request of the Anglo-Austrian Bank. On 6 February 1919 the retransfer of claims and credit balances as well as the retransfer of private creditors to Czechoslovak territory was forbidden by a decree of the Czechoslovak Banking Office. Consequently, the Czech branches were cut off from their head office in Vienna. Two days later the Prague branch of the Austro-Hungarian Bank was informed that further discounting of Treasury notes was prohibited unless authorized by the Banking Office.[24]

The question whether the Czechoslovak government would honour these Treasury notes was to become crucial to the negotiations between British and Czechoslovak representatives. According to unofficial information given to the Anglo-Austrian Bank from a Czechoslovak source shortly after the decree had been passed, its directors were told of the provisional character of this decree. However, although President Masaryk and his Minister of Finance had assured the Chairman of the bank, Dr Landesberger, that the bank's transfer of notes had been legal, the Banking Office continued to refuse to honour the Treasury notes. The directors of the Anglo-Austrian Bank insisted that they had acted legally in transferring the notes. The Czechoslovak government, on the other hand, stated that the issue of the notes had taken place in Vienna exclusively for the disposal of the Anglo-Austrian Bank's branches in Czechoslovakia.[25]

Since the Treasury notes constituted a considerable part of the Anglo-Austrian Bank's Czech assets and at the same time represented the security for the Bank of England's involvement in its reconstruction, Montagu Norman made them a condition for continuing his negotiations with its representatives. The subject of the negotiations was the take-over of the whole concern in full working order as it had existed until the end of the First World War.[26] The effort to secure and maintain the conditions set up by the Bank of England put increasing pressure on the representatives of the Anglo-Austrian Bank, while at the same time the Czechoslovak government was enforcing the measures to establish its independence of Vienna.

The only source of funds for the Anglo-Austrian Bank to carry on the business of its Czechoslovak branches was the advance of 61 920 000 Kč against the collateral of Treasury notes granted to it by the Banking Office. However, in February 1921 the Banking Office recalled the advance and demanded repayment in six 15 per cent monthly instalments. Owing to the depreciation of the Austrian crown, the remaining 10 per cent represented the value of the Treasury notes at that time. As the Banking Office accepted only Czech bills for rediscount, there was no possibility of providing the Czech branches with the necessary funds.[27]

In the Autumn of 1920 the directors of the Anglo-Austrian Bank had made a first attempt to solve the problems of the bank's Czechoslovak branches. This would have implied a 'Czechoslovak solution' on the lines adopted by all

Viennese banks, i.e. to merge their branches in Czechoslovakia with a local bank guaranteeing the strong support of the Czechoslovak government. The negotiations which had begun with the Hospodářskó úvěrní banka pro Čechy were immediately stopped once the Bank of England expressed strong disapproval. That is why the directors, though convinced that a merger with a local bank would have guaranteed the running of business in Czechoslovakia, had to refrain from any further attempts to arrive at their own solution of the Czechoslovak question.[28]

Without going into the matter of Czechoslovak legislation and its impact on the Anglo-Austrian Bank, the Bank of England insisted on its condition: the take-over of the bank in full working order without any of its assets being dissipated, guaranteed by its board directors. Montagu Norman feared that the Bank of England's participation in the project for the reconstruction of the Anglo-Austrian Bank would not be a viable proposition unless the substantial assets in Czechoslovakia, which formed the basis for the scheme, were secured.[29] In March 1921 Montagu Norman was informed that the Czechoslovak government had recalled the loan and had demanded that the Anglo-Austrian Bank immediately start negotiations with a view to transforming its branches into a Czechoslovak bank. It was even suggested that 40 per cent of the new bank's share capital of 100 million Kč be retained by the Anglo-Austrian Bank, 40 per cent be taken up by the Czechoslovak government and the remaining 20 per cent be offered to the British.[30] He immediately suspended negotiations because of the pressure the Czechoslovak authorities were putting on the management of the Anglo-Austrian Bank: 'It is out of the question to proceed with any scheme of reconstruction as long as there is the possibility of the assets in Central-Europe being dissipated.'[31] When reporting to Sir Basil Blackett of the Treasury, Norman even seemed to doubt the integrity of his Viennese negotiating partners when he wrote: 'It appears that some of their assets are being dissipated. Whether this is under pressure from Czechoslovak Government or for some domestic reason, or in order to put pressure on us, I am not sure, but it clearly ought not to be done.'[32]

At this time the policy of the Bank of England was still dominated by the aim of reorganizing the Anglo-Austrian Bank as a British concern, with the Bank of England as main creditor acquiring a controlling[33] interest and the Anglo-Austrian Bank being taken over with all its branches, irrespective of their location, in order to repay its sterling creditors and assist the restoration of the countries where it previously operated. Norman stressed this argument and the interests of British creditors when he made initial enquiries at the Treasury, the Foreign Office and the Board of Trade as to whether official representations with the Czechoslovak government were feasible.[34] Though aware of the problems that were making it difficult for the Anglo-Austrian Bank to maintain business as usual in Czechoslovakia, the Bank of England did not look into the underlying reasons for these problems. Indeed, it was the only Viennese bank at this time that had not reached an agreement with Czechoslovakia concerning its branches there. British representatives did not go into these matters of Czechoslovak legislative measures but attributed the problem instead to differences between the Austrian and Czechoslovak governments concerning the division of the gold assets of the Austro-Hungarian Bank. 'This pressure took the form of impeding the work of the Czech branches by legislation and threats. Owing to differences concerning the division of the gold assets of the Austro-Hungarian Bank' ... This account of the situation of March 1921, written in retrospect, shows little understanding, for none of the steps taken by the Czechoslovak authorities lacked the legal backing of either a law or a decree.[35]

There is no evidence that Montagu Norman had taken the position of Czechoslovakia into account either when he first initiated negotiations with Dr Landesberger, the Chairman of the Anglo-Austrian Bank (his death led to the suspension of negotiations), or when they were taken up again early in 1921. Norman stuck to his condition and left no room for initiative to the Viennese directors, in particular Dr Rosenberg, who was in charge of the negotiations on the Anglo-Austrian side after Dr Landesberger's death. Dr Rosenberg had informed Norman of the difficulties and had already asked for advice in late 1920. In March 1921, only one day after having received Norman's veto on any action taken by the Viennese directors, Dr Rosenberg – though unofficially – conferred decision-making powers upon Norman. In fact, only five days later Dr Hans Simon, a director of the Anglo-Austrian Bank, informed Montagu Norman that negotiations with the Czechoslovak authorities had already been adjourned, playing down the latest attempt to act according to their own priorities. 'The bank confined herself to give notice to the British creditors and in consequence of the answer from London, desirous to avoid all misunderstandings postponed in spite of the situation all further negotiations.' (sic)[36]

Only after the provisional agreement on the reconstruction of the Anglo-Austrian Bank as an English company had been signed on 4 May 1921 were the Austrians granted permission to inform the Czechoslovak authorities that the bank was going to be transformed into a British company. Norman obviously assumed that the Czechoslovaks would then stop exerting pressure, but agreed, as a concession, to inform the Czechoslovak ambassador to London, Mastný, of the provisional agreement. Norman did not seek a personal conversation with the Czechoslovak ambassador but sent a representative who was 'to discuss banking facilities' in Czechoslovakia.[37] Nevertheless, Norman had contacted Sir Basil Blackett of the Treasury asking whether it would be possible to persuade the Foreign Office to intervene through Sir George Clerk, the British ambassador to Prague. Blackett reminded Norman of the Enemy Trading Act and of the fact that Czechoslovakia was an associate state; according to him it was out of the question for the Foreign Office to take any official step in favour of an ex-enemy country. The Foreign Office confirmed the Treasury's view and remarked that any steps taken by the British ambassador would of necessity be unofficial; they should be regarded only as explanatory talks with the various Czechoslovak government authorities, and Sir George Clerk was instructed accordingly. Norman, however, was advised to arrange any possible intervention in connection with the settlement of prewar debts through a representative of the Board of Trade, who might then take up the matter when negotiating a settlement on these debts with the Czechoslovak authorities. The Board of Trade refused any such action on the grounds that there was no prospect of a definite arrangement. The Treasury also declined Norman's alternative suggestion that the Czechoslovak ambassador to London be invited to act as an intermediary, on the grounds that he might lack the necessary authority as well as the necessary knowledge of details.[38] Only two possible courses were left: either to try the Foreign Office again and to entrust negotiations with the Czechoslovak officials to Sir George Clerk; 'or whether the more expeditious method would not be to send, as you suggested, someone to Czechoslovakia to sit on the doorstep of the Ministry concerned until he has gained his point.'[39]

Towards the end of June 1921 the Viennese directors informed Norman of a further deterioration in the position of the branches in Czechoslovakia. Dr Simon, a director of the Anglo-Austrian Bank and a member of the Austrian negotiating team, went to London to leave a memorandum with Norman and to persuade him personally to get the British authorities involved. British representatives abroad obviously assumed that the nub of the problem was nationalism and pointed out that this was contrary to their aims:

> The Czech Government is doing its best to make the working of the Czechoslovak branches impossible in order to sell them to Czech banks. If the Bank is to become a British institution it is obviously in our interest that it should be able to take over the very numerous and important Czecho-Slovak branches in full working order; on the other hand, the Czech authorities, as in other similar cases, are likely to object to the Czech company being in any way dependent on or subordinate to any institution in Vienna, whether controlled by British capital or not.[40]

The banking concession of the branches had been renewed by the Czechoslovak authorities only up to the end of 1921 and so the management of the Anglo-Austrian Bank faced the threat of practically having to cease business unless negotiations with a Czechoslovak bank or financial institution were started immediately. The Banking Office had indicated that it might issue a decree restricting the volume of deposits to the level of the working capital of the Czechoslovak branches. This would have meant that the Anglo-Austrian Bank would have had to repay about 70 million Kč to Czechoslovak creditors as deposits had risen to 150 million Kč, representing nearly twice the sum of the working capital. The ensuing obligation to repay would have meant a perceptible loss but to make matters worse, the head office was in no position to control the situation, for the only way to provide the branches with the sums they needed was to buy Czech crowns; this, however, was out of the question because of high inflation.[41]

Not willing to risk the success of his far-reaching project, Norman considered the only feasible action to be taken, which was to send Michael Spencer-Smith as his own representative and confidant.[42] Bruce Lockhart gives a vivid picture of Michael Spencer-Smith, a typical representative of the City, in his memoirs. He not only provided a description of the genuine English banker but also offered an explanation for the problems during the negotiations: 'At that time Spencer-Smith was the youngest director of the Bank of England ... he was regarded as the most promising of all younger financial lights in the City of London ... a typical Englishman, he knew no foreign languages and had no experience of dealing with Continental Europeans.' Spencer-Smith was sent to Prague to secure the interests of the Bank of England by negotiating with the Czechoslovak authorities. He left for Prague on 7 July 1921 with all diplomatic credentials. London officially informed Prague and made sure that the British Legation provided him with any support he needed.[43]

The meagre correspondence between Spencer-Smith and the Governor of the Bank of England during Spencer's stay in Prague as well as Bruce Lockhart's reports to the Board of Trade indicate that Spencer-Smith had come with exact instructions. The lines of his negotiations had obviously been well prepared beforehand. The directors Dr Hans Simon and Dr Wilhelm Rosenberg had been summoned to Prague to provide Spencer-Smith with any background information he might request.[44] From the very beginning of his talks Spencer-Smith had to face the strong determination of the Czechoslovak authorities to avoid any dependence on the formerly dominant financial centre of Vienna. He seemed deeply impressed by this fact when reporting to Norman about his negotiations in Prague: 'The hatred of the Czechs for the Austrians is intense and colours every thought and action. The Austrians are treated like dirt and without our intervention the Anglo-Austrian Bank would have been helpless.'[45] On this interpretation, the Austrians might well appear to be helpless, for they had tried to solve the problems in the same way as many Viennese banks after the introduction of the Czechoslovak legislative measures. Since, however, it had been a crucial condition of the British to take over the Anglo-Austrian Bank in full working order with all former branches and since the Austrians were unable to 'convince' the Czechoslovak authorities of the advantages of the British scheme, the British had to intervene as their predominant interests were at stake.

On 18 July 1921, only a few days after his arrival, Spencer-Smith presented the Czechoslovak negotiating party with a first draft of an agreement comprising the British conditions for a future settlement.[46] Its last point, the extension of repayment of the wheat bills, which was to become an important bargaining counter, refers to a British loan to Czechoslovakia for the purchase of wheat, which was part of a scheme of food credits to the Central European countries associated with the Entente. In February 1921 the British government had granted to the Czechoslovak government a short-term loan of £2 million in the form of Treasury bills for the purchase of flour. In June the Czechoslovak government asked for a renewal of the maturing bills due on 7 August 1921 and offered at the same time to pay the accrued interest. The Treasury refused on the very day Spencer-Smith set out on his mission to Prague. Correspondence between Montagu Norman, the Treasury and the Foreign Office, as well as the fact that Spencer-Smith had had a long meeting with officials at the Treasury before going to Prague, suggest that Spencer-Smith had full authority to use the renewal of the wheat bills in order to put pressure on the Czechs.

Although he seemed quite sure that the Czechoslovaks would agree to the provisional draft, Spencer-Smith nevertheless, turned to Norman for advice on the next move in his negotiations with the Czechoslovak authorities. Indeed, he admitted that the negotiations would have come to a deadlock earlier had he not used the renewal of the wheat bills as the strongest weapon to break the resistance of the Czechoslovaks towards the Bank of England project. The Czechoslovak negotiators had insisted on the formation of a separate bank and were able to convince Spencer-Smith that the repayment of the 156 million Kč Treasury notes would need parliamentary consent, which could hardly be obtained because of the strong opposition of the National Democrats and the far-reaching influence of the Živnostenská banka. Aware that the Czechoslovak government was in need of foreign capital, he had coupled the question of the Treasury notes with the possibility of Czechoslovakia raising a loan in Britain. Thus, according to Spencer-Smith's draft, the new bank would be able to get hold of its valuable assets in cash before the maturing wheat bills were due. Understandably, he did not want the question of a loan to be linked with a possible agreement about the Anglo-Austrian Bank's branches in Czechoslovakia. The attempt to couple a loan issue in Britain with the payment of the Treasury notes was at once an offer and a threat since he was convinced that it would be impossible for the Czechoslovak government to survive without raising a loan within the next ten years; consequently this would simply imply the de facto recognition of the Treasury notes by the Czechoslovak government.[47] The question of Czechoslovakia raising a loan in Britain, he admitted, was due to some linguistic misunderstanding. Therefore he had broken off the negotiations for he wanted to consult Norman on whether to insist on his original intention that the new bank be released from the obligation to repay the advance of 156 million Kč if the Czechoslovak government contracted a loan abroad. This seemed to be the weakest point in Spencer-Smith's negotiations. He quite frankly admitted that if the Czechoslovaks turned elsewhere, for instance to Berlin or Paris – though he assumed, they did not want to be driven into the German or

French sphere of financial influence – they could call his bluff, since the Treasury would have to renew the wheat bills in any case. Moreover, the new bank would not get a penny. Having arrived at this point, he dared not go on without further instructions from Norman.[48] The question of the renewal of the wheat bills was to remain Spencer-Smith's most effective means of arriving at a settlement and he admitted frankly that he had had to use it quite brutally to get as far as he had.[49]

Spencer-Smith faced Czechoslovak opposition to the intended take-over of the Anglo-Austrian Bank's branches and had to acknowledge Czechoslovakia's nationalism and strong wish for total independence from Vienna. The Czechoslovak side considered this was not guaranteed unless the branches were established as a separate entity. In spite of this he remained adamant. To meet some of the Czechoslovak demands he agreed that Czechoslovakia should participate in the new bank's share capital – he considered that £100000 would be an appropriate sum – and one Czechoslovak representative be appointed to the board of directors. The reconstituted bank's name should be altered to Anglo-Continental Bank. At the end of July Dr Edward Beneš informed Spencer-Smith that, because of the reshuffle of the Czechoslovak government, it would be some time before it could give him an answer on the draft and resume negotiations.[50]

As the Austrian parliament had unexpectedly postponed the passing of the Länderbank and Anglobank Bill, by which these two institutions were to be transformed into a French and British bank respectively, Spencer-Smith went on to Vienna in order to impress on the Austrian authorities the need to expedite the passing of these two bills. As a result of these unexpected delays it now fell to the representatives of the Foreign Office to work for Norman's project. Spencer-Smith was summoned to London to report and discuss further steps. Norman wanted to take advantage of the temporary halt caused by the situation in Austria, which gave him time to consider further steps to be taken in Czechoslovakia. He did not expect that Beneš would be unable to resume the negotiations with Michael Spencer-Smith until the end of September 1921.[51]

In the meantime Norman, Spencer-Smith, and General Herbert Lawrence, a director of Glyn, Mills & Currie and representative of the British banking syndicate, were obliged to recognize that no further action could be taken regarding the Treasury notes and the reconstitution of the Anglo-Austrian Bank until the new Czechoslovak government had been formed and the Austrian parliament had passed the necessary laws. Spencer-Smith was sent to the Treasury to give an account of his negotiations. Consequently the maturity of the bills was extended until 6 October 1921 and it was indicated that a further extension might be agreed as soon as the Czechoslovak government reached an agreement with the Bank of England.[52]

All the British parties concerned were aware of the difficult situation in Czechoslovakia, caused by opposition to the ambitious project and the eventual repayment of the Treasury bills, both within the government, and from the Agrarian Party and the Banking Office. In August, however, Norman was still adamant about achieving his objective unaltered.[53] Despite the difficulties, the Foreign Office representatives were optimistic that Czechoslovakia would not reject the chance of a close connection with the Bank of England. In fact, whenever they conferred with Dr Beneš they stressed the advantages of an agreement with the Bank of England and the resulting direct connections with London.[54]

Shortly before negotiations were resumed, Beneš assured Sir George Clerk and Bruce Lockhart of his intentions to keep the negotiations in his own hands; Czechoslovak financial circles would not start negotiations concerning a foreign loan before he had come to an agreement with the Bank of England. Furthermore, he was prepared to reach a settlement with the Bank of England regarding the Treasury notes.[55] The new Czechoslovak government having agreed on an answer to Spencer-Smith's draft, negotiations between Beneš and Spencer-Smith were resumed. The latter returned to Prague only after it had been confirmed that a solution to the problem of the Treasury notes could be obtained by Czechoslovakia guaranteeing prewar debts due to the Anglo-Austrian Bank. On 1 October 1921, the Czechoslovak government officially asked for a further extension of the wheat bills and was informed on 10 October, the day an agreement between Beneš and Spencer-Smith was signed, that the British government had granted the Czechoslovak request. The Bank of England's interests regarding the repayment of the 156 million Kč Treasury notes were secured because the Czechoslovak government guaranteed to pay an advance of prewar debts of up to 156 million Kč due to the Anglo-Austrian Bank. The government had agreed to pay a first instalment of 25 million Kč on the advance, repayable within 75 years at a 2 per cent rate of interest. The balance of the advance was to be paid to the new Anglo-Czechoslovak Bank by 20 January 1922 after the government had granted the banking concession.[56]

The Bank of England had to accept the Czechoslovak demand that an Anglo-Czechoslovak Bank be founded out of the branches of the Anglo-Austrian Bank. Nevertheless, this was consistent with its original objective since the Anglo-Czechoslovak Bank was the only foreign bank operating in Czechoslvakia and the Bank of England was thus assured of a financial foothold there. Despite the Czechoslovak representation on the board of the new bank, the link to the Vienna branch was kept by nominating Spencer-Smith, G.M. Young and Pierre Bark as the Bank of England's representatives on the board of the Anglo-Czechoslovak Bank as well as on the board of the Anglo-Austrian Bank.[57]

The Anglo-Czechoslovak Bank started business after the Czechoslovak loan was floated in London on 6 April 1922. Negotiations had been wearisome and the British had to put further pressure on Beneš, whose intention it was to couple the presentation of the agreement with the Bank of England in parliament with the announcement that a Czechoslovak loan was launched on the London market. Though Spencer-Smith had strictly refused to recognize any direct connection between the agreement and the loan, the Bank of England was prepared to support Czechoslovakia's endeavours to raise a loan in the City and initiated talks with Barings Bros. Beneš, however, encountered difficulties in parliament mainly because of the opposition from the National Democrats, the Agrarian Party and the Živnostenská banka, who were against the establishment of a bank operating with foreign capital in the state of Czechoslovakia. Therefore the guaranteed concession to the Anglo-Czechoslovak bank and the 156 million Kč advance were both delayed.[58]

Czechoslovak negotiations about raising a loan in London lasted until Spring 1922 when the first tranche was finally floated in London and New York. Only then was the Anglo-Czechoslovak Bank granted its banking concession and the payment of the 156 million Kč secured. The Anglo-Czechoslovak Bank was paid half the advance by the Czechoslovak government on 23 March 1922 and the balance was paid through Baring Bros. out of the first proceeds of the loan. The Treasury had again provided the basis for Spencer-Smith's talks with the Czechoslovak government concerning the final agreement on the establishment of the Anglo-Czechoslovak Bank and the payment of the 156 million Kč advance. The maturity of the wheat bills, due on 31 March 1922, was extended for another year and they were to be repaid out of the loan granted to Czechoslovakia.[59]

Despite the intentions of Michael Spencer-Smith to keep the question of a loan issue on the London market separate from the agreement between the Bank of England and the Czechoslovak government, the crucial points became closely intertwined.[60] Thanks to close cooperation from the British Treasury and the Foreign Office, the Bank of England's aims and intentions were essentially fulfilled. Although Czechoslovakia acquired a first-class introduction to the London market and succeeded in achieving some of her original aims, it was the British side that had gained most.[61]

The Anglo-Czechoslovak Bank was constituted on 12 April 1922 with a share capital of 120 million Kč, which was wholly held by the reconstituted Anglo-Austrian Bank in London and its successor the Anglo-International Bank up to 1927. In accordance with Czechoslovak law, Kuneš Sonntag, a former Finance Minister, became President and Pierre Bark, a former Russian Finance Minister, Vice-President of the Anglo-Czechoslovak Bank. London appointed three more members of the board of directors including Spencer-Smith and Young, who were to keep the link between the Prague and Vienna offices. The bank intensified its connections with the export-oriented industries of Czechoslovakia and thus continued to provide a means of channelling British capital to Central–South–Eastern Europe.[62]

When the process of mergers started among the Viennese banks in 1924 as a result of the financial crisis, the Bank of England's original policy with regard to the takeover of the Viennese Bank was soon abandoned. This led to the amalgamation of the Anglo-Austrian Bank's branches and business with the Creditanstalt in 1926.[63] However, the Bank of England retained part of its direct influence in the Anglo-Czechoslovak Bank throughout the interwar period. In July 1927 the Anglo-International Bank in London sold most of its shares in the Anglo-Czechoslovak Bank. The Czechoslovak government, not having participated originally in the bank, now acquired 25 per cent of the shares; the rest were taken up by the Petschek–Schicht–Liechtenstein group, the Czech Agricultural Cooperative and in 1929 a further amount was taken up by the London banking house Samuel & Co and the New York investment bank Harriman & Co. The Anglo-International Bank retained its participation of 16.6 per cent in the Anglo-Czechoslovak Bank's share capital until the Second World War.[64]

Looking back on the partial withdrawal of the Bank of England one can see a certain logic in the transfer of shares to the Czechoslovak group: it is to be interpreted as a sign that the Czechoslovak Republic had achieved the financial independence it had sought ever since its foundation. It was also a consequence of the Bank of England's withdrawal from Vienna where it participated instead in the Creditanstalt.[65]

Conclusion

This chapter seeks to show that the Bank of England, despite being a bank of issue, pursued a policy which was aimed at getting direct control of a Viennese bank and thus establishing a financial foothold in Central and South-Eastern Europe. The economic stipulations of the Treaty of Saint-Germain served as the legal framework for the penetration of Entente capital into the region of Central and South-Eastern Europe and were aimed at forestalling Germany's resurgence and preventing its economy from regaining its former markets. The Bank of England, in seeking to secure the prewar debts of the London branch of the Anglo-Austrian Bank, launched a far-reaching project that was to serve as a means of opening up new fields for British investments and to compensate for some of the losses resulting from the nationalization of foreign assets and investments by the Russian government. On the one hand, the clauses of the Paris Treaties legitimized the political changes resulting from the defeat of the Central Powers – the breakup of the Austro-Hungarian Empire and the establishment of national successor states – and guaranteed Czechoslovakia the status of an associate state. On the other hand, the allies' political and financial institutions tried to realize some of their economic and financial aims through capital participation in the Viennese banks, on the assumption that the economic unity of the former monarchy would survive.

Czechoslovakia's ambitious endeavours to establish an efficient national economy were taken into consideration only when the Bank of England encountered difficulties in executing its Central European plan. Still, Czechoslovakia had to make concessions when such a powerful institution as the Bank of England offered it a chance to enter the London market, because it was in need of foreign capital. This applies to Austria and the Viennese banks to an even greater extent. Thus it is not surprising that the directors of the Anglo-Austrian Bank very soon gave up any initiative in negotiating with the Bank of England and simply tried to comply with Montagu Norman's demands. In order to secure a settlement concerning the Treasury notes once they were forbidden to negotiate on their own, the directors of the Anglo-Austrian Bank transferred all their legal rights to the Bank of England, i.e. to Norman. So Norman was entitled to negotiate on behalf of the Anglo-Austrian Bank after Spencer-Smith had submitted the first draft of an agreement between Czechoslovakia and the Bank of England.

The aim here is to show that the Bank of England, a representative institution of a victorious nation, pursued its Central European objectives with determination and was prepared to take into consideration the policies pursued by Czechoslovakia, an associate state, only when the realization of its plan was threatened. For this purpose the cooperation of the Treasury and the Foreign Office was sought and the wheat bills were used as an instrument of political and economic pressure.

Notes

1. For the important role of Czechoslovakia as a link between British and French economic interests on the one side and the South-East European region see Alice Teichova, *Wirtschaftsgeschichte der Tschechoslowakei 1918–1980*, Wien, 1988, pp. 59–68; '… a quarrel in a far-away country between people of whom we know nothing…', 40 years after: 'An Economic Re-assessment', Inaugural Lecture delivered before the University of East Anglia on 27 September 1978; *An Economic Background to Munich. International Business and Czechoslovakia*, Cambridge, 1974, pp. 24, 377.
2. György Ránki, *Economy and Foreign Policy. The Struggle of the Great Powers for Hegemony in the Danube Valley 1919–1939*, New York, 1983, p. 7; Alice Teichova 'Versailles and the Expansion of the Bank of England into Central Europe' in N. Horn and J. Kocka (eds), *Recht und Entwicklung der Großunternehmen im 19. und frühen 20. Jahrhundert. Studies in the history of industrialization in Germany, France, Great Britain and the United States*, Göttingen, 1979, p. 368, Alice Teichova, *Kleinstaaten im Spannungsfeld der Großmächte. Wirtschaft und Politik in Mittel- und Südosteuropa in der Zwischenkriegszeit*, Wien, 1988, p. 77 Marie Luise Recker, *England und der Donauraum 1919–1928*, Stuttgart, 1976, pp. 11,128.
3. For the Anglo-Austrian Bank's links to its industrial concern see Charlotte Natmeßnig, 'The Industrial Concern of the Anglo-Austrian Bank', in Budapest University of Economic Sciences, *Report from the International Conference* 1992.
4. P.L. Cottrell, 'London Financiers and Austria 1863–1875: The Anglo-Austrian Bank', in *Business History*, vol. XI, no. 2, July 1969, pp. 108–119; Carl Morawitz, *50 Jahre Geschichte einer Wiener Bank. Vortrag gehalten in der Gesellschaft österreichischer Volkswirte anläßlich des 50 jähringen Jubiläums der Anglo-Oesterreichischen Bank*, p. 6; A.S. Baster, *The International Banks*, London 1935, p. 6; Eduard März, *Österreichische Industrie- und Bankpolitik in der Zeit Franz Josephs I*, Wien, 1968, p. 123.

5. Eduard März, *Österreichische Bankpolitik in der Zeit der großen Wende 1913–1923. Am Beispiel der Creditanstalt für Handel und Gewerbe*, Wien, 1981, pp. 52–65; see also Bank of England Archive C(BoE), C40/116 Memorandum by Pierre Bark on the Anglo-Austrian Bank, 27 December 1921; Bark provides a detailed description of the Anglo-Austrian Bank's mixed banking business.

6. Archiv der Republik (AdR), Bankkomission, Karton 19, Anglo-Oesterreichische Bank, Geschäftsberichte der Anglo-Oesterreichischen Bank 1913, 1914; 'Die Bilanzen', *Beilage zum Österreichischen Volkswirt (Die Bilanzen)*, 17 April 1915, p. 125.

7. BoE, C40/119, Notes on the Bank of England's scheme for the reconstruction of the Anglo-Oesterreichische Bank. (Notes on the Bank of England's scheme.)

8. BoE, C40/116, statements on the advances made to the London branch of the Anglo-Austrian Bank by the Bank of England, 21 December 1921, and 9 January 1922; BoE, OV52/28, Outline of the General Scheme for the financial and economic rehabilitation of Austria with special reference to the part played by the Bank of England.

9. The Länderbank scheme had been evolved before and a provisional agreement had been achieved as a result of the close cooperation of Montagu Norman and the French authorities. BoE, C40/123, provisional schemes on the reconstructions of the Länderbank of 9 August 1920 and 8 October 1920; G3/177 letters Norman to Blackett 4 May 1920, 18 May 1920, 29 July 1920; C40/119 Brief Outline of the Scheme of Reconstruction, Appendix A to Notes on the Bank of England's scheme. *Österreichischer Volkswirt*, 3 January 1920; *Die Bilanzen*, 18 September 1920, p. 124; *Die Bilanzen*, 17.12.1921; P.L. Cottrell, 'Aspects of Western equity investment in the banking systems of East Central Europe', in Alice Teichova and P.L. Cottrell (eds), *International business and Central Europe 1918–1939*, Leicester University Press 1983, pp. 316–319.

10. Public Record Office, (PRO) FO 371/5785/C16831 memorandum by Bruce Lockhart 18 August 1921; Teichova, op. cit., note 2, pp. 369–387.

11. BoE, G3/177, letter Norman to Ter Meulen, 16 June 1921.

12. Teichova, op. cit., note 2, p. 368; Cottrell, op. cit., note 9, p. 311; Recker, op. cit., note 2, p. 132.

13. PRO, FO 368/2056/C16605, Philpotts to Board of Trade (BOT) 12 December 1919; C176534 Philpotts to BOT 30 January 1921; FO371/3558/C192241 Philpotts to BOT 12 April 1920; C198057 Philpotts to BOT 17 May 1920; FO 371/5785/16831 memorandum Bruce Lockhart 18 August 1921; Hans Kernbauer and Fritz Weber, 'Multinational banking in the Danube Basin: the business strategy of the Viennese banks after the collapse of the Habsburg Monarchy', in Alice Teichova, Maurice Lévy-Leboyer and Helga Nußbaum (eds), *Multinational enterprise in historical perspective*, Cambridge 1986, p. 189.

14. 'Die neuen Aufgaben der tschechischen Banken und das fremde Kapital', in *Berichte aus den neuen Staaten*, vol. 29–31, 3 year, 11 February 1920, p. 215.

15. The sale of shares of Alpine Montan A.G. to an Italian group provides an excellent example; for further details see März, op. cit., note 5, pp. 307–317; P.G. Fischer, 'The Österreichisch-Alpine Montangesellschaft, 1918-1938', in Alice Teichova and P.L. Cottrell (eds), *International Business and Central Europe 1918–1938*, Leicester University Press, 1983, pp. 253, 259.

16. AdR, BMF, Z1.83.613/1919/Gegenwärtiger Stand und Zukunft der Banken Österreichs, memorandum by Paul Hammerslag; März, op. cit., note 5, p. 284; Kernbauer and Weber, op. cit., note 13, p. 187.

17. AdR, MdI, GZ. 13910/1910, Z1. 43.863/1919; PRO, FO 368/2056/C166105, Philpotts to DOT 12 December 1919; FO 371/7420/C2609 reports on banks in Austria, 18 February 1922; FO 371/5786/C13714 report on Austria in 1920 by Lindley, 23 June 1921.

18. The state of Czechoslovakia was proclaimed on 28 October 1918, in December T.G. Masaryk was elected first President of the Republic.

19. Teichova, op. cit., note 1, p. 60 and 'A comparative View of the Inflation of the 1920s in Austria and Czechoslovakia', in Nathan Schmuckler and Edward Marcus (eds), *Inflation through the ages: Economic, Social, psychological and historic aspects*, Brooklyn College Press, New York, 1983, p. 536; for the main reasons that induced the Czechoslovak National Committee to introduce preparatory steps for the currency seperation see: Alois Rašin, *Die Finanz- und Wirtschaftspolitik der Tschechoslowakei*, München and Leipzig, 1923, pp. 17–23; Richard Kerschagl, *Die*

Währungstrennung in den Nationalstaaten. Die Noten der Oesterreichisch-Ungarischen Bank ihr Schicksal, Wien, 1920, p. 10.

20. Teichova, op. cit., note 2, p. 58; Peter Robert Berger, *Der Donauraum im wirtschaftlichen Umbruch nach dem Ersten Weltkrieg. Währung und Finanzen in den Machfolgestaaten Österreich, Ungarn und Tschechoslowakei 1918–1929,* Dissertationen der Wirtschaftsuniversität Wien 35, Wien, 1982, p. 239.

21. *Compass 1922, Tschechoslowakei, Währungspolitische Maßnahmen,* p. 5; Teichova, op. cit., note 1, p. 60; Rašin, op. cit., note 19, pp. 17–23; Berger, op. cit., note 20, p. 236.

22. *Compass 1922 Tschechoslowakei, Währungspolitische Maßnahmen,* p. 6; Friedrich Steiner, *Die Währungsgesetzgebung der Sukzessionsstaaten Österreich-Ungarns. Eine Sammlung einschlägiger Gesetze, Verordnungen und behördlicher Verfügungen von 1892 bis 1920,* Wien, 1921, pp. 198–236; Teichova, op. cit., note 2, pp. 58, 59; op. cit., note 19, p. 537; op. cit., note, 1, p. 98; op. cit., note 2, p. 59; Rašin, op. cit., note 19, p. 141; Recker, op. cit., note 2, pp. 67; Staatsvertrag von Saint-Germain-en-Laye vom 10. September 1919, 249.

23. BoE, C40/119, Notes on the Bank of England's scheme; März, op. cit., note 5, p. 57; The leading role of Vienna and its banks is pointed out by W.T. Layton and Charles Rist, *Die Wirtschaftslage Österreichs. Bericht der vom Völkerbund bestellten Wirtschaftsexperten, Deutsche Übersetzung,* Wien, 1925, p. 86.

24. The transfer of the Treasury notes was split up: the first part was retransferred on 31 January 1919, the second on 5 February 1919; BoE, C40/119, Notes on the Bank of England's scheme; C40/115, letter Rosenberg to Norman, 23 March 1921 and enclosure: memorandum by Simon 21 June 1921 and appendices K–O 21.6.1920; Berger, op. cit., note 20, p. 289.

25. C40/115 ibid; C40/119, Notes on Bank of England's scheme.

26. BoE, C40/115, Anglo-Austrian Bank, Estimated analysis of the approximate sterling position as at 31 December 1920. This estimation by Binder & Hamlyn, the Bank of England's auditors was based on the figures of the balance-sheet of 1919.

27. BoE, C40/119, Notes on the Bank of England's Scheme; C40/115, Banking Office to Prague Branch of the Anglo-Austrian Bank, 26 February 1921.

28. BoE, C40/115, letter Rosenberg to Norman, 23 March 1921; memorandum by Simon, 21 June 1921.

29. BoE, G3/177, letter Norman to Blackett, 17 March 1921; BoE C40/115, memorandum with reference to the proposed reconstruction of the Anglo-Österreichische Bank 5 April 1921.

30. BoE, C40/115, telegram Schwarz to Simon, 15 March 1921.

31. BoE, C40/115 telegram Norman to Rosenberg, 17 March 1921; telegram Binder to Rosenberg, 18 March 1921.

32. BoE, C40/115, letter Norman to Blackett, 17 March 1921.

33. BoE, C40/115, general outline of proposed scheme 24 March 1921; Norman aimed from the very beginning at direct control by requesting the right to nominate seven directors out of eleven as long as a certain amount of certificates of indebtedness remained outstanding. At this point he tried to reduce the necessary amount from £210000 to £100000. The number of directors was reduced from seven to six out of eleven. The directors in charge were to be British citizens and former directors of the Anglo-Austrian Bank were to be attached to the board of directors mainly for the purpose of making the transition from one nationality to the other as smooth as possible. BoE, G3/177, letter Norman to General Lawrence, 13 April 1921; letter Norman to Blackett, 7 November 1921; C40/115, memorandum with reference to the proposed reorganization of the Anglo-Austrian Bank, 5 April 1921; FO 371/5776/C18847, report Keeling to FO, 23 September 1921.

34. BoE, C40/115, letter Norman to Blackett, 17 March 1921.

35. BoE, C40/119, Notes on the Bank of England's scheme.

36. BoE, C40/115, memorandum by Simon, enclosure to letter Rosenberg to Norman, 23 March 1921; 'Please take it for sure that we would not do anything against your intentions and that we have absolutely acknowledged that you have to be asked for your permission,' telegram Rosenberg to Norman, 18 March 1921.

37. BoE, C40/115, letter Norman to Mastný, 11 May 1921 and enclosed copy of the scheme; no details were revealed, all the relevant figures were left out and the Bank of England's involve-

ment was not mentioned at all; ibid., letter Mastný to Norman, 13 May 1921; memorandum Paget 20 May 1921.

38. BoE, C40/115, Fass to Norman, 4 April 1921; PRO, FO 371/5827/C7075, Fass to Waterlow, 6 April 1921; FO 371/7075/C7075 minute by Cadogan, 8 April 1921; BoE, C40/115, letter Fass to Norman, 30 June 1921.
39. BoE, C40/115, letter Fass to Norman, 30 June 1920.
40. PRO, FO 371/5785/C13400, Philpotts to BOT, 15 June 1921.
41. BoE, C40/119, Notes on the Bank of England's scheme; BoE C40/115, memorandum by Simon 21 June 1921; notes on meeting at the Bank of England, 25 June 1921.
42. 'I am so glad to think that you are working after our interests in Prague and Vienna and feel sure that before you leave a satisfactory conclusion will have been reached.' BoE, C40/115, letter Norman to Spencer-Smith, 15 July 1921.
43. It has to be pointed out, that Lockhart, in retrospect, considered his impact on the negotiations to have been much greater than it really was. Bruce Lockhart, *Retreat from Glory,* London, 1934, p. 159. BoE, C40/115, note on Spencer-Smith's trip to Prague, 7 July 1921; C40/119, Notes on Bank of England scheme.
44. The difference between the typical London banker and a Central European banker is described by Lockhart in his memoirs, op. cit., note 43, p. 163, BoE, C40/116, Bruce Lockhart to BOT, 18 August 1921.
45. BoE, C40/115, letter Spencer-Smith to Norman, 18 July 1921.
46. The most important points were: (1) The information of the Czechoslovak government that a British group headed by the Bank of England was going to take over the Anglo-Austrian Bank reconstituted as a British bank consisting of sterling capital. (2) The Czech government was to grant to this new bank the concession to take over and run all branches of the Anglo-Austrian Bank in Czechoslovakia. Czechoslovak capital was to be allowed to participate and Czechoslovak representation on the board of the new bank was to be arranged. (3) To assist the bank to develop trade between Great Britain and Czechoslovakia, the government should make an advance of 156 mill. Kč, repayable within ten years at an interest rate of 2 or 3 per cent. This sum was to be given to the British minister at Prague before 10 August 1921. (4) If the Czechoslovak government raised a loan or advance in England, the new bank would not have to repay the advance and repayment of interest should also cease from the date such a loan became effective. (5) The repayment of the £2 000 000 Treasury bills for purchase of flour was to be extended for a further six months. Ibid., draft of proposed agreement, enclosure to letter Spencer-Smith to Norman, 18 July 1921.
47. 'This appeared to me to cover our Interests fully as we should get our cash at once and it seems out of the question that the Czech Government should carry on for 10 years without a foreign loan.' Furthermore, he was quite sure that in either case – a loan raised in London or elsewhere – that he could force the Czechoslovaks to agree to an interest rate of 2 per cent. Ibid.
48. Ibid.
49. Ibid.
50. Ibid; C40/116 letter Beneš to Spencer-Smith, 29 July 1921; C4/119, Notes on the Bank of England scheme.
51. BoE, C40/116, Notes on meeting in the Bank of England, 22 July 1921; telegram Norman to Spencer, 22 July 1921; letter to Norman to Spencer-Smith, 22 July 1921.
52. BoE, C40/116, notes on meetings at the Bank of England, 2 and 4 August 1921.
53. 'The scheme is the reorganization of the Anglo-Austrian Bank and whatever arrangement must fall in with that.' Handwritten note by Norman, ibid.
54. BoE, C40/116, memorandum by Bruce Lockhart, 18 August 1921; PRO, FO 371/5785/C18336 memorandum by Bruce Lockart, 15 September 1921; FO 371/5786/C18842 memorandum by Bruce Lockhart, 22 September 1921.
55. PRO, FO 371/5786/C18842 memorandum by Bruce Lockhart, 22 September 1921.
56. BoE, C40/116, Agreement between the Czecho-Slovak government and the Bank of England, 10 October 1921; further points of the agreement were: the Czechoslovak government granted a concession for a new bank which was to take over all the branches of the Anglo-Austrian Bank in the Czechoslovak Republic together with their assets and liabilities; the articles of the

new bank had to conform with the Czechoslovak laws but the constitution was to be entirely at the discretion of the Bank of England; a proportion of 20 to 30 per cent should be allotted to the Czechoslovak government which was not to dispose of the allotted shares without the consent of the British, who were to have a right of pre-emption; at least six members of the board were to be Czechoslovak citizens, one of them to be appointed by the Czechoslovak government; a British citizen was to be in charge of the management of the Prague office; the Bank of England was to submit the articles of the new bank to the Czechoslovak government no later than 31 December 1921 and the Czechoslovak government would grant the banking concession to the new bank within a fortnight after the receipt of the articles.

57. *Compass 1923*, Bd. 2, *Tschechoslowakei, Anglo- Tschechoslowakische Bank*, p. 142; Bd. 1, *Österreich-Ungarn, Liquidation, Anglo-Austrian Bank*, p. 289.

58. BoE, C40/119, Notes on the Bank of England's scheme; PRO, FO 371/5829/23034, private letter Clerk to Crowe, 29 November 1921; memorandum Bruce Lockhart, 14 April 1922.

59. BoE, C40/116, letter Spencer-Smith to Norman, 23 March 1922; C40/119 Notes on the Bank of England's scheme.

60. 'You could not avoid to some extent mixing up the Bank settlement and the repayment of the wheat bills, while at this end the repayment of the Wheat Bills and the issue of the loan were inextricably mixed up, hardly less in the minds of Barings and myself than of the Treasury. In point of fact, whatever we all might pretend to one another, these three questions were really parts of one.' BoE, G3/178, letter Montagu Norman to Spencer-Smith, 25 March 1922; and letters dated 22 March and 24 March 1922.

61. 'As regards the results achieved, there can be no doubt that British interests have reaped a great triumph. ... The Bank of England has had its wishes met in every way. It has received what is almost equivalent to a gift of 156,000,000 Czech crowns, and it is the only foreign bank in the republic which has been allowed to own more that 50 per cent of the Czech bank in which it is interested.' PRO, FO 371/7385/C5637, memorandum by Bruce Lockhart, 14 April 1922.

62. Ibid. Teichova, op. cit., note 1, pp. 338–352.

63. 'A conviction has been growing there that the position of their offices in Austria as branches of an alien institution is far from satisfactory and that it would be better from all points of view that these branches should be handed over to a responsible institution established under Austrian law and having its headquarters in Vienna.' BoE, C40/116, *Financial News*, 12 August 1927; Norman made first enquiries regarding sale of the Anglo-Austrian Bank's branches in Austria in April 1924; BoE, C40/120 Norman to Kay, 9 April 1924; In the course of financial transactions with Austria's leading bank, the business of the Anglo-Austrian Bank was transferred to the Creditanstalt on whose board the Anglo-International Bank was represented. The Bank of England acquired about 20 per cent of the Creditanstalt in 1926. *Hans Kernbauer, Währungspolitik in der Zwischenkriegszeit. Geschichte der Oesterreichischen Nationalbank von 1923 bis 1938*, Wien, 1991, p. 273; BoE, C40/119, *Financial News*, 19 May 1926. 1 June 1926; *The Times*, 4 June 1926; the transaction with the Creditanstalt in 1926 was a further step of the Bank of England's withdrawal from Central Europe for the same line was adopted regarding the branches of the Anglo-Austrian Bank in Italy and Yugoslavia and in 1930, when the Budapest branch was amalgamated with the British and Hungarian Bank, BoE, C40/119 Notes on the Bank of England's scheme; agreement between the British-Hungarian Bank and the Anglo-International Bank, 27 January 1930.

64. PRO, FO 371/12097/C1836; *Compass 1928, Čechoslovakei, Anglo-Československá banka*, p. 282; 1930, *Anglo-Československá banka*, p. 300; *Die Bilanzen*, 9 April 1927, 19. Jg., Nr. 28, p. 741; 9 July 1927, Nr. 42, p. 467; 16 July, Nr. 42, p. 487; Teichova, op. cit., note 1, pp. 350, 358.

65. BoE, C40/119, *Financial News*, 15 June 1926; 'We have thus taken a further step in carrying out the policy we have adopted of developing our relations with Central Europe through the medium of local banking connections, instead of through branches of our own.' Speech of the chairman after the amalgamation of the Budapest branch with the British and Hungarian Bank, undated.

116·28

9 The failure of crisis management: banking laws in interwar Austria
Gertrude Enderle-Burcel

In comparison with other relatively economically advanced European states the First Austrian Republic was unsuccessful in providing an effective legislative framework to curb unsound banking and excessive speculation. Only in times of crisis have there been serious attempts to control banks by legislation. The establishment of the Banking Commission in 1921 and the draft of a banking law in 1932 represent the most extensive but frustrated approaches to this kind of crisis management. The reasons for the failure of legislative controls on the Austrian banking system are discussed in historical context in this chapter.

Until the First World War supervision of banks was mostly intended to prevent abuses, which was sufficient in normal times. The Sparkassenregulativ (savings bank regulations) of 1844, the Vereinspatent (association code) of 1852, the Gewerbeordnung (trade regulations) of 1859, the General Commercial Code of 1863, the Vereinsrecht (association law) of 1867, the Genossenschaftsgesetz (cooperative association law) of 1873 and the Aktienregulativ (joint-stock company law) of 1899 only regulated single elements. An overall bank supervision, however, did not exist (Fröhlichsthal, 1990, pp. 10–46), which was not unusual at that time. In the nineteenth century there were no legal controls of banks in most European countries, which meant that 'everybody had the right to found banks and to conduct banking operations in accordance with certain legal provisions that had nothing to do with banking supervision' (Honold, 1956, p. 38).

After the First World War the laws of the nineteenth century continued to be in force in Austria. The association code of 1852 provided an obligation to obtain a licence for cooperative societies and joint-stock companies, as well as introducing a rather vague form of economic control. State authorities could examine the business practice of every association and appoint a state commissioner. However, this only applied to public law associations, joint-stock companies and limited liability companies conducting banking business. Other legal forms of banks were classified as unrestricted trading. They did not need a licence to set up business, but had only to register at the Trades Inspectorate (Heller, 1912, p. 1727). The General Commercial Code of 1863 provided control clauses for joint-stock companies, the legal obligation to disclose results as well as to present the balance sheet to the shareholders within six months of the end of the business year. The company law contained only guidelines, designed to help companies to obtain official authorization (Noell, 1927, p. 4). The licence system in Austria provided that every establishment of a joint-stock company and every amendment of a statute required official authorization. Once the licence was granted, the authorities did not interfere further. A state commissioner participated in every general assembly. However, these commissioners often attended general assemblies unprepared and could judge neither the management nor the adequacy of balance sheets. As controllers they were ineffective. The licence system and the state commissioners gave the impression of a state control which did not exist in practice. By establishing a system of official authorization, the state took over a responsibility it could not cope with, because the participation of state officials in formal acts such as company formation, the amendment of statutes, or an increase of capital was no real supervision (Noell, 1927, pp. 1–5).

The end of the monarchy severed traditional financial relations and led to radical political and economic changes. It only needs to be pointed out that the new borders cut through the network of branches, which changed both the capital structure and profitability of the major Viennese banks. At the same time difficulties increased for the Austrian universal banks during the period of transition from a war- to a peacetime economy. The interdependence of state and banks should be stressed, since the state had to provide the legal framework to facilitate the influx of foreign capital into Austria. The banks, on the other hand, helped the state to raise money by participating in the issue of government securities and in the taking up of loans (Ein Jahrhundert, 1957, pp. 161–71). The period of adaptation of the Austrian banking sector to the new conditions in the Republic coincided with the postwar crisis. In Austria this crisis manifested itself in a growing budget deficit, an unbalanced trade account, rapidly growing money supply, a rise in prices and the enormous depreciation of the Austrian crown on international markets (Kernbauer, März and Weber, 1983, p. 348). The state had repeatedly to print more money. Until the Summer of 1922 the value of the Austrian crown fell dramatically, which resulted in speculation on foreign exchange markets and in the 'sell-out' of Austrian stock. The inflation boom masked the structural weakness of the economy and made almost every investment profitable. At the end of the inflation period Austria had twice as many joint-stock and other banks as in 1919 and 1200 more enterprises. Speculation in foreign currency, goods and securities which peaked in 1923 led to enormous misinvestments. The deflationary effect of the currency stabilization by the League of Nations Loan in 1922 made most of the banks and firms founded during the inflation disappear (Weber, 1981, pp. 593–7). Also a significant part of the capital, which had been shifted abroad during the inflation, was not invested in domestic production when it returned to Austria after the Geneva reconstruction but was used to further speculation on the stock exchange where enormous losses were incurred as a result of the franc speculation of 1924 (Weber,

1981, p. 599). This led to credit tightness and extremely high interest rates which made industrial financing more difficult. In addition, the major banks, such as the Depositenbank, the Lombard- und Escomptebank and the Zentralbank deutscher Sparkassen, had to close and the Postal Savings Bank needed financial help from the state. Kernbauer, März and Weber define the years after 1923 as a period of permanent crisis in the Austrian banking sector and see the causes for this situation in the collapse of the Austro-Hungarian Monarchy, in the losses of assets during the inflation and the faulty decision making of bank managers.

The Austrian state quickly made use of its legislative power in order to cope with the crisis initiated in 1919 by the inflation of the crown and the specula-tion in foreign currency. The response, however, was less effective than in other countries (Ausch, 1968, p. 134). As early as 1921, long before the uncontrolled creation of banks, the stock exchange boom of 1923 and the franc speculation of 1924, the Bankkommissionsgesetz (Banking Commission Law) established a special Banking Commission. This intervention by the state was considered to be particularly important in Austria, since the banks were issuing houses, providers of credit and partners in industrial enterprises.

Whereas the neighbouring states Hungary and Czechoslovakia reacted in a calm and efficient way, the Austrian attempt to regulate the banking sector by establishing a Banking Commission was a failure. In October 1921 the Federal Parliament passed a law establishing a Banking Commission for a term of five years. However, the situation was complicated by other measures for single banks: the Länderbankgesetz (Länderbank Act), which converted the Länderbank into a French company; the Anglobank Act, which made the Anglobank an English institution; the Centralbank Act of July 1926, which established a guarantee fund; the Postal Savings Bank Act of 1926; and the Credit-Anstalt Acts of the early 1930s.

The activity of the Banking Commission had three main tasks: the continuous supervision of the business activities of Austrian banks; the examination of their operations in the light of economic needs; and reporting to a special committee of the Federal Parliament on the protection of economic interests. In the five years of its activity, the Banking Commission produced fifteen memoranda and drafts. As an auditing body, it examined about 100 joint-stock banks and 160 private banks. The results were transmitted to the Credit Department of the Federal Ministry of Finance. On behalf of the Federal Parliament special studies were carried out, e.g. on the movement of the Alpine-Montan shares in 1922 (Weiss, 1984, pp. 13–15). The work of the Banking Commission shows that it was not a control commission but merely prepared legal measures and was restricted to observation. The Commission even experienced difficulties in establishing a register of banks, because the lists of the Chamber of Commerce (Trade Register) and of the tax authorities were faulty and incomplete. A study of bank charges showed that even major enterprises were not sure about the real costs of raising money, because banks charged a large amount of different services which were variously calculated and accounted at different times. This rendered industrial financing more difficult.

The Commission also proposed a reduction in the number of institutions and their inflated administrations, which was to be achieved by state-aided mergers. Another proposition was that the licences of new joint-stock companies should only be granted after careful examination, and for private banks a general obligation to obtain a licence was recommended. The designation of 'bank' and 'banker' was to be legally protected, while the number of firms dealing in foreign currency was to be drastically reduced. In order to guarantee correct accounting the annual reports of companies were to be systematized; and in order to curb the practice of banks of using security deposits as collateral for raising capital, a Protection of Depositors Act was to be passed by parliament (Weiss, 1984, pp. 17–20).

The Commission also pointed out that there were more members on boards of directors than necessary and that membership of state officials, mostly from the Ministry of Finance, on them was illegal. The Ministry, however, did not even provide the Commission with a list of officials working for banks or affiliated industrial companies.[1] The central question for the Commission: 'Should the state take over the role of a supervisory authority or should there be an independent auditing institution between the state and the banks?' was not answered, revealing the true relationship between the Commission and the Ministry of Finance. It was obvious that the Ministry was not interested in establishing an independent supervisory authority. The relationship between the Banking Commission and the Ministry of Finance was further complicated by the fact that there was a special parliamentary committee to which the commission had regularly to report. Thus the Commission was caught between the politicians and civil servants and neither side was seriously interested in putting its recommendations into practice.

In May 1926 the promoter of the Banking Commission, Hofrat Georg Stern, Vice-Chairman of the Commission and leading financial specialist and Social Democrat, appealed once more to parliament that 'it was a fundamental necessity to continue the supervision of banks…'[2] This appeal fell on deaf ears. Despite the commission's meticulous and correct observations on the problems of the banking sector its mandate expired after five years of fruitless activity at the end of 1926. In the 'Epilogue of the Banking Commission' we can find one last attempt to rescue the institution: a proposal to develop the Commission's audit department into a bank inspectorate on the Scandinavian model.[3]

There were several reasons for the failure of the proposals made by the Banking Commission. The Ministry of Finance responsible for the supervision of joint-stock companies and banks often did not provide it with the necessary information and frequently neglected its recommendations. The members of the

Commission, mostly bankers or accountants, would have needed help from administrative law specialists to realize their ideas. For the officials in the Ministry of Finance, however, the Commission was a superfluous institution restricting their own control activity. Consequently, they refused to help whenever they could do so. When, in 1925, the Commission demanded help from the Ministry of Justice for working out the penal clauses of a Bankbetriebsgesetz (banking operations law) Jakob Ahrer, the Minister of Finance, was strictly against such a cooperation:

> I am of the opinion that it would be dangerous if a ministry participated in the preparation of drafts by the Banking Commission without the agreement of the Ministry of Finance, because the drafts would then seem approved by the state authorities, although there might be economic reasons or reasons of credit policy forcing the Ministry of Finance to reject the drafts. The Ministry of Finance is extremely interested in maintaining the actual regulation leaving the full right to decide on drafts by the Banking Commission to the Ministry of Finance or to the government.[4]

It was the banks, however, that most resisted state intervention. When the Banking Commission was founded, its members already foresaw that the banks would use the international financial situation as an argument against their work;[5] namely that their deliberations would harm the credit-worthiness of Austria abroad (Weiss, 1984, p. 82). It was also argued that the public would be unnecessarily worried. Because of the close connections between the banks and the newspapers, people were informed wrongly or in an incomprehensible manner, if at all, about the activities of the Banking Commission (Ausch, 1968, pp. 166, 204, 245, 299). Last but not least, the growing dependence of the government on the banks discouraged state intervention of all forms. The Austrian state needed the increasing cooperation of banks to take up the League of Nations Loan and to finance the budget deficit.

Although the Banking Commission pointed out the problems in the banking sector and also drew up effective solutions for them some basic ideas were not even discussed. Nobody ever questioned the Konzessionssystem (franchise system) for joint-stock companies or tried to replace it by the Normativsystem (general company law) which was finally introduced by force after the violent *Anschluss* in 1938 as a part of German law. Nobody ever questioned the role of Austrian banks as universal banks. There was no fundamental attempt to introduce legislation on limits of banks shareholding, enabling the state more efficiently to control banks and their *Konzerne* (combines). The banks were never required to disclose the amount of credits granted to industrial enterprises. Yet some laws in the 1920s could be considered as indirect results of the work of the Banking Commission. The commission carried out important preparatory work but the final drafting was done by the Ministry of Finance and the Ministry of Justice often disregarding the Commission's proposals. The Bankhaftungsgesetz (Law on the Liability of Banks), the Geldinstitutezentralegesetz (Law on the Central Office of Money Institutes), the Konzessionsergänzungsgesetz (Supplementary Licensing Law), the Bankgewerbekonzessionsverordnung (Banking Licence Order) and finally the Goldbilanzengesetz (Gold Balance Act) were the legal instruments of the state introduced to overcome the crisis in the banking sector in the postwar years.

The Bankhaftungsgesetz provides the best demonstration of how the proposals of the Bank Commission were avoided. According to the provisions of this law (BGB1.284 of 29 July 1924) the members of the managing boards of joint-stock banks were to be responsible to their banks and required to conduct business as defined by the Commercial Code. If they neglected their duties they were to be personally liable to the bank for any losses. The original proposal drawn up by the Banking Commission in July 1923 – i.e. before the bank collapses in 1924 – had been much more extensive, since the Bankhaftungsgesetz was intended to apply to all banks, not only to joint-stock banks, and personal liability was to have been extended to managers and all members of supervisory boards.[6] Although these suggestions were not taken up, the proposals of the Commission regarding the protection of minority shareholders, reporting of masked accounts, and staff regulations were used in the final law after some modifications. To a certain extent the Bankhaftungsgesetz devised by the Ministry of Finance tried in a rather inadequate way to establish some special cases of liability (Bondi, 1933, p. 36). When banks collapsed later, it was the basis for the prosecution of certain members of the managing boards, but in the main this action came to nothing (Ziegler, 1933, p. 42), because no implementing order had been passed.

The Bankhaftungsgesetz was the first of a number of inadequate legal attempts to cope with the problems in the banking sector. The law enabling the government to use emergency powers enacted in the period of financial crisis (Geldinstitutezentralegesetz, BGB1.285 of 29 July 1924) provided for the setting up of a central office of money institutions on the Hungarian model. However, the creation of an institution of 'the lender of the last resort' provided by law never came to life. Instead the already existing Bank for Public Enterprises and Works, a majority state institution, was temporarily transformed into a trustee or into a receiver, e.g. in the cases of the Depositenbank, the Zentralbank deutscher Sparkassen, the Bauernbank and the Industrie- und Handelsbank. However, in none of the laws passed during 1924 and 1925 – the licensing law for the conduct of banking and the setting up of branch offices (BGB1.427 of 3 December 1924) and the law defining banking as the professional conduct of banking business by individuals, general and limited partnerships (BGB1.263 of 11 August 1925) – were the changes proposed by the Banking Commission in the preparatory stages taken up (Knett, 1985, pp. 74–80).[7]

The last law enacted as a result of the postwar crisis was the Goldbilanzge-setz which became necessary after the stabilization of the crown at 1:14400 in April 1923 and which applied not only to banks but to all joint-stock enterprises. Germany had introduced the legal requirement to balance accounts in gold imme-diately after the stabilization of the mark by an order of 28 December 1923. Austria, however, needed more than two years to make the publication of gold balance sheets a legal requirement. Günther Noell concluded in his comparison of the Austrian and German situations:

> In the postwar period the banks in Austria controlled nearly the whole of industry. Their influence was so great that they could prevent the passing of legislation which they held to be against their interests. The introduction of gold balances would have made visible the lack of capital in the economy, and so they tried to delay this step as long as possible. (Noell, 1927, p. 9)

Indeed, the gold balances showed the enormous indebtedness of Austrian joint-stock companies, on the one hand, and the extensive credit-financing of enterprises by banks, on the other (Noell, 1927, 198f.). More detailed exami-nation shows that the Gold Balance Act did not lead to greater clarification of the financial situation of banks. Generally, only insiders knew what was really behind the published balance sheets (Bondi, 1933, p. 26).

The attempts at legislating to strengthen sound banking in the first half of the 1920s obviously failed. Even in the years of economic growth from 1925 to 1928 (Mosser and Teichova, 1991, p. 126) further banks became illiquid. This led to a wave of mergers in the Austrian banking sector ending in 1934 (Kernbauer, März and Weber, 1983, p. 364; Teichova, 1988, p. 13). However, this could only temporarily alleviate economic difficulties (Weber, 1991, p. 23).

At the time of the world economic crisis and in the wake of the crash of the Credit-Anstalt the Austrian state launched a further attempt to gain legal control. Critical situations in the financial sector had always concentrated politicians' minds on the necessity of state intervention. Reactions to the international financial crisis in the 1930s were diverse, but all of them involved the engagement of public finance. As the Credit-Anstalt, and later the Wiener Bankverein as well as the Niederösterreichische Escomptegesellschaft, needed public funds of an estimated 1087 million Schillings,[8] a legally effective bank supervision was again called for. On the occasion of the presentation of the report of the Credit-Anstalt Reconstruction Committee the Council of Ministers decided to consider seriously the formulation of a banking law based on the Czechoslo-vakian draft bill of April 1932;[9] in addition, the German emergency law of 1931 was taken into consideration. However, objections to the draft drawn up by the Ministry of Justice came from all sides – the banks, the Chamber of Labour, the Chamber of Commerce, the Chambers of Agriculture and the agricultural cooperatives. In the main, 'bad timing' was the reason given. For example, Josef Joham, a member of the managing board and later managing director of the Credit-Anstalt, who was then advising the Ministry of Justice, stated 'that the time was unfavourable for a new banking law because of the danger of causing public disquiet,'[10] despite the fact that the changes he proposed had been fully incorporated into the draft.[11] Even in the various files of this draft in the Ministry of Finance we find the statement that 'none of the officials in charge of drawing up the draft thought that the time was favourable for passing a bank law, leaving aside parliamentary considerations'. The officials were of the opinion that causing disquiet among the population should be avoided and that the surviving Austrian banks did not need a law as strict as the draft. According to them the Czechoslovakian law was so radical because of its guarantee fund earmarked to subsidize ailing banks by the state. Besides, they urgently warned the state, i.e. the Ministry of Finance, against enforcing audits of banks as this could saddle the state with new responsibilities which it would be unable to meet under the prevailing financial difficulties.[12]

The draft bill, known as the 9th CA-Bill, in calling for expert reports by public bodies, demanded a new regulation of the entire company law, since a banking law alone offered no solution because of the interlocking of banks and industry. In the following the main features of the draft bill will be discussed in order to examine and clarify the intention of the proposed banking legislation. Its first part provided for accounting regulations: prescribed schemata for balancing accounts were to be adhered to, quarterly business reports were to be published – as in Czechoslovakia – and monthly reports to the National Bank were to lead to greater openness. Compensation of assets and liabilities was to be forbidden and an agreed method of creating reserves was to be maintained. Against these measures it was argued that banking secrecy could not be preserved and competitors might be able to profit from too radical a disclosure. Other critics referred to the fact that the relations between banks and their subsidiary enterprises (Konzernfirmen) had not been taken into consideration sufficiently, and that the profits of the subsidiaries should also be included in the balance sheet. There was no attempt to define a subsidiary company as was the case in England, Germany and Czechoslovakia. This question was to be resolved later by a reform of the company law (Ottel, 1933, p. 84).

The greatest problem in the drafting stage was how to control the management. The Austrian draft tried to combine two methods: an examination of the annual accounts; and audits at any time of the year. The draft provided that inspections of annual accounts had to refer to the contents of the profit and loss account *and* to the observation of legal norms. The Ministry of Finance would then pass an order stipulating which control institution would be entitled to carry out audits. This was a combination of the German and Czechoslovakian solutions. In Germany annual balance sheets were examined by an appointed accountant, whereas in Czechoslovakia the banks were required by law to form a cooperative the office of which was responsible for the inspection of accounts. Since Austria had no tradition in this field, like for example auditors (chartered accountants) in England, the independence of accountants was not assured. Bankers vehemently opposed the Ministry of Finance on this issue.

The problem of credit reports was to be resolved by an order similar to German and Czechoslovakian provisions. Credits were to be reported not in detail but merely whether they exceeded a limited amount to be fixed by law. An important opportunity was missed here, since the banking crisis in the 1930s was mostly based on a credit crisis. The Austrian draft, however, neither provided for the reporting of credits to the National Bank nor to one of the accounting or trust companies appointed by it. Thus the question was left undecided (Ziegler, 1933, p. 59). Critics maintained that management control always came too late and even the best supervision was of little use as the example of Kreuger had shown. It was argued that this kind of control would only be detrimental to the creditworthiness of Austria abroad.

One entire clause in the draft bill defined unlawful business, that is commodity trade which was very risky. The draft followed the Czechoslovakian and Polish example in this respect: commodity trade would only be permitted to the extent to which banks were already conducting it according to their statutes at the time the law became effective. Further it was to be unlawful to conduct business with members of the managing and supervisory boards, with bank employees and their families. However, this provision did not apply to the members of the board of directors because they 'were not involved in management affairs' (Ottel, 1933, p. 87).

The second part of the draft dealt with the personal position of managers, the central issues of which were the number of posts on boards of directors, the reduction of excessive salaries and the more extensive liability of managing boards. The excessive number of posts of one person on boards of directors had been a point of public debate for years. Also in this matter the Austrian draft followed the Czechoslovakian example which treated the issue in greater detail than the German emergency law of 19 September 1931. After first setting a limit of ten posts a director could hold, fifteen posts were finally authorized. There were many objections also to this regulation, because the banks were afraid to lose their influence over the companies dependent on them. In the report on the draft law this argument was refuted. It was argued that banks had enough influence over the subsidiary enterprises of their *Konzern* due to credit contracts and audits. Further, the draft provided that the banks themselves should pay the board members whom they delegated to client companies, while the subsidiary companies would have to pay directors' fees for administrative work to the banks. As to directors' incomes, contrary to the German emergency law which reduced excessive salaries only for the period of great losses, the Austrian draft wanted a lasting reduction. It accepted the Czechoslovakian designation 'managing employee' for persons having to make commercial and administrative decisions of great importance. Salaries were to depend on the performance of the bank and in cases of doubt an arbitration court would decide. Also the question of liability of the managing board was treated according to the Czechoslovakian example. Managers accused of violation of the law were obliged to produce proof that there was no causal connection between the unlawful act and losses incurred in the bank. Critics claimed that such a regulation would paralyse initiatives by managers and that no qualified person would want to take on such a position.

The third part of the draft bill provided for changes of the Geldinstitutezentralegesetz, making it easier to dismiss managers of institutions in difficulties. The legal period of notice was suspended, and a period of notice of three months was substituted. This section also included an amendment on trade supervision. Since a banking crisis could lead also to a run on active, solvent companies, the new trade provision would protect these against unmotivated repayment claims and give them the possibility of suspending payments temporarily. Such a trade supervision – granted on the application of a solvent institution – would be considered an exceptional temporary arrangement providing a moratorium to viable institutions, as mentioned in the statement of arguments for the Czechoslovakian law in 1924.

The fourth and last part of the draft provided extensive penal clauses.[13] The draft drawn up in April 1932 had already been rejected in the following September, although the Lausanne Protocol contained the duty to 'amend the general legislation on banks'.[14] The banks' personalities like Josef Joham and Viktor Kienböck,[15] the ministries participating in the preparation of the draft, the public bodies giving expert opinions and, last but not least, the 'worrying Financial Committee of the League of Nations', had prevented the draft becoming law (Kernbauer, 1991, p. 380).[16]

Until 1938 interventions by the state were limited to a few legal measures assisting banks in financial difficulties. A Kapitalreduktionsgesetz (law on the reduction of capital), a Bankentlastungsverordnung (order to relieve banks) and a Bankpensionsverordnung (order on bank pensions) only regulated parts of the banking sector. At the instigation of the President of the Austrian National Bank a federal law on the reduction of the capital of joint-stock companies was enacted in July 1932 (BGB1. 213/1932). The law provided better conditions for joint-stock companies enabling them to decrease their equity to the level of their real liable capital in order to make balances more authentic. Until then, this had only been possible via Art. 248 of the Commercial Code with a long application procedure to protect creditors. The law copied the 3rd German emergency law of 6 October 1931 and applied in particular to joint-stock banks. This law had been even more urgent, since the Mercur Bank had rapidly to reduce its capital, because it was not able to satisfy its creditors. The situation of the Wiener Bankverein was similar. The deadline for capital reductions was set at 30 June 1933 but this had to be deferred several times until 1938 because, among others, the subsidiary companies of the Bankverein and the Niederösterre-ichische Escomptegesellschaft also had to make capital write-downs.[17] The law on capital reduction was adopted by parliament only after furious debate and against the opposition of the Social Democrats. On the other hand, the contro-versial Article III, which limited the number of posts on boards of directors to ten and contracts of employment to two years, was adopted only because of social-democratic pressure (Bondi, 1933, pp. 16 and 41). The order on bank employees' pensions of 23 August 1933 (BGB1.377) and the order to relieve the banks, the Bankenlastungsverordnung of 19 March 1933 (BGB1.68), were introduced without parliamentary process on the basis of the war economy legislation of 1917. They finally provided the long desired relief for banks. These measures were still not sufficient for the banks and so the Bankpensionsverordnung even altered collective agreements on pensions between the following banks and their employees: Wiener Bankverein, Austrian Credit-Anstalt, Niederösterreichische Escomptegesellschaft, Wiener Giro- und Cassenverein, Zentraleuropäische Länderbank/Zweigniederlassung Wien, Mercurbank, Bank für Oberösterreich und Salzburg and Steiermärkische Escompte Bank.[18]

As we can see, state legislative intervention during the crisis of the 1930s was limited to measures in the interest of the banks and not in the public interest. The state invested huge sums to reconstruct some major banks but did not obtain any real control, supervision or influence over the banking sector. The attempts in Spring and Summer 1932 to gain stronger influence by estab-lishing a new banking law were not successful. Even the enormous public investment to rescue the Credit-Anstalt and the ten Credit-Anstalt bills did not restrict the independence of the bank. Sometimes government officials considered the Credit-Anstalt to be a state bank,[19] but, when Josef Joham took over the management of the Credit-Anstalt in 1936, he stated that this was not the case, although there had been certain attempts to obtain state control over its business activities.

The consequences of the crisis of the 1930s in Austria were that banks reacted cautiously to credit demands from the economy. The restrictive bank policy was justified by the financial sacrifices of the state to save the Credit-Anstalt (Stiefel, 1988, p. 309). The Austrian banks had survived thanks to public money without granting any control or influence to the state.

Notes

1. Parlamentsarchiv. Bestand der Bankkommission. Konvolut Protokolle über die Sitzungen der Ausschüsse, II und III.
2. Ibid., Konvolut Protokolle über die Sitzungen des Ausschusses I. Sitzung des Finanz- und Bud-getausschusses der Bankkommission, 18 May 1926, p. 6.

3. Ibid., Epilog der Bankkommission, p. 5.
4. Archiv der Republik. Ministerratsprotokolle der Ersten Republik, MRP 415/9, 30 December 1925, p. 9.
5. Parlamentsarchiv: Bestand der Bankkommission. Konvolut Protokolle über die Sitzungen der Ausschüsse II und III. Sitzung, 23 March 1922.
6. Archiv der Republik. Bundesministerium für Finanzen. Bestand Bankkommission, Karton 18. Beilage zur Denkschrift IV.
7. This applies to the Konzessionsergänzungsgesetz (BGBl. 427 of 3 December 1924) as well as to the Bankgewerbekonzessionsverordnung (BGBl.263 of 11 August 1925).
8. *Der österreichische Volkswirt*, no. 32, 5 May 1934, p. 682.
9 Allgemeines Verwaltungsarchiv. Bundesministerium für Justiz, Signatur 1 P Z, G Zl 11.126/1932.
10. Ibid., Zl 11.127/1/1932. Amtserinnerung betreffend Richtlinien für ein Bankengesetz.
11. Archiv der Republik. Bundesministerium für Finanzen Zl 35.515-15/1932 Richtlinien für den Entwurf eines Bankgesetzes (IV. Fassung).
12. Allgemeines Verwaltungsarchiv. Bundesministerium für Justiz. Signatur I P 2, G Zl 11. 126/1932, Zl 11.443/1932 Amtserinnerung betreffend den Entwurf eines Bankengesetzes.
13. Archiv der Republik. Bundesministerium für Finanzen. Zl 50.028/1932 Regierungsvorlage samt Begründung; Allgemeines Verwaltungsarchiv, Bundesministerium für Justiz, Signatur I P 2, G Zl 11.126/1932, Zl 11.536-1/1932 Amtserinnerung betreffend Pressemitteilung bei Versendung des Bankengesetzentwurfes.
14. Allgemeines Verwaltungsarchiv. Bundesministerium für Justiz, Signatur I P Zl 11.126/1932, Zl 11.756-1/1932 Amtserinnerung betreffend Bemerkung des Industriellen E. Foradori über den Entwurf eines Bankengesetzes.
15. *Protokolle des Ministerrates der Ersten Republik. Abteilung VIII. Vol. 1*, Vienna, 1980, MRP 807 of 15 June 1932, p. 214.
16. MRP 826 of 29 September 1932, p. 571.
17. Allgemeines Verwaltungsarchiv. Bundesministerium für Justiz. Signatur I II I. G Zl 11. 045/1932.
18. 'Neugestaltung und Zusammenfassung im österreichischen Bankwesen', *Mitteilungen des Verbandes der österreichischen Banken und Bankiers* No. 1/2, February 1935, p. 26.
19. Archiv der Republik. Ministerratsprotokolle der Ersten Republik, MRP 1016/2 of 2, 3, 4 December 1935, p. 51.

References

Ausch, K. (1968), *Als die Banken fielen, Zur Soziologie der politischen Korruption*, Wien, Europaverlag.
Bondi, A. (1933), *Neue Wege des Aktienrechtes, nach einem am 14. Dezember 1932 in der Wiener Juristischen Gesellschaft gehaltenen Vortrag*, Wien/Leipzig: Manz'sche Verlags- und Universitäts-Buchhandlung.
Frölichsthal, F. (1990), *Geschichtliche Entwicklung der Österreichischen Bankenaufsicht*, Diplomarbeit am Institut für Wirtschafts- und Sozialgeschichte, Wien.
Heller, E. (1912), *Kommentar zur Gewerbeordnung*, 2. Band, Wien, Manz'sche Verlags- und Universitäts-Buchhandlung.
Honold, E. (1956), *Die Bankenaufsicht*, diss., Mannheim.
Kernbauer, Hans (1991), *Währungspolitik in der Zwischenkriegszeit Geschichte der Österreichischen Nationalbank von 1923 bis 1938*, Österreichische Nationalbank (ed.), *Das Österreichische Noteninstitut*, Third Part, Vol. 1 (Vienna, 1991).
Kernbauer, Hans, Eduard März, and Fritz Weber (1983), 'Die wirtschaftliche Entwicklung' in Erika Weinzierl and Kurt Skalnik (eds), Österreich 1918–1938, *Geschichte der Ersten Republik*, Band 1, Graz/Wien/Köln, Styria.
Knett, H. (1985), *Die Bankkommission, Eine Fachkommission für das Bankwesen von 1922 bis 1926*, Diplomarbeit, Sozial- und wirtschaftswissenschaftliche Fakultät der Universität Wien.
Mosser, Alois and Alice Teichova (1991), 'Investment behaviour of industrial joint-stock companies and industrial shareholding by the Österreichische Credit-Anstalt: inducement or obstacle to renewal

and change in industry in interwar Austria' in Harold James, Håkan Lindgren and Alice Teichova (eds), *The role of banks in the interwar economy*, Cambridge, Cambridge University Press.

Noell, G. (1927), *Die Ergebnisse der Goldbilanzierung bei den Aktiengesellschaften in Österreich*, Libau: Buch- und Steindruckerei Gottl. D. Meyer.

Ottel, Fritz (1933), 'Der österreichische Bankgesetzentwurf', *Betriebswirtschaftliche Blätter*, 3, März.

Pollak, M. (1932), *Bankensanierung und Bankenrekonstruktion*, Brünn/Prag/Leipzig/Wien, Verlag Rudolf M. Rohrer.

Puxbaum, H. (1929), *Das mitteleuropäische Bankenwesen*, Berlin/Wien, Industrieverlag Spaeth & Linde.

Stiefel, D. (1988), *Die große Krise in einem kleinen Land, Österreichische Finanz- und Wirtschaftspolitik 1929–1938*, Wien/Köln/Graz, Böhlau.

Teichova, Alice (1988), 'Rivals and Partners, Banking and Industry in Europe in the First Decades of the Twentieth Century', Uppsala papers in economic history, *Working papers*, No 1.

Weber, Fritz (1991), 'Universal banking in interwar Central Europe' in Harold James, Håkan Lindgren and Alice Teichova (eds), *The role of banks in the interwar economy*, Cambridge, Cambridge University Press.

Weber, Fritz (1981), 'Hauptprobleme der wirtschaftlichen und sozialen Entwicklung Österreichs in der Zwischenkriegszeit' in Franz Kadrnoska, *Aufbruch und Untergang, Österreichische Kultur zwischen 1918 und 1938*, Wien, Europaverlag.

Weiss, B. (1984), *Die Bankkommission als Instrument der staatlichen Bankenaufsicht in Österreich 1922–1926*, Diplomarbeit am Institut für Wirtschafts- und Sozialgeschichte Wien.

Ziegler, J. (1933), *Bankensanierung und Bankenaufsicht, Ein Beitrag zur Bankenkontrolle und Bankenreform in Mitteleuropa*, Wien/Berlin, Österreichischer Wirtschaftsverlag/Carl Heymanns Verlag.

PART III

UNIVERSAL BANKS AND INDUSTRY

10 Banking system changes after the establishment of the Independent Czechoslovak Republic

Vlastislav Lacina

Czech Republic
Slovakia
621
N24

Basic trends in the development of the credit system and industrial financing in Czechoslovakia were similar to those of Germany, Austria and Hungary. Nevertheless significant changes were brought about by the disintegration of the Habsburg Monarchy and the emergence of an independent Czechoslovak state. These changes were more profound and had a form different from those of Austria and Hungary, the capitals of which had constituted the financial centres of the former monarchy. Both parts of Czechoslovakia – the Czech Lands and Slovakia – had depended on these centres. The dimensions of Prague banking, which developed after 1900, were still essentially provincial. Most of the largest industrial enterprises retained their credit links with the big banks of Vienna and a substantial part of them had their head offices there.

This state of affairs survived into the first months of the new Czechoslovak Republic. The decisive influence was still exerted by the large Viennese banks. In the Czech Lands, ten had 76 branch offices and 26 agencies, substantial shareholdings and constant credit links with nearly all the leading enterprises in mining, metallurgy, engineering and arms production including the most significant textile and chemical plants. After the collapse of the Habsburg Monarchy, these banks attempted to become multinational enterprises active in all successor states.[1] Such plans, however, clashed with the aims of the economists and the government of Czechoslovakia and ultimately failed. Though Viennese banks were allowed to operate in Czechoslovakia, the conditions for acquiring credit worsened considerably after Czechoslovakia had declared herself an independent customs territory on 20 February 1919 and introduced her own Czechoslovak currency on 25 February,[2] in order to avoid being drawn further into the galloping inflation in Austria.

Enterprises with plants in the Czechoslovak Republic but with head offices in Vienna or Budapest, from which they drew their credit, found themselves in a difficult position. Neither the centres nor the Viennese banks could continue providing the necessary credits. Consequently, these enterprises had to seek credit from the domestic banks, which disposed of sufficient funds. Of the German provincial banks, only the Czech Bank Union could supply larger advances. German commercial and savings banks had considerable sums immobilized in war loans. Moreover, Czech banks had good contacts with state institutions and the new Prague government, a great advantage in the turbulent postwar period. For this reason such enterprises sought new credit links with the banks of Prague and Brno as early as Spring 1919. Among these were such important corporations as the Škoda Works, Ringhoffer Works and the Association for Chemical and Metallurgical Production. In addition to this, more than a hundred middle-sized enterprises once in credit connections with Viennese banks obtained the credit necessary for the transition to peacetime production from Prague banks in 1919. Credit links naturally resulted in the banks obtaining influence over these enterprises and, in most cases, in representation on the boards of directors.

For the big firms, the most important partner was the largest bank of Czechoslovakia, Živnostenská banka. In addition to ranking first among the commercial banks, it had close contacts with the Ministry of Finance and with government circles generally. In July 1919, the Živnostenská banka concluded an agreement on the financing of firms belonging to its Czechoslovak 'concern' with the Viennese Boden-Creditanstalt, and both banks pledged to coordinate their activities in relation to Czechoslovak industry. All this opened the way for Živnostenská banka to gain influence in the largest industrial firms of Czechoslovakia, hitherto a position enjoyed by the big banks of Vienna.[3]

The establishment of constant credit links constituted a departure point for the further growth of influence on the part of the domestic banks. To a substantial extent, they participated in the transformation of originally private enterprises into joint-stock companies and especially in the increase of capital taking place in all the joint-stock companies because of rampant inflation during 1919–21 and the needs of postwar construction. A typical feature of this situation was that for the purpose of issuing new stock, Czech banks formed syndicates with 'maternal' Viennese banks,[4] as well as with Česká eskomptní banka (Böhmische Escomptebank) of Prague, representing the Austrian-oriented group of German capital in the Czech Lands.[5] The issue of new stock enabled domestic banks through purchases of shares to obtain a direct capital participation in major industrial and commercial companies once dominated by the Viennese banks. The Živnostenská banka, Česká průmyslová banka (Bohemian Industrial Bank), Agrární banka (Agrarian Bank) as well as the Böhmische Escomptebank also organized purchases of shares from Austrian owners.

The most significant changes in the banking system, however, were brought about by nostrification, promulgated for industrial, commercial and transport enterprises by the law of December 1919 and, within the banking sphere, codified by the regulation concerning the branch offices of Viennese banks of September 1920. Though the law expressly demanded no more than transfers of the head offices of joint-stock companies to Czechoslovakia, the true impact of the nostrification went much deeper. First and foremost, nostrified enterprises built up new credit links and had to be supplied with sufficient basic capital which was eroded by progressive inflation. Nostrified companies had to increase their capital stock through new issues. This stock was usually issued by banks with which the enterprises maintained credit contacts. Such banks also acted as agencies for the sale of shares which gave them an influence over their distribution.[6]

However, a major factor in the transformation of the banking system was the nostrification within the banking business itself. The original idea in Czech financial circles was to liquidate the branch offices of Viennese banks and absorb them into domestic, mostly Czech banks. This strategy, however, materialized only in the case of the branch offices of the relatively insignificant Verkehrsbank, which was incorporated into the Česká průmyslová banka, one of the big banks of Czechoslovakia.[7] In most cases other measures were taken to avoid liquidating Czech branches of the big Viennese banks, such as the agreement of 1919 between the Creditanstalt of Vienna and the provincial German Böhmische Escomptebank of Prague concerning the takeover of the Creditanstalt branches. The fusion and restructuring of this Prague bank involved a considerable increase of its capital stock. This was realized under the patronage of the Ministry of Finance with the participation of the Živnostenská banka which purchased 52 per cent of the new shares. Thus the outcome of this union was the mixed Czech–German Česká eskomptní banka a úvěrní ústav – Böhmische Escomptebank und Kreditanstalt (BEBKA), which in its initial stage was closely connected with the Živnostenská banka. It shared a number of subsidiary enterprises with it and concluded an agreement on the coordination of activities in February 1920.[8] As time went on, this mixed bank rose to second position among the banks of Czechoslovakia in terms of capital size, offering a base for the cooperation of Czech and German enterprises throughout the whole of the 1920s.

The fusion of the Creditanstalt branch offices and the Böhmische Escomptebank was a first-grade nostrification act preceding the Ministry of Finance's regulation concerning the branch offices of the Viennese banks. In its consequences, this regulation implied the establishment of independent head offices for the Czechoslovak branch offices. The first nostrification under this regulation was that of the offices of the Merkur Bank of Vienna. In December 1920, these formed a mixed Czech–German Česká komerční banka (Bohemian commercial bank), which in 1930 amalgamated with the Anglo-Pragobank. In 1921, the branch offices of the Wiener Bankverein merged with the cooperation of a Belgian partner into the Všeobecná česká bankovní jednota – Allgemeiner Böhmischer Bankverein.[9] In the course of the 1920s, the influence of Austrian capital in this bank gradually increased and in 1930 it was incorporated into the biggest former Austrian bank, the Böhmische Bank Union (Česká banka Union). Again, in 1921 the nostrification of the Viennese Länderbank branch offices led to the creation of Banka pro obchod a průmysl (Bank for Commerce and Industry), with the decisive French influence of the Banque de Paris et de Pays-Bas. For the entire interwar period it remained a mixed Czech–German bank and the basis of Bohemian–German–French economic cooperation, having found a safe anchorage in Czechoslovak foreign trade with France and other Francophile countries.[10]

The case of the branch offices of the Anglo-Austrian Bank of Vienna on the territory of the Czechoslovak Republic became part of complicated negotiations between Austria, Britain and Czechoslovakia in the course of the transformation of the Viennese bank into a British company, the Anglo-Austrian Bank of London (cf. Charlotte Natmeßnig, Chapter 8 in this volume). As a result of an agreement between the British and Czechoslovak governments all branches of the former Viennese bank were brought into the newly founded Anglo-československá banka (Anglo-Czechoslovak Bank) of Prague (constituted on 12 April 1922). Its capital stock remained exclusively British until 1927 when the British group represented by the Anglo-International Bank sold 25 per cent of the stock to the Czechoslovak state and ceded a further 50 per cent to a Czech group of companies (the Škoda Works, the agrarian Kooperativa, R. Petschek and J. Schicht) and to the Prince of Lichtenstein.[11]

Transformations following the establishment of new credit links and nostrification resulted in substantial adjustments of the banking system and of the traditional interconnections between industry and the banks. Of course, this was not the only factor at work: a considerable role was played by the vigorous growth in banking after the First World War. As a consequence of the postwar boom, the number of commercial banks in the Czech Lands grew from 22 in 1918 to 38 in 1922 while the amount of capital stock rose from 529 million Czechoslovak crowns (Kč) to 1 905 million Kč.[12] The core of the banking system no longer consisted of Viennese banks but of formerly provincial Czech, German and, to a lesser extent, Slovak banks. Although these banks were mostly established on the ethnic principle, business relations of Czech banks after the emergence of the Republic included also German and Slovak enterprises. But German banks also did business with Czech enterprises. Nevertheless, the ethnic division of the banks was disadvantageous for Czechoslovak economic life and a major integrative role was played by the three big mixed Czech–German banks which emerged from the nostrification process with the capital participation of the Allied countries. None of the large number of banks newly founded in the four postwar years rose to any position of prominence, save for the Banka československých legií (Bank of Czechoslovak Legions).

After the boom of 1918–22, Czechoslovak banking was hit by a short-term crisis during which three Bohemian banks were bankrupted, while others merged with stronger banks (in terms of capital) and a number of firms had to be salvaged by state aid. After 1925, the banking system became stabilized in Czechoslovakia. One can distinguish four main bank groups according to the languages spoken in their head offices: Czech; mixed Czech–German; German;

and Slovak. In 1929, there were again no more than 22 banks with a total capital of 1 845 million Kč[13] in the Czech Lands. Table 10.1 lists the main banks of Czechoslovakia in rank order.

Table 10.1   Capital stock and total balances of the main commercial banks in Czechoslovakia

Bank	Czechoslovakia capital stock (in million Kč)		Total balances (in million Kč)	
	1919	1922	1929	1929
Živnostenská banka Industrial Bank	120	200	300	5 676
Česká průmyslová banka Bohemian Industrial Bank	80	120	210	2 448
Pražska úvěrní banka* Prague Credit Bank	50	75	235	4 509
Moravská agrární a prům. banka Agrarian and Industrial bank of Moravia	36	120	120	1 919
Česká banka Bohemian Bank	20	60	60	637
Banka československých legií Bank of Czechoslovak Legions	–	70	70	1 020
Agrární banka Agrarian bank	12	60	60	913
Česká eskomptní banka** Bohemian Escompte Bank	48	175	250	4 397
Anglo-československá banka** Anglo-Czechoslovak Bank	–	120	–	–
Banka pro obchod a průmysl Bank for Commerce and Industry	–	80	160	1 966
Böhmische Bank Union[†] Bohemian Bank Union	80	160	200	4 404
Deutsche Agrar- und Industriebank[†] German Agrarian and Industrial Bank	–	–	60	750
Tatra banka[††] Tatra Bank	2	–	75	730
Slovenská banka [††] Slovak Bank	9	–	70	692

Notes:
* In the year 1929 Anglo-Prague Bank.
** Czech–German banks.
† German banks.
†† Slovak banks.

Source: Statistická příručka Republiky československé II, Praha 1925, pp- 212 and 213; ibid., vol. IV, Praha 1932, p. 259.

The data in Table 10.1 indicate that at the end of the 1920s, big and medium banks of Czechoslovakia included seven Czech, three Czech–German, two German and two Slovak banks. There were four large banks with a capital exceeding 200 million Kč, which had a large number of subsidiary companies and an extensive banking business: the Živnostenská banka, Pražska úvěrní banka (transformed later into the Anglo-Pragobank), Česká eskomptní banka and Böhmische Bank Union. Though the leading role in Czechoslovak banking was played by Czech bank capital, significant positions were occupied by mixed banks and by domestic German capital. Slovak banks remained weak even though their capital stock and banking business showed relatively the most substantial growth.

The creation of a smoothly functioning money market became an element of extraordinary importance in the economy of the newly emerged Czechoslovakia. This system rested on two pillars: commercial banks; and savings banks. The other financial institutions – banking houses, land and mortgage banks – had a complementary function. The lack of capital, so painfully felt in the first postwar years, was an incentive in the creation of a system capable of concentrating both the capital acquired by industrial, agricultural and commercial enterprise and the savings of common people. This role was taken over by a swiftly expanding system of popular money institutions: community and private savings banks and credit cooperatives of the Kampelík and Raiffeisen types. In 1929, the deposits of these institutions totalled 25.1 billion Kč. They financed small- and medium-sized businesses, transferring a part of their deposits to the banks. In the savings accounts of the commercial banks no more than 10.1 billion Kč were deposited.[14]

The extraordinary economic power wielded by the biggest Czechoslovak financial institution, the Živnostenská banka, followed from the fact that in addition to its own capital, private savings banks transferred large sums of money to it. These deposits amounted to about twice as much as the total of its own savings accounts.[15] Other banks drew money from people's savings banks, as for instance the Agrární banka from the Kampelík credit cooperatives. Thanks to this system and especially to the interconnection between banking and people's savings institutions, a remarkable degree of mobilization of internal financial sources, which subsequently became the foundation of a successful modernization of Czechoslovak industry in the 1920s, could be achieved.

In spite of the extraordinary importance of the people's savings institutions the most significant component of the money market in Czechoslovakia consisted of commercial joint-stock banks. They held 57 per cent of the balances of all financial institutions and oriented their business, first and foremost, towards large- and middle-sized industrial enterprises and the wholesale trade. The commercial and credit activities of the banks increased considerably over the first decade of the existence of the Republic. This was reflected by the expansion of the system of branch offices. The increase in capital and the extent of reserves and balances, are shown in Table 10.2.

Table 10.2   Commercial banks in the Czech Lands, 1918–28

Year	Number of:		Capital stock	Reserves	Total
	institutions	branch offices		(in million Kč)	balances
1918	22	163	529	197	6 661
1922	38	423	1 906	769	31 865
1924	31	420	1 870	1 005	28 619
1929	22	416	1 845	1 636	31 345

Source: Almanach československého peněžnictví v prvním desetiletí ČSR, Praha 1928, pp. 108–123; *Statistická příručka* RČS IV, pp. 258–9.

The commercial banks of Czechoslovakia were universal because they combined both deposit and investment banking. In addition to this, they continued the extensive trading activities introduced before the war, especially the wholesale marketing of sugar and coal, as well as landed mortgage banking. After the bank laws of 1924, which forbade such activities, the wholesale business was transferred to subsidiary commercial enterprises.

The period immediately after the First World War brought to the fore a new field of activity, hitherto reserved for the big banks of Vienna or for the trading companies of Trieste, Vienna and Hamburg in prewar times – the financing and organization of imports and exports. The chief problem for Czechoslovakia's postwar industry was lack of raw materials, such as cotton, wool, oil, chemicals and non-ferrous metals which had to be imported and mostly financed by credits abroad. In the turbulent postwar period. the large Prague banks endeavoured to get their business and for this purpose, they formed a syndicate of seven banks. The leading bank and pilot enterprise of this syndicate was Živnostenská banka. In mid-April 1919, its directors, Messrs A. Tille and J. Horák, left for the USA in an attempt to obtain credit for the syndicate of about 25 million US dollars. In view of the general uncertainty of the situation then prevalent in Central Europe they met with a rather hesitant attitude from US banks and returned with a substantially lower credit of 6.3 million US dollars for the purchase of cotton.[16] Other necessary supplies had to be procured with credit obtained from banks in France, Britain, the Netherlands and, again, in the USA.

The banks of Czechoslovakia, which had been provincial institutions before 1918, had considerable difficulties in mediating the financing of foreign trade. On the one hand, their experience with this kind of business was rather limited; on the other, the pressure exerted by governments of the other newly established successor states resulted in a substantial reduction in the number of branch offices abroad (from 39 to 11) and direct contacts between the territories of the former monarchy were thus limited. Together with foreign companies, Prague banks established a number of commercial companies abroad for the support of foreign trade. The most significant were the Obchodní sdruženi českosloven-ských bank (Commercial Association of Czechoslovak Banks) in Berlin, the Bank für auswärtigen Handel, also of Berlin, and the Dutch–Czechoslovak Holbo company.[17]

Although the range of business expanded, the operations of Czech, mixed and German banks remained largely in the field of credit-financing of industrial companies and the wholesale business. The banks' capital came from four sources: their own stock and reserve capital; savings deposits; sums on current account; and finances entrusted to the banks. The proportion of reserve capital and money deposited on current account of industrial and commercial companies grew considerably in comparison with the prewar period. In 1919 and 1920, the bank balances on company current accounts showed a surplus of 5621 million Kč while savings-book accounts increased by only 1017 million. This trend, however, lasted only until 1922, when the currency was stabilized and ratio-nalization of industry had begun. Companies invested their current-account surpluses and during the economic boom their total diminished. During the peak of the recovery period in 1928, it rose again to the 1922 value, surpassing 19 billion Kč.[18] As the banks' interest in credit-financing industry and trade rose, they tried to increase deposits on savings-book accounts. By setting up a wider network of branch offices and by raising interest rates, they succeeded in increasing deposits on savings books by 65 per cent. These could then be used for providing credits to industry and commerce.

After the First World War, bank credit became an integral component of industrial enterprise. Immediately after the war, it mainly facilitated the conversion to peacetime production and the purchase of raw materials. After 1922, the range of credit employment was substantially expanded and, instead of granting individual credits, long-term stable credit contracts came to pre-dominate even in the case of middle-sized industrial firms. Before the war, this practice was confined to large firms or the subsidiary enterprises of banks.

This interpretation of the way credit was provided for industrial companies is mainly based on the abundant archive materials of the biggest bank of Czechoslovakia – the Živnostenská banka. The bank occupied a dominant position within Czechoslovak banking thanks to both its capital strength rep-resented by 300 million Kč of capital stock and 5676 million Kč in total balances as well as to its good relations with the government and elite of the state. The first finance minister of Czechoslovakia, Alois Rašín, was a member of its board of directors and its executive committee. Most of the Živnostenská banka's clients represented companies of such industries as textiles, sugar, iron and steel works, chemicals and mechanical engineering; in the course of the 1920s, the bank formed an extensive 'concern' which included the most important companies of Czechoslovakia.[19]

The Živnostenská banka was the only domestic bank with the capital to provide larger investment credit itself. However, it only did so in exceptional circumstances, for example in the form of consortial credits with several other banks, and first and foremost, with the Česká eskomptní banka. The companies resorted to large current-account credits to cover their investments. The head office of the bank set the credit limits on which the enterprises could draw according to their needs. Large long-term investment credits were scarce in Czechoslovakia. This was why the banks extended them to their 'concern' enterprises, their promising and long-term clients, and those few companies in which the bank head offices had special interests.

The vast majority of credits were made up of short-term credits. In most cases, these were working-capital credits, advances for the purchase of raw materials (principally cotton, wool and oil), short-term credits for pre-sales of products, lombard (guarantee) credits and diverse internal credits for other banks and various investments. The range of clients for these kinds of credit varied, but regular clients with credit contracts prevailed. In addition to these, credit was furnished to firms without regular trade contracts with the bank.[20]

Regular customers predominated in the case of other services provided by the banks to industrial enterprises. These were, first and foremost, guarantees of various kinds. Most frequently, banks took over guarantees in the course of loans by foreign banks, in the course of offer procedures both at home and abroad, as customs guarantee loans and guarantees *vis-à-vis* the tax-collecting offices. In about 10 per cent of all cases, the extension of guarantees and credit increases was granted on condition of 'concentration of all business in our institution'. The banks used investment credits, regular credit contacts and the takeover of guarantees to tie industrial and commercial firms to their business.[21] There was a trend towards extensive but loosely organized concerns. In addition to the Živnostenská banka's concern, which was by far the largest one, strong concerns were built up by the Česká eskomptní and Pražská úvěrní banks and by the Böhmische Bank Union over the 1920s.

The banks' activities in founding and promoting companies gained momentum after the emergence of Czechoslovakia. These met the needs of the nascent economy of independent Czechoslovakia and of postwar economic recovery. At the same time the pressure of the postwar inflation produced surplus money seeking investment. In the course of the 1920s, branches of production which had not been established in the new state were set up. This resulted in the establishment of electrotechnical firms 'Osram' and 'Elektra' factories (Prague), 'Telegrafia' (Pardubice), aircraft factories (Kbely), explosives production (Explosia in Semtín at Pardubice), among others. From 1918 to 1922, the number of joint-stock companies increased from 605 to 1089 and the amount of their capital from 2.5 billion Kč to 5 billion. The banks assisted in the establishment of nearly every joint-stock company, whether they were new undertakings or private companies converted into public ones. They took over the establishment of the companies, issues and sales of shares, keeping a part of the stock in the bank's own (nostrum) account or selling it to their clients. Only two industrial companies were helped in their initial phases by foreign capital: Osram and Explosia.[22]

In the first postwar years, most of the business of founding and promoting firms was taken up more by the Czech or mixed banks, rather than the German banks, which distrusted the new state. However, German banks fully participated in the second phase of encouraging the establishment of joint-stock companies after 1921. In that year, there was a split in the activities of the Czech banks. One part of them, represented by the Pražská úvěrní banka, continued the intensive promotion of companies bordering on a 'foundation rush or fever'. The other part, stronger in terms of capital and led by the Živnostenská banka, put a temporary limit on these activities, concentrating on capital penetration into nostrified enterprises and on the large-scale increase of capital by existing firms, necessitated by the postwar inflation.[23] A temporary suspension of the business of establishing companies by the strongest Czech banks invigorated Czech enterprise but had an adverse impact on the introduction of new branches of industry and on technical rationalization.

Significant changes in the banking system and in bank–industry relationships can be seen in Czechoslovakia after the First World War. Intensification of contacts between commercial banks and industrial enterprises both in terms of credit and in company formation went hand in hand with nostrification and the transfer of the new state's banking to Prague. The position of Czech and mainly Prague banks which, together with mixed and domestic German institutions, played a decisive role in Czechoslovak banking and in bank–industry relationships as early as the end of the 1920s, grew stronger. The influence of Viennese banks was substantially weakened, though it lasted until the fall of the Creditanstalt in 1931.

Notes

1. The attempts of Viennese banks to maintain their commercial contacts with enterprises of the successor states were discussed in H. Kernbauer and F. Weber, 'Multinational banking in the Danube basin: the business strategy of the Viennese banks after the collapse of the Habsburg monarchy', in A. Teichova, M. Lévy-Leboyer and H. Nussbaum (eds), *Multinational enterprise in historical perspective*, Cambridge, 1986, pp. 185–99.
2. Cf. V. Lacina, *Formování československé ekonomiky 1918–1923* (The emergence of Czechoslovak economy 1918–1923), Praha, 1990, pp. 81–8.
3. Archive of the Státní banka československá (furthermore abbreviated as ASB), ŽB-S-I.c. Minutes of the executive committee of the Živnostenská banka, 30 September and 9 November 1919.

4. These were mainly: Boden-Creditanstalt, Creditanstalt and Niederösterreichische Escompte-gesellschaft.
5. A. Pimper, *České dochodní banky za války a po válce* (Bohemian commercial banks in the war and postwar times), Praha, 1929, pp. 491–501.
6. For the most extensive analysis of the nostrification of industrial and commercial ventures, see Lacina (note 2), pp. 10–14.
7. Ibid., p. 115.
8. ASB, ŽB-S-I.c., Minutes of the executive committee of Živnostenská, 15 December 1919, 12 February and 17 June 1920.
9. Pimper (note 5), pp. 485–90 and 514–27.
10. A. Teichova, *An Economic Background to Munich*, Cambridge, 1974, pp. 348–50.
11. Ibid., pp. 350–56; *Hospodářská politika 1930* (Economic policy), pp. 232–3; for further details see A. Teichova, 'Versailles and the Expansion of the Bank of England into Central Europe' in N. Horn and J. Kocka (eds), *Recht und Entwicklung der Großunternehmen im 19. und frühen 20. Jahrhundert*, Göttingen, 1979, pp. 366–87; and Charlotte Natmessnig in this volume, Chapter 8.
12. *Almanach československého peněžnictví* (A review of Czechoslovak money affairs), Praha, 1928, p. 108.
13. *Statistická příručka Republiky československé* (Statistical manual of the Republic of Czechoslovakia), vol. IV, p. 259.
14. Ibid., p. 258.
15. Annual report of the Živnostenská banka for the years 1922, 1929.
16. ASB, ŽB-S-V. a-13/9. Syndicate 'Cotton'. For more details on negotiations concerning the cotton purchase credits cf. J. Novotný, 'Americké bavlnářské úvěry z roku 1919 a československý bavlnářský puůmysl' (American cotton credits of 1919 and the Czechoslovak cotton industry), *Z dějin textilu* (The History of textiles), 3, 1982, pp. 56–66.
17. Lacina (note 2), p. 99.
18. Cf. Pimper (note 5) and M. Ubiria, V. Kadlec and J. Matas, *Peněžní a úvěrová soustava ČSR za kapitalismu* (The money and credit system of Czechoslovakia under capitalism), Praha, 1958.
19. Cf. V. Lacina, Živnobanka a její koncern v letech velké hospodářské krize 1929–1934' (Živnobanka and its concern in the years of the great economic crisis 1929–1934), *Československý časopis historický*, pp. 350–77.
20. These conclusions are based on the minutes of the Živnostenská banka's executive committee of 1919–1923 and on detailed analyses of credit sums above 100000 Kč furnished by the Živnostenská banka in 1923.
21. Ibid.
22. On the participation of foreign capital in Czechoslovak banking and industry cf. Teichová (note 10).
23. Analysis of foundation activities of the banks is based on materials of the boards of directors and executive committees of the Živnostenská and Pražská úvěrní banks of 1919–1923. These are deposited at the ASB, fonds ŽB and PÚB.

11 Bank–industry relations in interwar Slovakia

Jozef Faltus

It is widely known that interwar Czechoslovakia was in economic terms a relatively advanced country in which industry was the leading sector of the economy. This fact influenced all other aspects of economic and social life. It is, however, less well known that this general characterization applies, above all, to conditions prevailing in the Czech part of the state inhabited by the majority of the population (in 1930 the population of the Czech Lands – Bohemia, Moravia and Silesia – amounted to 10.7 million out of a total of 14 million [excluding the population of Carpatho-Ukraine]). The economic character of the eastern part of the state, Slovakia, was qualitatively different. In this area over 60 per cent of the population were occupied in agriculture and forestry in 1921 and industrialization was at the beginning of its development. In addition, the uneven political and cultural level inherited by Czechoslovakia from the main parts of the Dual Monarchy – Austria and Hungary – affected Slovakia unfavourably (e.g. the absence of a national Slovak intelligentsia was critical). During the interwar period the inherited differences in the political and cultural spheres between the Czech and Slovak part of the state diminished, but in the economic sphere only very few changes occurred.

The uneven levels of industrialization in the Czech Lands and in Slovakia, which were reflected in the different intensity of agriculture and services, also found their expression in the differences in the systems of banking and finance inherited from the former Austria and Hungary respectively. In the Czech Lands a wide variety of banking institutions had developed long before 1918 whose main representatives were relatively influential commercial banks. At the beginning of the existence of Czechoslovakia the credit system of Slovakia consisted of three components: joint-stock banks totalling 228 institutions in 1918;[1] credit cooperatives totalling 235 in number; and branches of banks whose head offices were in Hungary, amounting to twelve branch offices of eight banks.[2] In addition commercial banks from Vienna, Budapest and Prague as well as Brno operated on the territory of Slovakia without establishing branches. However, the domestic credit system of Slovakia was insufficiently developed at the time of the establishment of Czechoslovakia and important areas were not covered, such as long-term credits provided by banks, modern type of people's savings banks, rediscount centres and clearing houses.

A modern banking system capable of financing large factories of wholesale and export-oriented enterprises was not found in Slovakia but in the big banking institutions of Budapest, Vienna and Prague (the latter operating either directly or through branches). Only a few local joint-stock banks were able to provide certain credit facilities to a limited number of small and medium-sized industrial and trading enterprises. Practically all the joint-stock banks domiciled in Slovakia resembled people's savings banks which drew upon temporarily free resources of the local population, mainly peasants, craftsmen, tradesmen, and members of the petty intelligentsia. Moreover, their financial operations were limited to this sphere. This is evident from the proportionate amounts in the balance sheets of Slovak banks, i.e. of deposits on savings accounts, on the one hand, and other credit balances on the other, which in economically advanced systems are usually in inverse proportion. Even in the case of the biggest of these institutions large industrial and commercial enterprises had no significant place in their credit and debit business.

A further characteristic feature of banking in Slovakia was the division of institutions according to the nationality of their shareholders which was reflected in the language spoken at the respective banks. Out of the 228 banks which existed at the inception of the Czechoslovak state only 32 were Slovak[3] but, at the same time, their interest in industry was smaller than that of banks where the language spoken was Hungarian or German.

The establishment of Czechoslovakia, and especially the introduction of a new currency and customs system, brought about a number of fundamental changes in the economy of Slovakia. While the integrative tendencies in Slovak economic life had taken a southern direction in the former Monarchy, they changed towards the west, that is towards the Czech Lands and Western Europe. Old markets were lost; new ones had to be found. Slovak agriculture was able to change its orientation comparatively easily (food production in the Czech Lands was insufficient), but the industrial capacity of Slovakia was reduced and the consequences of this deindustrialization were overcome only after the Great Depression of the 1930s.

Gradually also the credit system changed in the framework of the new socio-economic and political conditions. In the first place the branches of Hungarian banks disappeared: branches of six banks went into liquidation, two owned by the Uhorská eskontná a zmenárenská banka (Hungarian Escompte and Exchange Bank) were taken over by the Eskontná a hospodárská banka (Escompte and Agrarian Bank), the bank of the local German-speaking population in Bratislava, the majority of whose equity was transferred to the Tatra Bank in Martin.[4] Two branches of the Uhorská všeobecná úverová banka (Hungarian General Credit Bank, a sister institute of the Vienna Credit-Anstalt) were under the provisions of the Nostrification Act transformed into the separate Slovenská všeobecná úverová banka (Slovak General Credit Bank), for which the bank acquired a concession: the Americko-slovenská banka (American-Slovak Bank, the bank of American Slovaks founded in 1919), the Česká eskontní banka a úvěrní ústav (the Bohemian Escompte Bank and Credit Institute–BEBCA in Prague which nationalized the branches of the Viennese Credit-Anstalt in the Czech Lands under the nostrification legislation) and the former parent bank in Budapest.[5]

Until 1918 the number of banks in Slovakia steadily grew. However, after the establishment of Czechoslovakia centralization gradually increased and this provided opportunities for the biggest banks in Slovakia to widen their credit operations in the sphere of industrial and commercial enterprise. The legislation of the new state supported the process of centralization, especially the introduction of licensing for new banking firms, which also applied in Slovakia.[6] Above all, the banking laws of 1924 and 1932 as well as the law affording tax relief for mergers of joint-stock companies, furthered concentration.[7]

Table 11.1 shows the progress of concentration of joint-stock banks in Slovakia in benchmark years selected from the business cycle. During the 1920s buoyant growth can be observed, which was followed by dramatic reductions in all items of the banks' balance sheets during the 1930s.[8] The biggest banks increased their share of total bank balances during the process of concentration. Whereas in 1921 the fourteen biggest banks in Slovakia accounted for just under half of total bank liabilities, their share had risen to almost 80 per cent by 1929; this share had risen only slightly to 83 per cent by 1937. However, this share appears to be somewhat underestimated since many of the minor banks, whose equity was held by the bigger banks, were in effect their branches.

Table 11.1   Number of banks and main balance items of all banks in Slovakia (in million crowns at the end of year)

	1921	1924	1929	1933	1937
Number of joint-stock banks	181	128	76	49	47
Amount of debits	3568.1	4024.8	4703.0	3460.4	3614.3
Joint-stock capital	316.3	434.3	375.0	247.7	244.1
Reserve loss funds	158.6	152.7	192.6	148.1	128.4
Deposits	1847.8	2157.2	2946.2	2248.4	2386.4
Creditors	982.1	960.8	1077.4	753.7	788.9
Bills of exchange	514.1	709.1	1170.2	702.0	578.5
Loans	1748.3	1997.2	2500.4	1792.8	1817.4
Lasting capital participations	85.9	123.3	114.7	78.2	85.0
Securities	618.8	472.5	259.8	363.0	418.5

In the context of the democratic political conditions which characterized the new Czechoslovakia the pressure of magyarization disappeared and the Slovak language became customary also in banking. As a result the significance of the grouping of banks according to nationality declined. In spite of this, a small group of banks situated in areas inhabited by a mixture of nationalities retained a majority of Hungarian- or German-speaking clients, including Yiddish-speaking customers. During the 1920s the bigger national Slovak banks were able to strengthen their capital position substantially. Their influence grew not only because they belonged politically to the constituent elements of the new state but also because of the losses suffered by the local Hungarian–German–Jewish banks after part of their assets had become frozen in the big Budapest banks and devalued by inflation; also because of their losses through their substantive engagement in war loans as well as losses in consequence of the disarray of postwar conditions (losses caused by movements in the rate of exchange and prices, and the bankruptcies of their debtors).[9] The bigger Slovak banks succeeded in acquiring that part of the savings of the population as well as of enterprises which before 1918 had been directed to local banks competing with them but also to banks in Budapest and Vienna. They were also strengthened by the generous support from the 'restitution fund' established by the law of 1924 which was to compensate losses suffered as a result of postwar conditions,[10] as well as by favourable credit conditions provided by the Czech banks and the central bank of issue (before 1918 the Slovak banks had no rights of rediscount at the National Bank of Austria–Hungary).

The capital of American Slovaks played a special role in furthering the expansion of the national Slovak banks during the 1920s.[11] The money was imported in several ways after the First World War. One way was in the form of savings brought into the country by returning emigrants, and also as remittances by Slovak emigrants to their families at home; the overwhelming part of these funds was used for consumption, the lesser part was invested directly into agricultural or other business activities, and part of these payments found their way into the savings accounts of various banks. The second way was in the form of investments of American–Slovak capitalists into already existing industrial and other enterprises (mainly in the woodworking and food industries); and the third was in the form of direct capital participation in banks. Here, the foundation in 1919 of the American–Slovak Bank in Bratislava by taking over one of the small Slovak banks, is best known.[12] In this way American resources significantly strengthened the national Slovak banking business in the 1920s. However, American–Slovak capital began to withdraw with its profits in the second half of the 1920s. In addition by 1931 the American–Slovak Bank was liquidated.[13]

Concentration in the banking system

Table 11.2 shows the development of the capital resources of the biggest banks in Slovakia.[14] By 1918, the leading national Slovak banks were already among the larger banks in Slovakia but during the 1920s they grew to such an extent that they could be compared with the medium-sized Prague banks. During the postwar decade a group of local banks was transformed from people's savings banks into modern commercial banks. The Slovenská banka's (Slovak Bank) own resources (equity and reserves) as well as its creditors increased sixfold. Even more outstanding was the 'spurt' made by the Tatra Bank (see Table 11.2). The continuing process of concentration in the banking system was further underlined by the successive takeover of the majority shares of the equity of smaller banks by the leading banks, so that a number of outwardly independent banks were in reality subsidiaries of the leading big banks. For example, one of the bigger banks, the Eskontná a hospodárska banka in Bratislava, was affiliated to the Tatra Bank which possessed the majority of its joint-stock capital (see Table 11.2). Concurrently the network of branch offices which concentrated on deposit acquisition increased. It is, however, necessary to emphasize that in spite of this buoyant growth even the biggest Slovak banks remained institutions of only provincial significance. Thus, for example, the total liabilities of all Slovak banks were at the end of 1929 4.7 million Kč, whereas the total liabilities of the joint-stock banks of the Czech Lands amounted to 30 thousand million Kč. While the assets of the biggest Slovak bank in Bratislava amounted to around 670 million Kč, the Živnostenská banka in Prague had in 1929 5.680 million Kč at its disposal.

Table 11.1 indicates among other things an extraordinary increase in savings accounts during the 1920s, but other areas of the credit system in Slovakia also registered exceptional growth. Indeed, the increase in the sum of deposits was significantly larger than that of economic growth. In view of the nature of the general economic conditions in Slovakia it is more likely that the increase in savings accounts was not the result of a greater propensity of the population to save but a transfer of individual and family hoards to credit institutions.

During the postwar years, new spheres of activity were introduced into the credit system of Slovakia. These were, above all, new types of people's savings banks. Business was expanded on the cooperative principle, especially by the Raiffeisen-type credit cooperatives operating within individual villages, and further by peasants' mutual savings banks of the Schultze-Delitsch type operating within individual districts and tradesmen's credit institutions acting within counties. In addition, a group of communal savings banks was founded. Another important part of the credit system in Slovakia consisted of branch offices of the Zemská banka česká (Bohemian Country Bank) and Hypoteční banka (Bohemian Mortgage Bank) in Bratislava, whose equity was financed from state funds. These began to offer services which so far had been unknown in Slovakia by providing communal, mortgage and building credits on the basis of issuing obligations. In this way the structure of the credit system of Slovakia began to resemble that of the Czech Lands.

Table 11.2 Capital resources of the biggest banks in Slovakia (in million crowns at the end of year)

	1921 A	1921 B	1924 A	1924 B	1929 A	1929 B	1933 A	1933 B	1937 A	1937 B
1. Americko-slovenská banka, Bratislava	27.2	93.4	37.7	122.8	37.9	124.7	–	–	–	–
2. Slovenská banka Bratislava	113.1	542.1	114.3	367.4	116.7	550.3	37.3	472.1	38.3	457.7
3. Tatra banka Turč. Sv. Martin	90.0	365.7	91.0	443.9	91.7	624.5	46.0	459.4	46.4	505.7
4. Národná banka, Banská Bystrica	20.3	86.8	14.3	91.9	14.8	129.9	20.3	132.9	19.0	137.3
5. Ľudová banka Ružomberok	9.4	44.6	9.1	27.0	11.5	46.9	17.0	43.8	17.9	57.3
6. Dunajská banka, Bratislava	29.0	53.2	29.5	93.1	27.4	276.9	32.9	255.5	23.7	267.7
7. Slov. všeob. úverová banka Bratislava	55.0	263.7[a]	57.8	343.8	59.2	451.2	69.9	391.2	61.6	456.1
8. Trnavská I. banka, Trnava	3.6	46.0[a]	6.1	61.6	6.6	90.5	6.6	81.2	6.6	80.8
9. Eskontná a hospodárska banka Bratislava	2.0	40.8	13.5	130.3	22.2	151.0	12.0	59.1	12.0	60.2
10. Tekovská banka Levice	3.2	26.3	4.2	50.7	8.8	124.6	11.9	104.5	12.9	113.1
11. Bratis. všeobecná banka Bratislava	15.6	114.6	16.4	175.2	27.5	283.2	28.0	231.6	28.6	234.3
12. Spišská banka Kežmarok	6.3	26.1	6.5	46.0	9.3	86.7	9.6	66.5	9.9	68.5
13. Bratisl. I. sporivá banka Bratislava	11.2	92.3	11.6	114.4	14.3	156.2	20.8	183.3	24.8	172.8
14. Košická banka, Košice	–	–	6.6	37.8	6.5	39.9	6.6	38.8	6.6	39.2

Notes:
[a] 1922.
A Joint-stock capital and reserves.
B Deposits and creditors.
Nationality of the banks.
1–5 Slovak
6–10 Mixed
11–12 German
13–14 Hungarian.

One of the most important new facets of the Slovak credit system was the Czech banks' branches. As early as 1919 the following banks established branches in Slovakia: the Živnostenská banka Praha, the Moravská agrární a průmyslová banka Brno (Moravian Agrarian and Industrial Bank, later Moravská banka = Moravian Bank), the Ústřední banka českých spořitelen (Central Bank of Czech Savings Institutions), Banka Bohemia (Bohemian Bank), which went bankrupt in 1923, and the Pražská úvěrní banka (Prague Credit Bank, which from 1930 was the Anglo-Czechoslovak and Prague Credit Bank). Somewhat later further branches were opened by the Agrární banka (Agrarian Bank), the Česká banka Union (Bohemian Union Bank), the Česká průmyslová banka (Czech Industry Bank) and especially the Banka československých legií = Legiobanka (Bank of the Czechoslovak Legionaries). In 1930 there were seventeen branches of eight commercial banks whose head offices were in the Czech Lands.[15] Furthermore, because of the dramatic expansion of the Banka československých legií in Slovakia by the end of the 1920s its capital was predominant in thirteen local banks in which two big banks were included: the Slovenská všeobecná úvěrová banka and the Americko-slovenská banka (which liquidated its business in 1931). Both these banks had together 40 branches and nineteen affiliated credit institutions. During the 1930s the Legiobanka succeeded in gaining the majority in another comparatively large bank, the Trnavská I. banka, with its branches. A further large institution, the Bratislavská všeobecná banka (Bratislava General Bank), was already in 1921 drawn into the orbit of the Bohemian Escompte Bank and Credit Institute (= BEBCA) and also somewhat later of the Anglo-Prago Bank. Viennese, Belgian and Czech capital participated shortly after 1918 in a relatively large Slovak bank, the Dunajská banka (Danube Bank) in Bratislava (which in 1930 participated as a majority shareholder in seven further local banks), but soon Viennese capital (through the firm of S. and M. Reitzes) predominated.

The branches of Czech banks in Slovakia became an extraordinarily important factor for the Slovak capital market, and among them the Živnostenská banka and Banka československých legií held the dominant position. At this time exact quantitative information about the credit facilities provided by this network of branches is not available. It is difficult to reach a reliable estimate because it is well known that a number of credits in Slovakia was provided directly by the Prague head offices of these banks, and also by some of their subsidiary enterprises situated in the Czech Lands. The branches of Czech banks in Slovakia not only channelled financial resources from the Czech Lands into Slovakia, but also gathered up deposits from the local population, including resources from business enterprises. There is very little information about these activities. A contemporary expert estimated in 1930 that the deposits in Czech bank branches in Slovakia amounted to about 500 million Kč.[16] The significance of their business may be judged by the fact that, for example, the branches of the Živnostenská banka employed 120 staff at the end of the 1930s. This number of employees equalled the total employed by the head offices of two biggest Slovak banks – the Slovenská banka and the Tatra banka.[17] Whereas the branches of Czech banks in Slovakia became common place there were hardly any branches of Slovak banks to be found in the Czech Lands; the exception was the Americko-slovenská banks, which between 1920 and 1926 had a branch in Prague.

Slovak industry was traditionally more dependent on financial resources from outside Slovakia than industry in the Czech Lands. It is therefore obvious that the events of 1918, which resulted in the drying up of credit supplies from Vienna and Budapest, led to a steep rise in demand for credit in the new Czechoslovakia. In Slovakia this demand was necessarily greater. Therefore the interest rate for loans was significantly higher than in the Czech Lands. While joint-stock banks in the Czech Lands charged interest rates for overdrafts on current accounts of between 7.5 and 9.5 per cent during the 1920s, banks in Slovakia charged 11 to 14 per cent, but much higher interest rates were also common. While in the Czech Lands the interest rates charged to industrial customers of the big banks were, on the whole, agreed and controlled by cartel agreements (which included also interest on deposits), nothing of the sort existed in Slovakia and attempts to equalize interest rates for deposits failed at the end of the 1920s. The Slovak banks generally incurred higher costs and also the higher rates of interest paid on deposits were reflected in the higher rates of interest on loans. The different levels of interest on deposits and on loans were also a result of the different relationships between banks and popular savings institutions in the Czech Lands and in Slovakia. In the Czech Lands the people's savings institutes permanently provided the banks with funds from their deposits and, at the same time, the sphere of their credit operations was more or less defined and divided between them. In Slovakia the division between customers of banks had not yet developed; the people's savings institutions did not provide the joint-stock banks with funds from their deposits (often they did not have any such funds to spare) and, indeed, in the struggle to attract deposits they were competitors. The possibilities of mobilizing funds collected from small savers were limited both for people's savings institutions and for the banks even though they were interested in the credit-financing of industry.

Expansion of banking into industry
The new political and economic situation in Slovakia after the break-up of Austria–Hungary created favourable conditions for the expansion of banking into industry. In addition to the objective circumstances following upon the disintegration of the Monarchy legislative conditions favoured this expansion by means of the so-called nostrification of enterprises which required the transfer of seats of companies whose head offices were abroad to the territory of the Czechoslovak state and which stipulated that the majority of members on

boards of directors had to be Czechoslovak citizens. An Interministerial Commission supervised and controlled this process and saw to it that simultaneously capital was transferred into Czechoslovak ownership and that also Czechoslovak banks gained greater opportunities to provide credit to such companies. This also presented opportunities for banks in Slovakia to expand their direct capital participation in industrial enterprises. They, however, took little advantage of these possibilities and when they realized their interest in industrial companies these usually did not belong to the most advanced and best in the respective branches of production.

Nostrification of the large industrial companies in Slovakia was carried out by the big banks of the Czech Lands and in this process they replaced the hegemony of the Budapest and Vienna banks.[18] Consequently, they also took over the business of credit-financing industrial firms. Thus the big banks of the Czech Lands which established their branches in Slovakia after the war became the financiers of Slovak large factory enterprises, commerce and foreign trade.

During the 1920s the number of direct capital participation of Slovak banks in industrial and commercial enterprises grew relatively fast, however not as a result of nostrification but as a result of the foundation of new companies by the banks. Also this activity was directed to enterprises of local significance, mainly in the wood industry, in food processing, hotels and spas, building firms and enterprises producing building materials, etc. In relation to these enterprises Slovak banks became the main providers of credit.

In connection with the reorganization of production and markets in Central Europe during the 1920s the capacity of large industry was temporarily reduced in Slovakia ('deindustrialization') and the recovery of employment in large enterprises progressed only slowly. On the other hand, small enterprises with up to 20 employees registered relative growth, supported by credits from Slovak banks. For the smaller firms conducting business in manufacturing, commerce and services the cheaper credit of the Czech big banks was often not obtainable as the Czech banks were not interested in this type of customer.

There can be no doubt that the industrial and commercial activity of Slovak banks increased substantially during the 1920s. However, they continued to be concerned with small and medium-sized enterprises. When large industrial enterprises appeared among their clientele the credit by a Slovak bank was often provided as part of a consortium with one of the big banks from the Czech Lands. Possibilities of independent credit-financing of the largest industrial companies in Slovakia were limited also by law which stipulated that credit extended to one single customer would not exceed 10 per cent of the bank's own equity (capital and reserves).[19]

In spite of the massive growth of their clientele and their credit turnover the character of the Slovak banks remained provincial. In the structure of their business operations agricultural credits ranked first. Objectively this was underpinned by the agricultural character of the Slovak economy and by the temporary check to the process of industrialization as well as by the land reform after 1918. Due to the division of former feudal estates and the increase in peasant ownership of land, large sums of money were mobilized in Slovakia. While in the process of nostrification Slovak banks remained an inferior outsider, they played a leading role in the financing of land reform in Slovakia, although the participation of some of the Czech banks was not negligible (e.g. the Banka československých legií, Agrární banka, and Moravská banka).

The types of credit granted by the Slovak banks corresponded to the character of their business. In the conditions of the industrially advanced Czech Lands after the First World War the importance of discounting bills of exchange as a source of financing industry declined. In Slovakia bills of exchange were commonly used as collateral for credits on current account. Bank records contain many cases of so-called registered bills of exchange which functioned in a similar way to mortgages as collateral for long-term credits.[20]

The Slovak joint-stock banks were severely shaken by the world economic crisis of the 1930s which challenged the results achieved in the previous decade. The full blast of the crisis hit the banks in 1931 when business bankruptcies intensified and bank losses reached multimillion currency units. Credit facilities were frozen; losses of banks were derived from the plummeting prices of securities and the cessation of dividends on their capital participation; the crisis led to runs on deposits and to the draining of credits on current accounts. As a number of commercial banks collapsed savers lost confidence in them and transferred their savings to people's savings institutions. Slovak banks experienced problems of liquidity and lost their ability to support even their best customers with loans. The National Bank as the bank of issue and some other institutions assisted by rediscounting bills and other transactions in order to prevent the collapse of the big banks. These measures were insufficient and equally inadequate was the assistance of the state which amended the banking legislation in 1932 and which enabled the carrying out of a second rescue action of banks.[21] It proved impossible to cover the losses of banks in this way and they had to write off large sums from their own resources.

Hardest hit by the banking crisis in Slovakia were the biggest banks which were based on Slovak capital. The Slovenská banka reduced its equity to a third, and the Tatra banka to a half, as did the case of its subsidiary bank, the Eskontná a hospodárska banka; the Americko-slovenská banka was liquidated as were a number of smaller banks. At the same time their deposits and credits on current account were substantially reduced which weakened their leading position in the banking system of Slovakia. On the other hand the financially weaker banks of the leading group of fourteen banks in Slovakia retained their position and some of them even gained in strength. In the case of the Slovenská všeobecná úverná banka in Bratislava a thorough reconstruction of its capital led to the withdrawal of the majority influence of the Česká eskontní banka a úvěrní ústav (BEBCA – Austrian–German–Belgian–Czech capital) and the capital participation bought by the Legiobanka became predominant while the positions of the national Slovak capital almost disappeared. Thus this bank became the third largest in Slovakia at the same time as behind the Slovak exterior the position of Czech capital in Slovakia was strengthened.[22]

If the course of the 1930s banking crisis in the Czech Lands is compared with that in Slovakia it emerges that, while the overall strength of banking capital was reduced, the relative importance of the biggest banks in the Czech Lands increased at the same time as that of the biggest banks in Slovakia was weakened. Already from the mid-1920s Slovak banks began to liquidate part of their direct capital participation in industrial enterprises in Slovakia, which they had acquired in the postwar years mainly through nostrification. These were chiefly minority holdings of shares acquired alongside the big Czech banks which frequently did not carry any direct participation in the credit-financing of these enterprises. For the Slovak banks it was more advantageous to sell these participations, usually to the big Czech banks cooperating with them, and to use the funds acquired by their sale for more lucrative and safer loans. The declining significance of capital participation as a means of financing industrial and commercial enterprises continued into the 1930s in spite of the fact that interest rates on loans to industry were substantially lower than in the 1920s and fell to the level customary in the Czech Lands (6–7 per cent from 1933, 5–6.5 per cent after 1935). In cases where Slovak banks had gained a majority participation and where it was possible to speak of a relationship of the bank to its subsidiary company they did not sell their participation; on the contrary, they cemented their influence by granting credits to these subsidiary enterprises. Therefore, the credit-financing of industrial enterprises by Slovak banks became a permanent feature of their business even though the largest industrial companies were only seldom in their sphere of influence. This business continued to be dominated by the branches of the big Czech banks.

In the second half of the 1930s a new competitor appeared in the capital market: agricultural credit cooperatives, especially their main organization, the Rolnické vzájemné pokladnice (Peasants' Mutual Trusts). They began to deploy large savings which they used through their head office for the financing of industry. The Zväz rol'nických vzájomných pokladnic (Association of Peasant Mutual Trusts) began to function like a bank (in fact it became the Sedliacká banka – Peasants Bank during the Second World War), founded new enterprises especially in the food industry, financed its production and participated in the purchase of agricultural products.[23]

During the 1930s the orientation of the Slovak banks towards small and medium-sized enterprises continued, since the reduction of their disposable resources during the Great Depression definitely ended their aspirations to penetrate the capital and credit business of large enterprises in Slovakia. Because of the great losses experienced during the crisis especially in the sphere of credit-financing of industry they became more cautious in this area.

Altogether, the experiences of the Great Depression led to measures which were to limit the speculation of debtors in the area of Czechoslovak banking. To this purpose the legal regulation of 1936[24] stipulated that financial institutions had to provide the National Bank of Czechoslovakia with a list of names of debtors who had received loans of 100 000 Kč and over (except for mutual loans between financial institutions) as well as a list of guarantors (collateral) for these loans. If the name of a debtor appeared on the lists of several banks the National Bank was obliged to inform the banks concerned about this fact. It is typical of the Slovak banks that they asked for the lowering of the limits of loans which were to be reported to the National Bank.[25]

During the years after the crisis of 1929–33 investments began to increase in Slovakia (contrary to the development in the Czech Lands) which renewed the process of industrialization in Slovakia. This was connected with the preparations for the possible outbreak of war. Great improvements in transport as well as partial electrification projects were financed by the state. New large industrial enterprises were financed by the big Czech banks or by the big industrial firms themselves. Slovak banks hardly took any part in this. In accordance with their character and orientation as well as their financial possibilities they participated in the financing (capital participation and loans) in secondary investments which resulted from the multiplier effect of the investments by the state, the Czech big banks and large industrial companies.

In spite of the development of industrialization in Slovakia after 1933 reports of the Slovak banks as well as other documents indicate a certain deindustrialization concerning the business, especially credit operations, of these banks at that time. This conclusion has to be qualified, for changes occurred which favoured agriculture and small businesses, while the banks directed their interest towards low-risk investments such as government securities. One could even say that their participation in financing the state led also to their participation in financing state investments in Slovakia.

A special statistical investigation shows the division of credits granted to the individual sectors of the national economy in Slovakia and in the Carpatho-Ukraine at the end of 1934. According to this investigation[26] the joint-stock banks in the eastern parts of the Czechoslovak state had provided a total of credits amounting to 2457.1 million Kč. Out of this total 999.7 million Kč was directed to agriculture, 582.0 million Kč to industry and trade, 447.5 million Kč to commercial business, 209.2 million Kč were taken up by mortgages and housing and the rest by other loans. Agricultural credit was and remained until the fall of the Republic the most important part of the credit operations of the Slovak banks. Finally, this was in accordance with the character of the Slovak economy after almost 20 years of Czechoslovakia's existence. The agrarian character of this part of the state continued. More than half of the population was dependent on agriculture and industry remained insufficiently developed.

Notes

1. 'Československé banky v roce 1918' (Czechoslovak Banks in the Year 1918), *Statistics of Ministry of Finance*, Praha, 1921.
2. See J. Faltus and V. *Průcha, Prehl'ad hospodárskeho vývoja na Slovensku v rokoch 1918–1945* (Survey of Economic Development in Slovakia in the Years 1918–1945), Bratislava, 1969, p. 240.
3. These are listed in I. Thurzo, 'Vývoj peňažníctva na Slovensku od politického prevratu do roku 1928' (Development of Banking in Slovakia from the Political Upheaval to 1928), in *Almanach československého peněžnictví* (Almanac of Czechoslovak Banking), Praha, 1928, pp. 293–4.
4. *Československý kompas – sborník peněžnictví* (Czechoslovak Compass – Volume of Banking), Praha, 1924, p. 304.
5. *Compass – Tschechoslowakei*, Wien, 1924, p. 185.
6. Vládne nariadenie 465 zo dňa 27.7.1920 (Order in Council 465 from 27.7.1920).
7. Zákon 151 zo dňa 4.7.1923 (Act of Parliament 151 from 4.7.1923).
8. Compiled from *Zprávy Státního úřadu statistického* (Reports of the State Statistical Office), Booklets 12–13/1923, 44–46/1926, 183–184/1930, 199–200/1934, 43–44/1938.
9. *III. Jahresbericht des Verbandes der Geldinstitute in Slovensko und P. Rus vom Jahre 1922*, Part I, pp. 35, 41, 48.
10. J. Faltus, *Povojnová hospodárska kríza v rokoch 1921–1923 v Československu* (Afterwar Economic Depression of the Years 1921–1923 in Czechoslovakia), Bratislava, 1966, pp. 227 and 250 f.
11. K. Stodola, 'Hospodársky rozvoj Slovenska od roku 1918' (Economic Development of Slovakia from 1918) in *Slovensko kedysi a teraz* (Slovakia Once and Now), ed. R.W. Seton-Watson, Praha, 1931, p. 272.
12. It was Rol'nicka a priemyselná banka in Bratislava (Peasants and the Industrial Bank, formerly in Malacky and in Vel'ké Leváre).
13. *Československé bursovní papíry* (Czechoslovak Stock Exchange Papers), ed. J. Kasppar, vol. VII, 1931/1932, p. 347.
14. See note 8. The average exchange rate of 1 Lstg was Kč 313 in 1921, Kč 164 in 1924 and 1929, Kč 112 in 1933 and Kč 125 in 1937.
15. *Československé bursovní papíry*, vol. VIII, 1931/32, at the individual banks.
16. F. Houdek, 'Bankovníctvo a peňažníctvo' (Banking and Finance), in *Slovensko kedysi a teraz* (Slovakia Once and Now), ed. R.W. Seton-Watson, Praha, 1931, p. 289.
17. Š. Horváth and J. Valach, *Peňažníctvo na Slovensku 1918–1945* (Banking in Slovakia 1918–1945), Bratislava, 1978, p. 137.
18. J. Faltus, 'Nostrifikácia po I. svetovej vojne ako nástroj upevnenia českého finančného kapitálu' (Nostrification after the First World War as an Instrument of Establishing Czech Financial Capital), in *Politická ekonomie*, vol. 1, 1961, p. 28–37.
19. Zákon 239 z 10.10.1924 (Act of Parliament 239 from 10.10.1924).
20. J. Faltus and V. Průcha, op. cit., – note 2, p. 254.
21. M. Ubiria, V. Kadlec and J. Matas, *Peněžní a úvěrová soustava ČSR za kapitalismu* (Money and Credit System of Czechoslovakia under Capitalism), Praha, 1958, p. 197.
22. J. Faltus and V. Průcha, op. cit., – note 2, p. 246.
23. Ibid., p. 258.
24. Vládne nariadenie 109 zo dňa 24.4.1936 (Order in Council 109 from 24.4.1936).
25. *Deset let Národní banky československé* (Ten Years of the National Bank of Czechoslovakia), Praha, 1937, p. 227.
26. K. Maiwald, 'Vývoj a skladba úvěrových vztahů' (Development and Structure of Credit Relations), in *Statistický obzor* (Statistical Review), vol. XVII, 1936, p. 52 f.

12 'Mushrooms and dinosaurs': Sieghart and the Boden-Credit-Anstalt during the 1920s[1]

P.L. Cottrell

> A day that hath no *pridie* no *postridie*, yesterday doth not usher it in, nor tomorrow shall not drive it out. *Methusalem*, with all his hundreds of years, was but a mushroom of a night's growth, to this day. And all the Four Monarchies, with all their thousands of years, and all the powerful Kings and all the beautiful Queens of this world, were but as a bed of flowers, some gathered at six, some at seven, some at eight, All in one Morning, in respect of this Day.

John Donne, lxxiii, 30 April 1626, Eternity.

Both mushrooms and dinosaurs play powerfully upon the human psyche, conjuring up a range of potent images. Their application to financial history may be regarded as unwarranted, but, none the less, even in this historical specialism, they can evoke appropriate images for assisting understanding, as with the collapse of the 'system' of Austrian investment banking during the 1920s. Mushroom is an appropriate metaphor for the inflation and hyperinflation of the early 1920s, which led to an enlargement of the Austrian financial sector, as more and more intermediaries came to play a role in the burgeoning monetary expansion. Staffs expanded, if only to enter more 'zeros' in the ledgers recording the process, whereas the consequent increase in personnel costs was to be a major problem during the subsequent liquidation. There was also a mushroom of a parallel new issues boom, arising from attempts to try to keep capitals in contact with paper values. Actually the market 'manufacture' of paper securities provided activity and, through related issuing commissions, yielded revenues for the banks to maintain their nominal profits. As supposedly happened in the USA in the late 1920s, life in Vienna came increasingly to be centred on the Börse during the inflation and, moreover, for a further fifteen months following monetary stabilization.[2]

There were also the dinosaurs, the Austrian investment banks established between the mid-1850s and the early 1880s. They were now dinosaurs as their world had changed beyond recognition, arising from the consequences of the First World War. These banks had been the premier financial institutions of the pre-1918 'imperial' economy, but that edifice had been shattered by the national revolutions of the Autumn of 1918. Despite the new geopolitics of Central and Eastern Europe arising from the collapse of the Dual Monarchy, none the less an expectation persisted amongst men of affairs that these banks could maintain their former role, so sustaining Vienna as the commercial and financial centre of the region. To some, such as Schumpeter in 1919, this was to provide in large part the foundation for the whole economy of the 'new' Austria. To Western financial interests, frequently for the first time encountering the region in depth, the Austrian investment banks appeared to offer the ideal entrée. Such attitudes were, understandably but ultimately misguidedly, confirmed by the paper activity of the inflation and its immediate aftermath – the Viennese stock exchange boom of 1923.[3] The changed reality only became clear from 1924, following the failure of a bear attack upon the French franc, in which many Austrian banks had played a substantial part.

The post-inflation situation consisted of the painful, both socially and politically, structural transformation of the economic base of the 'new' Austria. This lacked sufficient mineral sources of energy and was unable to feed the Republic's population, of which a third – some 2 million – resided in Vienna, the former imperial capital. Further constraints on required structural change were imposed in part by the continuing hostility of the successor states towards the 'new' Austria. Actually, within the financial realm, such centrifugal forces had been in play since the 1860s, marked by the rise of Budapest and Prague as secondary centres. This process was merely accelerated by the politico-economic consequences of the national revolutions of Autumn 1918. An overall, clear marker of the predicament was the slow growth of Austrian real national income per capita – at approximately 0.35 per cent per annum between 1913 and 1929 (national boundaries of 1919 to 1938).[4]

The Austrian economy did expand during the 'golden', although somewhat tarnished, years of the late 1920s – in terms of GNP per capita by 10 per cent overall. Such growth during the 'boom' of the second half of the decade was to prove of little assistance to the Austrian investment banks. From the Summer of 1924 their managements continually struggled with problems of illiquidity, caused by trying to support, and thereby maintain, their institutions' industrial 'concerns'. These attempts were only partially successful. As a result, there was an implosion of the system, comprised of both bank failure and bank merger, although the latter outwardly maintained the 'system', if in an increasingly diminished form, until May 1931.

This general experience of industrial investment banking will now be considered by examining the particular fortunes of the Allgemeine Österreichische Boden-Credit Anstalt, but largely from the somewhat unusual vantage point of the attitudes of one of its main post-1918 Western institutional shareholders – the Morgan group.[5] The first section considers briefly the origins of this Austrian bank, which only became a major industrial investment institution from 1900. The circumstances in which the Morgan group became big investors in the Boden-Credit-Anstalt are reviewed in the following section. The position of the bank during the mid-1920s is outlined thereafter, and then the response of Sieghart is discussed. The denouement constitutes the concluding sections.

Origins of the Austrian bank

During the 1920s the Boden-Credit-Anstalt was headed by the energetic but grandiose Dr Rudolph Sieghart. Personally, he was allied to the Christian Social Party, an affiliation which proved to be of some importance for his bank's development as the decade unfolded. Born in the mid-1860s, Sieghart had begun in journalism, when he had 'made himself very useful to various Austrian governments, particularly in "influencing" Deputies and bribing the press'. This activity may have been responsible for Sieghart's translation to the Imperial Civil Service in the 1890s, where he became the head of the Prime Minister's Office. As a reward for services to the Habsburgs, Sieghart was made Governor of the Boden-Credit-Anstalt, *the* bank of the imperial family and the Court. Although trusted by Franz Joseph, Sieghart was disliked by others of the House of Habsburg, to the extent that, after 1916, pressure from Emperor Karl brought about his resignation from the Boden-Credit-Anstalt. With this fall from imperial favour, Sieghart returned to his earliest forte, through becoming the proprietor of the *Neues Wiener Tagblatt*. However, with the collapse of the Dual Monarchy, he was able to regain control of the Boden-Credit-Anstalt.[6]

Until the mid-1920s the Boden-Credit-Anstalt was unique amongst the 'great' Viennese banks. Institutionally, it was clearly distinguishable through combining mortgage business, its original focus, with a degree of commercial banking. Furthermore, the Boden-Credit-Anstalt had remained aloof from the movement to develop branches that had occurred during the 1900s.[7] Its highly profitable business had largely stemmed from its exclusive privileges in the mortgage field, its close associations with the Habsburgs and the Imperial Court, and its connections with some of the largest domestic railway and shipping companies. Along with the other 'great' Viennese banks, it had also undertaken government loan issues. After 1900 the bank diversified to a degree, through acquiring greater links with industrial undertakings. This resulted in the Boden-Credit-Anstalt having, by the early 1920s, a significant 'concern', comprising 129 companies operating in eleven countries which had mainly arisen from the former territories of the Dual Monarchy. Of these industrial connections, the most important to the management of the bank were: AG für Mineralöl-Industrie vormals David Fanto & Comp., the kernel of a group of 29 oil companies, the Mautner textile combine controlling 804000 spindles and 12000 looms, the Verein für chemische und metallurgische Produktion at Aussig, and the Berg- und Hütten Werks-Gesellschaft in which the Archduke Frederick had had an interest.[8]

The Boden-Credit-Anstalt was able to retain influence over a large part of its 'concern', which after Autumn 1918 was situated in antipathetic, if not hostile, new nations, through agreements with both local banks in the successor states and Western financial interests. The latter type of arrangement led to a series of Western participations in the bank's equity being established immediately after the First World War. Most of the bank's understandings over its 'concern', reached from 1918, were related to its interests in what was now Czechoslovakia, but, as Bohemia and Moravia, these provinces had constituted since the 1880s the industrial heartland of the former Imperial economy.

In 1918 the Boden-Credit-Anstalt concluded an alliance with the Živnostenská banka in order to protect its interests in the Czech Lands.[9] In the case of Berg- und Hütten (Bánská a hutní společnost), a similar arrangement was followed by an agreement with the French Schneider concern. This involved the Boden-Credit-Anstalt transferring its 100 000 shares, so giving the French undertaking absolute control over the, now Czechoslovakian, industrial company. However, this in turn led to Schneider itself acquiring shares of the Boden-Credit-Anstalt, their subsequent quotation on the Paris Bourse in May 1924, and Eugène Schneider joining the board of the Austrian bank at the request of François Marsal, the Minister of Finance.[10] Although thereby losing its equity link, the Boden-Credit-Anstalt continued to be a banker for Berg- und Hütten and gained French intermediation in its dealings with the now Czechoslovakian company. Again, similarly, with respect to the Verein für chemische und metallurgische Produktion (Spolek pro chemickou a hutní výrobu), which had close ties with the Solvay works and Solvay & Cie, Brussels, it would appear that the Boden-Credit-Anstalt maintained its interest in this substantial Czechoslovakian chemical undertaking through an arrangement made with Mutuelle Mobilière et Immobilière of Brussels in 1921. This institution was effectively the bank of the Solvay group and had acquired approximately 140 000 shares in the Boden-Credit-Anstalt during either 1919 or 1920.[11] The connection was cemented in 1921 by Janssen of the Mutuelle joining the board of the Boden-Credit-Anstalt and the Belgian financial institution taking 'an interest in various undertakings associated' with the Austrian bank.[12] Further, the Boden-Credit-Anstalt was able to place its own shares with other Western financial institutions during the immediate postwar years – with the Amsterdamsche Bank, and Lippmann, Rosenthal – and with the Assicurazioni Generali, Trieste, which had been formerly part of the bank's 'concern'.

During the early 1920s the Boden-Credit-Anstalt needed to retain as much of its industrial 'concern' as was possible, because of a sharp contraction in some of its traditional business. Although still continuing to benefit in certain circles from the prestige and lustre of its former connection with the Imperial Court and family, the Austrian revolution of October/November 1918 had brought such business on any large scale to an end. Moreover, after the war, the bank's mortgage business had become negligible, whilst the postwar nationalization of the railways and the decline of Danube river shipping, due to economic nationalism and hostility, had 'practically wiped out profits from those sources'.[13] Sieghart coped with the problem of the Erste Donau-Dampfschiffahrts-Gesellschaft, the bank's main involvement with riverine transport, by transferring a sizeable packet of this company's shares to English shipowning interests during the Autumn of 1920.[14]

The bank sustained its 'concern' over the course of the Austrian inflation and hyperinflation, and the first year of stabilization, by undertaking new capital issues on behalf of its industrial clientele. Furthermore, commissions from this activity provided three-quarters of the bank's profits.[15] However, the collapse of the Viennese Börse between November 1923 and March 1924 closed this avenue of resort.

Investment by the Morgan group

The most marked financial feature of the Austrian economy during 1923 was a bull market on the Börse. This had begun in February and continued until November, with the market index rising from 395 to 1 631. The activities of foreign speculators were apparently particularly prominent in this heady rise. Such buoyancy resulted in a parallel flotations boom, with 4 500 million ö.K (Austrian crowns) of new shares created in 1923 and even a further 2 000 million during the first quarter of 1924. Again, foreign buying was to the fore. This activity was fuelled by the realization that the post-inflation monetary stabilization of the Austrian economy had resulted in stock market prices being left badly undervalued. Further, security operations were, to some, a substitute for foreign exchange speculation, now largely ruled out by the regained stability of the Austrian crown. However the previous experience gained with the Austrian crown was transferable to other inflation affected currencies, as with the French franc in the opening months of 1924.[16]

Not all foreign acquisitions of either newly created, or existing, Austrian equity during the 1923 Viennese bull market were of a speculative character. There were major Western investments in three of the 'great' Austrian banks and, also, in some of the middle rank financial institutions. These were a marker of Western confidence in Austria's regained monetary stability – the crown was now seen as the 'Alpine dollar' – as well as yet further indication of the expectation that Vienna would remain the financial and commercial centre of 'Danubian' Europe. In July 1923, the National Provincial Bank and Lazards of London took an 'important parcel' of Credit-Anstalt shares, while in November, Hambros, with Lloyds acquired 150 000 shares of the Niederösterreichische Escompte-Gesellschaft. Similarly the Union Européenne Industrielle et Financière, the financial holding company for the East European assets of Schneider-Creusot and the Banque de l'Union Parisienne, bought 100 000 shares of the Niederösterreichische Escompte-Gesellschaft.[17] Probably the largest of such investment operations was the acquisition of 500 000 shares of the Boden-Credit-Anstalt by J. Schröder of London and the Morgan group.

In December 1922 the management of the Boden-Credit-Anstalt decided to raise the capital of its institution by 1 million 300 ö.K shares at a price of 50000 ö.K per share. Sieghart offered approximately half of these new shares to Schröders, while an American house – James Speyer – was interested in acquiring those destined for the New York market. However Baron Schröder, closely connected with the Boden-Credit-Anstalt, suggested that it should approach Morgan in the first instance. Further, he recommended the Boden-Credit-Anstalt to Morgan's London partners – Morgan Grenfell – 'as the strongest and best managed institution in Austria with control over the principal textile, oil, railways, machinery, automobile and other concerns in Austria and the Succession States'.[18] The price of entry into this 'Trust Company holding large interests in industrial concerns in Old Austria and Near East' seemed small, being '200,000 to 250,000 shares at under four shillings a piece'. Morgans in New York immediately agreed to the proposal, cabling:[19]

> In addition to the hope that it may prove a profitable venture, we are influenced in our decision by our desire [to] assist Austria and hope that the public knowledge of our participation in this business may be of some influence in reviving general confidence in the ultimate economic recovery of Austria.

Consequently, J.P. Morgan & Co., who had been one of the principal bankers to the 1923 League of Nations Austrian stabilization loan, acquired, through Schröders, 250 000 shares in the Boden-Credit-Anstalt at a cost of £38 631 4s 2d.,[20] and Morgan Grenfell subsequently took up a quarter of this interest.[21] The initial arrangements for the transaction were for the 'Morgan' shares to be deposited in Vienna until 31 December 1925, while, thereafter, the Boden-Credit-Anstalt was to have an option on them at terms comparable to a third party bargain.[22] Morgans in New York agreed to this arrangement, provided it was approved by Baron Schröder.[23] However, the American bankers could not accept a subsidiary provision, making the Boden-Credit-Anstalt its sole Austrian correspondent, as they already had established agents in Vienna for the issue of 'letters of credit'.[24] This agreement was soon overturned by the opportunities stemming from the continuing rise in share prices on the Viennese market.

Morgans certainly benefited, on paper, from the Viennese bull market. They participated in a syndicate organized by the Boden-Credit-Anstalt for floating more of its shares,[25] and, with Schröders, took up their rights in the flotation.[26]

By October 1923 J.P. Morgan & Co. had seen an appreciation of $1.3 million on their interest in the Boden-Credit-Anstalt and within a further month this had risen to $1.6 million. Despite such a substantial book profit, T.W. Lamont of Morgans, New York, was anxious to sell nearly all of his house's holding at

$1.5 million, to either any other of the Western connections that the Austrian bank had acquired since 1918, or, more generally, 'acceptable London stock-holders'.[27] Morgan Grenfell in London agreed with this intent, but Schröder indicated that such a sale would have a detrimental effect. In the Baron's appreciation even its suggestion would upset the management of the Boden-Credit-Anstalt. For his part, Schröder remained convinced that the investment they had jointly made, and augmented, remained good. In his view it continued to be 'undervalued' by the market and he further pointed out that the Boden-Credit-Anstalt's shares had been introduced on the Paris Bourse, while an application for dealings had been made to the London Stock Exchange.[28] With such an opposing stance taken by their co-partner, Lamont let the matter drop, explaining his original rationale: 'we simply did not know but what, with the great rise in the shares, we might be doing a favour to somebody in the family, so to speak, if we let them take on some of our stock at a very great concession under the market.'[29]

Morgans would have done well, if they had foregone loyalty to Schröders, as November 1923 proved to be the apogee of the Viennese financial boom. By the end of May 1924 market quotations had halved.[30] It is difficult to establish how far the rise, and then the fall, on the Vienna Börse were products of foreign speculation – xenophobia is nearly always the basis for some to provide an explanation. None the less, in the case of the big Viennese banks, the course of the market over 1923, and responses to it, had led to Western financial interests acquiring further equity participations in these institutions – and some were larger than had been established during the inflation period.

The collapse of the Börse, coupled with the failure of the 'bear' attack upon the French franc during the early months of 1924, had very detrimental effects on the liquidity of the Viennese banks. This was heightened by a parallel withdrawal of foreign credits provided to them.[31] Their assets became frozen and depreciated. The consequences became rapidly apparent. With the effective rebuttal of the attack on the French franc, arising from a loan provided by Morgans to the Bank of France, the Allgemeine Industriebank collapsed immediately, together with six other significant banks, while even the outwardly respectable Postsparkassa Amt encountered severe difficulties. Within a year 100 Austrian banks had ceased business, of which 23 had been joint-stock institutions, including the sizeable Allgemeine Depositen-Bank. Subsequent parliamentary investigations revealed seamy relations in the franc speculation between Christian Social politicians and, particularly, the Austrian provincial banks. The ultimate toll for the Austrian financial sector of this ill-fated speculation was not to become clear until 1926.[32]

The illiquidity was met initially by Alfred R. Zimmerman, the League of Nation's Commissioner for Austria, releasing part of the proceeds of the 1923 stabilization loan to support the big Viennese banks. This provoked the wrath of Governor Norman of the Bank of England, who had played a key part in mobilizing Western financial resources for the stabilization loan: 'I see no reason why funds under your control should be used to avoid difficulties caused by speculators'.[33] Zimmerman also agreed to the Austrian National Bank organizing a stock market support syndicate, but the central bank went even further by freely discounting finance bills in order to provide yet further liquidity. Consequently the National Bank's holdings of bills rose from 123.3 million schillinge to 332.9 million schillinge over the course of the first half of 1924. These other diversions from the path of strict financial orthodoxy were also to be the subject of recrimination – at a meeting between Norman and Richard Reisch, head of the Austrian National Bank, held in December 1924.

From the Spring of 1924 the Austrian economy entered the 'doldrums', a situation both compounded by, and partially arising from, political factors, international and domestic. By mid-1925 Morgans had an official agent visiting Austria – F.C. Weems – a member of the statistical department of the New York house. Such an observer may indicate that some American bankers, especially as they had been responsible for the 1923 loan, were as concerned as French and English diplomats over the country's now apparent economic and political malaise.

The bank in the mid-1920s

Austria's economic and financial malaise rebounded upon the Boden-Credit-Anstalt. The bank made no profits in 1924 and was forced to draw on internal reserves to maintain its dividend. Its management had to resort to the same practice for the following year.[34] Until 1926 the Austrian bank's directors 'looked hopefully toward some kind of industrial revival in Austria and the succession states which would bring a return of profitable financing business, and in one ingenious way or another they have endeavoured in the meantime to support the bank's heavy overhead.'[35]

One example of this 'ingenuity' was the attempt to resurrect the bank's mortgage business. As a result of a visit to New York, Sieghart was able to arrange a dollar loan for the provision of agricultural credit. This was a complex transaction, but it began with the collection by the Boden-Credit-Anstalt of sufficient Pfandbriefe (mortgage letters) to establish the security, augmented by its own guarantee, for an undertaking from the European Mortgage & Investment Corporation of Boston. The $2.8 million loan was issued in New York by Lee, Higginson & Co and Schröders. Weems, Morgans' expert, thought initially that the Boden-Credit-Anstalt would be unable to amass sufficient mortgage letters and considered that the cost, a minimum of 14 per cent, would be beyond the reach of most Austrian farmers.[36] However the bank's mortgage business recovered from 1926, when the profitability of this sphere of its business doubled, although in its achievement, the bank had had to switch from 8 to 7 per cent mortgage bonds.[37]

More important were the attempts by the bank's management to sustain its 'concern' by supporting its client industrial firms, through the provision of foreign credits either to finance foreign trade, or to provide direct finance. Such resources for Austrian, and other Danubian, firms were difficult to obtain in the mid-1920s. They had been substantially withdrawn in the aftermath of the 'franc crisis', so compounding the Alpine Republic's post-inflation shortage of finance. For instance, 'Austrian' nominal monthly debit balances with the London acceptance house of Kleinwort Sons & Co. fell from £2.1 million in May 1924 down to £1.2 million by September 1924 and were not to exceed the £2 million mark again until December 1928.[38] It is only possible to establish in part the extent of the Boden-Credit-Anstalt's success in raising Western credits and loans to succour its industrial 'concern' during the difficult mid-1920s. Immediately following the 'franc crisis', this Austrian bank secured an account with Kleinwort, Sons & Co., which provided immediately a £0.1 million reimbursement credit. Some of the Boden-Credit-Anstalt's larger industrial clients could raise such credits without its intermediation and, for instance, Zuckerfabriken Schoeller & Co AG had had an account with Kleinworts before that of the Boden-Credit-Anstalt itself.

As credit and capital supply problems became graver in Austria during the mid-1920s, so more of the constituents of the Boden-Credit-Anstalt's concern directly sought facilities on Western markets. For instance, in December 1925 the International Export-und Import AG approached Kleinworts[39] and a month later Kux, Bloch & Co., Kleinworts's Viennese correspondents, relayed a request for a draft credit of £60 000 for twelve to fifteen months from the Öster-reichische Waffenfabriks-Gesellschaft (Steyr). This proposal perplexed the London house, which in any case disapproved of financing the export of motor cars over such a relatively long term. Above all, what Kleinworts partners could not comprehend was why the Boden-Credit-Anstalt was not arranging such business itself.[40] The apparent inability of the Boden-Credit-Anstalt to support its 'concern' financially had the danger that certain companies, partic-ularly the larger ones now situated in the successor states, would seek other local bankers and thereby totally break away from it. In 1924, for instance, the important sugar credit negotiations for Schoeller were finally concluded by the Živnostenská banka and the Česká eskomptní banka a úvěrní ústav.[41] In this situation, Sieghart searched everywhere for assistance and in August 1925 attempted to negotiate a $4.5 million 30-year loan at 7.5 per cent for the Danube Steam Navigation Company, the English company which, from 1920, had held the shares of the Erste Donau-Dampfschiffahrts-Gesellschaft. These talks were held with Lisman & Co. of New York, one of the second rate American houses handling Austrian provincial loan issues.[42]

Morgans of New York may have provided the Boden-Credit-Anstalt with commercial credits during the Spring of 1923; the question was certainly raised, along with raw material purchases, by Weiner, the bank's then general manager, with Anderson in April. The Austrian banker also held discussions with J.H. Schröder in London and with Morgan, Harjes & Co. in Paris.[43] Over the rest of the 1920s and with respect to 'the Morgan group', the Boden-Credit-Anstalt established the closest links with Morgan, Harjes & Co. for the provision of credits. Sieghart visited the Paris Morgan house in mid-1925, discussing a £0.4 million sugar export credit for Zuckerfabriken Schoeller & Co. AG, one of the major Czechoslovakian refineries, other sugar credit business, and a one-year loan for an Austrian brewery.[44] Ultimately the Schoeller credit was negotiated by a Prague bank, while the brewery loan transpired to be for five years, rather than one, and so was declined.[45]

Generally, after the Summer of 1923, the London and New York Morgan houses had few business dealings with the Boden-Credit-Anstalt, but, none the less, the New York house felt that it had acquired a 'moral' responsibility for the credit rating of the Austrian bank in the USA. By 1926 this proved to be a burden which the New York Morgan partners considered that they could no longer bear.[46] Accordingly, Morgans of New York decided to sell their shares in the Boden-Credit-Anstalt which were now released from the two-year deposit arrangement.

Other considerations, apart from moral responsibility, may also have played a part in reaching this decision. Morgans were not quite so innocent of the Boden-Credit-Anstalt's affairs as they occasionally implied, since in 1925 an attempt had been made to examine them on the ground by F.C. Weems. Weems's letters from Vienna were not encouraging and, for instance, he had been to discover, but not easily, something about the Boden-Credit-Anstalt's exposure with respect to the critical Polish financial situation during the mid-1920s. The Austrian bank had had a sizeable interest in the Bank Małopolski AG since 1921.[47] Moreover, the Boden-Credit-Anstalt had also extended major credits to this Polish bank. By September 1925, along with nearly every other Polish financial institution, the Malopolski was in difficulties and, furthermore, was unable to raise readily fresh resources. One of the directors of the Boden-Credit-Anstalt had persuaded a very unwilling Polish National Bank to provide a 0.5 million Zloty credit, although publicly the Polish Central Bank was unable to discount bills. Actually, while Weems was in Vienna, Rudolf Steiner and Ernst Garr of the Boden Credit-Anstalt were visiting Warsaw to discover if any other major shareholder in the Małopolski was prepared to provide it with fresh capital. All in all, unless the situation could not be contained, the Boden-Credit-Anstalt faced a large-scale disaster in Poland. While the Viennese bank had reduced its equity stake in the Małopolski, it none the less had provided secured credits, totalling $0.8 million, most of which had been granted since the Polish situation had turned sour. It appeared to Weems that the Boden-Credit-Anstalt's management were relying, in the last resort, on the Polish government to take an initiative to relieve the strain.[48]

Morgans' decision to extricate themselves from the Boden-Credit-Anstalt was explained to Sieghart by Weems on three counts. These consisted of a thinly veiled reference to the American bank's unsupportable moral responsibility; its practice of not identifying itself with other banking institutions, even in the USA, when Morgans played no active part in their management; and, lastly, the difficulties of comprehending the Austrian bank's 'concern'. Sieghart expressed surprise at Morgans' decision, maintaining that he had believed that Weems's investigations of 1925 had 'only strengthened your good opinion of our institution'. However, part of what transpired during Weems's direct discussions with Sieghart may only have increased the American's unease. The Austrian banker had tried to secure the more active cooperation of the New York house 'in the carrying through of the financial transactions of our combine'.[49]

A dilemma faced the Boden-Credit-Anstalt, caused, on the one hand, by the particular failure of the Morgan connection to provide a firm ongoing entrée to the New York market and, on the other, more generally, its own apparent inability to raise sufficient credits for its 'concern' on other Western financial centres. A way out was to change the nature of the bank. A greater emphasis on short-term commercial banking might provide both more liquid resources and diversification, thereby reducing the Boden-Credit-Anstalt's heavy postwar dependence on investment banking. There were opportunities for such a radical change of business policy, generated by the disarray within the Austrian financial sector after the 'franc crisis' of Spring 1924. However, any attempt to exploit this situation required further capital resources with which to acquire other Austrian banks in even graver straits. Yet the management of the Boden-Credit-Anstalt had some advantages, if such a radical course was to be pursued. It was well connected with both the Austrian National Bank, through Dr Reisch the President, who had formerly been the general manager of the Boden-Credit-Anstalt, and the Christian Social governments of the mid-1920s, not only as a result of Sieghart's long-standing political connections, but also through their institutionalization in Victor Kienböck's law practice acting for the bank.

Sieghart's response

The management of the Boden-Credit-Anstalt began to undertake this change in the nature of the bank during 1926. They were able to take advantage of Jakob Ahrers' bank merger policy. The Boden-Credit-Anstalt's acquisition of a series of provincial banks gave it a greater presence, albeit indirect, in the Austrian rural economy. Of more importance was its takeover of the Allgemeine Verkehrsbank, which had eighteen branches in Vienna and sixteen provincial branches, in addition to branches and associated institutions in the successor states.[50] This 'middle' bank was initially acquired by the Boden-Credit-Anstalt with support provided by the Schoeller group of companies and an industrialist, E. Hardmeyer.[51] However, initially the two banks remained apart, as the management of the Boden-Credit-Anstalt adhered to its traditional policy of a centrally organized bank without any branches. Rather, at first this step was used to transfer to the Verkehrsbank 'the class of business which did not fit in the Boden-Credit-Anstalt', while the two 'concerns' of the banks were rationalized to a degree through 'profitable combinations and mergers'.[52]

The initiative to completely transform the Boden-Credit-Anstalt into a bank with a considerable interest in commercial branch business came suddenly and swiftly. It consisted of the takeover of the Union Bank, followed by its complete fusion, together with the Verkehrsbank, into the Boden-Credit-Anstalt. Weems's appreciation for J.P. Morgan & Co. emphasized:

> how very sudden and how very bold a step it is on Dr. Sieghart's part. It evidences an aggressiveness on the part of the management and a determination to let no money-making opportunity escape through lack of flexibility or adaptability. Presumably, Dr. Sieghart, like the resourceful politician he is, recognized that the opportune moment had arrived for a complete change of front. The possibilities offered by the new line-up are very great, as are also the responsibilities. The problem of interior reorganisation in the Boden-Credit necessary to the administration of a system of branches in Vienna and in the various Austrian provinces will be very difficult, and the amalgamation of staffs and elimination of personnel ... will be rendered very burdensome by the necessity under Austrian law of indemnifying or pensioning released employees. Still, everything accomplished in the direction of simplification will be so much progress in improving economic conditions throughout Austria. And the same may be said with respect to the tasks the Boden-Credit will also have to undertake in merging and perhaps liquidating some of the competitive industrial concerns in the respective combines of the three banks participating in the fusion.[53]

The Union Bank, with ten Viennese agencies, a branch in Innsbruck, and a capital of 4000 million ö.K, was categorized as one of the Viennese 'great' banks during the early 1920s. None the less it had fallen as a direct victim of both the crash of the Viennese Börse and the 'franc crisis' of Spring 1924. The majority of its shares during the early 1920s had been acquired by Sigmund Bosel, one of the notorious speculators of the postwar period. This young man had built up his fortune during the war by supplying *matériel* and, then, during the early years of the republic he opened his own banking house.

The takeover of the Union Bank allowed and assisted the business restructuring of the Boden-Credit-Anstalt, though the transaction was substantial and required financing. It seems likely that this was facilitated, partially, by the Postsparkassa Amt holding Boden-Credit-Anstalt shares. These resulted from a direct swap for the Union Bank shares that had constituted Bosel's collateral for loans from the Postsparkassa.[54] None the less, the Boden-Credit-Anstalt's bid for the Union Bank was attractive to the Postsparkassa Amt on two counts. First, the savings bank was given a participation, running for five and a half years, in any profits arising from the disposal of the interests of the Union Bank, primarily shares held directly, or through syndicates. Second, the Boden-Credit-Anstalt provided the Postsparkassa Amt with a loan, enabling it to liquidate a debt of $5.3 million to the Comptoir d'Escompte, Geneva. This had been outstanding for some time, bore a high rate of interest and arose from Bosel's affairs. The arrangement with the Boden-Credit-Anstalt would save the Postsparkassa Amt about $0.2 million in annual interest charges.[55]

Formally, the Boden-Credit-Anstalt acquired the Postsparkassa's 3 million Union Bank shares by exchanging them for Boden-Credit-Anstalt shares at a rate of one Boden-Credit-Anstalt share for every three Union Bank shares. This was an advantageous ratio for Sieghart, as the average medium-term market quotation of three Union Bank shares had been 31.20 schillinge, as opposed to 14.90 schillinge for one Boden-Credit-Anstalt share. Similarly, the Boden-Credit-Anstalt acquired the balance of the share of the capital of the Verkehrsbank relatively cheaply, as the price struck was two Boden-Credit-Anstalt shares for every eleven of the Verkehrsbank.

The merger of the three banks was financed through raising the issued capital of the Boden-Credit-Anstalt by 15 million schillinge. It was intended that the parcel of shares that the Postsparkassa Amt thereby outwardly and publicly acquired – merely some 167000 – would not be a permanent investment. However, in the prior negotiations, Sieghart further protected the position of his bank by having the savings bank's holding deposited with the Boden-Credit-Anstalt, securing their voting rights at general meetings, and obtaining an option, as well as the pre-emption right, on them for a number of years.[56]

The complete absorption of the Union Bank and the Allgemeine Verkehrsbank was complicated by the necessary post-inflation conversion of the Boden-Credit-Anstalt's equity capital from crowns to schillinge, the new currency units. This resulted in the bank having a capital of 45 million schillinge consisting of 900 000 50-schillinge shares, of which the Morgan group held 350000, following the sale of 25 000 during February and March 1927.[57]

Finding funds

Despite the radical change in its outward nature, the Boden-Credit-Anstalt still required resources to support its now much enlarged industrial 'concern'. It might have become a multi-branch bank, but the restructuring mergers had also brought with them sizeable packets of industrial interests, thus augmenting the Boden's investment banking activities. At the bank's general meeting in May 1927, its equity capital was further increased – to 55 million schillinge – by a rights issue of 200000 new 50-schillinge shares. Sieghart was conscious of the dilution of earning power that this potentially involved, but wrote to Anderson of J.P. Morgan & Co. expressing his confidence that the bank would be able to sustain its current dividend of 7.2 per cent.[58] Although Morgan Grenfell, unlike

J.P. Morgan & Co., had fully retained its 1922/23 holding in the Austrian bank, both Anglo-Saxon houses of the Morgan group decided to sell their rights arising from their joint holding of 350 000 shares, yielding an overall profit of £153 2s. 6d.

As well as increasing the bank's capital, the Boden-Credit-Anstalt's management transferred parts of the investment portfolios of the Verkehrsbank and Union Bank to the Maatschappij vor Beheer und Effekten. This had been established by the Austrian bank's Dutch partners – the Amsterdamsche Bank and Lippman, Rosenthal – in conjunction with English and Swiss houses. Further, this Dutch 'holding' company also provided the Boden-Credit-Anstalt with an advance of 9 million florins at 9.75 per cent.

The enlargement of the bank would not appear to have been matched by a comparable expansion of the credits that it could obtain on Western markets. For instance, both the Allgemeine Verkehrsbank and the Union Bank had had accounts with Kleinwort Sons & Co., but, on their complete absorption by the Boden-Credit-Anstalt, they were closed.[59] During June 1927, the Boden-Credit-Anstalt was running three accounts with this London acceptance house, totalling only £158 505, as compared with the £0.1 million reimbursement credit that it had had since April 1924. An outline agreement was reached to raise the ceiling on these three credits by £0.1 million in October 1927 but, as with an industrial credit of £0.12 million in February 1928 and a further credit of £0.08–0.1 million, it was not put into effect. Consequently the Austrian bank's limit with Kleinworts remained at £158 505.[60]

While unsuccessfully trying to augment its Western credit lines, the Boden-Credit-Anstalt was also forced to maintain the value of its share quotation on the increasingly moribund Vienna Börse, a matter of prestige, if nothing else. This was undertaken through heavy purchases of its own shares. The resulting burden was increased by the bank undertaking a similar policy with regard to the shares of the principal companies of its 'concern'. Such policies immobilized a considerable proportion of the bank's resources and an air of desperation becomes evident as Sieghart attempted to peddle these 'bought-in' shares around the capital markets of Western Europe. In November 1927 he gave a short-term option on 50 000 of his bank's shares to Louis Hirsch, an arbitrageur.[61] Subsequently, during the Summer of 1928, a director of the Crédit Lyonnais, while in Vienna, was offered up to 175 000 shares, a packet which Sieghart was simultaneously trying to place in London. The Austrian banker expressed a preference for the shares to go to Paris, but the French authorities barred their introduction, while the real reason for the approach to the French bank would appear to have been a refusal in London. Sieghart then tried Berlin, where he discussed the possibility of the German government secretly purchasing shares in his bank, with the definite political purpose of increasing German influence within Austria.[62]

By the end of the decade further of the Boden-Credit-Anstalt's foreign share-holders now wished to withdraw, compounding the bank's financing problems. At the beginning of 1929 Sieghart returned to Paris to speak directly to officials at the Quai d'Orsay in order to find funds to take up shares that both Schröders and the Mutuelle Solvay wished to relinquish.

Pressure to merge

Sieghart's search for funds in any quarter, Paris or Berlin or London, during the early months of 1929 occurred when further mergers amongst the remaining 'great' banks were either the subject of rumour, or planned, in Vienna. Directors of the Niederösterreichische Escompte-Gesellschaft, in which there was a large French interest, were considering the desirability of a fusion with the Credit-Anstalt. Since 1927 Sieghart himself had been trying to acquire the Vienna branch of the Banque des Pays de l'Europe Centrale, a proposal which from its first airing had been firmly rejected by both the French Ministry of Finance and the Managing Director of 'Paribas'. Rebuffed in this direction, Sieghart then tried to bring off a marriage with the Wiener Bank-Verein.[63] Further banking con-centration was supported by some officials of the Austrian National Bank. It was also seen as desirable by some of the foreign institutional shareholders in the Viennese 'great' banks, as with the Banque de Bruxelles' backing for the proposed merger between the Niederösterreichische Escompte-Gesellschaft and the Credit-Anstalt.[64] By August 1929 members of Morgans' Paris house were also concerned about the position in Vienna, especially that of the Boden-Credit-Anstalt and its management by Sieghart.

It was generally acknowledged that one fusion between any two of the remaining 'great' banks would lead to the emergence of a financial institution which would then tower above the others. Such a result, together with 'pride and personal prejudice', had been the factors preventing any significant movement in this direction. Following a disquieting visit to Vienna, Benjamin Joy, of Morgan Harjes, Paris, suggested that a way to break this impasse was for Morgans to confront Sieghart with their dissatisfaction, so forcing the Austrian banker 'to make some constructive move to improve his bank's situation'. The alternative was for Morgans to sell the rump of their holding in the bank and for the Paris Morgan house to withdraw its credit at the end of the year. There was plain speaking between the Paris and New York Morgan houses, which ended with: 'Our checkings of Sieghart, even in Government circles, are not favourable so that he is of little use to us nor would his enmity be particularly harmful'.[65]

The aim of the Paris Morgan partners was to force a merger with the Wiener Bank-Verein. The time seemed ripe as the main Western institutional share-holders in both banks favoured the plan, likewise Heinz Leiner of the management of the Wiener Bank-Verein. It was expected that, if accomplished, it would introduce conservative management into the Boden-Credit-Anstalt. Anderson, for the New York Morgan partners, felt that he was unable to comment definitively and so consequently passed Joy's plan to Morgan Grenfell in London.[66] The compilation of their advice was complicated by the holiday season, but what was available struck the line that J.P. Morgan & Co. had 'no right to interfere', since the New York house had both sold a large part of its holding in the Boden-Credit-Anstalt and was currently undertaking little business with the Austrian bank.[67] However, those available within the senior management of Morgan Grenfell did not wish to be totally drawn on the matter since Morgans' co-partner, Baron Schröder, was absent from London. But, Joy's growing fears seemed to be at least partially substantiated by the Baron's own desire to resign from the Boden-Credit-Anstalt's board.

Joy accepted that the matter 'should be left until Baron Schröder returns to London in September', but even his own view of the Viennese situation was now becoming less clear. Replying to Grenfell on 20 August 1929, he stated the belief that the Paris Morgan house's credit line to the Boden-Credit-Anstalt was not 'a matter for worry at the present time, although the bank is certainly immobilized'.[68] However Joy was not prepared to allow the matter to rest, a month later reporting to Grenfell a conversation with Garr of the Boden-Credit-Anstalt. This had indicated that Sieghart had held discussions with the Wiener Bank-Verein, which had fallen through, but was now contemplating a merger with the Credit-Anstalt. This institution had been Joy's other possible marriage partner for the Boden-Credit-Anstalt. As he and Garr were both going to the USA, Joy saw an opportunity for further discussions and so he asked Grenfell to ascertain Baron Schröder's attitude. In all this, the American banker resident in Paris still accepted Grenfell's basic point that the Morgan group had no right to interfere, but he now believed that the banks in Vienna required 'some advice from a comparatively disinterested party'.[69]

Schröder fully confirmed Joy's views regarding both the general predicament of the Viennese banks and the particular position of the Boden-Credit-Anstalt. The Baron had already put pressure on Sieghart to conclude a merger, but this had only resulted in tentative negotiations, of which those with the Credit-Anstalt were the most recent. Despite this lack of success, Baron Schröder was prepared to write again to Sieghart urging the resumption of discussions with the Credit-Anstalt, but with the threat of the Baron's resignation from the Boden-Credit-Anstalt's board. The partners of Morgan Grenfell backed Schröder in this approach, pointing out that, although they felt unable to take the initiative, they would give any support, or assistance, if required.[70]

As well as outside pressure, there would appear to have been a plot for a 'Palace revolution' within the Boden-Credit-Anstalt during the late Summer of 1929. This involved a merger with the Wiener Bank-Verein under the management of Alexander Weiner, a former managing director of the Boden-Credit-Anstalt but who had left somewhat abruptly in October 1923.[71] Personal relations between Weiner and Sieghart, even in September 1929, were still very strained,[72] possibly because Weiner had been negotiating with Bosel in 1923 for a takeover of the Boden-Credit-Anstalt. Such a long-standing enmity seemed likely to limit drastically the chances of success, although the merger was backed by the Belgian institutional shareholders in the Wiener Bank-Verein. Whatever the outcome, Joy approved of pressure being brought to bear upon the Boden-Credit-Anstalt from a number of directions, 'as the situation is an increasingly serious one, and entirely apart from our stockholdings is a real concern to us all on account of the bad effect on Austrian credit in general'.

All these plans involving the Boden-Credit-Anstalt, together with others, such as the possible merger of the Niederösterreichische Escompte-Gesellschaft with the Credit-Anstalt, or the Vienna branch of the Banque des Pays de l'Europe Centrale, or, and a total different alternative, a share issue by the Niederösterreichische Escompte-Gesellschaft on the Paris market,[73] were stymied by the failure of the Boden-Credit-Anstalt. This was precipitated by a fresh upwelling of domestic political instability within Austria which had become increasingly marked since 1926. Rising friction between the Heimwehr and the Schutzbund led in September 1929 to domestic withdrawals of deposits from the Austrian banks and their conversion into dollars. This resulted in the National Bank losing over $7.5 million of *devisen* during the course of the month. The foreign exchange drain, coupled with a retreat of foreign short-term capital and rising short-term interest rates at other financial centres, forced the Austrian National Bank to raise its own discount rate from 7.5 to 8.5 per cent on 28 September. The domestic political crisis was calmed by the formation of the Schober cabinet, but the run on bank deposits and the refusal of the Austrian National Bank to continue to discount paper for the Boden-Credit-Anstalt in excess of its quota resulted in Sieghart's dinosaur closing its doors.

This drastic action on the part of the Austrian National Bank has to be put into perspective. Its holding of securities at the beginning of September 1929 had amounted to 240 million schillinge, as opposed to 183 million schillinge a year earlier and 171 million schillinge during September 1927. Over the course of September 1929 such holdings increased by 124 million schillinge, mainly as an expansion in its 'Portefeuille'. Accordingly, the central bank had attempted to take the overall strain upon the banking system, caused by both the domestic political and international monetary events of the month. However it was unable to continue to keep the Boden-Credit-Anstalt afloat. This bank's contribution to the National Bank's security holdings had risen from 18.9 per cent to 31.7 per cent over the course of 1927, the year of its full absorption of the Verkehrs-bank and the acquisition of the Union Bank. Thereafter this proportion had only fallen below 30 per cent once – at the end of June 1928 – and for the whole of

1929 had been of the order of 33.3 per cent. For two-and-three-quarter years before September 1929 the Boden-Credit-Anstalt had been substantially maintaining its liquidity through resort to the central bank.

It had become increasingly generally known during 1929 that the Boden-Credit-Anstalt was in a weak position, but in London, before the events of September, it had been expected by some that it would 'weather its troubles'.[74] As Joy had pointed out to his fellow Morgan partners in August, the bank was highly illiquid, while others, equally concerned, particularly stressed that three main constituents of its 'concern' – the Steyrwerke, the Erste Donau-Dampfschiffahrts-Gesellschaft, and the Mautner textile combine – had in aggregate at least 218 million schillinge in advances.[75]

Any 'knock-on' effects of the failure of the Boden-Credit-Anstalt upon the very fragile Austrian banking system were promptly nipped in the bud by the fusion of the now defunct bank with the Credit-Anstalt. This was brought about by the Austrian government, itself an indirect shareholder in the Boden-Credit-Anstalt via the Postsparkassa Amt, which some commentators in late 1929 reckoned might still have been holding as much as 30 per cent of the Boden-Credit-Anstalt's equity. There had been, fortuitously, some preparation for this amalgamation, arising from Sieghart's own private discussions, but the actual arrangements, in the crisis atmosphere of September, literally took the form of a shot-gun marriage. The Austrian gendarmery was used to locate Baron Rothschild, who was on a hunting trip in the mountains, and Chancellor Schober was later reported to have said 'not a revolver, but a machine gun was put at his [Rothschild's] chest'.[76]

Although the management of the Credit-Anstalt was given little time to assess the nature of the assets that they were being forced to acquire, the underlying transaction was not totally a case of 'force majeure'. The Credit-Anstalt was encouraged into undertaking the merger through the government granting extensive tax concessions, on the one hand, and the Austrian National Bank agreeing, on the other, both to prolong 50 per cent of its claims against the Boden-Credit-Anstalt and place, indirectly, foreign currency deposits with the Credit-Anstalt.[77] The General Council of the Austrian National Bank, at its meeting of 18 October 1929, agreed that the Credit-Anstalt should be given three years in which to liquidate half of the bills that the National Bank had discounted for the Boden-Credit-Anstalt. Further, up to $15 million of the National Bank's foreign currency reserves were to be placed with foreign banks, which, in turn would relay these funds back to the Credit-Anstalt as three months' deposits; such a mechanism would not directly increase the Credit-Anstalt's liabilities to the Austrian National Bank. Austrian central bankers expected that the foreign associates of the Credit-Anstalt would assist in the financing of the takeover of the Boden-Credit-Anstalt and thereby liquidate these 'cross-deposit' arrangements between the Credit-Anstalt and the National Bank.[78] This aspiration proved to lack any foundation. However, by the late Spring of 1931, the volume of 'cross-deposits' arising from the forced merger had been reduced to $8 million. Yet, with the collapse of the Credit-Anstalt itself, they were some of the first of this bank's liabilities to fall due, which immobilized a portion of the Austrian National Bank's reserve and thereby were a further complication in the May crisis of 1931.

The public terms of the forced takeover of the Boden-Credit-Anstalt by the Credit-Anstalt were severe, consisting of four 50-schillinge shares of the former being exchanged for one 40-schillinge share of the latter, a loss on nominal values of 80 per cent. As a result, for instance, the Morgan group's rump holding of now 35 000 Boden-Credit-Anstalt shares became a block of 8 750 shares in the Credit-Anstalt.[79] Not all the foreign shareholders consented quietly to this arrangement and there were loud protests, particularly from the smaller holders.

Conclusion
Although case studies are one of the main genres of business history, there is always, understandably, a tension for economic history as between the particular and the general, given that the wider domain is a discipline of the social sciences. However, what has been portrayed above in terms of the development of the Boden-Credit-Anstalt within the 'turbulent twenties' for the Austrian economy and its financial sector was not exceptional. Although the specific conditions may have varied, all the main Austrian financial institutions had a largely similar experience, in terms of acquiring Western institutional shareholders from 1919 and relying on Western credit lines for considerable support during the second half of the decade. As with the Union Bank and Bosel, the Allgemeine Depositen-Bank was taken over by another colourful yet notorious 'speculator' – Camillo Castiglioni – and it failed during the fateful year of 1924. Its liquidation, however, was managed by the National Bank in conjunction with a consortium of the 'great' banks. Morgans' hesitancy towards the Boden-Credit-Anstalt from 1925 was mirrored by similar English disquiet arising over the position of the Anglo-Austrian Bank. This 'great' bank had been 'anglicized' in 1922, but London's subsequent changed attitude led to consequent protracted negotiations for dissolution of the tie with this institution, which finally led, with the direction of the Austrian government, to the bank's Austrian branches being acquired by the Credit-Anstalt in July 1926.[80] This marked the inception of the Credit-Anstalt becoming the sole commercial bearer of the burdens of sustaining the industrial 'concerns' developed by the Austrian system of investment banking.

Some might take the failure of the Boden-Credit-Anstalt in September 1929 as Austria's own experience of the general financial strain which occurred at the upper turning point of the cyclical expansion of Western capitalism during the second half of the 1920s, mirroring, for example, the Wall Street crash and the Hatry crashes. Yet its origins lay somewhat further back and were of a different order – in the post-1918 structural problems of the Austrian economy and the inflationary experience of the first half of the 1920s. After the 'franc crisis', the 'imperial system' of Austrian investment banking went into liquidation, of which the failure of the Boden-Credit-Anstalt was but a stage in a process which continued until 1933, with the creation of the Creditanstalt-Bankverein out of the Credit-Anstalt itself, and the Niederösterreichische Escompte-Gesellschaft and the Wiener Bank-Verein. In this, the decade of the 1920s provides only particular evidence for some of the stages of the dismantlement of a financial system which had been created during the second half of the nineteenth century and was misplaced in the changed national economic environment of postwar East Central Europe. Ultimately the burden of that liquidation had to be borne, absolutely and overtly, by the Austrian National Bank and the Austrian federal government[81] – the state; it was part of the costs of readjustment to be paid by the new republic.

The 'great' Viennese banks have been pictured here as the dinosaurs of the 'imperial' economy, whose existence was maintained after 1918, for five years, by the mushroom of the inflation and the franc speculation. However, these events, by their very nature, in turn clouded the establishment during the first half of the 1920s of any long-term perspective of the development of the 'new' Austria. In all this too much historical inevitability may be being applied. There was a diverse range of paths available after 1918 to be pursued by the managements of the 'great' Viennese banks and, in the case of Sieghart, it has to be admitted that he was a bombast, attracted to the flamboyant. At the opposite end of the approaches actually taken from 1918 was that of the Wiener Bank-Verein, whose management took a far more conservative stance towards maintaining 'imperial' investment banking. This effectively sustained this bank until 1933, when its downfall was then largely a result of the Austrian's public distrust of *all* its banking institutions, following the events of May 1931 and their consequences.

Notes

1. This chapter is based upon archival research enabled by an SSRC personal research grant 'Foreign Investment, Multinational Companies and the Banking Systems of East Central Europe, 1919–1939'. I am also grateful to Morgan Grenfell for access to files held within their archive. The original paper has been revised in the light of comments made at the London workshop to which it was first presented and subsequently by Dr K. Burk.
2. C.A. MaCartney, *The Social Revolution in Austria,* Cambridge, 1926, pp. 216–17.
3. See, for one example: F.G. Steiner, 'Vienna as an Exchange market for the Succession States', *The Manchester Guardian Commercial* (20.iv.1922) – special Reconstruction of Europe issues, edited by J.M. Keynes and issued in conjunction with the Genoa Conference.
4. P. Bairoch, 'Europe's Gross National Product: 1800–1975', *Journal of European Economic History*, V, 1976, p. 276.
5. On the 'Morgan group', see V.P. Carosso, *The Morgans: Private International Bankers,* Cambridge, Mass., 1987, and K. Burk, *Morgan Grenfell 1838–1988*, Oxford, 1989.

6. Public Record Office, Kew, London (hereafter PRO), FO 120 1014 2238/-, 'Austrian Personalities', 17.ii.1927. For further background, see B. Michel, *Banques et Banquiers en Autriche au debut du 20ème Siècle*, Paris, 1976, especially pp. 128–35, 217–19, 250–55, 273–80, 343–9, and 367–8.

7. Before 1927 the bank had only one branch – in Paris – a reflection of the French interest in its equity from its establishment in 1864.

8. Morgan Grenfell Archive, London (hereafter MG); Boden-Credit-Anstalt File (hereafter B-C-A), undated, unheaded memorandum 'To JPM & Co. 21/3/23'; and, 'Memorandum for Mr Leffingwell. Mr Anderson by F.C. Weems', 4.ii.1927. See also Michel, op. cit., note 6, and E. März (translated by C. Kessler), *Austrian Banking and Financial Policy. Creditanstalt at a Turning Point, 1913–1923*, New York, 1984.

9. Archive of the Ministry of the Economy – the Ministry of the Budget (former Ministry of Finance), Paris (hereafter ME); F^{30} 627, French Commercial Attaché at Prague to Minister of Commerce and Industry, 10.x.1929.

10. ME: F^{30}, 628, 'Rapport au Ministre', 20.v.1924; F^{30} 629, François Marsal to E. Schneider, 29.iv.1924. See also A. Teichova, *An Economic Background to Munich. International Business and Czechoslovakia*, Cambridge, 1974, Chs 3 and 4; C. Beaud, 'The Interests of the Union Européenne in Central Europe', and E. Bussière, 'The Interests of the Banque de l'Union parisienne in Czechoslovakia, Hungary and the Balkans 1919–30', both in A. Teichova and P.L. Cottrell (eds), *International Business and Central Europe 1919–1939*, Leicester, 1982.

11. P.L. Cottrell, 'Aspects of Western Equity Investment in the Banking Systems of East Central Europe', in Teichova and Cottrell (eds), op. cit., note 10.

12. MG: B-C-A, undated, unheaded memorandum, 'To JPM & Co. 21/3/23'.

13. MG: B-C-A, 'Memorandum for Mr Leffingwell. Mr Anderson', by F.C. Weems, 4.ii.1927.

14. Ministry of Foreign Affairs, Archive, Paris (henceforth MAE): Autriche 137, Pontalis, French Minister at Vienna, to Ministry of Foreign Affairs, Paris, 18.viii.1920. PRO; FO 371 4653. See also A. Teichova and P. Ratcliffe, 'British Interests in Danube Navigation after 1918', *Business History*, XXVII, 1985.

15. MG: B-C-A, 'Memorandum for Mr Leffingwell. Mr Anderson', by F.C. Weems, 4.ii.1927.

16. C.A. Gulick, *Austria from Habsburg to Hitler*, I, *Labor's Workshop of Democracy*, 1948, rep. 1980, p. 684, S.A. Schuker, *The End of French Predominance in Europe. The Financial Crisis of 1924 and the Adoption of the Dawes Plan*, Chapel Hill, 1976, pp. 55–6, 92–4.

17. On the Union Européenne operation, see the essays by Beaud and Bussière in Teichova and Cottrell (eds), op. cit., note 10.

18. MG: B-C-A: Cable 22/4967, MG to JPM, 6.xii.1922.

19. MG: B-C-A, Cable 22/2475, JPM to MG, 9.xii.1922.

20. MG: B-C-A, letter, Baron Schröder to E.C. Grenfell, 18.xii.1922.

21. MG: B-C-A, Cable 23/2000, JPM to MG, 3.i.1923.

22. MG: B-C-A, 'Agreement between J.P. Morgan & Co. and the Allgemeine Österreichische Boden-Credit-Anstalt', Vienna, 6.xii.1922.

23. MG: B-C-A, letter, JPM to MG, 22.i.1923.

24. MG: B-C-A, letter, JPM to MG, 5.ii.1923.

25. MG: B-C-A, letter, A.M. Anderson, JPM, to E.C. Grenfell, MG, 5.v.1923.

26. MG: B-C-A, letter, J. Henry Schroeder to MG, 16.vi.1923.

27. MG: B-C-A, letter, T.W. Lamont, JPM, to E.C. Grenfell, MG, 8.xi.1923.

28. MG: B-C-A, letter, E.C. Grenfell, MG, to T.W. Lamont, JPM, 23.xi.1923.

29. MG: B-C-A, letter, T.W. Lamont, JPM to E.C. Grenfell, MG, 4.xii.1923.

30. O.S. Phillpotts, *Report on the Financial, Commercial, and Industrial Situation of Austria; Revised to July 1924*, Department of Overseas Trade, London, 1924, p. 13.

31. MG: File Series, Austria. Reconstruction. 1923/43 Loan, File 8, letter F.C. Weems to T.W. Lamont, 2.viii.1925, providing Zimmerman's retrospective views.

32. Gulick, op. cit., note 16, pp. 684–5.

33. Quotation in H. Kernbauer, 'The Policy of the Austrian National Bank before and during the 1931 crisis', SSRC Research Seminar Group in Monetary History Conference: 'The 1931 Crisis and its Aftermath', Cambridge, April 1982.

34. MG: B-C-A, 'Memorandum for Mr Andersen' by F.C. Weems, 30.xii.1925.

35. MG: B-C-A, 'Memorandum for Mr Leffingwell. Mr Anderson', by F.C. Weems, 4.ii.1927.
36. MG: B-C-A, letter (extract) F.C. Weems to E.C. Grenfell, 18.viii.1925.
37. MG: B-C-A, Memoranda and Documents, 'Confidential remarks to the Balance Sheet per 1926' (apparently supplied by Sieghart, or another member of the Boden-Credit-Anstalt's senior management).
38. Kleinwort Benson Archives, Newbury (hereafter KB): Monthly balances, 1921–1924, 1924–1929.
39. KB: Information Book No.1, th. v. 3.xii (1925).
40. KB: Information Book No.1, th.l. 26.i (1926), o.l. 26.i.(1926), th.l. 27.i. (1926), o.l. (1926).
41. KB: Information Book No.1, th.l. 21.vii (1924).
42. MG: B-C-A, letter (extract), F.C. Weems to E.C. Grenfell, l9.viii.1925.
43. MG: B-C-A, Letter, A.M. Andersen, JPM to E.C. Grenfell, MG, 9.iv.1923.
44. MG: B-C-A, Letter, N.D. Jay, MH to V. Smith, MG, 17.vi.1925.
45. MG: B-C-A, letter (extract), F.C. Weems to E.C. Grenfell, l9.viii.1925.
46. MG: B-C-A, Cable 26/2033, JPM to MG, 22.i.1926.
47. MG: B-C-A, Memoranda and Documents, Unheaded, undated memorandum 'To JPM & Co. 21/3/23'.
48. MG: B-C-A, letter F.C. Weems to N.D. Jay, MH, 24.ix.1925.
49. MG: B-C-A, letter, Sieghart to Weems, JPM, 12.iii.1926.
50. *Compass. Deutsch-Österreich, Österreich-Ungarn (Liquidation),* 1921, I, pp. 342–7.
51. ME: F³⁰ 628, French Minister, Vienna to Ministry of Foreign Affairs, Paris, 27.iii.1926.
52. MG: B-C-A, 'Memorandum for Mr Leffingwell. Mr Anderson', by F.C. Weems, 4.ii.1927.
53. MG: B-C-A, 'Memorandum for Mr Leffingwell. Mr Anderson', by F.C. Weems, 4.ii.1927.
54. MG: B-C-A, Memorandum, F.C. Weems, 12.i.1927.
55. MG: B-C-A, 'Memorandum for Mr Leffingwell. Mr. Anderson' by F.C. Weems, 4.ii.1927.
56. MG: B-C-A, letter, Boden-Credit-Anstalt to JPM, 18.i.1927.
57. It is possible that the shares resulting from J.P. Morgan & Co.'s disinvestment were acquired by the Boden-Credit-Anstalt's French shareholders, as, in April 1927, the Union Européenne Industrielle et Financière applied for official permission to acquire 60000 of this Austrian bank's shares (at a discount of 6 francs a share on the then current Paris quotation). MAE: Autriche 141, L'Union Européenne to M. le Président de la Commission du Controle de l'Exportation des Capitaux, Ministry of Finance, 8.iv.1927. The total sum involved was 4.6 million francs. There are indications that the Banque de l'Union parisienne, Schneider's banking partner in the Union Européenne, subsequently acquired these securities.
58. MG: B-C-A, Sieghart to Anderson, JPM, 15.iv.1927.
59. KB: Information Book No. 2, th.l. 15.iii.1927.
60. KB: Information Book, th.l. 14.vi.1927; th.l. 20.ix.1927; o.l. 23.iii.1927; th.l. 27.x.1927; 23.ii.1928; 23.i.1929.
61. MAE: Autriche 141, 'Note pour Monsieur de Beaumarchais', 7.xi.1927, f.119.
62. E.W. Bennett, *Germany and the Diplomacy of the Financial Crisis, 1931,* Cambridge, Mass., 1962, pp. 42, 102.
63. MAE: Autriche 139, French Minister at Vienna to Ministry of Foreign Affairs, Paris, 29.i.1929, ff.110–13; Telegramme to French Minister, Vienna, l9.iii.1929, f.125. ME: F³⁰ 627, French Minister at Vienna to Ministry of Foreign Affairs.
64. See MAE: Autriche 139, Ministry of Foreign Affairs, Paris, to French Minister at Vienna, 21.xi.1929, f.195.
65. MG: B-C-A, letter Benjamin Joy, MH to A.M. Anderson, JPM, 2.viii.1929.
66. MG: B-C-A, letter A.M. Anderson, JPM, to C.F. Whigham, MG, 2.viii.1929.
67. MG: B-C-A, letter, E.C. Grenfell, MG to B. Joy, MH l9.viii.1929.
68. MG: B-C-A, letter, B. Joy, MH to E.C. Grenfell, MG 20.viii.1929.
69. MG: B-C-A, letter B. Joy, MH to E.C. Grenfell, MG 20.ix.1929.
70. MG: B-C-A, M. Herbert, MG to B. Joy, MH 23.ix.1929.
71. See MG: B-C-A, letter N.D. Jay, MH to E.C. Grenfell, MG l.x.1923; and also A. Weiner, Boden-Credit-Anstalt to A.M. Anderson, JPM 28.ix.1923; A. Weiner, Boden-Credit-Anstalt to N.D. Jay, MH 28.ix.1923.
72. MG: B-C-A, letter B. Joy, MH to M. Herbert, MG 24.ix.1929.

73. MAE: Autriche 139, Ministry of Foreign Affairs to French Minister at Vienna, 21.xi.1929, f.195.
74. Bank of England, Archive, London (henceforth BOE): 'Austria at the time of the Boden-Credit-Anstalt affair', 30.i.1929.
75. BOE: 'Boden-Credit-Anstalt', 14.x.1929.
76. Gulick, op. cit., note 16, II, p.858.
77. BOE: Brauneis, Austrian National Bank, to Siepmann, Bank of England, 12.x.1929.
78. Austrian National Bank, Meeting of the Executive Committee, Referat Draemer, 18.xii.1932. I am indebted to Dr H. Kernbauer for this reference.
79. MG: B-C-A, Summary.
80. Cf. A. Teichova, 'Versailles and the expansion of the Bank of England into Central Europe', in N. Horn and J. Kocka (eds), *Law and the Formation of the Big Enterprises in the 19th and Early 20th Centuries*, Vandenhoeck & Ruprecht, Göttingen, 1979, pp. 366–87.
81. Cf. D. Stiefel, *Finanzdiplomatie und Weltwirtschaftskrise. Die Krise der Creditanstalt für Handel und Gewerbe 1931*, Frankfurt am Main, 1989.

Austria
N24
621

13 'For better, for worse ...': the Credit-Anstalt and its customers in 1931[1]

Dieter Stiefel

'It has certainly been a difficult task to run a large bank in Vienna over the past 10 years', wrote Walter Federn, economic journalist, in 1931[2] – and it must be said he was right. There had actually never been an 'easy' time for Viennese banks; in the nineteenth century they had been confronted with economic crises, speculation and possible losses, but that was not comparable with what awaited them after the First World War. Financing the War itself, investments in armaments and participation in the organization of the war economy constituted a great challenge for the banks. But the greatest problems started at the end of the war, and in the long run especially with the fall of the Habsburg Monarchy.

Viennese banks had been one of the central institutions of this economic structure in which the countries of the Monarchy had made up their unified and protected business; these were now split up into several areas with different currencies and separate restrictive, nationalistic – 'anti-Vienna' – legal systems. But this was not all. Inflation up to 1922, where the Austrian crown – measured by the standard of living index – fell to 1/15000 of its prewar value, and speculation in shares and currencies on the bourse right through until 1924, opened up opportunities for the banks to make profits unknown in such quantities, but on the other hand brought enormous risks and above all an extensive reversal of accustomed ways of doing business. With the introduction of the schilling currency in 1924 and the opening balance (Schilling-Eröffnungs-Bilanz) based on the value of gold in 1925, it seemed as if more peaceful times for the Viennese banks were about to begin. But now a time of reconstruction had to begin, with not only numerous speculative banks collapsing, but also large banks being forced to merge: the Union Bank and the Depositen Bank merged to form the Credit-Anstalt; the Anglo-Bank was taken over by the Credit-Anstalt, which in 1929 was 'forced' to take over the troubled Boden-Credit-Anstalt with the institution becoming a giant of Viennese banking.

This story has been recounted many times, above all from economic and political points of view. But for the banks, war and disintegration were not only political, but also management problems which, due to inflation, speculation and finally mergers, became considerably more complex and extensive from the mid-1920s. In a history of banking it cannot suffice therefore to deal only with large movements of goods and capital. One should at least attempt – in spite of difficulties with sources – to consider and judge the biggest political events and economic structural changes from inside a banking office, therefore from the point of view of the management. History has made clear how the situation developed. We know that the development in the interwar years led to the banking crisis of 1931 – but here the question of the bank manager's scope of action in the 1920s should be asked: to what extent did the large Viennese banks find an answer to the extreme demands on the banking sector after the First World War, and to what extent did problems of management and organization contribute to the bank collapses of the world economic crisis?

Expansion of business

The large Viennese banks' business policy seemed at first to be obvious. After the First World War there was a general tendency in Europe to re-establish the economic relations of the prewar period such as the reintroduction of the gold standard in the foreign exchange sector. The reconstruction of a *status quo ante* was however not only pursued for the economy as a whole but also in businesses, and therefore it came as no surprise that the Austrian banks were fairly optimistic at the beginning.[3] The collapse of the Monarchy would – according to most – cause problems but would not change anything fundamental to the central function of the Vienna financial centre. The collapse of the political system did not necessarily have to lead to the collapse of the economic system. Some economic positions had to be given up and many business relations had to be restructured, but the Viennese banks hoped to capture both formally and informally their traditional areas of business. Partners could be found – despite nationalistic views – in the successor states. The extent to which bankers were prepared to go was illustrated by an internal statement by the Credit-Anstalt in reply to the question as to why some shares had been credited to debtors' accounts:

> In a number of states (Yugoslavia, Romania) there are legal provisions where a certain minimum percentage of share capital must be found in the hands of residents. In order to satisfy this provision we had to transfer our ownership of shares in those companies in which we had a large stake to partner banks in the states concerned and to debit them with the value of the shares. In other cases we agreed to make it possible for our foreign friends to benefit from tax advantages (dividend received exemption) in their home country (Czechoslovakia). It also sometimes happened that options on these shares were granted to third parties. Finally, this method was used under orders from the managing director – for cosmetic reasons – to prevent the bank's share ownership from appearing in its entire amount on the balance sheet.[4]

The document contains a handwritten remark: 'All deliberate cover-ups are reprehensible to a high degree',[5] but this procedure was by no means an 'Austrian speciality.' As Teichova has pointed out there are examples from Germany, Great Britain and the USA of multinational companies – and large

Viennese banks in the 1920s were multinational companies – feeling above all responsible to internal business codes of conduct and then to rules and laws of the states where they were active.

It was soon discovered that 'cross-border' business transactions by the large Viennese banks might not only prove to be the revival of prewar relations but also represented a kind of expansion, purely on the basis of industrial expansion during the war and of forced industrialization by the successor states. The funds for this could only partly be raised in Austrian capital markets and to an even lesser extent in those of the successor states. The expansion of trade was supported mainly by foreign loans. Once expansion had been decided on in Vienna, there was nothing else to do in the 1920s except to fall back on these short-term foreign loans which were typical of this period and which, and here Austria was not alone, were used extensively for long-term purposes.[6] In 1931 such short-term foreign loans accounted for at least one third of the Credit-Anstalt's capital. In 1919 this strategy of the bank was described by leading Austrian financiers as 'a combination of foreign capital with the knowledge the Austrian businesses had of market conditions in the new states.' By this 'not only the Austrian economy was kept intact, but also the major powers were assured of the possibility of generous earnings'.[7] So the formula 'Austrian know-how plus Western capital' allowed the large Viennese banks to maintain their importance in Central Europe even after the First World War.

Organizational expansion
This ambitious banking strategy had to be reflected in some way in organizational measures. The clearest change was a considerable increase in personnel which reached a peak in the inflationary period. The planned economic guidelines of the wartime economy, exchange controls, the complication of business relations due to the new frontiers and more and more complex accounting and transaction processes at a time when inflation was accelerating in spurts, led to a sharp increase in the bureaucratization of the banking process. This was met mainly by the simplest method – by increasing personnel, for the simple reason that personnel costs could easily be passed on in times of fast monetary depreciation and did not particularly make a significant difference to the accounts. However, this changed when the value of money stabilized and when the mergers began. As a kind of inheritance of inflation, Viennese banks were left with problems of personnel and personnel costs which they were unable to solve throughout the interwar years. Bank tellers enjoyed their very privileged positions with good incomes, golden handshakes and pensions which reached some two-thirds of their earnings and were met by the bank itself. Thus measures to reduce personnel for example by merging with other banks could no longer be effective due to the costs involved. Thus in 1931 there were 1.5 pensioners for each active teller at the Credit-Anstalt; in 1932 the ratio more than doubled.

However, the burden of pensioners does not entirely describe the problem of mergers. It is not without significance that Chandler has observed that company mergers probably constitute the most difficult management problems.[8] Two different management hierarchies have to melt into one and thus the position of each individual manager has to be redefined. In the Viennese banks there were signs that reform attempts in the form of mergers came unstuck or were at least delayed due to particular interests within the business organization. The internal report of the Credit-Anstalt in 1931 complained:

> In the time of inflation and the numerous authoritarian rules connected with it, a large number of independent departments emerged causing a certain lack of perspective in delegating authority. In addition to this, over relatively short periods (July 1926 – November 1929), the affiliation of other institutions' business was affected, whereby – in spite of resistance – it could not be avoided that certain employees were given independent but ill-defined functions. In a number of departments there were employees who had made contributions to the institution for many years and whom it was important to save from being offended by substantial changes in their functions shortly before the end of their active service. ... Only after taking into consideration the decision in December 1930 to get rid of a number of old employees, and the announcement of notice to a further group as of 30 June 1931, could a string of reforms partly take effect and partly be planned.[9]

The internal organization of the bank seemed to have moved therefore in the direction of greater 'decentralization' which was confirmed all around. Some departments were given a considerable amount of independence which could be traced back to the common practice of the postwar period – 'discretion'. In this system, where there were often oral and confidential agreements, the management level below the board, i.e. the department heads and the managers had almost a monopoly of knowledge. This also explains why nearly all managers at this level personally survived the collapse and subsequent reorganization of the bank. Out of 28 leading managers only three were not taken on again; because who was to replace them? They were the only ones who were familiar with the bank and its complicated trade practices and even the managing director Van Hengel complained: 'I cannot claim that the help which was provided by the employees for this work (re-evaluation of investments) can be described as ideal, but on the other hand there is no one who has the complete authority to deal with a problem like this.'[10]

Therefore it is not surprising that the Viennese banks were accused of organizational complacency in the interwar period. There was talk of a 'conservative trait' in the organizational structure, 'which remains comparably behind that of the *reichsdeutsche* banks',[11] and of the fact that 'the bureaucratisation of the management was a side effect of the process of concentration and as a result led to a certain ponderousness of the management.',[12] British auditors at the Credit-Anstalt also stated that 'the organisation of the bank had become complicated and cumbersome',[13] an accusation which was confirmed by the later managing director Joham himself in the statement: 'One of the greatest mistakes of the bank's organisation was decentralisation, which went too far.'[14]

The principle of isolated decisions
But what of the management board? Why did the top management not put an end to this heterogeneous business structure and adopt a line-and-staff structure? Why didn't the Viennese banks respond, as some large companies in the USA were said to have done at this time, with organizational innovation and new company structures?[15] Why did the path lead to bank crisis and bankruptcy in Austria and not to organizational reform?

Answers to these questions can only be preliminary but there does seem to be some proof that even the top management was entrenched in this system of internal decentralization and in fact to such an extent that they could no longer get out of it. There seem to be times when organizations can no longer revive themselves – that is to say without crisis and intervention from outside. The bureaucratic wheel of the Viennese banks had developed during times of war and inflation and the management had, in exemplary fashion, led the way to the disintegration of the lower departments.

Here, above all, the exceptional role of the management secretariat should be mentioned. This body did not conform to the principal business structure and took on exceptional responsibilities. Correspondence about such important matters as investment loans, guarantees and syndicate participation was not conducted by the loans department responsible for it but by the secretariat itself. 'This procedure has the undeniable advantage', as an internal Credit-Anstalt report stated, 'that it withdrew correspondence about these often strictly secret matters from circulation in accounts and prevented unauthorized persons from looking into them.' On the collapse of the Credit-Anstalt it was shown that this secrecy had been effective. For example, a guarantee for the Amstel Bank for the (at that time considerable) amount of 100 million shillings appeared, which nobody outside the bank knew about. On the other hand, the loans department was not given much information, which led to attempts at the beginning of the 1930s – already under the pressure of the crisis – to reform the secretariat system. 'It was partly concerned with establishments which had remained principally the same for 40 years.'[16] But the position of the secretariat was still so strong that even now there could only be the beginnings of a reform.

> Here too there was resistance which led to the consortium loans business staying within the secretariat and just a few weeks ago – still with the exception of petroleum loans – being passed on to the loans section. ... The matter of guarantees is also connected with the reform of the secretariat. Correspondence about this line of business was entrusted to the secretariat and therefore reforms in this area were made much more

difficult, if not impossible. Only in the first months of 1931 was correspondence about guarantees transferred from the secretariat to the loans section.[17]

The autonomous position of the management board, which extended beyond the organizational principle of the bank, also came to light in other areas and seemed to represent a special form of 'business management by isolated decisions'. There were staff departments which formulated reports to guide decisions about debtors and groups of companies (Industry-Inspectorate), but these were not consulted for important customers, and in this way, as the British auditors found out:

> On looking at these reports you could see that they usually received sufficient information on smaller accounts, but they could not be approached in the same way for large debtors. The main faults can be put down to the lack of technical education of the personnel and to the superficial way in which audits are carried out, as well as the lack of completeness necessary to judge the debtor's real financial situation.

There were actually no reports available for the two largest debtors of the bank – Steyr-Werke AG and the Erste Donau-Dampfschiffahrts-Gesellschaft.[18]

In the Credit-Anstalt's internal statement there was an attempt to qualify this accusation:

> The fact that on the part of the Industry-Inspectorate no or only insufficient reports were available is indisputable; the cause lies in the fact that we are regularly represented in these businesses' administrative bodies by a board member who receives the necessary information from the internal sources of the business in question. Checks by this Industry-Inspectorate were only allowed in such companies on the request of an administrative board member and only to an extent as ordered periodically. ... The fact that in many cases only superficial information about the companies and businesses which we are interested in is available, is only valid if you do not take into consideration the personal knowledge of those board members representing us in the respective businesses and if you limit yourself exclusively to the reports contained in the files.[19]

'Board members' here meant administrative board members, that is supervisory directors rather than managers. This is evident from a note written by Van Hengel, the managing director, who described the situation as 'very strange', and doubted the effectiveness of personal knowledge for directors who sat on numerous supervisory boards: 'They have to have that in 50 to 80 supervisory board positions!' There are in fact extensive discussions about the position of the boards of large companies which were documented for the USA in the 1930s in the famous book by Berle and Means.[20] According to this source, the power and real decision-making possibilities in large companies increasingly shifted from the board to the executive management, therefore from the owners' representatives to the specialists. The concept of a 'managerial revolution' or 'managerial capitalism'[21] is based on this.

Discussions of this kind were nothing new in Austria in the 1930s. Indeed, after the collapse of the large Viennese banks, people became sceptical of the supervisory board's powers. Thus in 1934 Rutkowski wrote that the previous view that liberal loan granting was impossible due to this double function, 'had to be contradicted in view of experience'. 'The accumulation of supervisory mandates in the hands of bank representatives has made it almost impossible to meet the demands on them...'[22] The supervisory board's lack of knowledge of the companies was shown also in the often voiced accusation in the world economic crisis that engineers had dragged the banks along and this was why overcapacities and overproduction had emerged. 'What has come about since the time of crisis' asked the Länderbank report of 1931,

> since industrial problems have become more complex and since bank directors represented on the supervisory boards have no longer had the time to study this business? This is where misunderstandings between the banks' representatives and the management of the company itself are bred. The banks' representatives are subordinate to the technical council, the engineers for their part know that they are supported by the powerful banks and therefore do not feel involved in planning matters and are not worried about planning ambitious production programmes. What has happened since the war is that engineers have set up programmes and the bank's representatives have only been concerned about securing finances. Let us read the reports of the Austrian Credit-Anstalt once more. In each of them the bank expresses its satisfaction that it managed alone or with the help of its foreign friends to secure the financial demands of its group's activities. The result of an attitude like this is that, based on appraisals written by the best foreign engineers, one was led to overvalue the industrial plant of the companies.[23]

It was astonishing that the top management of the large Viennese banks believed in the possibility of guiding and controlling their large business clients through their positions on the supervisory boards. For they themselves had managed to a considerable extent to deprive their own supervisory board of real control. The weaker position of the shareholders' representatives revealed itself particularly harshly in the bank crisis of 1931. Supervisory board members were – just as the rest of the public – completely surprised by the collapse of the bank and some of them even learnt about it in the newspapers. Only at the beginning of August 1931 – some three months after the collapse – did the shareholders have the possibility to ask questions at a shareholders' meeting. The real balance of power was revealed during the recapitalization of the bank. There were no negotiations with the shareholders or their representatives (except the Rothschilds) about the reorganization of the institution, only with large foreign creditors and the Austrian government. For this reason Eugene Schneider (Credit Lyonnais, Paris) explained in a letter to the French Finance Minister in July 1931 that he was no longer prepared to keep his place on the board of the Credit-Anstalt which he had accepted on the request at the French Finance and Foreign Ministries:

> I regret to have to inform you today that the provisions of the new reorganisational plan of the Credit-Anstalt are of such a nature that the task given to me to represent and defend French interests has been made considerably more difficult. It seems indeed to be becoming increasingly clear that the supervisory board of the Credit-Anstalt is, and will be in the future, cut off from every effective influence on the management. It seems as if the foreign members of the supervisory board have been kept in complete ignorance of the real situation of the bank and have learnt of the sudden announcement of the present difficulties in the newspapers[24]

The history of the reorganization of the Credit-Anstalt which is full of illusions and disappointments will not be elaborated on here. What did become clear was the modest influence of the supervisory board; from their lack of knowledge about business activities in the 1920s to their actual ignorance of the world economic crisis. The bank's restrictive policy on financial statements and information which was stylized under the principle of banking secrecy, facilitated this procedure. And in connection with this it was astonishing how foreign ministers from France or from the German Reich[25] kept pushing the idea of strengthened representation on the boards of the large Viennese banks in order to gain considerable influence on the Austrian economy and partly also on industry in the successor states.

The organizational development of the large Viennese banks in the 1920s seemed therefore also to be heading towards strengthening the top management's independence; and not only – as had been the case in other countries – in view of the supervisory board. Through the principle of secrecy and through the exclusive position of the management secretariat, the business organization's ability to control its own management was reduced. An increase in personal power might have been connected with this, but on the other hand it may also have been the result of a reduction in the feedback within the company and the restricted flow of information, and therefore less likelihood of meeting the political and economic structural changes with organizational change, since this undoubtedly would have challenged the dominance of the top management. Thus one can make the assumption that in the large Viennese banks of the 1920s the position of the top management itself had become a considerable obstacle to organizational reform.

Excursus: admiration and hate

The large Viennese banks after the First World War were not institutions where decisions were made impersonally only according to the rules and regulations of an organization. Rather they were run by a 'small, highly paid and exclusive group of bank managers'[26] in the absolute style of a financial elite. The economic and political power connected with this, together with international ties, explain also the admiration and the extraordinary social position which bank managers and financiers could still enjoy in the 1920s.

It was, then, all the more noticeable and personal when the attacks in the 1930s were made when failure eventually became obvious. Debates on the management's responsibility were held in parliament, the Styrian militia tried to start a petition to fine those responsible for the bank collapses, but even people who had usually been in favour of the Viennese banks started to criticize them heavily. Walter Federn, economic journalist, spoke of a 'fair amount of the bank manager's own fault', who neglected the most primitive fundamentals of banking.[27] Rutowski recognized many violations of the principles of a cautious banking policy.[28] Even Sir Robert Kindersley, a Bank of England director ascertained, '... that he was shocked to find how bad the abuses in the Credit-Anstalt had been. The management had been both extravagant and incapable....'[29] One of the British auditors mentioned to an ambassador of his home country that he had not found any significant signs of dishonesty and fiddling at the Credit-Anstalt, but he had constantly come across an extensive 'matey circle' and a lack of experience and knowledge which to someone who was familiar with Western business practices would have appeared completely incredible. A relative of a director, for example, had caused losses of about 20 million shillings in four companies where he had successively been appointed as chief executive, through his pure inability and lack of willingness to acquaint himself with the most fundamental business rules. And the British ambassador continued:

> If my informant continues to be right, then the primarily Jewish element of industry and banking circles has no greater genius, experience or talent than the politicians who are today trying to break the Gordian knot of Austrian finance. Austria lacks prominent men in all areas and never before has the problem been as misled as by the thought that the Jewish bankers were clever men without scruples. Their lack of knowledge is, by and large, profound and their methods are mediaeval.[30]

Public criticism reached its peak when it was revealed that one of the managing directors was accused not only of having credited himself with excessively large loans but also of speculating with the bank's funds for his own benefit.[31] However, in general the particular organizational structure of the large Viennese banks and the dominant position which some of the top managers occupied within them, explains the exaggerated admiration of the 1920s and also – under justified criticism – the likewise exaggerated reproaches in the 1930s. In the corporative state the measures singling out former top finance managers were continued, above all by the collection of indemnity payments which may have cost some of them their fortunes.

The loss of perspective
Let us return to the problems of management and organization. After all that has been recounted so far, one can assume that in the large Viennese banks all

business perspective had been lost after the First World War. This supposition has been already expressed in the 1930s shortly after the beginning of the banking crisis, amongst others by the French Embassy which, being 'particularly well informed', stated: 'In the case of the Credit-Anstalt, the management gradually lost the necessary overview of the businesses dependent on it and only due to this shortcoming did the crisis and illiquidity of the institution finally arise.'[32]

The impression of a loss of perspective was also reinforced in the report of the British auditors on the internal organization of the bank. Here the debtors of the Credit-Anstalt were merely listed on a file which was 'updated' at the end of each semester. Therefore it was not customary – and only possible with great effort – to draw up an up-to-date list of all debtors. During the audit by British experts this was attempted at least for all debts of over one million shillings. At the same time, in order to gain a better idea of the creditworthiness of these debtors, a 16-page questionnaire was sent to most of the companies.

> The aforementioned list of those debtors whose total debt to the bank exceeds in each case AS 1,000,000 was considered to be inexact and incomplete, and there were many such debtors whose names did not appear on the list. In the end a complete list of these debtors had to be drawn up by officials of the Central Bank working together with us which meant a two-month task for these gentlemen. Even now mistakes and differences still appear when comparing these figures with the answers we received from the companies [33]

One of the British auditors clearly underlined that this situation did not match the usual practices of European bank management at that time: 'In the various banks which I know very well, the loan control service or a similar office is in a position at all times to give a complete view of outstanding debts. Usually this takes a quarter of an hour.'[34] But also many calculation errors and other inconsistences were revealed, which 'stem from an almost complete lack of cooperation between the different departments of the bank.' The conclusion was that the directors 'were probably incapable of getting, or not in a position to get, a rough idea of their bank's activities because decentralisation had been driven to an incredible extent and responsibility quite simply did not exist. Therefore they just let themselves be pushed along with the tide.'[35]

The Austrian Auditor General's office, which in 1932 for the main part agreed with the criticism of the British auditors, spoke of the fact that 'above all the almost complete failure of book-keeping had contributed to the collapse of the Credit-Anstalt.'[36] And the lack of internal perspectives definitely contributed to the fact that the government almost daily, had to make new capital available to the bank for so long – from May 1931 to January 1932. Over a longer period you simply could no longer tell where the holes were that needed mending. The many public reproaches about the institution's organization and its way of working were discussed and were understandably rejected by the management. But in the sober working atmosphere of the reconstruction committee the later long-serving managing director practically confirmed all the reproaches of the auditors: the absolutely necessary reorganization of the chief accountant's office, the lack of an overview on debtors and the need to strengthen both the Industry-Inspectorate and the information department.[37]

How large the organizational problems really must have been can be shown by the fact that the British auditors, after months of work, were able to give a report but not a complete view of the situation of the business, and that the new managing director, Van Hengel, almost one year after the collapse, could only state: 'Returning to figures I have to explain that I am not in the position to present figures on the bank's activities which I can actually call figures and which I could vouch for ...'[38]

But when did the Credit-Anstalt know about the crisis?
The problems of organization and information went closely together with the question which was asked most frequently about the collapse of the Credit-Anstalt: How long had the management of the company known about the threatening situation which finally led to disaster? This question was also asked several times at the 75th annual general meeting of the company in 1931. The shareholders present expressed their lack of understanding about the fact that 'difficulties had arisen so suddenly and that the balance sheet for 1929 had given no indication whatsoever of the dangers which were threatening the bank in 1930.'[39] With hindsight Rutkowski, like Federn, also stated 'the Credit-Anstalt, without a doubt, no longer had its own capital intact at the time of the acquistion of the Boden-Credit-Anstalt (i.e. 1929).'[40] The British auditors spoke of the suspicion that: 'Perhaps the unsatisfactory financial situation of the Credit-Anstalt in the past years in fact had been one of the causes of the continuing lack of compiled information which should have been researched immediately.'[41]

The first sign of awareness of a problem in the Credit-Anstalt can be traced to 1928, when the first discomforting entries in the financial reports appeared about individual group companies, like Krupp. But the real turning point came in 1929, when the first reorganizational measures were drafted. At the beginning of 1930, about a year before the collapse, there was an attempt to retire a number of bank employees, and an attempt was even made to get rid of the once mighty Friedrich Ehrenfest from head office and to 'demote' him to Paris. The *Neue Freie Presse* reported that the management at this time had begun to gather a number of expert reports from related companies and to recognize the problematic situation.[42] In 1930 some reorganizational measures were introduced and a company – the Continentale – was founded in Switzerland with the task of writing off the remaining assets and financial stakes and thus of providing the institution with new funds.

These efforts came much too late, however. That it could go on for so long – that the banks could cling to their business plans for so long without being forced to make radical internal reforms – was mainly due to the large undisclosed reserves which they had been able to accumulate during the war and the inflationary period. The *Österreichische Volkswirt* of 19 October 1929 made a strong attack on the system of undisclosed reserves which it considered a sore point of public limited companies at that time. The undisclosed reserves allowed incapable managers to cover up their bad management for years and to continue to pay out dividends. This in turn prevented shareholders from understanding the true position of the business. The magazine demanded: 'Undisclosed reserves must go!' Furthermore, Viennese banks were considered to be so strong as far as capital was concerned – and they did everything possible to reinforce this impression – that the thought that they might soon be in trouble seemed almost impossible. The *Neue Freie Presse* wrote: 'For decades it had been conviction and tradition for the Credit-Anstalt to have many undisclosed reserves and not to let a company which was under its protection go';[43] and Walter Federn argued

> If you ask why the leaders of both these banks (Boden-Credit-Anstalt and Credit-Anstalt. D.S.) for years dared to implement a policy which had to lead them closer to the brink of disaster, then you could say that they believed that nothing could happen to them and that, if ever difficulties should have become apparent, they would have been offered help.'[44]

Inevitability of the bank crisis of 1931

This chapter is not seeking to prove that the Viennese banks could have kept their position in Central Europe as it was before the First World War with more flexible organization or better management. This thought, however, was entertained by the *Neue Freie Presse,* which in the 1920s had been full of admiration for the business practices of the large Viennese banks and then in 1931 still insisted that 'it could have been different had the economic climate improved. If you had gritted your teeth and stuck it out, you would have been big.'[45] This view was merely nostalgia for the optimism of the 1920s. For the Viennese banks after the First World War there was certainly no more quick escape from temporary difficulties as it was no longer a matter of the economy, but of structural change.

The decline in the importance of large Viennese banks after 1918 could not be stopped. The original decision to maintain the old area of influence might have been reasonably based on the knowledge and expectations immediately after the war. But by the middle of the 1920s at the latest there were several signs that the old level of business could not be kept up in the long run. Protectionist difficulties in the successor states, the almost perpetual decrease in share prices and problems of profitability and sales in many companies to which capital and/or loans had been supplied all got in the way. But there was much to be said for the fact that in the 1920s an 'orderly withdrawal' of the Viennese banks could have been possible, thus reducing the extent and importance of business activities, but not causing the collapses and disastrous losses of the years 1929–34. 'Withdrawal' did not mean a complete abandonment of industrial financing (as was suggested by Anglo-Saxons or as was forced by law in the USA in the 1930s), since the large Austrian banks were for the most part founded to finance industry and this was their main purpose of business, but it would definitely have been possible to concentrate on a small number of companies and to withdraw in good time from some of the problematic investments in the successor states. With a sense of 'healthy shrinkage', the Länderbank report wrote that Central European banks could only achieve trust again 'if they voluntarily withdrew, in order to keep up at all costs the extent of their former business activities.'[46] Thus the bank crisis would have been merely a stage in the liquidation of the past; the dust which had enshrouded the entirety of large Central European banking institutions would have disappeared. In any case it would have been better 'to predict the creation of a situation which did not pass by some insighted observers in Central Europe or elsewhere abroad, and not to have been surprised by the events.'[47]

The problem of the Viennese banks lay in the discrepancy between their ambitions and an inappropriate internal organizational structure. The banks had been able to adapt themselves to the new situation after the First World War in their external relations, in their national and international political and financial connections and in the extension and restructuring of their business contacts. Internal adaptation, however, was incomplete. Organizationally, there were mergers, reshuffles and more personnel, but no innovations. Indeed the leaders of the Viennese banks considered themselves too much to be financial diplomats and not men of organization. The Austrian bank crisis of the interwar years was therefore both a management crisis and an organizational crisis. The banks were – as regards information processing and internal information – no longer in a position to recognize in time the need for structural changes in their complex and wide ranging area of business. Due to these shortcomings in organization and information – and some contemporary observers supposed also due to prestige[48] – they were not willing or sometimes not in a position to introduce these changes in time. So the catchword was not 'change' but 'sticking it out', and the management led the institution not down the path of an 'ordered withdrawal' but headlong to disaster.

In this way the idea of the inevitability of the Austrian banking crisis of the interwar years can be fundamentally questioned. This deep-rooted legend in Austrian economic history is either stylized by the Americans withdrawing their funds, and further distant forces which Austria could not influence being responsible for the collapse; or the French were to blame for everything, since for political reasons – the Schober–Curtius Plan of a customs agreement between Austria and the German Reich – they had recalled their capital from Austria in order to reduce the country to its knees via the banks. Both arguments contain an element of truth but they are either only valid for the German Reich or only for the later course of the crisis. One can refute them today as the trigger of the crisis for Austria, for the Boden-Credit-Anstalt as well as for the Credit-Anstalt. The French as capital investors were not so important in Austria that they could have triggered off such a disastrous outcome. There must have been aggravating circumstances from outside, for sure, but basically the Austrian banks slipped into the disaster on their own. This line of argument can be concluded by taking a look at the development of the large 'foreign' institutions of that time in Vienna. After the First World War two renowned Viennese banks – The Anglo-Austrian Bank and the Länderbank – were transferred into foreign ownership due to prewar debts which were relatively difficult to manage, and they transferred their headquarters to London and Paris respectively. They kept their traditional circle of business in Vienna and in the successor states but were undoubtedly influenced by their banking know-how and their new native countries. The Anglo-Austrian Bank gave up its activities in 1926. It was transferred to the Credit-Anstalt. In 1981 E. März wrote of this withdrawal of the British: 'This failure was definitely connected partly to the small amount of experience of British bankers in Central European business and with their notorious inability to adapt themselves to the business morale of this region.'[49] Even when you take into consideration the fact that industrial financing in Austrian universal banking style was not the same as the British banking system, then it still has to be handed to the British bankers that they recognized the intolerable situation as early as 1926 and thus avoided large losses and collapse. The abandonment of the Anglo-Bank was celebrated as a sign of the superiority of Austrian banking know-how in that a foreign bank system did not find it easy to do business. Critically approached, however, it could have been considered as an alarm for the other Viennese banks.

The fact that a different business policy was not possible was shown by the second Viennese institution in foreign hands: the Länderbank. According to März: 'The Central European Länderbank could … claim its independence until 1938, but at the price of a careful and restricted business policy. The voluntary self restriction imposed by the bank's management was the decisive reason for the institution surviving the heavy blows in the Central European banking world at the beginning of the 1930s.'[50] If the Länderbank was able to maintain its position by means of a 'voluntary self confinement', this can only confirm the opinion advanced here that, with appropriate internal company know-how, a reduction of business – which in the face of its capital was overproportional and was making heavy losses – an 'ordered withdrawal' would have been possible. The ways in which both 'foreign' institutions in Vienna behaved qualifies in the same way the opinion of the inevitability of the large banks' collapse in Austria during the interwar period. But they also show that internal organization, management and know-how deserve a much more important place in banking history than are usually afforded.

Notes

1. This chapter is based on my book on the Credit-Anstalt Crisis 1931: *Finanzdiplomatie und Weltwirtschaftskrise*, Schriftenreihe des Instituts für bankhistorische Forschung, Band 12, Knapp Verlag, Frankfurt, 1989.
2. W. Federn, 'Der Zusammenbruch der Österreichischen Credit-Anstalt', *Archiv für Sozialwissenschaft*, vol. 67, Berlin 1932, p. 406.
3. cf. E. März, *Österreichische Bankpolitik in der Zeit der großen Wende 1913–1923. Am Beispiel der Credit-Anstalt für Handel und Gewerbe*, Vienna, 1981, p. 284.
4. Credit-Anstalt's internal statement on the report of Chartered Accountants, 1932, Archives Economiques et Financières, Paris, 74.016/32 to managing director van Hengel. Apart from here, this study is built up from three further extensive documents: Report on the British auditors of Chartered Accountants Deloitte, Plender, Binder & Co. to the Austrian Ministry of Finance, Vienna, 3 October 1931. Landesgericht für Strafsachen, Vienna, Akt 26 d, vr. 6373/31. The British auditors had been charged with the audit by foreign creditors of the Credit-Anstalt and the Austrian government after the collapse. Report by the managing director of the Credit-Anstalt, A.J. van Hengel, to non-resident creditors, 19 November 1932, *Finanzarchiv*, Vienna, 77.685/32. Länderbank report 1931, 'Die Krise der Banken in Mitteleuropa', Archives Economiques et Financières, Paris, F30 624.
5. Remark supposedly by managing director van Hengel who in 1932 was employed by non-resident creditors and the Austrian government to rebuild the Credit-Anstalt.
6. That the banks should not grant such loans is a truism' asserted one of Austria's leading bank managers of this period, which, however, could only be appropriate in countries with high levels of capital. 'It is obviously a different matter in countries without much capital. ... The banks' distance from industrial risk remains in such poorer economies for the main part wishful thinking. The banks are rather forced by the circumstances to grant long-term industrial loans in the wrong way and when short-term funds from foreign or domestic creditors are hastily withdrawn this can end in serious damage.' E. Mosing, *Studien auf dem Gebiet der österreichischen Banken- und Kreditpolitik 1930–1934*, Vienna, 1934, p. 8.
7. März, op. cit., note 3, p. 353.
8. A.D. Chandler. *The Visible Hand. The Managerial Revolution in American Business*, Cambridge, Mass., 1977, p. 415.
9. Credit-Anstalt internal statement, 1931, p. 12.
10. Van Hengel's report. p. 4.
11. G. Weihs, *Die Beziehungen der Banken zur Industrie*, Vienna, 1921, p. 55.
12. H. Rutkowski, *Der Zusammenbruch der Österreichischen Credit-Anstalt für Handel und Gewerbe und ihre Rekonstruktion*, Bottrop, 1934, p. 72.
13. Report of the British auditors, p. 17.
14. J. Joham, 'Meeting of the executive committee of the Austrian Credit-Anstalt, 28.10.1932', *Finanzarchiv*, Vienna, 74016/32.
15. Chandler, op. cit., note 8, p. 455ff.
16. Report of the British auditors, p. l3.
17. Credit-Anstalt internal statement, p. 13/14.
18. Report of the British auditors, p. 13
19. Credit-Anstalt internal statement, p. 8.
20. A. Bearle and G. Means, *The Modern Corporation and Private Property*, New York, 1932.
21. Chandler, op. cit., note 8, p. 490ff.
22. Rutkowski, op. cit., note 12, p. 49.
23. Länderbank report, p.16.
24. Letter from Eugen Schneider to the French Minister of Finance of 30 July 1931, Archives Economiques et Financières, Paris, F30 629.

25. Likewise hefty political discussion arose about the question as to which nationality the managing director in charge of rebuilding the Credit-Anstalt should have. Microfilm archive of the Institut für Zeitgeschichte. Vienna, 11 Oe 2457 31.
26. März, op. cit., note 3, p. 15.
27. Federn, op. cit., note 2, p. 415
28. Rutkowski, op. cit., note 12, p. 49.
29. British Embassy to the Foreign Office, 15 June 1931, Public Record Office, London, F0371/15150/02382.
30. R.H. Hadow, British Embassy in Vienna to Arthur Henderson, Foreign Office, Vienna, 7 July 1931, Public Record Office, F0371/15151/02406.
31. As these speculations failed his informal debt account reached the sum of 1.4 million shillings which he could not possibly repay. Thus he had to give up his position in 1930 and, in order not to damage the bank's reputation by his dismissal he was transferred to a representative position in Paris. *Neue Freie Presse*, Vienna, of 15.5.1931, 26.10.1931, 28.10.1931.
32. French Embassy Vienna, 6 July 1931, Archives Economiques et Financières, Paris, E 450.003; also in connection with this: Rutkowski, op. cit., note 12, p. 72; *Neue Freie Presse*. Vienna, of 31.5.1931; Report of the British Embassy in Vienna to the Foreign Office, London, 7 July 1931, Public Record Office, London F0371/15151/02406.
33. Report of the British auditors, p. 17.
34. Correspondence by the British auditors, Deloitte, Plender, Binder & Co to Sir Robert Kindersley, Vienna, 28 June 1931, Archives Economiques et Financières, Paris, F30 624.
35. Ibid.
36. Auditor General's Office to the Federal Minister of Finance, Vienna, 4 August 1932, *Finanzarchiv Wien*. 52885/32.
37. Joham, Executive Committee.
38. Report by Van Hengel, p. 4.
39. *Neue Freie Presse*, Vienna, 17.5.1931.
40. Rutkowski, op. cit., note 12, p. 67.
41. Report of the British auditors, p. 17.
42. *Neue Freie Presse*, Vienna, 17.5.1931.
43. *Neue Freie Presse*, Vienna, 1.5.1931.
44. Federn, op. cit., note 2, p. 415.
45. *Neue Freie Presse*, Vienna, 31.5.1931.
46. Länderbank report, p. 30.
47. Ibid., p. 26.
48. Ibid., p. 23.
49. März, op. cit., note 3, p. 463.
50. Ibid., p. 464.

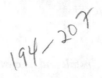

14 The Wiener Bank-Verein and its customers in the 1920s and 1930s[*]

Désirée D. Verdonk

The relations between universal banks and their customers, and their subsidiaries in particular, are still a largely unexplored area because of insufficient source material. In addition, it has been a closely guarded area of bank secrets and access to sources has in most cases been difficult to obtain.

When a set of so-called *Protokollbücher* (Minute books) of the Wiener Bank-Verein (henceforth WBV) became available – covering the years 1924 to 1934 – the chance of a more thorough insight into bank–industry relations was opened up. These books are quarterly volumes containing the minutes of board meetings of the WBV. Between August 1924 and March 1934 1 243 meetings were recorded, 489 of which included lists of credits granted to customers. And although the written information is not very conclusive quantitative analyses[1] of the credit data have revealed some interesting details of the WBV credit policy making it possible to shed some light on the disputed issue of continuity or discontinuity of credit ties with the successor states and to highlight the bank's special relationship with a group of privileged customers.

The history of the Wiener Bank-Verein[2]

The WBV was founded in 1869 as an associate of the Allgemeine Österreichische Boden-Credit-Anstalt (BCA), another important Austrian bank, and was to become one of the big Central European universal banks. After an increase in capital in 1881 the bank took up regular banking services. It established numerous branches all over the former Habsburg Monarchy and was also heavily involved in the foundation of industrial enterprises and in converting firms into joint-stock companies. In both cases the bank retained a large amount of shares and, as will be shown below, this group of customers, which became known as the *Konzern* (dependent subsidiary companies), was to play a vital role in the bank's history.

The bank, weathering the storms of the First World War, emerged weakened, as did the other big commercial banks of Vienna, to face the troubles of the

[*] The author wishes to thank the British Economic and Social Research Council for support during a research project under the direction of Professor Alice Teichova on 'Bank–Industry Relations in Interwar Europe: Austria, Czechoslovakia, Hungary and Sweden'. For advice and comment the author expresses her gratitude to Professor Alois Mosser and especially to Professor Alice Teichova – without whose constant support, encouragement and friendship this contribution would not have been written.

First Austrian Republic. In the course of the nostrification movement[3] sweeping through the successor states the General Bohemian Bank Union was created in 1921 incorporating the eighteen Czech branches of the WBV. Besides the Czech majority holding in the equity of the Bohemian Bank Union two Belgian banks – the Banque Belge pour l'Etranger and the Société Générale de Belgique – also participated with the WBV retaining 'a considerable interest'.[4] In 1922 the eight branches in Poland were turned into the General Polish Bank Union with the participation of the Banque Belge pour l'Etranger, the Basler Handelsbank of Switzerland and Polish capital; again the WBV retained shares in the newly founded bank. In 1928 the two Yugoslav branches in Zagreb and Belgrade became the General Yugoslav Bank Union and hence a Yugoslav bank. The Banque Belge pour l'Etranger and the Basler Handelsbank were also involved, as was the WBV which continued its interest in the new bank. Although the two Yugoslav branches were separated from the WBV the *Protokollbücher* continued to record advances of the Belgrade branch till 1930 and of the Zagreb branch until 1932. Despite the loss of most foreign branches (in 1918 the WBV had 31 branches outside the Austrian part of the Habsburg Empire, in 1925 the number had fallen to six)[5] the WBV was able to hold on to its very important Budapest branch and also the branch offices in Czernowitz (Romania), Bozen and Meran.[6]

Cooperation with the Banque Belge pour l'Etranger, the Société Générale de Belgique and the Basler Handelsbank was not restricted to the above-mentioned institutes. As the WBV increased its capital stock (1920–22, 1927, 1929 and 1932) all three banks acquired shares in its equity and they were also involved in multi-bank credits with the WBV (Konsortialkredite). Foreign shareholders of the WBV also included the Deutsche Bank- und Disconto-Gesellschaft whose share was 5 per cent in 1929 and the New York firm Dillon, Read & Co. which held 500 000 shares (18.2 per cent of the WBV share total) in 1927.[7]

The break-up of the Habsburg Monarchy and the resulting economic changes within Central Europe took a heavy toll on Austrian banks. The nostrification movement in the successor states not only stripped the big Viennese banks of most of their branches outside the newly created Austrian Republic (in 1918 the ten biggest banks possessed 143 branches outside Austria whereas in 1924 the number was down to nine) but also of many of their subsidiary companies.[8] In addition the composition of share ownership of the banks themselves changed with more and more equity being concentrated in foreign hands.[9] The dire economic situation in interwar Austria left the Viennese banking world in turmoil as the heavy credit demand from industry drained the banks' resources.[10] As can be seen from Table 14.1 the 1920s and 1930s were characterized by an unprecedented merger process. Table 14.1 also illustrates the important role of the WBV within the Viennese banking world. Its balance totals reveal a leading position (on average the third biggest bank) throughout the studied period.

Table 14.1   Balance totals of the seven biggest Viennese banks (in million Austrian shillings), 1925–34

	CA	BCA	Nö.Esc.	WBV	Union	Merc.	Verk.	LBª
1925	608	393	366	336	191	129	107	187
1926	927	506	391	416	178	133	139	203
1927	1 064	824	425	520	M	123	M	247
1928	1 198	846	460	527		141		283
1929	1 399	M	504	534		151		305
1930	1 885		580	532		138		327
1931	*		492	415		81		283
1932	635		401	365		82		273
1933	519		341	257		56		275
1934	799		M	M		62		292

CA: Österreichische Creditanstalt für Handel und Gewerbe.
BCA: Österreichische Boden-Credit-Anstalt.
Nö.Esc.: Niederösterreichische Escomptegesellschaft.
WBV: Wiener Bank-Verein.
Union: Unionbank.
Merc: Mercurbank.
Verk: Verkehrsbank.
LB: Zentraleuropäische Länderbank.
ª Balance of the Vienna branch of the Zentraleuropäische Länderbank (Banque des Pays de l'Europe Central), a formerly Austrian bank which became a French-based institution in 1921.
* In 1931 the CA did not present a balance.
M: Indicating the merger process taking place during the First Austrian Republic: The beginning of 1927 saw the merger of the Unionbank and the Verkehrsbank with the Boden-Credit-Anstalt. In 1929 the BCA merged with the CA. In 1934 the WBV was integrated into the CA. Also in 1934 the Niederösterreichische Escomptegesellschaft transferred its banking business to the CA, the remainder became the Österreichische Industriekredit A.G., an industrial holding company administrating the industrial *Konzern* of the former Escomptegesellschaft.

Source: Compass-Österreich, 1927 to 1936.

Increasing liquidity problems during the world economic crisis resulted in an attempted reorganization. When the 1931 balance was drawn up the bank's securities, participations and debts were revalued.[11] Despite these measures the WBV had to be integrated into the CA in 1934 which was renamed Österreichische Creditanstalt-Wiener Bankverein.[12]

Continuity or discontinuity – the geographical emphasis of credit distribution

A look at the number of client firms, number of credits granted and total amounts of credits issued over the period studied is instructive. It shows that the view taken by contemporary writers and economic journalists[13] as well as some authors of recent publications,[14] i.e. that Viennese banks continued to be too heavily involved in advancing credits to foreign industrial companies (thereby adversely affecting economic recovery and growth in interwar Austria and triggering the banking crisis), does not hold true for the WBV. Quantitative analysis of the years 1925–33 not only shows that 75.3 per cent of the total clientele were Austrian and that 85 per cent of all credits went to domestic customers but that Austrian customers received three-quarters of the overall sum of credits granted (see Table 14.2).

Table 14.2   The geographical distribution of WBV credits: number of firms, number of credits and credit sums in million Austrian shillings (A.S), 1925–33

	Total	Austrian	%	Foreign	%
Firms	3076	2313	75.2	763	24.8
Credits	10628	9032	85.0	1596	15.0
Sums	1417	1062	75.0	355	25.0

Source: Calculations based on data extracted from the WBV archive.

The emphasis of the WBV's credit business was without doubt to be found within the territory of the new Austrian Republic even though a quarter of the credits granted went abroad. Although the foreign clientele was scattered over sixteen countries three stand out in terms of number of firms and credits as well as the total amount of credits granted. The geographical direction of advances emphasizes the still existing traditional south-easterly outlook of the Viennese banking world: Hungary, Romania and Yugoslavia accounted for 20.2 per cent of all firms, 11.9 per cent of all credits and 15.8 per cent of the total sum granted over the period studied (see Table 14.3).

Table 14.3   The customers of the WBV in Hungary, Romania and Yugoslavia: number of firms, number of credits and credit sums in million Austrian shillings (A.S.), 1925–33

	Total	Hungary	%	Romania	%	Yugoslavia	%
Firms	3076	256	8.3	194	6.3	173	5.6
Credits	10628	651	6.1	351	3.3	268	2.5
Sums	1417	127.4	9.0	43.4	3.1	52.1	3.7

Source: Calculations based on data extracted from the WBV archive.

The importance of these credit ties can also be gleaned from the fact that after 1925 four of the six foreign-based branches of the WBV were located in these three countries. A detailed mapping-out of credit operations by the different branches shows that the one in Budapest was still granting credits in 1933 and also the figures for the first three months of 1934 seem to indicate that this branch continued its business until the WBV was taken over by the CA later that year. The Romanian branch in Czernowitz stopped business in 1932 while the two Yugoslav branches in Belgrade and Zagreb ceased the credit business in 1930 and 1932 respectively. But it is especially the amounts granted by these foreign branches that underline the importance of business connections with the former Austro-Hungarian territories even during the second half of the 1920s and the early 1930s. As opposed to other Austrian banks which had to give up most of their foreign-based branches in the successor states soon after the end of the First World War the WBV was able to hold on to its branches in South-Eastern Europe for a surprisingly long time. This confirms the multinational character which the Viennese banking sector retained after the break-up of the Habsburg Empire and – judging from the figures in Table 14.4 – was still in place during the period studied.

Table 14.4   Amounts of credits granted by domestic and foreign branches of the WBV, 1925–33 (in million A.S., current prices)

	1925	1926	1927	1928	1929	1930	1931	1932	1933
Zentrale*	127.2	136.0	165.5	132.2	137.1	124.0	97.4	65.4	58.3
Budapest	14.8	13.8	14.2	20.7	21.1	7.0	1.2	10.0	4.8
Zagreb	13.5	9.5	8.6	0.7	3.2	2.3			1.3
Belgrade	2.7	4.0	6.9	0.6	3.8				0.4
Czernowitz	2.3	1.3	2.2	5.0	5.7	0.7	1.1	0.2	
Graz	0.6	1.0	13.7	3.0	10.9	3.9	2.7	23.1	0.1
Klagenfurt	2.4	6.6	17.1	8.1	6.3	5.5	3.2	0.7	0.3

*Zentrale = Head Office.
Source: Calculations based on data extracted from the WBV archive

In the Austrian Republic the head office (Zentrale) in Vienna and the two branches in Graz and Klagenfurt played the key role in domestic business while Budapest was the second largest credit-granting business within the total WBV branch structure. As can also be seen from Table 14.4 the two Yugoslav branches in Zagreb and Belgrade showed a sharp reduction in 1928, the year in which they were turned into the General Yugoslav Bank Union whereas the two subsequent years indicate a rise in the credit business. Czernowitz seemed to have remained the only functioning Romanian branch of the WBV and until 1930 its business was quite substantial. The two branches in Northern Italy were of minor importance during the period. Bozen ceased business in 1928 and Meran last recorded a credit in 1932, all figures being low. The deepening crisis of the early 1930s evidently stymied the WBV's endeavour in the second half of the 1920s to strengthen its business in South-East Europe.

The customers

The relationship between banks and their customers has usually been shrouded in secrecy, as has already been pointed out in the introductory section of this chapter. As bank archives have not been accessible to researchers this relationship has been more a subject of speculation than precise knowledge including, of course, any quantitative assessment of credit distribution to client firms according to branches of industry, trade and finance. The *Protokollbücher* of WBV for 1925 to 1933 contain detailed information on the identity of the borrowers, the type and seat of their business enterprises and the amounts and dates of credits they received. From this information a database was created which sheds some light on the credit business of the WBV and the composition of its customers.

An analysis of the customers of the WBV in Tables 14.5[15] and 14.6 by sector shows several interesting aspects. The domestic clientele reflects fairly accurately the economic structure prevailing in Austria after the break-up of the Habsburg Empire. Traditionally, the Austrian part of the Empire had belonged to the industrially advanced areas whereas agriculture had played a comparatively minor role. During the immediate postwar years the successor states shunned trade with Austria and resorted to protectionism. The economic problems facing the newly created Austrian Republic were basically twofold, as shown in Tables 14.5 and 14.6. On the one hand agriculture[16] and the production and supply of food became one of the main economic challenges during the interwar period which is clearly seen in Table 14.5. Over the period 1925–33 the WBV had a total of 3076 customers, 2313 of whom were based in Austria; of these Austrian firms 228 (9.9 per cent) were involved in the food trade, 101 (4.4 per cent) in agriculture, 66 (2.9 per cent) in the production of food and 19 (0.8 per cent) in the production of sugar; in addition, 62 firms (2.7 per cent) produced beverages and another 14 (0.6 per cent) were breweries. The second problem was the enormous heritage of heavy industry now based in a small country and deprived of its traditional markets. Again this is reflected in Table 14.5: 156 firms (6.7 per cent) were involved in engineering and metal working and 124 (5.4 per cent) in the selling of these products. In addition the new Republic also received a fairly large share in the textile industry of the former Austro-Hungarian Empire: 137 WBV customers (5.9 per cent) were involved in textile production and 88 (3.8 per cent) in textile trade. The chemical and electrical industries (within the WBV clientele structure 52 or 2.2 per cent produced and 34 or 1.5 per cent sold chemicals and 35 or 1.5 per cent were involved in the electrical business) and also wood played an important role as it became a major export commodity especially during the inflation period[17] (145 firms or 6.3 per cent traded in wood and 66 or 2.9 per cent were involved in forestry and the production of products made from wood).

Table 14.5   Distribution of the number of Austrian and foreign customer firms of the WBV by industry, 1925–33

Branch of industry	Number of firms					
	Total	%	Austr.	%[1]	Foreign	%[2]
Food trade	276	9.0	228	9.9	48	6.3
Engineering/metal working	188	6.1	156	6.7	32	4.2
Textiles	172	5.6	137	5.9	35	4.6
Wood trade	170	5.5	145	6.3	25	3.3
Banking	161	5.2	26	1.1	135	17.7
Engineering/metal trade	160	5.2	124	5.4	36	4.7
Textile trade	155	5.0	88	3.8	67	8.8
Building	149	4.8	129	5.6	20	2.6
Agriculture	115	3.7	101	4.4	14	1.8
Paper	97	3.2	83	3.6	14	1.8
Food	85	2.8	66	2.9	19	2.5
Beverages	78	2.5	62	2.7	16	2.1
Chemicals	77	2.5	52	2.2	25	3.3
Wood	77	2.5	66	2.9	11	1.4
Entertainment	75	2.4	63	2.7	12	1.6
Leather and shoes	60	2.0	51	2.2	9	1.2
Chemical trade	55	1.8	34	1.5	21	2.8
Electrical	52	1.7	35	1.5	17	2.2
Transport	42	1.4	30	1.3	12	1.6
Sugar	25	0.8	19	0.8	6	0.8
Brewing	18	0.6	14	0.6	4	0.5
Mining and metallurgy	15	0.5	9	0.4	6	0.8
Financial firm/institution	6	0.2	3	0.1	3	0.4

[1] percentage in relation to number of credits given to Austrian companies.
[2] percentage in relation to number of credits given to foreign companies.

Source: Calculations based on data extracted from the WBV archive.

The fairly substantial foreign clientele also reflects the prevailing economic conditions of the time. Although foreign banks top the list (135 institutions or 17.7 per cent), a fair share of the 763 foreign customers of the WBV were found in the trade and production of textiles (67 or 8.8 per cent and 35 or 4.6 per cent, respectively) and food (19 or 2.5 per cent and 48, respectively), in the engineering and metal business (32 or 4.2 per cent in production and 36 or 4.7 per cent in trade) but also in the chemical industry (25 or 3.3 per cent in production and 21 or 2.8 per cent in trade). In addition transport (12 or 1.6 per cent), the electrical industry (17 or 2.2 per cent) and wood (25 or 3.3 per cent in trade and 11 or 1.4 per cent in production) prove that the customer structure of the WBV was highly diversified .

Table 14.6 shows the branch structure for the *Konzern* clientele. The following section will deal in greater detail with this particular set of customers. Suffice to say that within the domestic *Konzern* framework engineering and metal working (13 of a total of 43 firms, i.e. 30.2 per cent) top the list with the electrical industry (6 or 14 per cent) and textiles (5 or 11.6 per cent) also comprising a fair share whereas the foreign *Konzern* is dominated by transport (4 or 23.5 per cent of all foreign *Konzern* firms).

Table 14.6   Distribution of the number of Konzern firms of the WBV by industry, 1925–33

| Branch of industry | Number of *Konzern* firms | | | | | |
	Total	%	Austr.	%[1]	Foreign	%[2]
Engineering/metal working	14	23.3	13	30.2	1	5.9
Electrical	8	13.3	6	14.0	2	11.8
Chemicals	7	11.7	3	7.0	4	23.5
Transport	6	10.0	2	4.7	4	23.5
Textiles	5	8.3	5	11.6	0	0.0
Mining and metallurgy	3	5.0	2	4.7	1	5.9
Brewing	3	5.0	2	4.7	1	5.9
Engineering/metal trade	2	3.3	1	2.3	1	5.9
Chemical trade	2	3.3	2	4.7	0	0.0
Banking	1	1.3	0	0.0	1	5.9
Beverages	1	1.3	1	2.3	0	0.0
Building	1	1.3	1	2.3	0	0.0
Department store	1	1.3	1	2.3	0	0.0
Entertainment	1	1.3	1	2.3	0	0.0
Financial firm/institution	1	1.3	0	0.0	1	5.9
Food trade	1	1.3	1	2.3	0	0.0
Leather and shoes	1	1.3	1	2.3	0	0.0
Sugar	1	1.3	1	2.3	0	0.0
Wood	1	1.3	0	0.0	1	5.9
Total	60	100	43	100	17	100

[1] percentage in relation to number of credits given to Austrian companies.
[2] percentage in relation to number of credits given to foreign companies.

Source: Calculations based on data extracted from the WBV archive.

The *Konzern*

As my quantitative research into the credit operations of the WBV progressed it became obvious that a certain group of clients stands out in importance and must thus be given a closer and more detailed examination. This group of clients comprises the subsidiary enterprises, the *Konzern* firms (*Konzernbetriebe*) which in the following will be referred to as the *Konzern*. These firms – the majority of which were joint-stock companies, although also some private limited companies and some partnerships were included – enjoyed a very privileged position. In the case of joint-stock companies the bank usually held a considerable part of their shares while with the other types of firm the bank's interest is harder to determine although either capital or credit participation can be assumed. Detailed research into the exact financial ties between the WBV and its *Konzern* is still pending but there can be little doubt about the importance of this group of customers within the framework of the bank.

An examination of the *Konzern* reveals not only that most of these firms were actually founded by the WBV itself but that these foundations in part date back to the 1880s and 1890s. In some cases it was also the bank itself that turned former partnerships or private limited companies into joint-stock companies while retaining a large number of shares of the respective firms. After the end of the First World War the bank was able to hold on to its *Konzern* not only within the newly-created Austrian Republic but also managed to retain some of its ownership and credit ties with firms now based in the successor states.

In view of the unstable economic situation in Austria for most of the interwar period the credit-financing of the *Konzern* perennially endangered the liquidity of the bank, which had to draw mainly on short-term foreign loans to channel long-term funds to its subsidiary enterprises.[18] Moreover, the bank had amassed shares in its *Konzern* firms. Early in the 1920s the bank acquired shares to insure against the inflation-induced devaluation of advances, and later the bank was often left with shareholdings after overdue advances to industrial customers had to be converted into equity participations. In the course of the interwar years the WBV could not dispose of those shares but had to continue issuing frequent and substantial credits to the *Konzern* in order not to further jeopardize these firms and thus undermine confidence in its own credit worthiness .

It is within the *Konzern* group of customers that credits were particularly prolonged (411 credits or 43.3 per cent of all *Konzern* credits as compared with 1 654 or 13.7 per cent of all non-*Konzern* credits) or existing credits increased (314 *Konzern* credits or 33.3 per cent as compared with 1 330 or 13.7 per cent of all non-*Konzern* credits) . By allowing the debit balance of industrial customers to roll over and by increasing the credit granted, short-term advances became long-term ones thus further solidifying the ties between the bank and its *Konzern*.

The importance of the *Konzern* firms cannot properly be deduced when merely comparing the *number* of firms and *number* of credits. While the total number of firms receiving advances over the studied nine-year period amounted to 3 076 and the total number of credits granted came to 10 628 the *Konzern* consisted of a comparatively small number of 60 companies – 43 Austrian and 17 foreign which received 949 credits (about 10 per cent of the total) with 829 credits distributed in Austria and 120 abroad. The weight of the *Konzern* firms emerges from the *amounts* of credits granted to them in comparison with the sum total of credits advanced to all the bank's customers.

Credit distribution and the *Konzern*

An examination of the actual credit flow from the WBV to its *Konzern* confirms that these firms were given preferential treatment. As mentioned above only about 10 per cent of the total number of WBV customer credits went to the *Konzern* firms. But a more detailed breakdown of these credits demonstrates that they were large. As Table 14.7 shows, an average of 44 per cent of the sum total of all customer credits were granted to *Konzern* firms from 1925 to 1933.

Table 14.7   Total sum and percentage of credits to Konzern firms (in million Austrian shillings), 1925–33

	Total		All Konzern		Total Konzern		ÖKonzern		FKonzern	
	sum	%	sum	%[1]	%		sum	%[2]	sum	%[3]
1925	171	100	92	53.8	100		86	93.5	6	6.5
1926	186	100	92	49.5	100		89	96.7	3	3.3
1927	245	100	70	28.6	100		64	91.4	6	8.6
1928	190	100	71	37.4	100		56	78.9	15	21.1
1929	202	100	75	37.1	100		54	72.0	21	28.0
1930	149	100	60	40.3	100		35	58.3	25	41.7
1931	108	100	70	64.8	100		64	91.4	6	8.6
1932	101	100	54	53.5	100		47	87.0	7	13.0
1933	65	100	45	69.2	100		36	80.0	9	20.0
	1417	100	629	44.9	100		531	64.4	98	15.6

Notes:
Total: total sum of all credits.
All *Konzern*: total sum of credits to all *Konzern* firms.
Ö*Konzern*: total sum of credits to all Austrian *Konzern* firms.
F*Konzern*: total sum of credits to all foreign *Konzern* firms.

[1] percentage in relation to total sum of credits.
[2] percentage in relation to total sum of credits to all *Konzern* firms.
[3] percentage in relation to total sum of credits to all *Konzern* firms.

Source: Calculations based on data extracted from the WBV archive.

As a considerable number of credits was advanced in foreign currencies (27.7 per cent in US dollars, 9.9 per cent in Swiss francs, 4.4 per cent in pound sterling and 13.4 per cent in twelve other foreign currencies), I converted the total sum of credits for the period 1925 to 1933 into million Austrian shillings. Figure 14.1 compares the total credit volume in million Austrian shillings per year with the index of industrial production (1929 = 100). It is interesting to note that a certain counter-movement of credit flows and industrial production existed over the period. Figure 14.1 clearly shows that whereas the credit volume was highest in 1927 and declined from that year onwards (with a slight reversal in 1929), industrial production continued its upturn and peaked in 1929. From 1929 onwards both credit flow and industrial production show a downward trend with industrial production indicating a first sign of recovery in 1933. These figures warrant more detailed research into the credit policy of the WBV and also into the demand for credit by its customers in relation to the performance of Austrian industry, but this would exceed the scope of the chapter.

The dominant role of the *Konzern* firms can be deduced from the credit volume distributed by the bank to these clients. A look at Table 14.7, listing the total credit volume in million Austrian shillings to all firms, to the *Konzern* as a whole and to the *Konzern's* Austrian and foreign sections reveals an interesting picture and underlines what has been said earlier: of the total nine-year credit volume of 1417 million Austrian shillings 629 million or 44 per cent went to the *Konzern*. The yearly volumes and percentages vary over this period. The highest credit flow for the whole of the *Konzern* was reached in 1925 and 1926; 1927 marks a decline with a minor comeback in 1928 and 1929 and another drop in 1930 which is followed by a slight recovery in 1931 and a continuous decline in the following two years. More revealing seems the fact that, as compared with the overall credit flow, the years 1927 to 1930 mark a considerable reduction in the *Konzern's* share in credit volume. This seems to indicate that during the period of relative boom conditions and the first crisis year these big and important companies may have avoided borrowing from the bank and sought other sources of financing, including self-financing.[19]

When comparing the credits given to the Austrian and foreign firms of the *Konzern* the dominance of the Austrian share is striking. An average of 84.4 per cent or 531 million Austrian shillings went to the domestic part of the *Konzern* over the whole nine-year period while the foreign *Konzern* firms received 15.6 per cent or 98 million. But again a closer look at the details reveals some interesting aspects. While the credits to the Austrian part of the *Konzern* comprise the biggest share in the years 1925 to 1927 (between 93 and 96 per cent of the yearly credit flow to the whole of the *Konzern*) and experience a reduction in the following three years (between 58 and 78 per cent) the three crisis years see another shift back to the Austrian *Konzern* which absorbed 80 to 91 per cent of the total *Konzern* credits. The foreign *Konzern* firms show an opposite

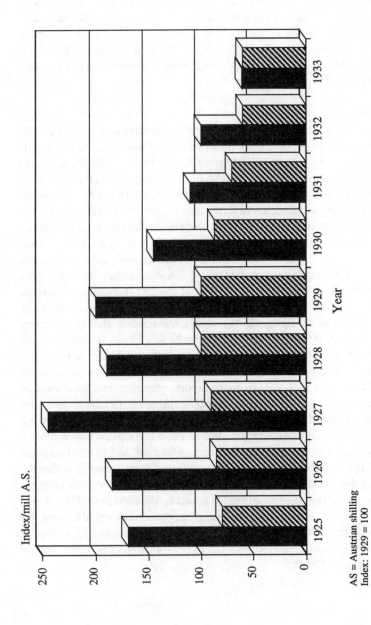

Index/mill A.S.

AS = Austrian shilling
Index: 1929 = 100

Source of index figures: *Monatsberichte des Österreich. Instituts für Konjunkturforschung, 12 (1938).*

Figure 14.1   Total credit volume (million A.S.) and industrial production index

movement with the largest credit flows in 1928, 1929 and 1930. These findings tally with the distribution of the total credit flow to domestic and foreign firms. Again the three years from 1928 to 1930 show a reduction in the credits to Austrian firms while the credits to foreign firms experience an increase. This shift in the amount, composition and distribution of credits during the relative boom years of the late 1920s and during 1930, at the end of which the economic crisis hit the world, tends to confirm the speculative view that the big Vienna banks, especially the CA, the BCA and the WBV, tried unsuccessfully to recapture Vienna's former role as the financial centre of the Danube basin.[20] However, the direction and amounts of credit flows will need to be examined more closely by further research.

Conclusion

This chapter has presented a first attempt at a quantitative analysis of the relationship between the WBV, one of the big universal banks in Austria, and its customers during the second half of the 1920s and the early 1930s. Its results underline several important aspects. First, this case study shows that as regards the question of continuity or discontinuity of credit ties between Austrian banks and their customers in the successor states after 1918 the WBV did indeed retain close relations with its customers, particularly with those parts of the former Habsburg Empire which as successor states consisted of Hungary, Romania and Yugoslavia. But in spite of this continued south-easterly outlook of the business policy of the WBV during the studied period it was nevertheless the domestic clientele that was granted the vast majority of credits. This seems to indicate that although the WBV did continue business with the neighbouring successor states the bank's credit-financing of industry was concentrated in the newly founded Austrian Republic. Second, as the bank's business shifted to the Austrian heartland it concentrated mainly on agriculture and food, on the engineering and metal working industry and its associated trading companies but it also provided credits for textile firms, transport companies, and the chemicals and electrical industries. Third, the *Konzern* firms, i.e. the dependent subsidiaries, were indeed a privileged set of customers receiving the largest share of the total credit volume over the studied period. As there was a mutual dependency between the bank and its *Konzern* the bank had to grant frequent and large credits to these firms to keep them from failing, especially after the outbreak of the world economic crisis in 1930 when *Konzern* firms received between 50 and 70 per cent of all credits granted. Although the WBV seemed to have slowly come to grips with the changing situation in Central Europe, the early 1930s with its economic crisis in general and its banking crisis in particular took too heavy a toll, finally ending the existence of this important Central European universal bank.

Notes

1. Only the years 1925 to 1933 have been taken into account as the years 1924 and 1934 are incomplete. In addition, 1925 marked the currency reform with the Austrian shilling substituting for the inflationary Austrian crown.
2. The history of the Wiener Bank-Verein still remains unwritten as attention concerning Austrian banks has mainly been focused on the Österreichische Credit-Anstalt für Handel und Gewerbe (CA). For lack of literature and sources this short history is primarily based on information extracted from the *Compass-Österreich,* a yearbook listing all relevant information concerning joint-stock companies. Further scattered information has been gained from the *Protokollbücher.*
3. Cf. Alice Teichova, *Kleinstaaten im Spannungsfeld der Großmächte: Wirtschaft und Politik in Mittel- und Südosteuropa in der Zwischenkriegszeit,* Munich, 1988, p. 57ff.
4. Cf. *Compass-Österreich, 1927,* p. 350. For share participation of Western banks in Central European banks see P.L. Cottrell, 'Aspects of Western Equity Investment in the Banking Systems of East Central Europe' in Alice Teichova and P.L. Cottrell (eds), *International Business and Central Europe, 1918–1939,* Leicester, New York, 1983, pp. 309–47.
5. *Compass-Österreich, 1918* and *1925.*
6. Cf. Herbert Matis, 'Disintegration and Multi-national Enterprises in Central Europe during the Post-war Years (1918–1923)' in Teichova and Cottrell, op. cit., note 4, pp. 88 and 90.
7. Cottrell, 'Aspects of Western Equity Investment ...', op. cit., note 4, p. 338.
8. Cf. Alice Teichova, 'Comments on Commercial (Universal) Banking in Central Europe: From Cisleithania to the Successor States', unpublished paper, p. 9.
9. Cf. Cottrell, op. cit., note 4, pp. 309–47
10. On Austrian banks in the interwar period see also Fritz Weber, 'Die österreichischen Großbanken in der Zwischenkriegszeit' in *Christliche Sozialdemokratie,* no. 4/85, pp. 323–57.
11. On the attempted reconstruction cf. Dieter Stiefel, *Finanzdiplomatie und Weltwirtschaftskrise. Die Krise der Credit-Anstalt für Handel und Gewerbe 1931,* Frankfurt, 1989, pp. 214–25.
12. Cottrell, op. cit., note 4, p. 328; Hans Kernbauer and Fritz Weber, 'Multinational banking in the Danube basin: the business strategy of the Viennese banks after the collapse of the Habsburg monarchy' in Alice Teichova, Maurice Lévy-Leboyer and Helga Nussbaum (eds), *Multinational enterprise in historical perspective,* Cambridge, 1986, p. 196.
13. Cf. e.g. W. Federn, 'Der Zusammenbruch der österreichischen Kredit-Anstalt' in *Archiv für Sozialwissenschaften und Sozialpolitik,* 67. Band/4. Heft, Tübingen, 1932, pp. 407, 411.
14. E.g. Kernbauer and Weber, op. cit., note 12, p. 195; but also Stiefel, op. cit., note 11, pp. 97–8, 124.
15. Table 14.5 includes only the most important branches of industry, trade and finance serviced by WBV credits. Those omitted from Table 14.5 played a minor role within the credit structure of the bank.
16. In 1920 agricultural production did not even attain a third of the 1913 output whereas until 1929 agricultural production output surpassed the 1913 level by 10 per cent. Cf. 'österreichs Volks-einkommen 1913 bis 1963', *Monatsberichte des Österreichischen Instituts für Wirtschaftsforschung,* Vienna, 1965, 14. Sonderheft, p. 5.
17. Peter Berger, *Der Donauraum im wirtschaftlichen Umbruch nach dem Ersten Weltkrieg. Währung und Finanzen in den Nachfolgestaaten Österreich, Ungarn und Tschechoslowakei 1918–1929,* Dissertationen der Wirtschaftsuniversität Wien; 35/1, Vienna, 1932.
18. P.L. Cottrell with C.J. Stone, 'Credits, and deposits to finance credits' in P.L. Cottrell, H. Lindgren and A. Teichova (eds), *European Industry and Banking Between the Wars. A Review of Bank–Industry Relations,* Leicester, London, New York, 1992, pp. 43–78. Cf. also Weber, op. cit., note 10, pp. 334–8.
19. Cf. Alois Mosser and Alice Teichova, 'Investment behaviour of industrial joint-stock companies and industrial shareholding by the österreichische Credit-Anstalt: inducement or obstacle to renewal and change in industry in interwar Austria' in Harold James, Håkan Lindgren and Alice Teichova (eds), *The role of banks in the interwar economy,* Cambridge, 1991; and Alois Mosser, Chapter 15 in this volume.
20. Cf. Kernbauer and Weber, op. cit., note 12, p. 195.

15 Financing industrial companies in interwar Austria: working capital and liquidity

Alois Mosser

The economic development of Austria during the First Republic has been increasingly judged by academic literature as deviating from the long-term development trend between the two world wars. Although opinions are still divided, as far as the reasons are concerned, the role of industry has gained more and more importance.[1] The economic decline of the interwar period was the result of structural changes, primarily of the reduced importance of industry and the trends towards agriculture, although services like banks and insurance increased their contributions to the Gross National Product during certain phases of the period. As I have pointed out elsewhere, it was not until 1950 that the industrial sector regained the share of Gross National Product which it enjoyed in 1913.[2] And it was industry, having recovered its strength, that was responsible for the rapid economic growth after 1950.

The 'failure' of Austrian industry during the interwar period has therefore been of great interest in historical research, especially as in 1918 a very high proportion of industrial plants of the Monarchy was inherited by Austria. These industrial enterprises were obviously not able to adjust themselves to the new market conditions and to develop successful development strategies. In this context the blame is often put on lack of capital which made it impossible for these enterprises to make the necessary investments. I have frequently dealt with this question and have arrived at the conclusion that 'the existing potential productive forces could not effectively develop because of the paucity of investment'.[3] However, this seems not to have been a result of a lack of capital but was due to the absence of promising opportunities for investment. If these existed the enterprises preferred internal sources of capital or – as was the case with joint-stock companies – financing by issuing shares. Long-term external capital (bonds, loans, credits, mortgages) played a comparatively subordinate role. Only large enterprises with corresponding access to the capital market used these means of financing. The Austrian entrepreneur of the interwar period usually avoided this kind of fixed burden with high rates of interest and repayment. This can also be regarded as a sign of a lack of confidence in the economic upturn starting in the mid-1920s as can the fact that investment was primarily aimed at reducing costs (rationalization), whereas increased production was only an objective for a few years (before 1929). Does the existence of a low level of investment in the First Austrian Republic, which cannot be ostensibly explained by an inadequate supply of capital, prove that the availability of capital to industrial enterprises did not generally pose a problem during this period? The following considerations will deal with the supply of working capital, i.e. with the liquidity of enterprises.

The sources contain very little to help us determine liquidity, i.e. the ability of enterprises to keep available disposable assets at the extent of existing liabilities at any given time. Annual reports of joint-stock companies allow the study of the liquidity of enterprises over the longer run – but only at the time when the annual balance sheet was drawn up. In addition, the total balances of between 70 and 90 per cent of all industrial joint-stock companies, as compiled by the Bundesamt für Statistik for the years from 1919 to 1936, make it possible to examine the relationship between disposable assets and existing liabilities. However, the data only provide an insight into assets which could be liquidated and the maturity of liabilities. As far as the above-mentioned 'total balances' are concerned this is only true for the years 1923–32 which will be dealt with in the following analysis.

The maintenance of liquidity is the most important aim of all the financial management measures of an enterprise. These are reflected in the balance of assets drawn up at the end of each business year. When studying liquidity it is advisable to exclude tangible and financial assets since their disposal is generally neither intended nor can it be assumed. Also long-term liabilities are to be excluded. The liquidity problem can thus be reduced to the extent of covering short- and medium-term liabilities by part of the current assets.

Although the existing material does not allow an exact determination of the overlapping of terms of part of the current assets and liabilities, a distinction can be made between assets to be realized on a short- or medium-term basis and obligations to be met. By using different methods of calculation the liquidity aspect can be approached in several ways. First, the relationship between the enterprise's own assets, which can be liquidated at any time (cash in hand, bank credit balances, remittances) and mature liabilities (bank credits, acceptances) is to be dealt with (liquidity I). Second, the relationship between those claims and liabilities which derive from sales and services (i.e. debtors and creditors) is also instructive (liquidity II). However, it cannot be ruled out that these positions might include other assets or obligations. Third, current assets not including stock (raw materials, semi-finished and finished goods) are to be compared with the overall number of short-term liabilities (liquidity III). This approach is justified since stock – although not completely – forms an integral part of the enterprise's assets which must be considered illiquid from an operational point of view. Fourth, rough estimation of a company's liquidity can be based on the ratio between the overall current assets and the total of short- and medium-term liabilities (liquidity IV), although in this case the aforementioned principle that operational parts of the current assets are to be regarded as illiquid cannot be taken into account.

When interpreting these index numbers it has to be considered that the data used only allow a rough division of assets and outside capital according to disposability and maturity; as the criteria on which these divisions are based remain unchanged during the period reviewed, a comparison over this period can give reliable indications as far as the development of liquidity is concerned. However, it is not possible to make a precise judgement for a randomly selected year. It must also be pointed out that it was only after the Austrian shilling was introduced in 1925 that the collective balances for the years 1923 and 1924 were calculated by converting the existing values in Austrian crowns according to the official exchange rate. As each position in the balance had been 'inflated' differently because of varied levels of investment a conversion based on the same exchange rate changed and falsified the values and their magnitudes. The liquidity figures for the years 1923 and 1924, which in parts strongly deviate from the other years, thus not only reflect the special conditions prevailing in the years before the currency stabilization but especially give proof of the peculiar method of drawing up the collective balances .

Liquidity IV (see Table 15.1) shows that for the whole period from 1923 to 1932 the value of current assets of industrial joint-stock companies exceeded the amount of mature liabilities. In 1925 this additional coverage amounted to one-third but declined continually during the years of increased economic activity until reaching 15 per cent in 1928; during the crisis years it fluctuated between 11 and 16 per cent. Accordingly, liquidity existed at any time although it did clearly decline during the economic upturn (until 1929) and at the beginning of the downturn. In 1932, without doubt the height of the economic crisis, liquidity was improving.

If stock is not seen as adequate cover for liabilities, as is the case with liquidity III (see Table 15.1), then the liquidity of industrial joint-stock companies was not sufficiently covered in any year. Also this method indicates a deterioration of liquidity in the second half of the 1920s; in 1925 every fourth shilling of the mature liabilities exceeded the liquidity of industrial joint-stock companies, in 1929 every third shilling. An increase in liquidity during the downturn of the business cycle in 1929 is more clearly seen, as with liquidity IV.

The relationship between debtors and creditors (liquidity II – see Table 15.1) generally presents an excess of debts with the suppliers over the debts arising from goods supplied. However, this relationship became increasingly balanced in the course of time. This trend continued unabated during the economic depression and in 1932 the liquidity situation can be regarded as satisfactory.

Liquidity I (see Table 15.1) is of special importance as it most clearly presents the state of actual liquidity at the time when the balance was drawn up. The first balance drawn up in Austrian shillings, i.e. the one in 1925, demonstrates that on average the industrial joint-stock companies were only in the position to cover two-fifths of the mature liabilities with liquid assets. In the following year liquidity decreased to 16 per cent of the liabilities. During the following period of economic upturn, which resulted in increased investments, liquidity could only be increased to a meagre 20 per cent. Liquidity was strengthened more rapidly during the crisis years than during the period of economic upturn. In the year 1932 liquid assets amounted to 28 per cent of mature liabilities.

Table 15.1   Liquidity of industrial joint-stock companies, 1923–32

Year	Liquidity I	Liquidity II	Liquidity III	Liquidity IV
1923	0.74	0.76	0.72	1.18
1924	0.57	0.60	0.59	1.01
1925	0.42	0.79	0.74	1.33
1926	0.16	0.89	0.68	1.22
1927	0.18	0.86	0.65	1.16
1928	0.20	0.85	0.66	1.15
1929	0.20	0.92	0.66	1.15
1930	0.24	0.95	0.68	1.14
1931	0.27	0.93	0.68	1.11
1932	0.28	0.98	0.72	1.16

Notes:
Liquidity I: Ratio of liquid assets (cash in hand, bank credit balances, remittances) and mature liabilities (bank credits, acceptances).
Liquidity II: Ratio of debtors and creditors.
Liquidity III: Ratio of current assets excluding stock and short-term liabilities.
Liquidity IV: Ratio of current assets and short-term liabilities.

Source: Statistisches Handbuch für die Republik Österreich, ed. Bundesamt für Statistik 1 (1920)–17 (1937). Chapter: 'Erwerbsgesellschaften und Genossenschaften: Aktiengesellschaften'.

Before arriving at further conclusions it has to be stressed once again that values for single years and liquidity indexes taken on their own are not very conclusive. Only the trends and different developments of the four liquidities studied can provide a useful indication of the determination of the liquidity of industrial joint-stock companies.

Despite these reservations two facts stand out relatively clearly: the first is that industrial joint-stock companies were inadequately supplied with working capital. Only if raw materials are completely included in liquid assets, which doubtless does not apply in reality, do these exceed short- and medium-term liabilities. If stock is not taken into account liquidity appears seriously jeopardized. In particular, cash assets and equivalent means of payment for settling liabilities seem to have been lacking. Second, the data show that the deterioration of liquidity during the economic upturn (until 1929) could not only be stopped during the crisis years but that liquidity was even improved. All index numbers show this development.

Industrial enterprises therefore did not dispose of enough working capital and until 1929 developed an increased demand for short-term bank credits. According to the sources demand decreased after 1930. A look at the development of short-term bank credits supplied to industrial joint-stock companies underlines this trend. In 1925 the average enterprise accounted for 155 000 shillings in credits of this kind. Until 1929, i.e. within a four-year period, this amount showed a five fold increase to 857 000. The end of the economic upswing in 1930 marked a decrease in business and also a reduction in the demand for working capital by a fifth within a two-year period (until the end of 1931); the year 1932 did not show any significant changes. (All amounts are given in current prices.)

To see a causal connection between a decrease in sales and a reduction of working capital is only permissible to a very limited extent. A lower turnover of capital, which is connected with a negative business trend, makes it quite often necessary to increase cash in order to keep up liquidity. Some light can be thrown on this aspect if changes in the use of the total capital are taken as an indicator for the course of business. The use of the total capital decreased on an average of 6.5 per cent between 1929 and 1931. This could be interpreted as a result of decreased turnovers. The demand for short-term bank credits decreased by about 20 per cent which means that for 13.5 per cent of this reduction another explanation has to be found.

The crisis years led to a change in the structure of capital (see Table 15.2). The ratio between equity capital and loan capital shifted from 0.84 (in 1929) to 1.12 (in 1931); on average the use of equity capital increased by 8.5 per cent during these two years whereas loan capital fell by 19 per cent. Short-term borrowed capital was responsible for this reduction, since long-term credits were actually increasing. The industrial joint-stock companies were able to increase their equity capital absolutely and relatively and to reduce their liabilities during the crisis years (this trend continued more intensively in 1932).

Three circumstances promoted this, at first glance, surprising development. In many cases the bad business results of 1931 and 1932 – the reported losses exceeded the profits of industrial joint-stock companies by 38 per cent in 1931 and 160 per cent in 1932 – enforced stabilizing measures (devaluations, new issues of shares, the conversion of credit capital into participation capital, etc.) which positively influenced the capital structure. From today's point of view it has to be stressed that these measures for overcoming the crisis took effect very rapidly. Comparing the balances of profits and losses of all industrial joint-stock companies the business figures for 1932 already surpassed the figures for 1929. It would be rewarding to deal with the different reasons for this.

Table 15.2   Structure of capital and profits of industrial joint-stock companies (JSC), 1923–32 (in current prices, thousand Austrian shillings)

Year	No. of JSCs	Balance total (average)	Equity capital (average)	Loan capital (average)	Short-term bank credits (average)	EC: LC	Losses in % of profits
1923	583	1567	383	1088	56	0.35	10.53
1924	554	2305	520	1701	44	0.31	61.76
1925	414	6183	3299	2732	155	1.21	17.40
1926	515	5732	2949	2649	452	1.11	35.55
1927	522	6122	2966	3002	556	0.98	25.81
1928	540	6394	2981	3225	568	0.92	34.58
1929	525	6949	3088	3686	857	0.84	87.08
1930	470	6865	3283	3425	785	0.96	84.92
1931	452	6474	3356	3005	693	1.12	137.56
1932	455	6694	3494	3108	709	1.12	259.82

Source: Statistisches Handbuch für die Republik Österreich, ed. Bundesamt für Statistik 1 (1920) – 17 (1937). Chapter: 'Erwerbsgesellschaften und Genossenschaften: Aktiengesellschaften'.

A second reason for the decreasing indebtedness of industrial joint-stock companies during the crisis years seems to be the fact that a number of enterprises were able to repay outside capital. This is clearly seen in the analysis of the financial management processes of single industrial enterprises and also certain industrial branches. In the early 1930s the majority of breweries, for example, were able to reduce the number of expensive short-term bank credits.

Third, it has to be taken into account that in the course of the stabilization measures, but also outside of these, short- and medium-term bank credits were turned into long-term ones. In contrast to short-term credits long-term ones were used more, absolutely and relatively, during the crisis years. This trend can be very clearly discerned in 1932 when long-term outside capital increased on an average of 48 per cent whereas short-term credits dropped by 6 per cent. These developments certainly helped to improve the liquidity of enterprises as now short-term credits, which were necessary to keep up business on a long-term basis, could at least be partly disposed of over a longer period of time without being subject to call.

As a result of the above discussion, the question posed at the beginning of the chapter, whether industrial enterprises were sufficiently supplied with working capital during the interwar period, has to be mostly answered in the negative even when interpreting the results very cautiously. Enterprises often tried to avoid the imposing threat of illiquidity by prolonging short-term credits – and even increasing them during the economic upturn – which in fact meant turning these credits into long-term ones. When the economic crisis broke and banks themselves faced financial difficulties calling in outstanding short-term credits or putting up for discussion their prolongation many enterprises had to stop production for lack of working capital. The resulting stabilization measures caused an improvement of the capital structure and an increase in the share of equity capital or the conversion of short-term credits into long-term ones. As the crisis progressed the liquidity situation of industrial enterprises eased. This development must be attributed in part to the above-mentioned stabilization measures but it must also be explained by the often neglected phenomenon that many enterprises were able, with or despite of a reduced course of business (decreasing turnover), to achieve a balanced structure of costs and profits which for instance can be seen in the increasing adjustment of debtors and creditors in terms of value.

Notes
1. Cf. A. Mosser and A. Teichova, 'Investment behaviour of industrial joint-stock companies and industrial shareholding by the Österreichische Credit-Anstalt: inducement or obstacle to renewal and change in industry in interwar Austria', in Harold James, Håkan Lindgren and Alice Teichova (eds), *The role of banks in the interwar economy,* Cambridge, 1991, containing further literature.
2. Ibid., p. 123.
3. Ibid., p. 134.

16 The industrial clientele of the Hungarian General Credit Bank, 1920–26

Agnes Pogány

The role of the commercial banks in industrial business, especially the personal ties between banks and industrial enterprises, have always attracted a great deal of attention in economic history, economics and even in sociology. For example, John Scott refers to the economic power concept of Marxism and the anti-trust concerns of the American liberal tradition as two independent sources of this interest.[1] Seeking to avoid ideological barriers recent research has tried to clarify the phenomenon by analysing its historical background and comparing the past experiments of various European countries.[2] The aim of this chapter is to investigate the contents of bank–industry relations in the Hungarian General Credit Bank in the period 1920–26.

The Hungarian General Credit Bank's industrial activity before 1914

The Hungarian General Credit Bank,[3] founded in the year of the Ausgleich (1867), had a crédit mobilier character from its beginning. Its business was broadly defined by its statute, and comprised all branches of banking activity, including participation in industrial and commercial enterprises, commissions and share issue.[4] The Credit Bank granted current account advances and accepted current account deposits from 1867 on. *Kontokorrent* was the innovation which spread quickly in Hungary during the second half of the nineteenth century. It proved extremely suitable for industrial financing, as it could either be in credit (deposit) or in debit (overdraft) and reliable clients were allowed regular overdrafts. The current account credits, formally short-term but permanently renewed, proved one of the most lucrative businesses of the Credit Bank.

The Credit Bank acquired the biggest 'sphere of influence' among the Hungarian banks at the turn of the century. Before 1869 railway investments were the most characteristic but some mines and earthenware industrial firms were also founded by the bank in this early period. The crises of 1869 and 1873 stymied the bank's interest in promoting business and industrial finance for a number of years. In the early 80s the Credit Bank was the only Hungarian commercial bank which dealt with the founding of industrial firms; but it preferred promotions when the government also participated in them. At the beginning of the decade it took part in the government development programme of the seaport Fiume (Rijeka) by promoting the Fiume Rice Mill (1881), Fiume Mineral Oil Refinery (1882) and three other smaller companies. In Transylvania the Kronstadt Wood Pulp Mill was established by the bank, also with government approval, in 1888.

The turn of the century was marked by a new phenomenon in industrial finance: the Credit Bank established its industrial concerns in the milling and sugar industry where its commodity department had already served as the sales agency and head office of cartels for the Hungarian milling and sugar industry for some time.[5] In 1875 the bank merged two mills which had become insolvent during the crisis of the previous years. The milling concern was broadened by acquiring majority shares in other mills as well. The Credit Bank's milling interests were unified in a giant enterprise called 'Hungaria United Steammills Co. Ltd' in 1897.

The Credit Bank established a contractual connection with the biggest Hungarian engineering firm Ganz in 1894–95 when the company was granted a bigger loan by the bank, which had already had some interest in Ganz. In the 1890s, the Credit Bank bought the Ganz family's shares, which were offered to it by the Swiss banking house Thois Söhne.[6] In 1895, the president of the bank, count Ede Pallavicini, was nominated by the bank to chair the Ganz board of directors. In 1900, Zsigmond Kornfeld took over the presidency. Ganz was one of the most important clients in the Credit Bank's concern which was demonstrated by the fact that the bank was represented on the company's board by high-ranking officials, with Kornfeld succeeded by Adolf Ullman. The firm had been mostly self-financing until the end of the nineteenth century, but from that time on it became necessary to obtain a permanent overdraft from a bigger bank.

In the first decade of the twentieth century the Credit Bank's interest turned to the textile industry, which it had hitherto neglected. As a consequence of the industrial support policies of successive Hungarian governments several textile works were established by the bank.

Industrial activity in the 1920s

Trying to reconstruct the Credit Bank's industrial clientele in the 1920s, I used the protocols of the meetings of the Credit Bank's board of directors, which contain all the important information concerning the clients of the Credit Bank (credits, promotions, increases of capital, changes of ownership, acquisition of new subsidiary companies, the formation and dissolution of syndicates, etc). My other important source was the lists prepared by the accounting department of the bank enumerating the companies that belonged to the bank's concern (*Konzern-Unternehmungen*) or to the bank's participations in syndicates (*Consortialbeteiligungen*). In this chapter I use both to produce a reconstruction of the bank's customers.

According to the protocols, 590 companies were granted credits by the Hungarian General Credit Bank between 1920 and 1926. (In the analysis that follows, I have excluded private persons, banks, insurance companies, transport and agricultural firms from the data-base.) Only half of the 590 firms were registered as joint-stock companies. Beside the biggest Hungarian enterprises, one can find the names of many small and medium-sized firms in the credit lists. Private banking houses with well established names like (König – Strausz) or the famous private mills of Schmidt and Császár were also clients of the Credit Bank. The story of the Schosbergers (a private banking, wholesale merchant and landowning firm), which ended with the incorporation of the Schosbergers' sugar works at Selyp in the sugar concern of the Credit Bank in 1926 has already been told by the late György Ránki.[7]

Table 16.1 The most frequently mentioned industrial companies in the credit protocols of the Credit Bank, 1920–26

Company	Frequency
1. Hungaria Vereinigte Dampfmühlen AG	33
2. Pannonia Hanf und Flachsindustrie AG	31
3. Joss & Löwenstein AG	26
4. Ungarische Baumwolle – Industrie AG	25
5. Ungarische Allgemeine Maschinenfabrik AG	22
6. Ganz'sche Elektrizitäts AG	21
7. Rokka Strick und Wirkwarenfabrik AG	21
8. Porzellan-, Steingut- und Ofenfabrik AG	20
9. Ganz & Co. Danubius Maschinen-, Waggons- und Schiffbau AG	19
10. Magyaróvárer Kunstseidefabrik AG	19

Source: NA Z50 77/8, 78/8.

The majority of companies had only very loose connections with the bank: they were granted credit or had other dealings with the bank on no more than one or two occasions over the seven years. Only 13 per cent of the companies were mentioned more frequently than five times in the protocols of the board of directors and scarcely more than 25 firms were mentioned more than ten times. The first ten of the most frequently mentioned companies are listed in Table 16.1. This analysis of relative frequency appears to support the critical arguments of Richard Rudolph and Richard H. Tilly on the Gerschenkron theory. Rudolph argued:

> The Vienna Great Banks were not the venturesome substitutes for entrepreneurs that the brothers Pereire would have had in mind. Rather the Great Banks selected plump, juicy firms with favourable prospects, firms with the difficulties and risks of their early years already completed; they then built up expanded credit dealings with the firms, in many cases granting unsecured bank credit in fairly large and possibly increasing sums.[8]

Or as R.H. Tilly has pointed out, the essence of the German universal banking was 'development assistance for the strong'.[9]

All the enterprises that were mentioned most frequently (which meant the most intensive credit links with the bank) belonged without exception to the Credit Bank's concern (*Konzern-Unternehmungen*). The Credit Bank had share-holdings in them, and had taken part in the promotion of most of them (see Tables 16.1 and 16.2). On the other hand, there were giant companies which hardly had a mention. Urikány-Zsilthaler Ungarische Kohlenbergwerke and Ungarische Allgemeine Kohlenbergbau AG had only one credit from the Credit Bank, while the AG für elektrische und Verkehrsunternehmungen, which incorporated more than a dozen electricity works, was mentioned only eight times in the protocols. In spite of this, in my opinion, share ownership and intensive credit activity did positively correlate in the case of the biggest clients of the Hungarian General Credit Bank.

Table 16.2   The Credit Bank's industrial concern (31 December 1924)

Company	Year founded	Founded by	Total credit[*]	Share capital[*]	Owner-ship	NOCRD
Steel and engineering industry						
1. Ung. Allgemeine Maschinenfabrik AG Budapest	1911	HGC[1] CA[2] Daimler[3]	11 242.6	500	6.2	1
2. Ganz-sche Elektrizitäts AG Budapest	1906	HGC Ganz- Dan	5 212.5	2 520	7.0	2
3. Ganz & Co. Danubius AG Budapest	1869	Private merchants of Pest	6 006.5	3 780	9.3	2
Sugar industry						
4. Ung. Zuckerind. AG Budapest	1889	Bleichr. Disc. Ges.	8 056.8	3 600	11.9	2
5. Mezöhegyeser Zuckerind. AG Budapest	1890	Stummer[4] governm	1 000.0	900	10.0	1
6. Georgia AG Budapest	1894	HGC	4 063.6	6 000	22.4	2
7. Bácsmegyeer Zuckerfabrik AG Novi Vrbas	1911	HGC PMKB[5] ŽIVNO[8]	7 692.1	25[6]	4.7[7]	1

Company	Year founded	Founded by	Total credit*	Share capital*	Owner ship	NOCRD
Textile industry						
8. Joss & Löwenstein AG Budapest	1920	HGC	1298.7	130	26.6	1
9. Pannonia Hanf- und Flachsind. AG Budapest	1907	HGC Georgia	4470.8	1242	31.1	3
10. Rokka Strick- und Wirkwarenfabrik AG Budapest	1920	HGC UBWI[9] BSPV[10]	1197.0	82	35.7	2
11. Ung. Baumwolle Ind. AG Budapest	1884		5400.9	33	42.9	2
12. Kattundruck- Ind. AG Budapest	1906	HGC	544.3	1800	15.0	3
13. Linum Spinnerei AG Budapest	1922	Panno[11]	2161.6	300	17.5	2
14. Vaterländische Kammgarnspinnerei AG Budapest	1922	HGC[12]	5889.1	380	3.9	2
15. Magyarovárer Kunstseidefabrik AG Budapest	1923		3447.4	300	22.1	2
Mines and earthenware industry						
16. Porzellan, Steingut und Ofenfabrik AG Budapest	1922	HGC[13]	3698.4	2000	20.0	1
17. Ung. Allg. Kohlenbergbau AG Budapest	1891		4575.6[14]	484	7.8	0
Wood industry						
18. Ung. Allg. Holzindustrie AG Budapest	1918		9883.7	86	11.0	4
19. Lignum Trust AG Zürich	1921	HGC Blank[15]	1801.3	7.2[16]	13.8	1
20. Zabolaer Holz industrie AG Zabola (Rom)	1905		0.5[17]	25[18]	4.9	0

Company	Year founded	Founded by	Total credit*	Share capital*	Owner-ship	NOCRD
Food industry and trade						
21. Hungaria Ver. Dampfmühlen AG Budapest	1897	HGC	10434.6	2100	7.6	1
22. Intern. Export und Import AG Budapest	1918		4703.0	1200	68.4	4
23. Excelsior Delikatessen- Konserven-	1920		2200.5	450	21.0	4

Notes:
[1] Hungarian General Creditbank (Ungarische Allgemeine Kreditbank AG).
[2] Österreichische Credit-Anstalt für Handel und Gewerbe.
[3] Österreichische Daimler AG.
[4] Karl Stummer.
[5] Ungarische Kommerzbank von Pest (Hungarian Commercial Bank of Pest).
[6] Million dinars.
[7] Data from 1911.
[8] Živnostenská banka.
[9] Ungarische Baumwolle-Industrie AG.
[10] Békéscsabaer Sparkasse Verein.
[11] Pannonia Hanf- und Flachsindustrie AG.
[12] Founded by: Hungarian General Creditbank, Adolf Kohner's Söhne, Waffen-Maschinenfabrik AG, Erste Ung. Wollwäscherei Ag, Ung. Baumwolle-Ind. Nederlandsche Wolen en Garen Maatschappij (Amsterdam), Kammgarnspinnerei Stohr & Co. (Leipzig), G. Schmidt jun. Söhne (Altenburg), Elberfeldtextilwerke (Elberfeld).
[13] Founded by the Ung. Allg. Kreditbank, Ung. Allg. Kohlenbergbau AG Budapest-Szentlörinczer Ziegelfabrik AG, Tataer Dachziegel- und Ziegelfabrik AG, Ofen- und Tonwarenfabrik AG (vormals Hardtmuth L & C, Wien).
[14] Creditor.
[15] Blankart & Cie.
[16] Million Swiss francs.
[17] Million Swiss francs.
[18] Million leus.
* million Hungarian crowns.
Ownership: per cent of Creditbank participation in the company's share capital.
NOCRD: Number of Credit Bank's representatives on the board of directors (supervisory boards incl.).

Sources: HNA Z 64/1 Hungarian General Credit Bank, Book-Keeping Department, Kormos féle Nagy Magyar Compass, vols 1923–25.

Of the Credit Bank's customers, 50 per cent consisted of industrial firms, and 44 per cent were commercial firms. The share of the industrial companies was relatively low compared with other Budapest banks' clienteles. According to Szádeczky-Kardoss, two-thirds of the subsidiary firms of the Budapest banks were industrial and only one-fifth were commercial in 1924.[10] The Hungarian General Credit Bank had the most clients in food processing (milling and sugar industry), textiles, chemicals and forestry. The share of engineering is strikingly low whereas many Hungarian authors considered the Credit Bank to be 'strong' in that industry. Nevertheless, the Credit Bank's clients in the engineering industry could be said to be the biggest in Hungary (Ganz & Co. Danubius, Hofherr-Schrantz-Clayton-Shuttleworth, Láng etc.). All the sugar works, flour mills, and machine building companies had belonged to the Credit Bank's sphere of influence well before 1914; the textile works, on the contrary, were mostly founded after 1918. Only four of the eleven textile works had been promoted before the Great War.

On reconstructing the credit lists of the Credit Bank, we can examine the regional structure of the bank's clientele too. The majority of the client companies had their centres in Budapest. Provincial and separated territories each had the same percentage (20 per cent). Comparing these percentages to the data of Szádeczky-Kardoss we can observe that other Budapest banks had less detached enterprises in 1924 than the Credit Bank. Having very close connection with the state, the Hungarian General Credit Bank took part in government programmes to develop some backward regions of pre-1914 Hungary (e.g. Transylvania and Fiume/Rijeka) and thus acquired many affiliated companies in these regions. In the years immediately following the war, one of the most urgent tasks was to settle the situation of the client firms in the territories separated from Hungary in the Trianon Peace Treaty. The Credit Bank tried many ways to avoid the effects of the nostrification laws of the successor states and to keep the companies under her umbrella. In some cases, it was sufficient to remove the firms' headquarters to the successor states (e.g. the Budapest office of the Stummer Sugar Works moved to Trnava). The shares of the Bácsmegye Sugar Works were sold with the first option to purchase if the Croatian Credit Bank (affiliated to the Credit Bank) wished to sell, and a few years later, the Credit Bank repurchased its former stock. The maintenance of relations with these separated companies was facilitated by the survival of a few branch offices in Romania. Some of the companies were sold for good but bankers' agreements remained valid and credits were granted to the former partners by the Credit Bank later on as well. There was also another frequently used method to evade nationalization: promotion of holding companies in neutral European countries (mainly in the Netherlands and Switzerland).[11] These holding companies took over the shares of the separated companies in exchange for their own equities, thus formally changing the Hungarian or Austrian ownership of the given firms to a Swiss or Dutch one. The equities of the Erste Ungarische Filz-, Tuch- und Fezfabrik AG were held by the Tarbouches AG, Zurich but the company was financed as before on a 50–50 per cent basis by Creditanstalt and the Credit Bank.[12]

In the paralysed economic situation of Hungary after the lost war, revolutions and counter-revolution, hardly any credit was needed in 1920–21. Only at the beginning of 1922 can we observe a revival in the lending activity of the Credit Bank. In 1922 and the subsequent years, the list of debtors became longer and longer and parallel to the accelerating inflation, credit limits rose higher and higher. Considerable overdrafts were approved for the most important clients. According to an aide-mémoire of 12 December 1923, with a K 26.5 million credit limit on current account Ganz & Co. Danubius Maschinen, Waggon- und Schiffbau AG was indebted to the bank to the extent of K 3 650 million, while the Ganz'sche Elektrizitäts AG, which had a credit limit of K 5 million on current account, had debts of K 1 350 million.[13]

The period 1922–23 was marked by increases in capital. The Credit Bank participated in 40 of these kinds of transaction concerning her clients in 1922 and 50 in the following year.[14] It was not unusual for the biggest companies to issue new equities two or three times a year. Besides bank credit, an increase in share capital was the only possible means to acquire new capital, since foreign capital was not available in the first years of the 1920s. In 1923, one of the oldest Hungarian banks, the Industrial Bank, was amalgamated with the Hungarian General Credit Bank, and in this way the bank's sphere of influence broadened with new industrial enterprises.

The savingscrown was introduced by government regulation in February 1924. Its value was fixed to the foreign quotations of the crown and to the rates of some Hungarian securities. Although the regulation made the use of the savingscrown compulsory, the Credit Bank hardly used it and credits were granted in inflated currency as before. After the monetary stabilization in June 1924, an end was made to the practice of granting credits in crown currency. The Hungarian stabilization, strongly influenced by Montagu Norman, brought about strict monetary restriction and high interest rates. Tight money encouraged the inflow of short-term foreign capital. The protocols show that the Credit Bank supplied its clients abundantly with short-term foreign currency credits, which they used for long-term purposes (as is shown by frequent credit extensions). That was hardly a new phenomenon in the business of the Hungarian universal banks but it involved enormous risks at this time. The Credit Bank did not always take the greatest care. In the cases of its favoured firms, it dispensed with collaterals, and the amount of credit was sometimes higher than the balances should have allowed (see Table 16.2). Big companies that belonged to the Credit Bank's concern were granted credit without collateral whereas smaller ones had to provide pledges, mortgages and/or sureties, in spite of the fact that some of the biggest enterprises, particularly in the milling and engineering industries, faced several problems (overcapacity, a small internal market, insufficient export outlets). Rescuing these giants – the cornerstones of the Credit

Bank's industrial concern before 1914 – required large-scale lending though it was sometimes rather hazardous as the case of Ganz-Danubius shows.

The contracting markets in the interwar Hungarian economy and the fierce competition among the large engineering companies forced Ganz-Danubius to grant long term commodity credits to its customers.[15] Ganz had to refinance these commodity credits mainly by short-term credits at high interest rates taken at the Credit Bank and several foreign banks (Pierson, Amstelbank, Goldman-Sachs, Irving Syndicate). Conversion from short- to medium-term credit was the main reason for the 1 million dollar loan given by the Amstelbank at 10 per cent interest in April 1926.[16] As a result of this policy Ganz became the most indebted client of the Credit Bank by the second half of the 1920s. The deteriorating financial position and the decreasing turnover (of 60–70 million pengös before the war, of 30–40 million in the 1920s)[17] prompted the Credit Bank to seek a solution to the problem. It suggested the development of the company's commercial activity by founding its own sales agencies abroad. By 1934, Ganz had representatives in Alexandria, Athens, Belgrade, Bratislava, Brussels, Bucharest, Cluj, Klagenfurt, Madrid, Milano, Sofia, Warsaw and Vienna.[18] The other mode of eliminating the severe problems was supposed to be the rationalization of production and the merger of large Budapest engineering firms. In July 1927, with the help of the Hungarian General Credit Bank, Ganz-Danubius merged with Schlick Nicholson Machine- Waggon- and Shipyard Ltd and with the Machine- and Railways-Equipment Factory Ltd of Kistarcsa. In December the same year, the Liptak Works also merged with them.[19] The fusions reduced the productive capacity of the Hungarian engineering industry and concentrated specialized production in mass production factories, making cost reductions possible.[20] The last years of the 1920s proved to be unsuitable for such reforms, however. In 1929, Ganz-Danubius showed a deficit which was financed through a merger with Ganz Electric. From 1930 to 1937, Ganz had a deficit each year. With the Hungarian payment moratorium having been proclaimed in the Summer of 1931 Ganz suspended payments on all its foreign currency credits.

Conclusion
Having analysed the structure of the Hungarian General Credit Bank's clientele we can distinguish three types of relationship between the Credit Bank and the client firms:

1. Debtor companies, obtaining permanent or temporary credits from the bank.
2. Members of the Credit Bank's shareholding, where the bank had a stake in the company's equity capital.

3. Members of the Credit Bank's concern, where the bank had a stake in the company's equity capital, a representative or representatives on the company's board and a credit relationship (see Table 16.2).

The most numerous was the group which had only credit relations with the bank. Approximately 20 per cent of the debtor companies were members of the Credit Bank's shareholding and even less, 25–30 companies, (approximately 5 per cent of the debtor firms in all) were members of the concern, which was the closest type of relationship between the bank and its clients. Analysis of relations between holding members and the bank (Table 16.3) shows that the majority of the holding members had neither credit at the bank nor belonged to the bank's sphere of interest. Only every third holding's member company had the strongest connection with the bank. Clients belonging to the holding or to the concern varied year by year, and it seems probable that there were no strict criteria set up for classification.

Table 16.3   *Types of relationship between the Credit Bank and members of its industrial concern (31 December 1924)*

Industry Branch	Number of companies	No other rel.	Only Credit	Only int.	Int. and credit
Steel and-engineering	9	3	0	0	6
Sugar and food processing	8	2	1	3	2
Textiles	17	5	2	0	10
Oil	7	6	0	0	1
Mines and earthenware	14	7	0	3	4
Wood	9	4	3	0	2
Others	27	19	2	1	5
Foreign value shares	10	8	1	0	1
Total	101	54	9	7	31
Per cent	100.0	53.5	8.9	7.0	30.6

Notes:
No other rel: The Credit Bank has a stake in the company's share capital but the company has no credit at the bank, and is not mentioned internally as a subsidiary company.
Only credit: The Credit Bank has a stake in the company's share capital and credit at the bank, but is not mentioned internally as a subsidiary company.
Only int: The Credit Bank has a stake in the company's share capital and is mentioned internally as a subsidiary company, but the company has no credit at the bank.
Int. and credit: The Credit Bank has a stake in the company's share capital and has credit at the bank, and is mentioned internally as a subsidiary company.

Source: HNA Z 64/1 Hungarian General Credit Bank, Book-Keeping Dept.

Shareholding and industry financing did coincide with each other only in the case of a few big firms which suggests that the selective character of the universal banks (Rudolph and Tilly) can be observed even as late as the 1920s. From the same facts we may conclude that the overwhelming majority of firms had only a very loose connection with the Credit Bank.

On the other hand, Rudolph's thesis on the conservative and risk-avoiding character of the crédit mobilier banks seems to be rather questionable, at least in the 1920s, and at least in Hungary in this period, since financing some of the 'well established firms' involved the highest risks for the bank.

Notes

1. John Scott, 'Theoretical Framework and Research Design' in *Network of Corporate Power. A Comparative Analysis of Ten Countries*, ed. by Frans M Stockman, Rolf Ziegler, John Scott, Polity Press & Basil Blackwell, Cambridge & Oxford, 1985, p. 3.
2. Alice Teichova, 'Rivals and Partners. Banking and Industry in Europe in the First Decades of the Twentieth Century', *Uppsala Papers in Economic History 1988*, Working Paper no. 1.
3. On the general history of the Credit Bank see G. Ránki, 'The Hungarian General Credit Bank in the 1920s', *International Business and Central Europe, 1918–1939*, ed. by Alice Teichova and P.L. Cottrell, Leicester University Press/St Martin's Press, New York, 1983, pp. 355–74.
4. *A Magyar Általános Hitelbank Igazgatóságának Üzleti Jelentése a 75. Üzletévröl*, pp. 8–9.
5. On the sugar industry see Ágnes Pogány, 'Bankers and families. The case of the Hungarian sugar industry', *European Industry and Banking between the Wars. A Review of Bank–Industry Relations*, ed. by P.L. Cottrell, Håkan Lingren and Alice Teichova, Leicester University Press, Leicester, London and New York, 1992, pp. 84–91.
6. Szekeres József-Tóth Árpád, *A Klement Gottwald (Ganz) Villamossági gyár története*, KJK, Budapest, 1926, p. 70.
7. Ránki, op. cit., note 3, p. 367.
8. Richard L. Rudolph, *Banking and Industrialization in Austria–Hungary*, Cambridge, 1976, p. 104.
9. Richard H. Tilly, 'German Banking 1850–1914. Development Assistance for the Strong', *The Journal of European Economic History*, vol. 15, no 1, 1986.
10. Szádecky-Kardoss Tibor, *A magyarországi pénzintézetek fejlödése*, Budapest, 1928, p. 191.
11. Herbert Matis, 'Disintegration and multi-national enterprises in Central Europe during the post war years (1918–23)', *International Business and Central Europe 1918–1939*, ed. by A. Teichova. P.L. Cottrell, Leicester University Press, 1983, p. 79.
12. HNA Z 50/77/5.
13. HNA Z 50/77.5.
14. HNA Z 64 Hungarian General Creditbank Book-Keeping Department 1/1.
15. Kádár Gusztáv, 'A bankok és az ipar egymáshoz való viszonya', *Magyar Gyáripar*, 1928, no. 10, pp. 4–9.
16. HNA Z 421 12 April 1926.
17. HNA Z 425/90 p. 443.
18. HNA Z 58/53/162, The Mannesmann concern also established its own sales agencies in the 1920s. See Alice Teichova, 'The Mannesmann Concern in East Central Europe in the Inter-war Period', in *International Business and Central Europe 1918–1939*, ed. by A. Teichova and P.L. Cottrell, Leicester University Press/St Martin's Press, New York, 1983, pp. 103–37.
19. HNA Z 425/90 p. 10.
20. HNA Z 421 20 June 1927 pp. 274–5.

PART IV

BANKERS AND BANK–INDUSTRY NETWORKS

17 Networks of bankers and industrialists in Greece in the interwar period

Margarita Dritsas

Greece
G21
N24
S24

Interwar sources point to the existence of powerful networks, some of which can be traced back to the previous century. The present chapter's scope is to formulate tentative hypotheses about the exercise of economic power through the formation of networks by focusing on bank–industry relations. More specifically it intends to look closely at the horizontal relations between the business sector in general and the banking sector; at network formation and joint directorships both among non-financial firms and between those and the banks.

In the nineteenth century networks operated in all sectors, not simply as bankers' groups, and were instrumental in the first phase of Greek industrialization, which however was short and led only to limited changes. Network formation was at the core of entrepreneurial strategy, whether in shipping or commerce, which were the main economic activities in the country. Large merchant houses in Syros for example dealt with transit, domestic and foreign trade through a network system that linked them with Marseilles, Livorno, Trieste, London, Liverpool, Smyrna, Constantinople, Odessa and Alexandria. At the same time they functioned as lenders for local shipowners, or were able to control the trade of particular products, e.g. cereals in Central Europe and beyond.[1] These networks had a strong kinship character and incorporated many members of the extended family who looked after business operations in various parts of the world. Relations among different networks were often cemented by marriage. Thus one network (family) could absorb another, appropriating at the same time its clientele and its economic basis, and gradually reinforcing its power structure. Shipping networks have even been credited with facilitating the expansion of the Greek merchant marine during the interwar years.[2]

As industrialization gathered pace in the twentieth century, banks became interested in the new sector and from 1924–25 credit became a sought-after resource but also a means of attracting new customers. Credit functions were now combined in many cases with ownership functions, the number of firms in which banks owned shares grew and bank-ownership rates within each firm also increased. Within the biggest bank, the National Bank of Greece (NBG) a new special department was organized to take care of industrial credit and then short-term accounts and long-term contracts, mostly linked to the attraction of foreign capital. At the same time, the bank's interest was reoriented towards, on the one hand, industries established in the centre (Athens–Piraeus area), rather than the periphery, and on the other, to particular industries such as chemicals, construction, electricity and railways. So other banks which also took an interest in industry such as the Bank of Athens, the Popular Bank and the Commercial Bank, by choice or by default, continued to finance more traditional sectors such as textiles, food and drink, carpets, paper, etc.

Many of the entrepreneurs involved in networks had set up joint-stock companies (JSC). This type of institution, giving the possibility of share ownership, proved extremely appropriate for the creation of networks. Many of the JSCs soon became customers of the major banks (NBG, Bank of Athens, Commercial Bank etc.) which owned part of their shares and also advanced credit. Others were established with the direct assistance of banks. However, whether customers were only or partly owned by a bank, these firms do not seem to have carried out their banking business exclusively with the same bank.

While in the nineteenth century networks incorporated mainly Greek diaspora and domestic resources, in the twentieth century, and more particularly during the interwar period, some reorientation occurred as networks also established links with foreign capitalists. Entrepreneurs and JSCs committed to this policy seemed to agree with the view that the country could only develop with the help of foreign capital.[3] For the NBG, the inclusion of foreigners also secured access to foreign markets. On the other hand, foreign banking institutions had shown their reluctance to arrange loans for the Greek market – government or other – without the participation of local financial groups. This procedure apparently minimized the risks associated with foreign investment. Local partners assisted foreign groups in overcoming cultural barriers, in acquiring information about the local scene and in providing communication channels.[4] The case of Hambros Bank of London and its relation with the NBG illustrated this point well.[5] Hambros had a very long presence in Greece as a government banker going back to the early nineteenth century. Later in 1893 they became mediators for the settlement of the Greek debt and advisers of the establishment of the Bank of Crete (1899). In the twentieth century they furnished most of the big Greek government loans. During the interwar period, they were involved in the issue of the Refugee Loan in 1924, the Public Works Loan of 1928, part of the Stabilization Loan and the establishment jointly with the National Bank of an Anglo-Greek trust to provide capital for Greek industry (1928–31). They had also approached the Banque de France (1932) on behalf of Greece for other loans, and signed a confidential financing agreement with Blair and Co. (N.Y.) which supported the Foundation Co., bidding for the Strymon irrigation projects.[6]

The Bank of Athens, initially an agent of French capital, was also active in similar fields. In 1925, it cooperated with the American firm Ulen & Monks Co. Ltd for a loan to finance the construction of a water supply system in Athens and other irrigation projects in Macedonia. Although Greek banks – rather than the state – 'activated' foreign direct investment for construction and public works,[7] and thus fed into both the political and the foreign dimension of networks, it is also true that to foreign circles the Greek network connection provided important benefits. In addition to lowering the cost of investment, it helped secure a firm foothold in the Greek market and, depending on the prestige and area of activities of the Greek members involved in the network, it allowed a high degree of control of the whole economy.

Despite these cases, the policy of Greek banks towards the local business sector in general was rather conservative, at least until the mid-1920s, and the gap was often filled by foreign exporters/importers who were ready to grant long-term credit to Greek firms[8] and by local private lenders' networks. At this time, many firms succeeded in independently negotiating important bond loans abroad. Even in the case of the cement industry, which had by then become oligopolistic in Greece and which maintained a very close relationship with the National Bank, parallel private networks competed with the banking sector. Private networks included shareholders and very often family members. The frequency and volume of private interfirm contracts were higher at the beginning of the interwar period (1913–15) and diminished over time as the presence of banks was strengthened and firms faced liquidity problems repeatedly (in 1921, 1926 and 1929–30).

From 1930, big firms relied less on private lending and banks increased the volume of credits granted to industries. They also lowered their interest rates and offered a number of other services. In the case of the NBG one could talk about a veritable campaign for the conquest of new customers/industrialists in addition to preserving as much of its old customer base as possible. On the other hand firms, in the face of fast changing conditions, not least of which were in technology, needed more capital both for short- and long-term obligations. Short-term credits most often rolled over to the next year so that they ultimately functioned like long-term loans. Exclusive cooperation between certain firms and one bank was common but often businessmen distributed their business among several banks, presumably to diminish control and to bargain for more favourable terms among competitors.

Networks of bankers and industrialists seem to have worked in each other's interests. One account of the period notes that as late as 1938, banking institutions '... have a strong personal character, their operations being directed closely by their founders and personal relations between bankers and their clientele are considered paramount for the maintenance and expansion of business'.[9] These comments appeared wholly applicable to smaller banks – regional or local – which were creations of a narrow circle of shareholders. Bigger banks, despite stricter accounting and controls and more objective systems of appraisal, also exhibited similar behaviour when negotiating credit contracts. The granting of loans to businessmen was done at the discretion of owners of banks or their executives who were assisted in their decisions by information acquired by 'intelligence bureaux' about the reliability of a client. Networks conveniently helped in providing such information.[10]

Bank–industry networks also had a political dimension. On one level this reflected the increasing formal state intervention in the economy but on another it confirmed that many politicians also held important positions in business. NBG governors were almost always political figures[11] and many politicians were shareholders and/or members of the board. Others figured in the founders' lists of joint-stock companies as well as on various boards of directors. This overlapping between politics and business was not only an indication of increasing state control but possibly also of strategies used to limit uncertainty stemming from contradictory state action, e.g. changing legislation. Networks also brought businessmen closer to supply contracts from various state agencies, e.g. the Army, or to commissions from international business deals. By including prominent personalities as members, they increased the prestige of banks or industries and were able to influence public opinion, thus enhancing the control function. An example, among others, is provided by the case of I. Eftaxias. A lawyer–economist, university professor and member of parliament, he was also Governor of the National Bank in 1914. By virtue of his office in the bank he also held directorships in several industries and other firms including the very important Athens–Piraeus Railway and the Astir Insurance Co., in which the NBG held a substantial number of shares. During the same period his brother served as minister in various cabinets.[12] The web of relations thus constructed not only secured information about government action but also allowed the exercise of control over a profitable transport company, and also deterred competitors from penetrating the same sector. On the other hand seats on the NBG board were given to other bankers in order presumably to minimize competition and to secure access to information.[13] Such practices could also be seen as strategic endeavours for an eventual expansion of the banks' customer base through the integration of other banks' customers. Participation most of all served to reinforce the prestige of operations that the bank sought to promote and to influence public opinion. In addition, in the case of the NBG, relations at government level reflected the fact that the state was an important – if not the most important – customer of the National Bank. NBG governors never hesitated to state publicly that the life of the bank could not be separated from the life of the country; that if '… a storm hit the Nation, the same storm would sweep through the Bank'. In practice, of course, they meant it rather the other way around, and history showed that whatever was good for the bank was also supposed to be beneficial to the nation.[14]

Looking at some of the groups behind another bank, the Commercial Bank of Greece, helps put network activity into a better perspective. Gregory Embedocles, founder and director general of this bank, shared many characteristics with other early entrepreneurs who had formed networks. He was born in Constantinople and was also educated outside Greece, in London. He held a Law Degree from the University of Athens and started his career in the Greek Postal Service and the Bank of Industrial Credit. When the latter went bankrupt he went to England where he started building a network with Greek, English and French bankers and other entrepreneurs. He returned to Greece at the end of the century and with his brother and a friend from Trieste, D. Cundumas, founded a broking office that soon became a small bank. Later, in 1905, the company acquired a new member, D. Petrokokkinos, also born and educated in London who had meanwhile married Embedocles's sister. The bank participated in and financed industrial firms (the most important of which was the Greek Gunpowder and Cartridge Co., Hellinikon Pyritidopoeion) in which Embedocles held a considerable number of shares. In 1908, the bank became a joint-stock firm under the new name of 'Commercial Bank of Greece'. Its founder preferred to remain general manager without becoming a majority shareholder, but kept his brother and brother-in-law as close associates. Until then, most JSCs' founders combined a majority share ownership with management functions. The Commercial Bank did not fit this pattern but seemed to follow an intermediate model between the individual and the managerial though the family dimension was prominent. Shares of the new bank were immediately bought by the National Bank of Greece, the Bank of Athens, Rodocanachi and Sons of London and a local bank operating from the town of Volos. The board reflected the catch-all character of the new institution and the orientation of its business, i.e. commercial and industrial communication with the big centres abroad, where Greeks also operated. The position of chairman was occupied by N.S. Serbos, ex-manager of the Odessa branch of the Crédit Lyonnais, the vice-chairman was M.I. Politis, an MP, chairman of the Athens–Piraeus Railway, and member of the National Maritime Co. Ltd; and the other directors were two more bankers and the manager of the Athens–Piraeus Railway. This structure proved efficient not only in day-to-day management but also in introducing innovations. Familiarity with city practices helped to introduce a new ethic in the Greek market based on efficient intelligence. Embedocles believed that 'as in every milieu, the best should be singled out, those who know their colleagues and think alike about them and those who usually know how much credit they obtain from the banks'.[15] He managed to obtain the credit lists of the other big commercial banks, the Ionian Bank and the Bank of Athens. By 1922, the network was extended further; following a two-pronged strategy, the firm included in the Greek board more representatives of firms from abroad and, later, created separate institutions outside Greece. The Commercial Bank of the Near East Ltd of Bishopsgate, London thus came into existence with the participation of Greek domestic and diaspora friends and sought to link with and serve the needs of Greeks operating in England, Constantinople, Alexandria and other Egyptian towns.[16] Other bankers joined in the business too like Rodocanachi and Sons who also did business in Egypt. The Commercial Bank was so successful that Hambros Bank of London became interested and bought a substantial number of shares.[17] By 1938, the network was more coherent and powerful than ever. This was reflected in the board of the bank: the governor of the National Bank of Greece was chairman; two more members of the NBG board were vice-chairmen, one director of the Popular Bank of Greece (which in 1936 had merged with the Ionian Bank); and the others were a representative of Hambros Bank, a shipowner, D. Petrokokkinos, the brother-in-law, a member of the board of 'Athinais' Silk Industry S.A., a landowner, Gregory Embedocles's brother and the manager of the commercial branch of the bank. Embedocles himself participated in various boards and firms, including the Gunpowder & Cartridge S.A. The network extended not only geographically but over time too into a second generation of descendants: G. Embedocles's son, Stefanos, in 1925, settled in London and until 1958 directed the business of the Commercial Bank of the Near East. Embedocles's daughters were married to the future vice-chairman and the future managing director of the Commercial Bank in Athens. The political dimension was not absent as the family was also related by marriage to Admiral P. Koundouriotis, ex-President of the Republic.

The preceding remarks were based on a limited indicative sample of entrepreneurs consisting of 250 names appearing from 1914 to 1938 in most of the big banks (totalling 20) and a total of 49 firms. Of those, 55, or 14 per cent, appeared several times as founders, shareholders and directors in more than one firm or bank. Ten had also held government and related political office for some of the time. Several among them belonged to up to ten different firms.[18] A separate sample of 1 279 shareholders in four industrial branches – chemicals, textiles, construction material and engineering firms – between 1912 and 1940 showed that 17.9 per cent were engineers, 8 per cent bankers, 24 per cent merchants, 22 per cent industrialists, and 6 per cent diplomats, lawyers or teachers.[19]

The 'Zürich Circle'
The information presented so far suggests that an important position among networks was held by one particular group which integrated big industry, public works and major banks with politics and influenced considerably the course of development of the country. It started as early as in the 1890s in Zürich, and consisted of most of the twentieth century pioneer industrialists and its activities spanned a long period, at least until the Second World War. It will be referred to as the 'Zürich Circle'.

Although it has been difficult to single out one pivotal figure around whom others revolved, one may talk about a limited number of businessmen who, each in his sector, took important initiatives. Most of them expanded their business and gradually moved into many other areas of economic life. Most of these entrepreneurs shared common characteristics. They came mostly from well-to-do or middle-class families in mainland Greece (both from towns and the countryside), or of the diaspora. They were all graduates or students of the Zürich Polytechnic, where they first met in the last decades of the nineteenth century and became friends and later associates. Around them moved a larger circle of entrepreneurs, scientists and state officials.[20] Key figures of the 'Zürich Circle' such as the Oeconomides brothers, N. Kanellopoulos, A. Zachariou, A. Hatzikyriakos, L. Arapides, A. Stylianides, A. Vlangalis, A. Papatheodorou and others maintained strong friendship bonds. Some transformed them into family bonds and most of them came to control banks and industries such as cement, dyestuffs chemicals, wine, textiles and railways. Their main areas of interest (and study) seemed to be chemistry and engineering. Most of them did not return home immediately after graduating but stayed on in Switzerland, Germany or elsewhere in Europe and held jobs related to their expertise either within the university or in private and state industry. Some of them had studied at German or French universities and shared with the former a common outlook about the need to introduce into Greece modern know-how, both in education and in the economy. Though some had succeeded in entering the academic world, most of them shared the disappointment, once back in their country, to be denied access to academia, as the cases of S. Oeconomides and N. Kanellopoulos show. They both tried to enter Athens University without success and not for lack, it seems, of adequate qualifications.[21] Another industrialist, S. Vezanis, who had also studied at Zürich Polytechnic, became an entrepreneur after failing to be elected to parliament and also failing to become a professor at Athens University.[22]

Apart from controlling the branches of industry already mentioned, this network integrated industry with the important area of public works construction and sought to benefit from foreign capital imports in the form of loans given for this purpose to the Greek state and negotiated by the big banks, especially the National Bank of Greece. Public works developed in the wake of increasing state intervention in the Greek economy, from the end of the nineteenth century, and had important political ramifications.

During the present century, and particularly during the interwar period, large development projects such as railways, the electrification of large towns, the supply of water, irrigation projects, port improvement schemes, communications, and road works became inextricably linked with state policy, especially after the influx of the Asia Minor refugees in 1922 and the need to introduce agrarian reform. Industrialization was perceived as part of this more general developmental activity, which included agricultural improvement and the stimulation of trade. Construction was directly linked with this effort and became a big business. Consequently, the banks also showed a lively interest in this sector. As a result, besides negotiations, network activity was related to contracting and consultancy services. Banks, and especially the NBG, were already reinforcing their control over public utility companies and were able to conduct efficient negotiations with the British and the Americans for large-scale loans and schemes such as the Power and Traction deal for the electrification of Athens and Attica, the modernization of urban transport, and the Foundation scheme for hydraulic and hydroelectric works. In 1923, a syndicate was formed with the participation of banks with the purpose of financing and supervising these and other projects.

Most of the core members of the Zürich Circle, as mentioned above, were civil or chemical engineers, while a wider circle of scientists with whom they related had been educated in Germany. Connections were also maintained with a yet broader circle of entrepreneurs who had created a name for themselves in important areas. A. Vlangalis,[23] for example, was born in Constantinople, studied engineering in Zürich, became involved in various industries and later established an engineering firm. His experience in these branches allowed him the time and the insight to better assess the chances of success in the new environment. He was instrumental in the organization of the Power and Traction Consortium which in 1926 secured the Athens power supply project. By holding several directorships, he was active in most public utility companies which were beginning to take shape in the country. He headed, for instance, as director, the Greek Electric Railways Co., also founded in 1926 with the participation of the NBG. He was also chairman of the Corinth Canal Co., the Athens–Piraeus Railway, the 'Hermes' Paper Mill Co., the Gas Company and a member of the board of the Telephone Co. S.A. In 1925–6 he was deputy chairman of the Chamber of Technology. The expertise he acquired was passed on to his son after the Second World War, who succeeded his father in directing the business of the electric railways. At the same time, however, a new figure emerged: Professor S. Andreades, who in addition to his position in the railway sector also became chairman in 1952 of the Commercial Bank of Greece, thus indicating the continuation of network ties beyond the interwar period. P.G. Macris belonged to the broader circle of entrepreneurs. A self-made man, he was after 1922 the agent of the Asiatic Petroleum Co. (later Shell Co. Ltd). He was influential both in the import of new materials like asphalt, and more importantly in the negotiations with the Greek government which led to the financing of a road network project.[24]

Another influential figure, A. Hatzikyriakos, was a member of a shipping family from the island of Samos which settled in Piraeus at the end of the nineteenth century. His is a case of deviation from the family tradition of shipping since after studying physics in Athens, he went to Zürich Polytechnic where he obtained a degree in chemistry. He then worked as assistant to Ludwig von Tetmayer in the area of construction material and cement. He was sent as an expert to France and Spain, he collaborated in the building of the Simplon tunnel and organized the Rezola cement factory in San Sebastian. His education was thus completed by practical application in new methods and technology. At the same time he witnessed the growing German nationalism that characterized this period and the efforts of that country to penetrate economically the Balkans and other areas. Gradually he realized the importance of new domestic technology as an element of national sovereignty for a small country like Greece and decided to invest his know-how by founding the first cement company there. He presented his initiative as vital for the survival of the nation and his friends from Zürich, Spelios and Leontios Oeconomides, N. Kanellopoulos, A. Zachariou, L. Arapides and two professors of chemistry in Greece, O. Roussopoulos and A. Christomanos – graduates themselves of German universities – agreed with his view. The cement industry was thus born in 1902 as a partnership between Hatzikyriakos and Zachariou. Kanellopoulos also joined in. It was renamed TITAN Cement Co. a few years later. The family came to the financial assistance of the group. Hatzikyriakos's father contributed generously to the capital as did his friend L. Oeconomides. A. Hatzikyriakos assumed the technical directorship and Zachariou the commercial and administrative side of the business. However, the local market was not yet prepared or was insufficient to host modern methods and allow for an optimum production of new materials. As a result the firm sought to develop alternative markets abroad, in Turkey, Egypt and the Balkans where German interests were strong and most big works were carried out by foreign firms.

Cooperation of the partners in the early stages of these initiatives allowed the survival and a certain expansion of the firms within the original sectors. The next step was to venture into completely new areas whose relationship with state development projects was not directly obvious. Thus expansion into the production of chemicals and fertilizers threatened for a while to jeopardize the cohesion of the network. Eventually the cement expert, Hatzikyriakos, moved out and founded his own cement company (this has operated ever since in competition with TITAN S.A.). It took six years for the new firm to be consolidated. Hatzikyriakos followed an alternative strategy. Rather than starting from the domestic market, he preferred to settle abroad once more. He travelled to Turkey where he invested in another cement factory in Nicomedea in which many Greeks from Turkey also participated. In 1911, he founded the General Cement Co. Heracles S.A. (AGET Heracles) as a successor of the commercial firm Zamanos & Zavogiannis in which Hatzikyriakos had bought shares. In 1916, he returned to Greece via Europe and in 1917 used his share ownership to become chairman of the AGET board. The previous traumatic experience of TITAN S.A. must have undoubtedly played a part in the structure of AGET Heracles, which remained for a long time a personal firm with strong family connections. TITAN S.A. also became a family firm (run by the Kanellopoulos family). The Zürich connection was strong in both. In the case of AGET Heracles, Hatzikyriakos was helped in the management of the business by his brothers and his in-laws and by expert friends who had also studied in Zürich, e.g. John Thomas Sassos, an engineer who had lived in Vienna and studied at Zürich Polytechnic; S. Agapitos and others. Hatzikyriakos thus came very close to being a pivotal figure in this offshoot of the central Zürich network. On the other hand, he maintained a very close relationship with the National Bank of Greece. This was not limited to obtaining credit only, but included a directorship in the bank's board. Apart from chairing and/or being member of many other boards (around ten), exhibiting a wide range of activities, he was also a political figure. He became an MP twice in 1905 and 1909 and was a senator between 1929 and 1932. He served as Minister of the National Economy in 1922–24, and 1936–37, caretaker Minister of Food (Episitismou) in 1923 and of Education later in the same year. Most importantly, in 1928, he became a member of the Hellenic and General Trust Co., the Anglo-Greek organization that was founded with the explicit purpose to assist Greek industry and which for the first time in Greece advanced long-term industrial loans to Greek firms and became involved in major public work contract negotiations. AGET Heracles was of course among the beneficiaries of such loans. Also in 1928 the firm, based on its network, carried forward a long-term strategy of expansion through mergers and cartels. Assisted by the National Bank, the firm was able to absorb 'Olympus', a smaller cement factory in Volos, thus securing 50 per cent of total Greek cement production by 1931. The move allowed the firm to improve its bargaining and negotiating position when the question of forming a cement cartel among competitors was raised.

One of those competitors was Hatzikyriakos's old partner, N. Kanellopou-los, who in addition to controlling TITAN Cement S.A., devoted his life to developing the chemical products and fertilizer industry in Greece. Kanel-lopoulos came from a wealthy Peloponnesian family of currant growers and producers and became aware of the need to improve agriculture in general. Although he originally studied medicine in Athens he eventually switched to chemistry when he went to Zürich Polytechnic. There he met other Greeks – L. Charilaos, L. Arapides, K. Syngros, A. Zachariou, A. Papatheodorou and L. Oeconomides. Upon graduation he volunteered to work as a chemical engineer in the chemical industry of Marseilles. He returned to Greece in 1892 and rather than continuing in the family business, went into partnership with L. Charilaos in order to modernize and operate an old oil factory in Eleusis (Charilaos & Rallis Co.). Soon the two partners were joined by their brothers, A. Kanellopoulos and E. Charilaos and the company was renamed Charilaos & Kanellopoulos, adding soap production to its activities. Only later did Kanel-lopoulos venture into wine production and organized what eventually became a huge concern, the S.A. Wine and Spirits Co., which was supported by most banks. Meanwhile the ground was already prepared for the next innovation, i.e.

the production of sulphuric acid and phosphoric fertilizers, through the purchase of cheap land for a plant and investment of 2 000 000 drs.[25] The group then appealed for funds to old friends who were already themselves well settled in various organizations. Their support was compensated by seats on the board: L. Oeconomides, A. Zachariou, N. Vlangalis, I. Drossopoulos (already an executive of the NBG) and others were present. The board also decided to appoint L. Arapides, another Zürich graduate working until then for the Gunpowder and Cartridge Co. S.A., to prepare a study of sulphuric acid production while Zachariou built the factory. Arapides remained with the new firm for the rest of his career as technical manager and director.

Modern technology was thus applied for the first time systematically in Greece for the purpose, on the one hand, of improving agriculture and, on the other, of using domestic agricultural raw materials (oil, currants) and substituting imports. By 1938 the complex expanded further to include a large glass foundry and several iron pyrites mines, exporting a good part of their output. All three firms, but especially the S.A. Chemical Products and Fertilizers, were among NBG's most important customers, benefiting from a wide range of banking services. In addition to short-term and long-term local loans the chemical plant had a bonded indebtedness to German firms and to London houses guaranteed by the NBG and the Greek government and bond issues were partly covered by its iron pyrites exports. Another innovation of the group was the operation for the first time of what could be considered an incipient research and development unit. This started as a workshop which was later converted into an institute that collected statistics and carried out research on soil and crop improvement. It enjoyed great support from the state and its work coincided with the agrarian reform and land improvement policy. In the 1930s state support was sought for a more efficient marketing of the products. Through an agreement with the newly established Agricultural Bank of Greece, the firm obtained a virtual monopoly for the supply of fertilizers to Greek farmers.

The personal histories of Hatzikyriakos and Kanellopoulos may be taken to illustrate the strain shown in and the risk of disintegration of core relationships. From a network perspective, however, these histories reveal a process of branching out, or reorganization and reproduction through the formation of alternative networks.

The cohesion of the Zürich Circle is best shown by the histories of A. Zachariou, L. Oeconomides and certain other entrepreneurs. Oeconomides started from the dyestuffs factory which his brother, Spelios, had founded at the end of the nineteenth century, while also teaching at the Military Cadet School in Piraeus. The two brothers had studied in Germany and Switzerland.[26] Upon his return to Greece, Spelios set up a firm importing distilling machinery and supplying mainly wine and spirits industries. He also began producing his own dyestuffs. The import firm brought the two brothers into contact with other industrialists, notably Zürich people, e.g. E. Charilaos. In 1898, Leontios Oeconomides and E. Charilaos became partners, founding their own wine industry. Meanwhile Spelios died and his brother succeeded him in the management of the dyestuffs factory (CHROPEI), which gave him a firm base from which to venture into other business. By 1902, he was co-founder of S.A. Chemical Products and Fertilizers, in addition to sitting on various other boards. In 1922, the composition of the S.A. Chemical Products & Fertilizers Board was almost identical to that of CHROPEI and it included most of the core members of the Zürich Circle. Cohesion was enhanced by two marriages designed to ensure the biological reproduction of the group and network. N. Kanellopoulos was married to E. Charilaos's sister and L. Oeconomides's sister married S. Sofianopoulos, who like herself came from the town of Kalavryta in Peloponnesos. Their sons became the managers of CHROPEI after 1922.

The Zürich network had another binding feature: a common ideology based on the belief that industrial pursuits were not only necessary but feasible and that the key was to integrate banking with industry. Undoubtedly their early 'Germanic' experience must have played an important part in shaping their outlook and in inspiring them to found their own bank in 1919, the Bank of Industry. This, however, had a short life. Perhaps the most important cause of its failure was the incapacity of the state to foster the creation of special institutions, along German lines, for supporting industry.

The public works dimension and the foreign capital connections of the Zürich Circle are revealed by studying the history of A. Zachariou, civil engineer, another graduate of Zürich Polytechnic. Before returning to Greece, Zachariou had worked for the Baden-Württemberg Railways and was for a while head engineer of the Bremen Port Committee. Once in Greece he joined forces with another engineer, A. Papatheodorou, also a Zürich Polytechnic graduate, and soon their firm became known as the industrial engineering firm *par excellence*. Zachariou's involvement in the cement industry can be seen as a strategic step which soon led to the local production of reinforced concrete (*béton armé*), until then imported from France. In addition to sitting on numerous boards, he acted as technical advisor to most of the major industries for which he built new plants.[27] At the same time, he maintained an import department that supplied the Greek market with kilns, traction engines, railway machinery and other equipment. During his earlier career in Germany he had secured the cooperation of big German industries such as Siemens-Schuckert, Siemens-Halske, Siemens Reiniger, Telefunken, Fr. Krupp, Maschinenfabrik Augsburg, Nuernberg and Babcok & Wilcox Ltd, Junkers-Flugzeug-Motorenfabrik for aviation material. In fact, Siemens considered Zachariou 'their man' in South-east Europe.[28] His firm had also installed 95 per cent of lifts functioning in Greece at that time, mainly Italian-made by Stigler of Milan, and most of the central heating facilities. As business increased the firm split into a construction department and an engineering one.

In 1920 a new firm, the S.A. Tekton, arose out of the construction department, in which the NBG and E. Charilaos, then chairman of the Bank of Industry, had a large stake. This was reflected also in the constitution of the board.[29] Tekton S.A. developed into one of the largest construction companies in Greece with a large staff of experienced engineers and architects. It participated in the installation of the underground railway in Athens and was one of the main partners in the Athens drainage project. The firm received extensive credit from the National Bank, though Zachariou never sat on the bank's board

Through Zachariou, the network maintained close relations with German industries and as a result was able to secure business for them in Greece. In 1930, two agreements were signed between the Greek state and Siemens-Halske for the establishment in Greece of an automatic telephone network. A special new firm was founded in that respect (S.A. Greek Telephone Co.) headed by Zachariou's old associate, A. Papatheodorou.

The National Bank of Greece seemed in general to seek cooperation with the various networks rather than antagonize them and accepted the *status quo* whereby parts of foreign capital were linked with specific areas of interest. There is growing evidence that it used networks to further its particular interests. One such instance was the development of hydroelectric power in Macedonia for which many groups competed. One of them was headed by C. Stylianides, a Zürich Polytechnic graduate, and a friend of Kanellopoulos and Zachariou. Stylianides seemed to favour a policy of cooperation with Siemens-Schuckert for the power supply of Thessaloniki. However counter-interests involving politicians and farmers were very powerful in the area and eventually NBG (supported also by Hambros Bank and other foreign interests) sided with alternative proposals. Those included nitrogen production related to fertilizer manufacture for the improvement of agriculture, which Stylianides considered unrealistic. This issue caused strain in the original group, since Kanellopoulos could see the important prospects in fertilizer production. Although there is no conclusive evidence, it is logical to assume that under the weight of Hambros financing of his S.A. Chemical Products and Fertilizers, Kanellopoulos eventually joined the NBG lobby. The S.A. Vermion founded by Stylianides and other Zürich members was subsequently wound up.[30] All studies were eventually shelved due to the impossibility of raising foreign capital after 1931.

Conclusion

The foregoing, based mainly on empirical research about the operation of business firms and banks in Greece during the first decades of the twentieth century, confirm the existence and operation of important networks. These networks consisted of a tightly structured core and a looser and wider web of relations maintained through a system of joint directorships in mainly different business firms. The purpose was to integrate several branches of industry with banking and commerce and thus minimize competition, allowing communication and the acquisition of information. Networks also facilitated access to areas such as public works construction and state agencies. In the particular case of the Zürich Circle, the network successfully sought to benefit from foreign connections, most importantly from foreign capital resources, foreign markets and foreign technology. Links at an international level generally followed either an ethnic pattern or exploited a pre-existing first link. Members of the network (Greeks from the mainland, diaspora Greeks or foreigners) seemed to share, apart from economic interests, cultural affinities and a common ideology that was just as important for the cohesion of the group at least in its early life. Once network links were secure, they were used in two ways. On the one hand, they functioned to benefit foreign partners who penetrated the Greek market and, on the other, they allowed Greek entrepreneurs to consolidate their position in all unpredictable environment. With regard to the banking sector, networks gave entrepreneurs the possibility to gain access to badly needed resources. Bankers also benefited by extending their customer base and by acquiring important information on them. In many cases, kinship ties were also functional for the maintenance and reproduction of networks.

Many of the ramifications of network activity have not been touched upon in this chapter. However, what has emerged rather clearly as a useful working hypothesis is that many of the networks operating in Greece during the interwar period included an important political dimension. This may reflect the increasing politicization of business due, among other things, to the increasing intervention of the state, but may also point to a more important and determining role of networks in the process of economic development. Though this chapter does not adhere to the idea that there is a dominant model of economic behaviour for peripheral countries like Greece and other areas of South-East Europe more generally, it is perhaps worthwhile to ask whether networks were – and to what extent – responsible for the route of development that these countries have followed over the last 100 years.

Notes

1. For a satisfactory account of the establishment of shipowners in Greece and Europe see Tzelina Harlaftis, 'The Role of the Greeks in the Black Sea Trade, 1830–1900' in Fischer and Nordvik (1990). For merchants of Syros, see Kardassis (1982). For the operation of Greek bankers in the Ottoman Empire see also Exertzoglou (1989).
2. Cf. Harlaftis op. cit.
3. The National Bank of Greece particularly supported this view. See NBGHA, series XXXIV, file N43-Z259 Hellenic and General Trust Ltd, 1939, and File N44-γ16 Support of Industry, Confidential Note by J. Drossopoulos to E. Venizelos, 16.12.1929.
4. See Kindleberger (1989). On the role of foreign capital in Greece see Dritsas (1990) and Pepelasis-Minoglou (1991).
5. See Dritsas (1990).
6. Ibid. (1990) and E. Tsouderos Archive 2/2 kai 46/21, Letter to E. Venizelos 6.3.1932.
7. See Minoglou (1991).

8. See Dritsas (1990) p. 360, 463(12). Also Department of Overseas Trade, *Report on the Economic Situation in Greece*, 1928, pp. 7–8, 'Generous Credit terms were given by German, Czechoslovak, American and other exporters while the Greek banks maintained their conservative attitude'.
9. Cited by N.P.I. Igglessis in his work *Guide of the Joint Stock Cos 1937–1938*, vol. 2, Part A., no. 5.
10. A report on *The Economy of Greece*, prepared in 1940 by H. Hill for the Coordinating Committee of American Agencies in Greece, mentions that the bank manager in Greece kept very close contact with the entire economy of the country. He also knew the whole life history of everyone of his clients and usually of the clients of other banks. 'There was a tendency in Greece for merchants and clients in general to turn to their banker as a Father Confessor ...' The bank manager advised on education of children, on doctors and medical treatment; he was also considered the authority for advising on investments, industries and business management.'...The handling of a client in accordance with his importance became a fine art'. See also Dritsas (1992).
11. Personalities like E. Kehagias in the nineteenth century, or I. Eftaxias, A. Diomedes, E. Tsouderos among others in the twentieth century.
12. It was not uncommon to read reports in the press and to follow debates in parliament about scandalous business deals involving politicians who were also shareholders in big firms. These cases were particularly frequent with regard to public works bids.
13. The composition of the NBG General Board for 1914 is enlightening: the board included top executives of all the other major banks, one vice-chairman of the Commercial Bank of Greece (M. Politis), the Director General of the Popular Bank of Greece (D. Loverdos), the Director General of the Bank of Athens (I. Eliasko), the General Manager of the Banque d'Orient (E. Kamaras). Two of the banks mentioned, namely the Bank of Athens and the Banque d'Orient, were subsequently absorbed by the NBG.
14. Remark made by I. Eftaxias, Governor of NBG in 1914. See Vovolinis (1957), MEBL (Biographical Dictionary) vol. 1 . Other Officials also referred to NBG's role in similar fashion, for example, P. Tsaldaris, Leader of the People's Party, Proïa, April 1927.
15. See Vovolinis, op. cit., note 14, vol. 3, p. 333–5. Other biographical and business details for most of the personalities mentioned have been extracted from the NBG Archives and from press sources.
16. See Politis (1935).
17. Igglessis, op. cit., note 9.
18. These figures can only be considered tentative at this stage as the full number of firms and entrepreneurs has not been analysed yet. However, this sample is sufficient to give us the trend that network formation followed in the early twentieth century.
19. See Dritsas (1990), p. 374.
20. Some of these personalities had a prominent presence in many sectors: e.g. J. Doanides, originating in Romania, physicist, graduate of Freiburg University, member of various boards; V. Katsigeras, from Kefallinia in the Ionian Islands, engineer, graduate of Zürich Polytechnic; several members of the banking sector e.g. A. Diomedes, I. Eliasco, A. Spourgitis, S. Loverdos, N. Paspatis etc.; eminent merchants and businessmen such as G. Stringos of Piraeus.
21. See Vovolinis, op. cit., note 14, vol. 1, relevant entries.
22. Ibid., vol. 1.
23. Vlangalis had a wide experience of many industrial branches, having worked, upon his return to Greece, for the pioneer firm Vassiliades Shipyards, for mining and other industries. His engineering firm obtained the first concession for the power supply of Athens, the completion of the Corinth Canal and the initial exploitation of the Peloponnesos railways.
24. Greece had still in the mid-1920s a rather primitive road network, with 9447 km of main roads and 3765 km of secondary roads. Macris set up a firm that supervised road construction around Athens. He later participated in the project financed by a 600 000 pounds sterling state loan, which, subject to repeated re-negotiations caused delays and an increase in the cost.
25. This amount was almost a standard start-up capital for most JSCs which rose to prominence.

26. After studying chemistry in Leipzig, Heidelberg and elsewhere and obtaining a doctorate, Spelios Oeconomides worked as an assistant of Adolf Bayer. While in Munich, he sent for his younger brother, Leontios, who also began studying chemistry in München before going to Zürich.

27. He used the new product for all of his modern constructions either in housing, hospitals or factories throughout Greece and Turkey. He built the sulphuric acid plant of S.A. Chemical Products and Fertilizers, the soap factory of Charilaos-Kanellopoulos Co. in Eleusis, the distilleries of their wine industry in Kalamata, Pyrgos and Eleusis, the 'Keramikos' plant, also founded by N. Kanellopoulos.

28. See H. Schröter, 'Siemens and Central and South East Europe between the two World Wars' in Teichova and Cottrell (1983).

29. Kanellopoulos and Papatheodorou were members of the Zürich Circle, while three more members were NBG high executives. There was also one wholesale merchant.

30. The issue of hydroelectric energy in Greece is very complicated and only a very brief account is given here, to illustrate one network dimension. Information is based on many sources, of which more indicative are articles by C. Stylianides and by his adversaries in the press. Also on articles in *Viomehanike Epitheorisis* (Industrial Review) by D.B. Hatzopoulos, no. 36, June 1937; no. 37, July 1937; no. 38, August 1937. For C. Stylianides's activities see Vovolinis, op. cit., note 4, vol. 1, p. 184. Other networks were also interested, particularly the 'Greek Syndicate for the Exploitation of Hydraulic Energy' which was made up of the Bank of Athens, the Popular Bank of Greece, the Bank of Industry, the Bank of National Economy, the Bank of Piraeus, the Bank of Chios and the Anglo-Financial Co. Ltd. Most of the businessmen already mentioned in this chapter belonged to one or more of these organizations.

Sources

Special reviews

Βιομηχανική Επιθεώρησις 1930–1939 (Industrial Review).
Δελτίο Ανωνύμων Εταιρειών 1937–1939 (Joint Stock Companies Bulletin).
Οικονομική Επετηρίς της Ελλάδος (Economic Yearbook of Greece), *1930–1939*, edited by G. Haritakis.

Newspapers

Ελεύθερον Βήμα, 1930.
Αθηναϊκά Νέα, 1930.
Πρωΐα, 1927.

Other

Εφημερίς της Κυβερνήσεως (Official Government Gazette) – parliamentary debates.

Archives

National Bank of Greece Historical Archives – Series: Industrial Credit.
National Bank of Greece Historical Archives – Annual Reports 1920–1936.
General Bank of Greece, Annual Report, 1934.
Emmanuel Tsouderos Archives, Bank of Greece.

References

Dertilis, G.B. (ed.), (1988), *Banquiers, usuriers et paysans, reseaux de crédit et stratégies du capital en Grèce 1780–1930*, Fondation des Treilles, Paris.

Dritsas, M. (1990), Βιομηχανία καί Τράπεζες στήν Ελλάδα τού Μεσοπολέμου (Industry and Banking in Interwar Greece), MIET, Athens.

Dritsas, M. (1992), 'Bank-industry relations in interwar Greece: the case of the National Bank of Greece', in P.L. Cottrell, H. Lindgren and A. Teichova (1992), *European Industry and Banking between the Wars*, Leicester University Press.

Exertzoglou, H. (1989), *Προσαρμοστικότητα καί Πολιτική ομογενειακών κεφαλαίων. Ελληνες Τραπεζίτες στήν Κωνσταντινούπολη* (Adaptability and strategy of diaspora capital. Greek Bankers in Constantinople), Research & Educational Foundation of the Commercial Bank of Greece, Athens.
Fischer, L.R. and H.W. Nordvik (1990), *Shipping and Trade, 1750–1950: Essays in International Maritime Economic History*, Lofthouse, London.
Harlaftis, G. (1988), 'The Greek Shipowners, the Economy and the State 1958–1974', PhD. Thesis, Oxford University, St Anthony's College, (unpublished).
Hill, Henry (1940), *The Economy of Greece*, Part I–VII, Greek War Relief Association, New York.
James, H., H. Lindgren and A. Teichova (eds), (1991), *The Role of Banks in the Interwar Economy*, Cambridge University Press.
Kardassis, V. (1982), 'Εμπορικές δραστήριότητες στη Σύρο 1843–1857', in *Deltion Historikes kai Ethnologikes Etaireias*, 25, pp. 321–94.
Kindleberger, Charles P. (1989), 'Summary, Reflections on the Papers and the Debate on multinational Enterprise' in A. Teichova, M. Lévy-Leboyer and H. Nussbaum (eds), *Historical Studies in International Corporate Business*, Cambridge University Press.
Pepelasis-Minoglou, Ioanna (1991), 'The Institutional Morphology of Foreign Capital Inflow in Greece during the Interwar period', in A. Teichova, H. Lundgren and M. Dritsas (eds), *L'Enterprise en Grèce et en Europe, XIXe–XXe Siècles*, Sophis, Athens.
Politis, E. (1935), *Annuaire des Sociétés Egyptiennes par Actions*, Alexandria.
Teichova, A. and P.L. Cottrell (eds), (1983), *International Business and Central Europe 1918–1939*, Leicester University Press.
Tsoukalas, K. (1975), *Εξάρτηση καί Αναπαραγωγή, ο κοινωνικός ρόλος τών εκπαιδευτικών μηχανισμών* (Dependence and Reproduction, the role of educational mechanisms), Themelio, Athens.
Veremis, Th. (1980), *Μελετήματα γύρω από τόν Βενιζέλο καί τήν εποχή του* (Studies on Venizelos and his Era), Athens.
Vovolinis, S. (1957), *Μέγα Ελληνικό Βιογραφικό Λεξικό* (Greek Biographical Dictionary), Viomichaniki Epitheorisis, Athens.

18 Interlocking directorships between banks and industry in interwar Sweden[1]

Jan Ottosson

The emergence of new networks and changes in network structures have been a central issue in the research on industrial networks.[2] Networks are dynamic: new relationships emerge, others are terminated and old allies become bitter rivals. Elements of stability also occur in industrial networks, where the relationships are often characterized by longevity. Until recently, little interest has been paid to the question of bank–industry relations in this theoretical context. Here, the interrelationship between the industrial and financial sectors is in focus. Banks can thus be viewed as actors within a financial market network.[3] The application of the concept of markets as networks facilitates a more detailed and systematic analysis of these phenomena. As a result, the historical study of such relations will provide an improved understanding of the evolution, and the resulting structure, of relations between the financial and the industrial sector. The suggested historical approach, therefore, can be expected to generate new insights both into organizational theory and into finance history. In this chapter, personal relationships between banks and industry in interwar Sweden are examined, with special reference to the longitudinal development.

Longitudinal studies of the dynamics of interlocking directorships, illuminating different aspects of the process of change, have been performed mainly on American and Canadian sources. In these studies, most of the analysis focuses on the question to what extent links have been broken, and whether these personal links were reconstituted. Thus, a high degree of reconstituted ties would confirm the hypothesis that interlocking directors play a significant role, since they are replaced. On the other hand, a low degree of reconstituted ties would suggest that these links are more likely to be random. Earlier studies indicate results in both directions. In addition, the American studies show a lower degree of reconstitution, compared with the Canadian studies.[4]

Some researchers have also examined the formation of new interlocking directors in a network. Mizruchi and Brewster-Stearns studied new links between 22 companies during the years 1956–83 in the USA. The authors suggested that the financial links would tend to increase when companies' solvency and profit decreased and long-term debt increased. Their results were, however, mixed. They found support both for the above-mentioned hypothesis (long-term debt was, however, not statistically significant), as well as an increased number of financial interlocks in producing companies' boards of directors during periods of economic growth and expansion. In this study the authors also drew attention to the historical conditions that the companies worked under, with special reference to the credit market.[5] Related to this topic also is the classical 'Finanz–Capital' discussion, where aspects of the power of banks are emphasized. Personal links between banks and industry have often been regarded as closely associated with bank dominance over the industry.[6]

The above-cited studies, however, have not been concerned with all aspects of the process of change of interlocking directors. Not only the formation of new and broken links deserves attention, but also the question of persistence has to be taken into consideration in order to study the whole process of change in the bank–industry network.[7] Here, all three aspects are analysed in a historical, institutional context against the background of the crises in the early 1920s and 1930s in Sweden.[8] In this study, the issue of formation, stability and broken personal links between the largest banks and industry in Sweden during 1918–24 and 1928–34 will be examined. The focus of this chapter is therefore to describe and compare the transformation process of financial networks in interwar Sweden.

The crises of the 1920s and of the 1930s
The early 1920s were dominated by a deep financial crisis which originated after the First World War. The depression had far-reaching consequences for the complex web of bank–industry relations. During the crisis, the banks took over shares to secure their commitments. As a result of these actions, the banks became the owners of a number of Swedish firms.[9] Also, the credits granted to the bank-dependent or bank-owned firms reached substantial levels. However, the banks themselves also became more dependent on industry.[10] Thus the relations between banks and industry seemed to be getting closer and more intense during the years after 1918. In 1924 economic activity was intensified. The consequences of the crisis were, however, far-reaching for the rest of the 1920s.[11]

The crisis and the depression in the 1930s also changed the relations between banks and industry, but several authors have pointed out that bank–industry relations probably underwent a greater shift in the exchange relationships towards the banks during the early 1920s. Thus, bank–industry relations did not intensify during the crisis in the 1930s, compared with the 1920s.[12] However, the worldwide depression and the start of the international financial crisis during the Summer of 1931 also hit the Swedish economy as well as the financial system. This was especially notable in the Spring of 1932, when the concern of the financier and businessman Ivar Kreuger collapsed. This event had severe implications especially for the second largest bank in Sweden at that time, Skandinaviska Kreditaktiebolaget, due to the intimate relations between the bank and Kreuger's businesses.

One neglected aspect, which has not been studied systematically until recently, is the development of personal networks between banks and industry during these two crises.[13] Two questions are especially interesting. The first concerns the patterns and development of personal networks between banks and industry during the crisis in the early 1920s and the early 1930s. Were elements of dynamics or stability evident? The second relates to the question of the different development of the two crises. Was there any difference in the process of change in these networks during the two crises? In this chapter these two questions are examined.

Method

The study is based on a sample of 69 companies. Ten of these companies represented the largest commercial banks, the other 59 were the largest industrial companies in interwar Sweden. The sample was selected from firms which belonged to the 125 largest financial and non-financial companies in 1918, and which were also among the largest firms in 1939. This cohort of the largest companies in interwar Sweden was studied during two seven-year periods: 1918–24 and 1928–34.[14] All interlocking directors between the companies were examined every year during these two periods. The latter period has been examined by my colleague Staffan Westerström in an unpublished study.[15] The periods chosen made it possible to examine the networks during the last years of rapid economic growth directly after the First World War and in the late 1920s, before the depression started.

The sources for the two periods, however, differed in quality. For the period 1918–24 no name register was found in the main source *Svenska Aktiebolag och Enskilda Banker*. Therefore, lists of every company's board of directors during these seven years were made, each year's list consisting of about 600–700 directorships. The links between banks and industry between 1918 and 1924 were identified with a network computer program.[16] The links – a link can be one (single link) or several (multiple links) interlocking directors between banks and industry – were followed between 1918 and 1924 by studying the composition of the companies' and banks' boards of directors year by year.[17] The second period, 1928–34, was examined by Westerström with the help of a name index in *Svenska Aktiebolag och Enskilda Banker*. In this index, every board director's memberships of different boards were listed, with the exception of deputy members, who were included in the earlier period.

The links between banks and industry were divided into two broad categories: stable links and changed links. Companies having a stable link during the whole period were defined as having an unchanged link with the bank. The last category was subdivided into the following grouping: new links, broken links, and temporary links. A new link means that the company did not have any link to the banks in 1918, but the link was created after 1918. A broken link is one where the interlocking director/directors no longer fulfils the criteria of an interlock – when a director no longer holds two or more directorships. Temporary links are links which were created and broken during the period.

Results

Stable and changed links

The distribution of personal links shows that a majority of the links – 54 per cent in the 1920s and 61 per cent in the 1930s – were changed during both crises (Table 18.1). The personal network was characterized by a process of change during these two periods of external strain. The network was transformed more during the crisis of the 1930s, since a larger share of the links was changed during this crisis.

Of the four largest banks, Stockholms Enskilda Bank had the largest share of persistent links with the companies in the sample during both periods. The bank had more stable links during the 1920s (71 per cent compared with 63 per cent in the 1930s). The second bank with 59 per cent (1918–24) and 50 per cent (1928–34) stable links was Skandinaviska Kreditaktiebolaget, the second largest bank after Svenska Handelsbanken. About one third of Svenska Handels-banken's links were stable, a percentage which was the second lowest among the large banks. Only Göteborgs Bank had a smaller share of persistent links, falling from 27 per cent in the 1920s to 20 per cent in the 1930s. The provincial banks had fewer stable links during both periods (Table 18.1). Table 18.2 shows the same data in the form of the total number of personal links between banks and business enterprises in each year and for each bank, 1918–24 and 1928–34. The total increased to a peak of 75 links in 1924, then fell to 48 in 1933 and 1934 (Table 18.2).Skandinaviska Kreditaktiebolaget (SKAND) held between 33 and 38 per cent of all links during this period. The regional banks had a somewhat larger share of the links between 1918 and 1924. Only in a minority of cases in the 1920s was there just one single link between a bank and a company. In most cases the bank had links together with other banks. In the second period, Stockholms Enskilda Bank (SEB) became the leading bank in 1932, and Skandinaviska Kreditaktiebolaget ranked second. Göteborgs Bank's share fell to 6 per cent after the Kreuger crash and Svenska Handels-banken (SHB) showed a slightly smaller share – 17 per cent in 1934, compared with 19 per cent in 1928. Östgöta Enskilda Bank was the only regional bank which had a larger number of personal links in 1934, compared with 1928 (Table 18.2).

More new links were created in the first period studied. Broken and temporary links were more common in the later period. In Figure 18.1 the changed links are compared over the two periods. The total number of changed links reached a peak of eighteen cases in 1932, compared with a peak of thirteen changed

Table 18.1   Distribution of personal links between banks and industry in Sweden, 1918–24 and 1928–34

	1 Same links				2 Changed links (3+4+5)				3 New links		4 Broken links		5 Temporary links		Total	
	1918–24	%	1928–34	%	1918–24	%	1928–34	%	1918–24	1928–34	1918–24	1928–34	1918–24	1928–34	1918–24	1928–34
Banks operating on a national level																
Göteborgs Bank	4	27	2	20	11	73	8	80	6	1	4	4	1	3	15	10
Stockholms Enskilda Bank	10	71	10	63	4	29	6	38	3	6	1	0	0	0	14	16
Svenska Handelsbanken	6	35	5	31	11	65	11	69	3	3	5	3	3	5	17	16
Skandinaviska Kreditaktiebolaget	19	59	10	50	13	41	10	50	5	2	5	5	3	3	32	20
Sum, banks on a national level	39	50	27	44	39	50	35	56	17	12	15	12	7	11	78	62
Regional banks																
Östergötlands Enskilda Bank	0	0	2	33	0	0	4	67	0	2	0	0	0	2	0	6
Wermlands Enskilda Bank	0	0	1	25	4	100	3	75	1	1	0	1	3	1	4	4
Smålands Enskilda Bank	1	20	1	17	4	80	5	83	2	0	1	5	1	0	5	6
Sundsvalls Enskilda Bank	2	50	1	33	2	50	2	67	2	0	0	2	0	0	4	3
Upplands Enskilda Bank	0	0	0	0	0	0	2	100	0	0	0	0	0	2	0	2
Sum, regional banks	3	23	5	24	10	77	16	76	5	3	1	8	4	5	13	21
Total	42	46	32	39	49	54	51	61	22	15	16	20	11	16	91	83

Sources: Svenska Aktiebolag och Enskilda Banker, years 1919–25, 1929–35, n = 59

Table 18.2   Number and percentage of personal links between banks and industry by bank, 1918–24 and 1928–34

	GÖBA	SHB	SEB	SIGAB	SKAND	SMÅLENBA	SUNDENBA	WERMBA	UPENBA	ÖSTGÖTBA	TOTAL
1918	8	13	11	3	25	3	2	0	0	0	65
1919	6	12	11	4	24	3	2	1	0	0	63
1920	6	12	13	5	24	3	2	3	0	0	68
1921	12	12	13	5	26	2	2	1	0	0	73
1922	12	10	13	4	27	2	2	2	0	0	72
1923	13	10	13	4	27	2	3	2	0	0	74
1924	10	11	13	5	25	4	4	3	0	0	75
1928	6	11	10	0	17	5	3	3	0	2	57
1929	6	10	13	0	19	4	3	2	0	3	60
1930	5	12	13	0	16	4	2	2	2	5	61
1931	6	13	13	0	15	4	2	2	2	5	62
1932	8	11	16	0	15	2	2	3	0	5	62
1933	3	9	16	0	12	1	1	2	0	4	48
1934	3	8	16	0	13	1	1	2	0	4	48
	%	%	%	%	%	%	%	%	%	%	
1918	12	20	17	5	38	5	3	0	0	0	
1919	10	19	17	6	38	5	3	2	0	0	
1920	9	18	19	7	35	4	3	4	0	0	
1921	16	16	18	7	36	3	3	1	0	0	
1922	17	14	18	6	38	3	3	3	0	0	
1923	18	14	18	5	36	3	4	3	0	0	
1924	13	15	17	7	33	5	5	4	0	0	

	GÖBA	SHB	SEB	SIGAB	SKAND	SMÅLENBA	SUNDENBA	WERMBA	UPENBA	ÖSTGÖTBA	TOTAL
1928	11	19	18	0	30	9	5	5	0	4	
1929	10	17	22	0	32	7	5	3	0	5	
1930	8	20	21	0	26	7	3	3	3	8	
1931	10	21	21	0	24	6	3	3	3	8	
1932	13	18	26	0	24	3	3	5	0	8	
1933	6	19	33	0	25	2	2	4	0	8	
1934	6	17	33	0	27	2	2	4	0	8	

Notes:

GÖBA	Göteborgs Bank
SHB	Svenska Handelsbanken
SEB	Stockholms Enskilda Bank
SIGAB	Stockholms Inteckningsgaranti AB
SKAND	Skandinaviska Kreditaktiebolaget
SMÅLENBA	Smålands Enskilda Bank
SUNDENBA	Sundsvalls Enskilda Bank
WERMBA	Wermlands Enskilda Bank
UPENBA	Upplands Enskilda Bank
ÖSTGÖTBA	Östergötlands Enskilda Bank

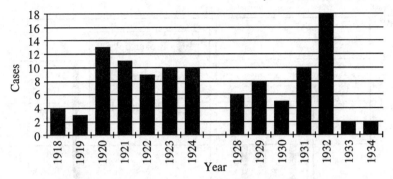

*Figure 18.1   Changed links between banks and industry in Sweden,
1918–24 and 1928–34*

links in 1920 (Figure 18.1). The number of new links was considerably higher
during the first period of crisis, especially from 1920 onwards. Broken links
were more common during 1932. In the first period these links were more common
in 1921 and 1923. Temporary links reached substantial levels in 1930–32
(Figure 18.2). A large number of companies retained the same bank link and
added more bank links during the 1920s.

In the case of broken links – in any of the above-mentioned categories – most
were broken at the bank's board of directors. In several cases a director lost his
multiple function, but remained a member of the company board. This was
especially the case with banks which encountered serious difficulties during the
crises.

Conclusions
Earlier longitudinal research about interlocking directorships focuses mainly
on broken links. In this study other categories of links were also examined. In
addition, changes in the personal networks between the largest banks and
companies in Sweden were analysed.

The first of the two questions posed in this chapter relates to whether elements
of dynamism and stability were discernible. The Swedish financial network
consisted both of elements of dynamism as well as elements of stability during
the interwar period, the element of change slightly dominating during both crises.
Earlier American studies concerning the postwar period were unable to conclude
whether new links were created during periods of recession or periods of
economic booms. In this study the personal networks were more turbulent
during periods of crisis, a tendency being more distinct during the early 1930s.

The second question deals with differences in the process of change of these
networks. New links were created more frequently during the depression years
– though the largest number of new links was created during 1924 when the

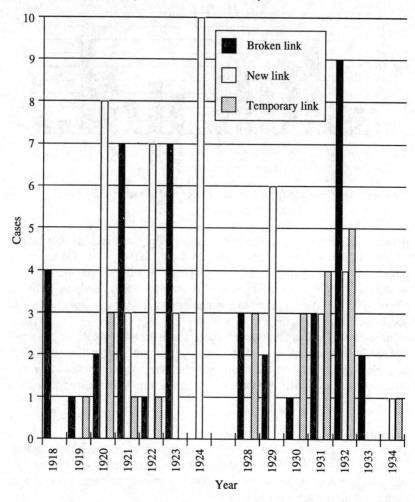

*Figure 18.2   Changed links between banks and industry in Sweden by type,
1918–24 and 1928–34*

worst period of the crisis was giving way to greater economic activity. In the
second period the largest number of new links was created in 1929 – before the
crisis started. The peaks were obviously concentrated, on the one hand, at the
end of a depression phase and, on the other hand, at the start of such a period.
Thus, as in American studies, it is plausible that new links between banks and
industry were established both during depression and boom periods. There was
a stronger tendency to create new links during the depression years in the 1920s

than in the 1930s. In the latter case, such links were created to a greater extent in the first years of the investigated period. Broken links were more common during the years of crisis, with a peak in 1932 after a sharp rise. Broken links were also more frequent during the depression years of the 1920s rising from only one broken link in 1919 to seven cases in 1921. No links, however, were broken during the last years in the two investigated periods when the Swedish economy in both cases showed signs of recovering.

The crisis of the early 1920s was more severe in its consequences for the banking sector. Several banks were forced to reconstruct or to obtain reconstruction loans, especially some of the banks included in this sample, the Stockholms Handelsbank (from 1920 Svenska Handelsbanken), Smålands Enskilda Bank and Wermlandsbanken. These banks' personal networks were all affected by this crisis. In addition, the Skandinaviska Kreditaktiebolaget felt the strain. Thus, the changes and turbulence in personal relations between banks and industry during the crisis of the early 1920s was to a large extent a result of the crisis of the financial sector. Close links between banks and industry already existed in 1918, thus the crisis changed an already existing structure. In the case of the 1930s the collapse of the Kreuger empire tended to explain the largest part of the changed links in the peak year 1932.

One aspect which is constant in both periods is the dominance of one single bank in the network, the Skandinaviska Kreditaktiebolaget. The position of the bank was, however, neither stable nor constantly rising. Its position as a star among the companies in the network tended to shift, and other banks became more centrally placed in the rank order of personal networks. Most notable is the rise of the Stockholms Enskilda Bank to a central position in 1932. However, even after the chaotic period following the fall of Kreuger the Skandinaviska Kreditaktiebolaget remained one of the central actors, yet it no longer took up its former dominant position in this group of large industrial companies and banks.

The crisis in the beginning of the 1920s led to severe structural changes both in industry and in the financial world. According to earlier Swedish research the banks extended their influence in industry during the early 1920s, by providing more credit and acquiring larger shareholdings in industrial companies. Bank-control theories also maintain that interlocking directorships should increase since they are seen as an instrument for monitoring functions. That means, first, that the number of interlocking directors should increase, second, that broken links would be replaced by new persons. How did the Swedish experience correspond to this hypothesis during the crisis?

The aspects studied in this chapter tell us that a more complex pattern than expected constituted the personal network in Sweden during the crisis of the early 1920s and 1930s. Only a small number of companies were outside the personal network of banks and industry in 1918. The links already existed in 1918. During the crisis several of the companies changed their links with the banks, commonly by adding an interlocking director representing a new bank on the board. In several cases, changes in the composition of the bank's board of directors due to the financial crisis constitute an important factor in explaining changes in the network. Thus the Swedish network was more characterized by a restructuring process during the crisis of the 1920s rather than a completely new network structure.

Different banks had different strategies in using interlocking directors with the largest firms, as evident from the sheer number of interlocking directors coming from banks. In particular, one of the largest banks, the Stockholms Enskilda Bank, had long-lasting links with its customer firms. The other three largest banks tended to have a less stable personal network.

Which factors explain the patterns of network relations? Two variables were chosen by Westerström: credits granted and ownership relations between banks and industry. According to Westerström, during the 1930s ownership relations were more important in explaining interlocking directors than direct credit relations. In ten companies credit relations coexisted with interlocking directors during the 1930s. Smaller and more regionally based banks were more vulnerable to changes in the network.

Recent research on Swedish bank–industry relations has underpinned the long-term character of different contracts – e.g. credit contracts, bond contracts and ownership bonds – between banks and industry. Compared with the picture of relatively unchanged relations given in the study of contracts between banks and industrial companies, the patterns of interlocking directorships presented in this study seem to be more changeable and more complex during periods of crisis. Also, the different development of the banks in the network was considered here.[18] Monitoring functions and information channels are some of the complex roles these personal links fulfilled. Harold James has recently pointed to the risk- and uncertainty-reducing functions of interlocking directors as a means of meeting a high degree of competition.[19] The actors in the network could change these roles depending on the financial situation facing the specific firm. In this perspective, Sidney Pollard claimed that interlocking directorships could be seen as reflecting the duality and interdependence in bank–industry relations. One director – and one link – could perform several of these activities. Thus no single theory can help us to understand the complex pattern of personal links between banks and industry.[20] The Swedish experience can probably best be understood with the help of several different theories explaining the complex and fascinating phenomenon of interlocking directorships. By studying this phenomenon, new important aspects can be discussed concerning the function and role of different bank systems, thus illuminating a crucial part of the process of dynamics of the economy.

Notes

1. I would like to express my gratitude to the participants of the Nordic seminar 'Banks and industry in Scandinavia 1914-1940', Sandvika, Norway, 13–14 June 1991, and the participants of the conference 'Banks and Customers: Institutional Theory and Banking Practices', held at the London School of Economics and Political Science, Business History Unit, 11–14 September 1991. I would especially like to thank Alice Teichova, Terry Gourvish, Håkan Lindgren, Ra Lundström, Ulf Olsson, Mats Larsson and Hans-Christian Johansen, whose helpful comments have been of benefit to this contribution.

   My colleague Staffan Westerström conducted a study of the personal relations between banks and industry 1928–34 in an unpublished paper. Thanks to his generosity and encouragement, I have been able to cite and refer to his results, as well as use his tables and sources when comparing his period with the period of 1918–24. Our discussions have been a great help to me. Thanks are also due to Mrs Annika Wallroth-Nordlander who checked the language in this contribution.

2. Geoffrey Easton, 'Industrial Networks: a Review', in: *Industrial Networks. A New View on Reality*, ed. by Björn Axelsson and Geoffrey Easton, Routledge, 1992, pp. 21; Anders Lundgren, *Technological Innovation and Industrial Evolution – The Emergence of Industrial Networks*, EFI, Stockholm School of Economics, (diss.), Stockholm, 1991.

3. Lars Engwall and Jan Johansson, 'Banks in Industrial Networks,' *Working Paper 1989/2*, Department of Business Studies, Uppsala University, Uppsala, 1989.

4. See e.g. Thomas Koenig, Robert Gogel, and John Sonquist, 'Models of the Significance of Interlocking Directorates,' *American Journal of Economics and Sociology*, vol. 38, no. 2, April 1979, pp. 173–86; Donald Palmer, Roger Friedland and Jitendra V. Singh, 'The Ties that Bind: Determinants of Stability in a Corporate Interlock Network.' *American Sociological Review*, vol. 51, 1986 and Donald Palmer, 'Interpreting Corporate Interlocks from Broken Ties', *Social Science History*, vol. 7, no. 2, Spring 1983, pp. 217–31.

5. Mark S. Mizruchi and Linda Brewster Sterns, 'A Longitudinal Study of the Formation of Interlocking Directorates,' *Administrative Science Quarterly*, 33, 1988, pp. 194–210.

6. See e.g. Michael Soref and Maurice Zeitlin, 'Finance Capital and the Capitalist Class', in: *Intercorporate Relations. The Structural Analysis of Business*, ed. by Mark S. Mizruchi and Michael Schwartz, Cambridge University Press, 1987, pp. 61–2, and B. Mintz, and M. Schwartz (eds), *The Power Structure of American Business*, The University of Chicago Press, Chicago, 1985.

7. One excellent example of a study of stability in personal networks is Frans Stokman, Jelle Van Der Knoop and Frans W. Wasseur, 'Interlocks in the Netherlands Stability and Careers in the Period 1960–1980.' *Social Networks*, 10, 1988, pp. 183–208. One of the main findings was that primary (the director has an inside position in one of the companies) and multiple interlocks tended to be more stable.

8. For an interesting discussion of the importance of expanding the domain of institutional theory to include areas such as financial markets, see Walter W. Powell, 'Expanding the Scope of Institutional Analysis', in Walter W. Powell and Paul J. DiMaggio (eds), *The New Institutionalism in Organizational Theory*, University of Chicago Press, Chicago, 1991, pp. 183–203. Edwin Neave proposes the need for an institutional approach to explain changes in financial systems, especially those between alternative governance structures. Here, uncertainty and information becomes important in determining the choice of governance structure (Edwin H. Neave, *The Economic Organisation of a Financial System*, Routledge, 1991, pp. 30–31).

9. Mats Larsson and Håkan Lindgren, 'Risktagandets gränser. Utvecklingen av det svenska bankväsendet 1850–1980,' in: *Bankmarknader i förvandling*, ed. by Carl G. Thunman and Kent Eriksson Lund, 1990. For a detailed examination of the financial crisis in the early 1920s, see Mats Larsson, 'State, banks and industry in Sweden, with some reference to the Scandinavian Countries' in: *The Role of Banks in the Interwar Economy*, ed. by Harold James, Håkan Lindgren and Alice Teichova, Cambridge University Press, 1991, pp. 85–91.

10. For a detailed discussion on this matter, see Ragnhild Lundström, 'Banks and Early Swedish Multinationals' in Alice Teichova, Maurice Lévy-Leboyer and Helga Nussbaum (eds), *Multinational Enterprise in Historical Perspective*, Cambridge University Press, 1986 [1989], pp. 211, 213.

258   Universal banking in the twentieth century

. The increased dominance of the banks during the crisis in the early 1920s has been discussed earlier by, e.g. Anders Östlind, *Svensk samhällsekonomi 1914–1922*, Stockholm, 1945, Statens Offentliga Utredningar, *SOU 1927: 11*, Stockholm 1927, and Karl-Gustaf Hildebrand, *I omvandlingens tjänst*. *Svenska Handelsbanken 1871–1955*, Stockholm, 1971; Ragnhild Lundström, 'Banks and Early Swedish Multinationals' in Teichova, Lévy-Leboyer and Helga Nussbaum, op. cit., note 10, pp. 210–11 and Håkan Lindgren, *Bank, investmentbolag, bankirfirma*. *Stockholms Enskilda Bank 1924–1945*, Stockholm, 1988.

12. See, e.g. Mats Larsson, 'Government Subsidy or Internal Restructuring? Swedish Commercial Banks during the crisis years of the 1920s', in *European Industry and Banking Between the Wars. A Review of Bank–Industry Relations*, ed. by H. Lindgren, P.L. Cottrell and A. Teichova, Leicester University Press, 1992, p. 130 and Larsson, op. cit., note 9, p. 92. James, op. cit., note 9.

13. Staffan Westerström, 'Gemensamma styrelseledamöter i bank och näringsliv 1928–1934', unpublished mimeo, Uppsala University, Department of Economic History, Uppsala, 1992.

14. The chosen criterion was share capital, based on Swedish sources and the possibility of comparing results from this study within the scope of a larger research project. For a discussion of the chosen criteria, see Ottosson (1992). Let me conclude that other criteria of size, e.g. stock market value, sales etc. certainly are more desirable from a theoretical point of view. The problem here, however, was to find criteria which could be used during the period 1903–39, the only existing one was share capital. This period was chosen for my dissertation, *Stabilitet och Förändring i personliga nätverk, Gemensamma styrelseledamöter i bank och näringsliv 1903–1939, Uppsala*, 1993.

15. I would like to express my gratitude to Staffan Westerström for his help and comments on earlier manuscripts.

16. The PC program used for this analysis was Gradap, PC-version 2. 1, supplemented with Ucinct. With this software, matrices for every year were created from database files. These matrices were analysed both in Gradap and Ucinet. Sprenger & Stokman, *GRADAP, manual, PC-Version 2. 1*, iec, Progamma, The Netherlands, 1989.

17. A *personal link* between banks and industries is defined in this study as one or several interlocking directors sitting on two or more boards. Therefore, a *single link* consists of one interlocking director. If several directors constitute a link, this is called a *multiple link*.

18. Hans Sjögren, *Bank och näringsliv*, (diss.), Uppsala University, Uppsala, 1991. Sjögren also points out a tendency for the banks to increase the number of credit contracts during periods of recessions, a short-term trend during the crisis. As noted before, a tendency to increase the number of bank–industry interlocks was also seen during periods of crisis.

19. Harold James, 'Introduction' in James, Lindgren and Teichova, op. cit., note 9, p. 10, Sidney Pollard in Lindgren, Cottrell and Teichova, op. cit., note 12, p. 224. Lindgren has also pointed out the role of the industrialists on the bank's board in the case of Stockholms Enskilda Bank, Lindgren, op. cit., note 11, p. 43.

20. For a more detailed discussion, see e.g. Linda Brewster Stearns, 'Capital Markets Effects on External Control of Corporations', in. *Structures of Capital. The Social Organization of the Economy*, ed. by Sharon Zukin and Paul DiMaggio, Cambridge University Press, 1990, pp. 175–201.

Sources

Swedish National Archives
Patent- och registeringsverkets arkiv
Bolagshandlingar
Bank och Fondinspektionens arkiv
Undersökningsberättelser för affärsbankerna
Engagemangsregistret.

Patent- och registeringsverket, bolagsbyrån, Sundsvall:
Bolagshandlingar

References

Brewster-Stearns, Linda and Mark S. Mizruchi (1986), 'Broken-Tie Reconstitution and the Functions of Interorganizational Interlocks: A Reexamination', *Administrative Science Quarterly*, 31, pp. 522–38.

Ornstein, Michael (1984), 'Interlocking Directorates in Canada: Intercorporate or Class Alliance?' *Administrative Science Quarterly*, 29, pp. 210–31.

Östlind, Anders (1945), *Svensk samhällsekonomi 1914–1922*, Stockholm.

Ottosson, Jan, 'Network Analysis and Interlocking Directorships: interwar Sweden', in H. Lindgren, P.L. Cottrell and A. Teichova (eds), *European Industry and Banking Between the Wars. A Review of Bank-Industry Relations*, Leicester University Press, 1992.

Ottosson, Jan, *Stabilityt och Förändring i personliga nätverk. Gemensamma styrelseledamöter i bank och näringsliv 1903–1939*, Dissertation published by Department of Economic History, Uppsala University, 1993.

Palmer, Donald (1983), 'Interlocking Directorates and Intercorporate Coordination', *Administrative Science Quarterly*, 28, pp. 40–55.

Svenska aktiebolag och Enskilda banker, red. Key-Åberg, 1919–25, 1929–35.

19 Interlocking directorships between commercial banks and industry in interwar Vienna

Peter Eigner

Around the middle of the 1890s the great Austrian universal banks began to shift their business relations to the industrial sector and were soon highly involved in a number of industrial companies.[1] Financial ties in the way of participation, granting or procuring credits then led to the appointment of bankers to the boards of industrial joint-stock companies and to the accumulation of 30 or more seats.[2] These interlocking directorships have to be seen as the essential formal means for banks to acquire influence in industry.

Nevertheless, the personal influence of Austrian finance capital on industry in the Habsburg Monarchy and its successor states has attracted remarkably little interest in discussions of the economic development of the huge empire.[3] This neglect has led to an overestimation of the influence of the Viennese banks because little distinction was drawn between potential chances of influence and actual influence exerted by bankers. A systematic analysis of the role and the functions of interlocking directorships (to be analysed from a network perspective) may be seen as a contribution to an international debate which considers the question why and how different forms of networks in different European countries have developed and in which historical context.[4] To investigate the reasons, the amount, the consequences and the limits of the personal involvement of directors in banking and industry was the aim of a project entitled 'The Concentration of Decision-Making Power. Interlocking Directorates between Banks and Industry in Austria 1895–1938', which was conducted by the author under the leadership of Professor Alois Mosser.

The study concentrates on the ten largest Viennese commercial banks, i.e. the Anglo-Österreichische Bank (AB), the Allgemeine Österreichische Boden-Credit-Anstalt (BCA), the Österreichische Credit-Anstalt für Handel und Gewerbe (CA), the Allgemeine Depositenbank (DB), the Österreichische Länderbank (LB), the Mercurbank (MB), the Niederösterreichische Escompte-Gesellschaft (NEG), respectively after 1934 its successor organization, the Österreichische Industriekredit-Aktiengesellschaft (ÖIKAG), the Union-Bank (UB), the Allgemeine Verkehrsbank (VB) and the Wiener Bank-Verein (WBV). In 1913 they represented more than 85 per cent of the equity of all eighteen Viennese joint-stock banks. A database was constructed which includes all members of the bank boards from 1895 to 1938 (894 persons; 92 of them were working for more than one bank of the sample) taking into account their function in the bank hierarchy and the duration of their bank career. This longitudinal study was used for analysing the dynamics in the process of the formation of links and broken interlockings. It was combined with complete networks of the bank board members' interlocking directorships with industry and other banks at four cross-sectional years, i.e. 1908, 1917, 1928 and 1937. The data-base of the decision makers in banks and industries thus serves as the basis of a network analysis having the aim of recording the potential of influence, communication and control.[5]

The source used was the *Compass*, the financial yearbook of Austria–Hungary (after 1918 of Austria and the successor states of the Habsburg Monarchy), which contains detailed information on the banks and industrial joint-stock companies and in the *Personenverzeichnis* lists the interlocking directorships of bankers and industrialists. The industrial companies were provided with a code of regional affiliation to show what happened to the multinational holdings of the Viennese banks after the establishment of the successor states. In the first – quantitatively oriented – part of the investigation the extent and the distribution of the interlocking directorships among single banks and branches were established.

Number of interlocking directorships – position of the banks

The number of interlocking directorships with industrial joint-stock companies nearly doubled from 533 in 1908 (no earlier data were available) to 1 050 in 1917 (Table 19.1). A rank-order of banks in 1908 showed that the Credit-Anstalt had already taken the lead with almost one-quarter of all interlockings. The Niederösterreichische Escompte-Gesellschaft was in second position followed by the Wiener Bank-Verein. The middle-sized banks (DB, MB, UB and VB) had not yet turned to the financing of industry. A modification of its statutes had enabled the Boden-Credit-Anstalt to intensify its industrial business so that with 144 interlockings it was in third position in 1917. The middle-sized banks were still at the end of the rank-order but they too had established substantial industrial concerns. After the disintegration of the Habsburg Monarchy the Austrian industrial structure underwent substantial adjustments. Nevertheless, the Viennese banks continued and extended their services for their industrial clients and their control of the financial processes in the companies grew. Mergers and other concentration movements were in the interest of the big banks and in some cases the banks worked out recovery strategies for their heavily indebted subsidiary enterprises.[6] In spite of these activities the banks did not seem to conduct a specific industrial policy.

The number of interlockings increased by a further 34 per cent to 1 406 in 1928.[7] The Credit-Anstalt remained in first place in terms of total interlocks in that year, followed by the Boden-Credit-Anstalt and the Niederösterreichische

Escompte-Gesellschaft. The growth of BCA interlockings was due to the merger of the bank with the Union-Bank and the Verkehrsbank, which had increased its industrial holdings enormously. By 1937, the year in which the database, because of Austrian banking concentration, only consisted of four banks, the number of interlocking directorates decreased, as expected by 71 per cent to 407. The banking giant, the Credit-Anstalt, held more than one-third of these. The impressive number of interlocks between banks and industry, however, remains of relatively minor significance unless the functions exercised by a banker are taken into account. The accumulation of 40 or even more seats on boards of directors set narrow limits to the quality of business expertise if we think alone of the limited time available to bank representatives. Personal relationships between banks and industry have thus to be seen in the context of numerous power-restricting factors.[8]

Table 19.1   Total number of interlocking directorships of ten Viennese joint-stock banks with industrial joint-stock companies

Bank	1908 Number	1908 Rank	1917 Number	1917 Rank	1928 Number	1928 Rank	1937 Number	1937 Rank
AB	57	5	125	4	–	–	–	–
BCA	54	6	144	3	333	2	–	–
CA	130	1	178	1	379	1	146	1
DB	4	10	62	8	–	–	–	–
LB	61	4	114	5	163	5	124	2
MB	13	9	49	10	57	6	40	4
NEG	96	2	148	2	302	3	–	–
ÖIKAG	–	–	–	–	–	–	97	3
UB	29	7	54	9	–	–	–	–
VB	18	8	81	7	–	–	–	–
WBV	71	3	95	6	172	4	–	–
Total	533		1050		1406		407	
Average number per bank	53		105		234		102	

Source: Database, Peter Eigner; *Compass 1909* vols I, II; 1918, vols I, II, III (*Verzeichnis der Verwaltungsräte und Direktoren*); 1929, vols *Österreich, Čechoslowakei, Ungarn, Jugoslawien, Rumänien, Personenverzeichnis*; 1938, vols Österreich, *(Verwaltungsräte und Direktoren)*.

Specialization in specific industries

An analysis by industry (see Table 19.2) reveals that mining and metallurgy held first position in 1908, closely followed by engineering and metal working, which took the leading position in all other cross-sectional years. Some branches such as the shoe and leather industry and the glass industry seemed to have been largely independent of the banks. It would be wrong to speak of a specialization of the banks' industrial clients in 1908 though some banks began to establish priorities. Thus, the Credit-Anstalt held 30 of its 79 interlockings in engineering and metal working, and the Niederösterreichische Escompte-Gesellschaft was connected with the most important mining and metallurgy companies of the empire.

Table 19.2 Distribution of interlocking directorships by industry

Industry[1]	1908 Number	Rank	1917 N.	R.	1928 N.	R.	1937 N.	R.	Total N.	R.
Hotels	8	13	24	12	6	16	6	16	44	16
Building (Materials) ind.	26	9	45	11	48	12	16	9	135	11
Glass industry	7	15	15	15	36	14	8	14	66	14
Mining and metallurgy	81	1	98	5	171	3	57	3	407	2
Engineering and metal working	79	2	198	1	208	1	69	1	554	1
Spirits and brewing ind.	21	10	51	8	64	9	18	7	154	9
Chemicals and gas ind.	44	6	106	4	109	5	35	5	294	5
Mineral oil, petrol industry	46	4	51	8	65	8	12	10	174	8
Food industry	11	12	20	14	41	13	11	12	83	13
Electrical industry	39	8	58	7	145	4	62	2	304	4
Wood industry	19	11	50	10	53	10	8	14	130	12
Leather and shoe ind.	1	16	15	15	24	15	9	13	49	15
Paper industry	46	4	63	6	53	10	17	8	179	7
Textile industry	56	3	120	2	183	2	36	4	395	3
Sugar industry	41	7	115	3	105	6	31	6	292	6
Miscellaneous	8	13	21	13	95	7	12	10	136	10
Total	533		1050		1406		407		3396	

[1] Industrial classification according to *Compass* volumes.
Source: As for Table 19.1.

In 1917 the bank board members had nearly one-fifth of all their industrial interlockings with engineering and metal working. This branch was followed by the textiles and sugar industries. The close connection of the textile industry with the Austrian banks was a surprising result compared with other European countries. There are strong indications that the business policy of the Viennese banks – originally determined by the principle of a wide dispersion of risks for investments – was gradually restrained by a policy of specialization. The Viennese banks seemed to have secured their interests by turning to an industry-specific policy. The Boden-Credit-Anstalt was now known as 'textile bank';

the Länderbank specialized in the sugar industry. Austria–Hungary's industrial development took place with increasing concentration in major branches of manufacturing. The activities of the banks have therefore to be seen in the context of cartelization and concentration which culminated in the establishment of the Österreichische Kontrollbank in 1914.[9]

While the textile industry was able to maintain its position behind engineering and metalworking until 1928 (one-third of 183 interlockings with this branch held by members of the Boden-Credit-Anstalt), the sugar industry, which had been mainly located in Czechoslovakia and Hungary, lost importance. The Viennese banks now showed a stronger tendency towards the specialization of their business activities. Each of the banks, however, had interests in most of the industrial branches so that it would be misleading to speak of one bank controlling one or the other branch. The Credit-Anstalt extended its influence over the engineering and metal working companies, and in the sugar industry it displaced the Länderbank from its leading position. The majority of the interlockings of the Niederösterreichische Escompte-Gesellschaft were concentrated in the electrical industry. This industry was the second largest in 1937 according to the number of interlocking directorships, which implies a stronger concentration of directorships on Austrian companies, whereas engineering and textiles showed a sharp decline. Three industries may be identified as the most interlocked with the ten universal banks in the period investigated: engineering and metal working (554); mining and metallurgy (407); and textiles (305). They were followed by the electrical industry, chemicals and sugar. So it seems that, with the exception of the textile industry, the representatives of banks had more influence in the more complex, capital-using industries than in less technological, less capital-using industries.

Continuity and change in bank boards
A high degree of stability characterizes the composition of the bank boards. The interlocking directorships were often held over two or three decades. Of the 250 persons registered in 1917 38 per cent had already been represented in 1908 (when the database included 188 bank board members). In 1928 (296 persons registered) 18 per cent of the bank board members had belonged to the sample of 1917, and a further 11 per cent had already been represented in 1908, 20 years before. One hundred and seventeen persons were included in the database in 1937. None of these persons were directors in 1908, 7 per cent were included in 1917; 43 per cent in 1928; and 59 persons (50 per cent) were recorded for the first time in 1937. If we think of the dramatic political turning points during the period investigated the composition of bank boards showed a surprisingly high continuity.[10]

The BCA and the NEG, 1917–28
In the second part of this study the functional effects of disintegration after 1918 will be investigated for two Viennese universal banks, the Allgemeine Öster-

reichische Boden-Credit-Anstalt (BCA) and the Niederösterreichische Escompte-Gesellschaft (NEG), with regard to the composition and structure of their boards as well as their concerns. Before the First World War the big Viennese universal banks had secured strategic positions in almost all branches of industry, their groups of affiliated companies consisting of possessions in all parts of the monarchy. In 1917 the industrial concern of the Boden-Credit-Anstalt (if we define concern through interlocks) consisted of 93 companies with which the bank was connected through 144 interlocking directorships. The bank had turned to industrial business relatively late but had intensified its efforts and nearly trebled the number of interlocking directorates as well as the number of companies in which it was represented over the last ten years (Table 19.3).[11]

Table 19.3   BCA's interlocking directorships and companies, 1908–17

	Number of interlocking directorships	Number of companies
1908	54	36
1917	144	93

Source: Database, Peter Eigner

This process was connected with the new governor of the BCA, Rudolf Sieghart. Under his leadership the sugar companies of Schoeller & Co. and the waggon-building company Ringhoffer in Prague came under the bank's influence. The number of interlockings with the textile industry alone increased from twelve in 1908 to 35 (almost one-quarter of all BCA interlockings) in 1917. In order of importance there were interlocks with mining and metallurgy, engineering and metal working, and sugar. Compared with the other banks the BCA had a strong presence in the Austrian paper industry. Continuity was also evident: 29 of the 36 companies belonging to the BCA's industrial group in 1908 were again found in 1917. Among its main industries were the Mautner group of textile companies, the Fanto mineral oil industries, the Österreichische Waffenfabriks-Gesellschaft, the chemistry giant Österreichischer Verein für chemische und metallurgische Produktion (Association for Chemical and Metallurgical Production) and the huge Österreichische Berg- und Hüttenwerksgesellschaft (Mining & Metallurgy Co.). Karl Leth, a former governor of the Post Office Savings Bank and a former minister of finance, stood at the head of the bank as Sieghart had to relinquish his position at the beginning of 1917. But Sieghart still presided over the boards of directors of the Association for Chemical and Metallurgical Production and of the Mining & Metallurgy Co. The other members of the bank's top management in 1917 were the executives Alfred Herzfeld, Richard Reisch and Alexander Weiner.

The industrial group of the Niederösterreichische Escompte-Gesellschaft consisted of 87 companies in 1917. One hundred and forty-eight interlockings built the link between the bank and its industries. In 1908 the NEG was linked with 64 industrial companies through 96 interlockings. The distribution by industry was different from that of the BCA. One quarter of the personal links were concentrated in engineering and metal working. Even more impressive were the holdings in mining and metallurgy companies mainly located in the later Czechoslovakia where the NEG dominated in comparison with the other nine banks. The influence of the Prager Eisen-Industrie-Gesellschaft (Prague Iron Co.) had intensified during the last years so that its general manager Wilhelm Kestranek (also president of the Österreichisch-Alpine Montan Gesellschaft) was appointed vice-president of the bank and Sieghart even speaks of Kestranek and his group controlling the bank.[12] The 'new' industries, i.e. the electrical industry, where the NEG acted as a pioneer, and the chemical industry, followed. Of the 87 companies forming the industrial group of the NEG in 1917, the bank had already been connected with 47 of them in 1908. Some industries had almost no connection with either bank: shoes and leather, wood, food, and glass.

The distribution of the interlocking directorships among the bank board members revealed considerable differences between the hierarchical levels of the bank boards.[13] The board of directors was in most cases only formally the highest body of decision making of a company, but in fact the power of decision making had passed to the managing board (Vorstand) as far as vital and long-term questions were concerned.[14] This tendency was more pronounced in the case of the NEG. The members of the managing board held alone more than 50 per cent (76) of all interlockings. Grouping them with the president and the vice-presidents of the board of directors of the NEG they were represented on the most important industrial boards, i.e. the Österreichisch-Alpine Montan Gesellschaft (Alpine Montan Co.), the Prague Iron Co., the Poldihütte (Poldi Works), the Hofherr-Schrantz-Clayton-Shuttleworth companies, etc. The bank assembled prominent industrialists on its board, for example the general manager of the Alpine Montan Co., Oscar Rothballer, and the general manager of both Felten and Guilleaume companies, Adalbert Bergmann. There was no high degree of specialization of the board members in certain industries. Some members of the board of directors, however, seem to have acted as experts, like Leopold Teltscher (president of the Vereinigte Elektrizitäts AG, VEAG) in the electrical industry or Ludwig Urban in the engineering companies. A strong link was built to the bank's sister, the Böhmische Escompte Bank (Czech Escompte Bank). Max Feilchenfeld presided over the board of directors of both banks. Besides, he was the chairman of the Poldi Works and the vice-president of the Alpine Montan Co.

The Boden-Credit-Anstalt showed a different pattern of distribution. Its governor and the three executives had 52 interlockings, but only five of them could be defined as leading positions.[15] The seventeen members of the board of directors enjoyed 82 interlocking directorships, but more than half of them were held by only three board members: Georg Günther, Isidor Mautner and Heinrich Miller-Aichholz. In 31 companies they were in leading positions. Fourteen members of the board of directors had been titled or were of noble birth (barons, knights, earls or princes) which was due to the bank's character as bank of the Court.[16] The board members of the BCA showed a higher degree of specialization: Mautner represented the huge Mautner textile concern and held six leading positions in the textile industry. Richard Schoeller (president of the sugar companies Schoeller & Co. and of the Leipnik-Lundenburger sugar company) and Ferdinand Bloch-Bauer were sugar industrialists. Günther, the general manager of the Austrian Mining & Metallurgy Co., seemed to have been responsible for the armament plants. He was the president of the Austrian Waffenfabriks-Gesellschaft (later Steyr-Werke) which had taken over the whole equity of the Steirische Gußstahlwerke AG and of the Zündhütchen- und Patronenfabrik in Prague (both companies were also presided over by Günther).

After the establishment of the successor states with the collapse of the Austro-Hungarian Monarchy the process of nationalization (or 'nostrification') began, which meant the dissolution of the banks' industrial holdings and networks of branch banks. In 1917 the industrial combine of the NEG consisted of 87 industrial joint-stock companies, 62 were designated Austrian, 21 Hungarian. In 1921 only 40 companies (45 per cent) were named in *Compass* as Austrian, and 12 as Hungarian; 21 were now Czechoslovak companies. This process of nationalization was connected with an alteration in the composition of the bank boards as in 1921 seven of the 29 board members of the BCA in 1917 had lost their function, in the case of the NEG seven out of 20.

The Viennese banks faced the alternative of either 'Austrification', which meant their retreat from the South-East and Central European area by restricting their business to the new Republic of Austria, or 'multinationalization' which meant trying to uphold their traditional spheres of influence. The banks decided in favour of the multinationalization of their activities.[17] The early postwar years were thus characterized by a transformation of the foreign branch banks into independent banks and their contribution into already existing credit institutions respectively. Since the activities of the Viennese banks had 'tended to replace the capital market the banks became the centre of interest of the great West European banks and business combines after 1918'.[18] For their capital support they were invited onto the boards of the Viennese banks.

The banking network of the Boden-Credit-Anstalt

In 1918 the Boden-Credit-Anstalt made an arrangement with the Živnostenská Banka in order to cover the position of its industrial interests within the new Czechoslovak Republic. The Czechoslovak companies were from now on controlled on a joint basis.[19] Because of the dominant position of the Viennese banks West European capital groups had soon realized that cooperation with these banks meant an entry into the most important industries and companies of East–Central Europe. There were two ways of gaining influence: a direct share-participation in these enterprises; or the indirect way by acquiring part of the equity of the Viennese banks. In the case of the BCA the French held about a quarter of the bank's capital in 1919 dating from before the war. The Belgian group Mutuelle Solvay purchased a considerable block of shares in 1919/20. In 1922/23 J. Henry Schröder & Co. of London in conjunction with J.P. Morgan & Co. of New York acquired an interest. In 1924 Eugène Schneider, the president of the Schneider–Creusot combine, the Union Européenne Industrielle et Financière (UEIF), joined the board of the BCA. The influence was increased when the combine bought another parcel of 60 000 shares in 1927. The Italian Assicurazioni Generali of Trieste and the Amsterdamsche Bank in conjunction with Lippmann and Rosenthal had also taken an interest in the bank.[20]

The acquisition of both the Union-Bank and the Verkehrsbank was the most important event in the development of the industrial holdings of the bank. In 1926 a syndicate under the leadership of the BCA consisting of Schoeller & Co. and Heinrich Hardmeyer, Winterthur, bought the majority of the shares of the Verkehrsbank. Underlining this ownership relation the Boden-Credit-Anstalt put three representatives on the board of directors (Alfred Herzfeld, Ernst Garr and Adolf Stern). In the next year, in Spring 1927, the BCA merged both with the Union-Bank, which had formerly been controlled by Sieghart's arch-rival, Siegmund Bosel, and the Verkehrsbank. The BCA bought three million shares of the Union-Bank (coming from the Post Office Savings Bank's holdings caused by Bosel's speculation) against 200 000 shares (nominal value 50 A.S.) of its own shares. For raising the necessary resources to finance the merger the bank's equity had to be increased twice, and Schneider's group was able to acquire further securities.[21] In 1926 the Boden-Credit-Anstalt was involved in the foundation of the American, British & Continental Trust (ABC Trust), an investment company founded by Schröder of London, its American subsidiary, Blith, Witter & Co., New York, and the Hungarian Commercial Bank of Pest. In 1927 the Dutch Maatschappij voor Beheer v. Effekten was formed by the Dutch partners of the BCA with the purpose of acquiring the portfolios of the Union- and the Verkehrsbank.[22] It also took over the holdings of the bank in the Fanto petrol group. After 1925 Sieghart enlarged the bank's network of relations to other banks by acquiring some provincial banks. The BCA took over part of the equity of the Bank für Oberösterreich und Salzburg (through a credit connection two representatives were on the board in 1928). Its strong interest in Austrian provincial banks was underlined by its participation in the merger of the Tiroler Hauptbank with the Bank für Tirol und Vorarlberg in 1926 which created the Hauptbank für Tirol und Vorarlberg (1928: four board members of the BCA). The BCA also took part in the foundation of the Bank für Steiermark

(1928: four board members) which was a result of a merger of the Agrarbank with the former branch of the VB, the Steirerbank and the Graz branch of the liquidating Centralbank deutscher Sparkassen in 1927. In 1928 the BCA bought half of the shares of the Bank für Kärnten (two board members).[23]

The bank also participated in banks of the successor states. It was involved in the merger of the Kroatisch–Slavonische Landes-Hypothekenbank (Croatian–Slavonian Mortgage Bank) with some other Yugoslav banks in 1928 which resulted in the foundation of the Yugoslav Union-Bank AG (two board members). The Boden-Credit-Anstalt further acquired interests in the Bank Malopolski (two board members) and in the Banque Générale de Bulgarie (two board members).[24]

The next step was to look at the composition of the bank's board in 1928 (Table 19.4). There was one difficulty concerning the nationality of the board members. As *Compass* lists their addresses this was the criterion chosen in case of doubt.[25] For the representatives of West European capital groups I used the symbol 'W'.

Table 19.4   The Board members of the BCA and their interlocking director-ships, 1928

	1	2	3	4	5	6	7
Managing board							
a) Chair or Presidency							
President: Sieghart, Rudolf	A	9	5	–	–	–	–
Vice-President: Herzfeld, Alfred	A	29	5	2	1	–	–
b) Members of the executive board							
Chairman: Steiner, Rudolf	A	31	3	3	1	–	–
Mosing, Ernst	A	20	2	5	1	–	–
Widmer, Emil	A	5	–	1	–	–	–
Garr, Ernst	A	7	–	3	–	–	–
Stern, Adolf	A	16	1	2	–	–	–
Total		117	16	16	3		
Board of directors							
Auspitz, Stefan	A	7	1	–	–	VP, MB	–
Bloch-Bauer, Ferdinand	A	14	4	1	–	–	–
Croy-Dülmen, Leopold	A	–	–	1	–	–	–
Friedländer, Eugen	A	14	9	–	–	–	–
Giannelia, Basilio	A	–	–	–	–	–	–
Graetz, Viktor	A	6	–	–	–	–	–

	1	2	3	4	5	6	7
Günther, Georg	A	16	5	1	–	–	–
Hankar-Solvay, Robert	W	11	–	3	–	–	–
Hardmeyer, Heinrich	A	–	–	1	–	–	BoD
Hofstede de Groot, P.	W	–	–	1	–	–	–
Janssen, Emanuel	W	8	3	2	1	–	–
Langer, Leopold	A	7	1	1	–	–	VP
Liebieg, Theodor	C	12	8	2	1	–	–
Mautner, Isidor	A	10	4	–	–	–	–
Mayr, Maximilian	A	3	–	1	1	BoD	–
Morpurgo, Edgardo	W	7	1	6	–	–	–
Raux, Fernand	W	–	–	–	–	–	–
Ringhoffer, Franz	C	6	3	–	–	–	–
Schneider, Eugène	W	6	3	4	1	–	–
Schoeller, Richard	A	10	2	1	–	–	–
Schonka, Franz	A	1	–	–	–	–	–
Schröder,* Bruno	W						
Skene, Richard	A	12	6	–	–	–	P
Stern, Julius	A	2	1	1	–	MB	–
Strakosch-Feldringen, Siegfried	A	1	–	–	–	–	–
Taussig, Karl	A	2	–	–	–	–	–
Weissenstein, Emanuel	A	3	1	–	–	–	–
Total		158	52	26	4		
Controllers							
Gassauer, Anton	A	–	–	–	–	–	–
Reich, Otto	C	1	–	1	–	–	–
Stein, Adolf	A	2	–	1	–	–	–
Total		3	–	2	–	–	–
Appointed deputy directors							
Blitz, Otto	A	2	–	1	–	–	–
Fischer, Ernst	A	2	–	–	–	MB	–
Hochapfel, Julius	A	28	3	2	–	–	MB
Popper-Artberg, Adolf	A	7	–	1	–	–	ChMB
Wilhelm, Max	A	5	1	2	–	–	–
Total		44	4	6	–		
Whole board		322	72	50	7		

Notes:
1 Origin.
2 Number of industrial interlockings.
3 Leading positions (defined as president, chairman, general manager or owner) in industrial companies.
4 Number of interlockings with other banks.
5 Leading positions in banks.
6 Former member of the Unionbank.
7 Former member of the Verkehrsbank.
Abbreviations:
  A – Austrian representative
  C – Czechoslovak representative
  W – Representative of Western capital group
  BoD – Member of the Board of Directors
  P – President of the Board of Directors
  VP – Vice-President
  MB – Member of the Managing Board
  ChMB – Chairman of the Managing Board.
* Baron Bruno Schröder was not mentioned in the *Personencompass*, vol. 1929. He was head of the London banking house J. Henry Schröder.

** The five directors' representatives which are not included in the table held seven seats in other banks (all of them Austrian provincial banks) and six seats in industrial companies. There were also ten entitled directors' representatives which had together eleven seats in industrial joint-stock companies of which eight were held by one single person, Alexander Marmorstein, who was chairman of the credit department and a former board member of the Verkehrsbank.

Source: *Compass 1929*, vol. *Österreich*, list of the board members of the Boden-Credit-Anstalt on pp. 278–9; vol. *Personenverzeichnis (Verwaltungsräte und Direktoren)*.

Seven members were easily identified as the top management of the Boden-Credit-Anstalt. Four of them had already belonged to the bank's board in 1917. One-third of the members of the board of directors had been represented on the board of the BCA in 1917. Sieghart's career had only been interrupted for two years (1917 and 1918). He was now president of both the managing board and the board of directors of the bank and held the position of president in the most important companies connected with the BCA, the Staats-Eisenbahn-Gesellschaft, the Österreichische Siemens-Schuckert-Werke, the Verein für chemische und metallurgische Produktion (now Spolek pro chemickou a hutní výrobu), the Wiener Lokomotivfabrik, the Cosmanos textile company and the Veitscher Magnesitwerke AG. Almost the same was true of the bank's vice-president, Herzfeld. He was the president of the boards of the AG für Mineralöl-Industrie vorm. D. Fanto, the Hanf-, Jute- und Textil-Industrie AG, the Textilwerke Mautner AG (now Mautnerovy textilní závody a. sp.), the Pottendorfer Knüpfteppich Industrie and the Falkenauer Kohlenbergbau AG (now Falknovská akciová společnost pro dolování uhlí). He also held this position in the Wiener Giro- und Cassen-Verein. The majority of the interlocking directorships were held by members of the managing board. There was a certain degree of specialization as in the case of Rudolf Steiner, who had thirteen interlockings with textile companies. Among the appointed deputy directors (*Titulardirektoren*) there was one 'multi-functionary', Julius Hochapfel, a former member of the managing board of the

Verkehrsbank, with 28 interlockings. The list of board members of the former Verkehrsbank included, besides Hochapfel, Leopold Langer, Richard Skene, Heinrich Hardmeyer, and Adolf Popper-Artberg. Three of the BCA directors, Garr, Herzfeld and Stern, had been entrusted with directorships at the Verkehrsbank for only one year (1926 – when the BCA had acquired the stock majority of the Verkehrsbank). On the board of the BCA there were four former members of the Union-Bank, too: Stefan Auspitz, Ernst Fischer, Julius Stern and Maximilian Mayr. Having a seat on a bank board often meant a job for life, e.g. Basilio Giannelia had joined the board in 1898; Langer had begun his bank career as a member of the board of directors of the Verkehrsbank in 1901.

The Austrian members of the board of directors were nearly all important and prominent industrialists coming from distinguished families in many cases.[26] Eugen Friedländer was the general manager of the Böhler companies in Vienna and Berlin. Günther was the president of the Österreichische Bundesbahnen and the Steyr-Werke AG. Schoeller held this position in the Schoeller-Bleckmann steelworks and the Grazer Waggon- und Maschinenfabrik. Mautner built a strong link with the textile interests of the BCA (nine interlockings). Franz Schonka was the president of the Donaudampfschiffahrts-Gesellschaft. Skene sat at the head of the boards of five sugar companies, the Steyrermühl AG and the insurance company Anglo-Danubian Lloyd.

Among the 27 members of the board of directors seven were representatives of Western capital groups which had taken interest in the bank. Robert Hankar-Solvay and Emanuel Janssen came from the Belgian Solvay industrial group. Hankar-Solvay was also found on the board of the affiliated banks of the BCA, the Polish Bank Małopolski and the Yugoslav Unionbank AG. Hofstede de Groot was an executive of the Amsterdamsche Bank. The Italian Edgardo Morpurgo was the general manager of the insurance company Assicurazioni Generali. He belonged to the type of a specialized board member or expert and had 25 interlockings with insurance companies. Fernand Raux was a French minister plenipotentiary. Schneider represented the Schneider–Creusot industrial group. He was the president of the Union Européenne Industrielle et Financière, a holding company that had been established to control the former Austro-Hungarian assets acquired by Schneider. Schneider had been associated with the Škodovy závody (Škoda Works) since before the war and after a new purchase of shares Schneider held 61 per cent of Škoda's capital and had thus obtained a controlling holding. At about the same time Schneider had come into contact with the BCA through his acquisition of at least part of the bank's interest in the now Czechoslovak Mining and Metallurgic Co. (Báňská a hutní společnost).[27] Baron Bruno Schröder was the head of the London banking house J. Henry Schröder & Co. Two members of the board of directors were Czechoslovaks: the industrialists Theodor Liebieg, also president of the Böhmische Unionbank (Bohemian Bank Union), who showed seven interlockings with textile joint-stock companies, and Franz Ringhoffer, the president of both the Ringhoffer and the Tatra Works.

The industrial combine of the Boden-Credit-Anstalt in 1928
By 1928 the BCA, which had begun as a mortgage bank, had, under the direction
of Sieghart since the Winter of 1919, completed its transformation into a 'full
industrial "mobilier"'.[28] Between 1917 and 1928 the number of interlocking
directorships had doubled (Table 19.5). The Boden-Credit-Anstalt was represented through its Austrian board members in 161 industrial companies. The
bank was connected with these undertakings through 285 interlocking direc-

*Table 19.5   Distribution of interlocking directorships of the BCA by industry,
1917 and 1928***

Industry[1]	1917			1928		
	NoI	NoC	NoLP	NoI	NoC	NoLP
Hotels	2	2	–	3	3	1
Building (materials) industry	5	5	–	10	7	2
Glass industry	1	1	1	–	–	–
Mining and metallurgy	17	11	8	40	25	14
Engineering and metal working	17	8	3	45	26	9
Spirits and brewing industry	4	3	1	13	8	1
Chemicals and gas industry	12	7	2	12	8	1
Mineral oil, petrol industry	11	7	1	14	8	2
Food industry	2	1	1	7	5	–
Electrical industry	6	3	2	15	9	3
Wood industry	–	–	–	6	4	–
Leather and shoe industry	–	–	–	8	3	–
Paper industry	15	13	4	20	11	1
Textile industry	35	21	10	53	23	8
Sugar industry	17	11	3	30	16	8
Miscellaneous	–	–	–	9	5	3
Total	144	93	36	285	161	53

NoI   Number of interlockings.
NoC   Number of companies.
NoLP   Number of leading positions (defined as in Table 19.4).

Notes:
*Omitting interlocking directorates of Czechoslovak citizens and representatives of Western capital
groups.
[1] Industrial Classification according to *Compass*.

Source: Compass 1918, vols II, III (*Verzeichnis der Verwaltungsräte und Direktoren*); *Compass
1929*, vols *Österreich, Personenverzeichnis* (*Verwaltungsräte und Direktoren*).

torships. Thus, almost 85 per cent of the interlockings, accounting for all BCA-board members (including the foreign representatives), were held by Austrians, which is an impressive figure. In 53 undertakings the bank held a leading position. Nearly half of all interlockings were concentrated in three industries: textiles, engineering and metal working, and mining and metallurgy. The number of interlockings had increased in all industries except one: glass.

Three indirect sources, two of them listing the concerns of the Viennese universal banks,[29] were taken for a sample of companies representing the industrial group of the BCA and the NEG. By including all information in the *Compass* volumes from 1895 to 1929 a complete list of the banks' activities[30] from their beginning was compiled. The sample of the concern of the Boden-Credit-Anstalt consisted of 63 companies; seventeen had formerly belonged to the concern of the Verkehrsbank, and nine to the concern of the Union-Bank. In twelve undertakings the bank(s) had taken the role of the founder (six BCA, four UB, two VB). In ten companies the *Compass* mentioned bank participation in the companies' equities. Ten companies were transformed into joint-stock companies with the help of the bank(s). In one case the bank was responsible for the reorganization of a company, in another the bank had been active in a merger. In almost two-thirds (41) of the companies the bank activities consisted in increasing their capital or purchasing part of their shares. In eighteen companies shares were either issued by the bank or introduced to the stock exchange. These bank activities enabled bank representatives to obtain seats on the boards of industrial joint-stock companies.

The textile industry was one of the sectors where the bank was engaged traditionally. This involvement had led to the bank's reputation as the 'textile bank', which is underlined by the fact that in both cross-sectional years the textile industry had the majority of interlockings. The most important component of the 'textile imperium' of the BCA was the Mautner group of companies (see Table 19.6). In spite of the nostrification of a number of enterprises the bank's strong influence survived after 1917, though the Živnostenská Banka was involved in the Mautner concern in the postwar period. At the head of the Mautner textile group in 1928 were the textile works Mautner in Prague which had a number of subsidiary companies in Czechoslovakia, the Fr. Mattausch AG (presidency, one board member [b.m.]), the Rosenberger textile works Mautner (three b.m.) and the Kammgarnspinnerei Schmieger AG (one b.m.).[31] The Austrian members of the concern were the Vereinigte österreichische Textilindustrie AG (three b.m.), the AG der Baumwollspinnereien zu Marienthal (two b.m.), the Felix-dorfer Weberei und Appretur (two b.m.), the Pottendorfer Baumwoll-Spinnerei und Zwirnerei (two b.m.) and the Pottensteiner Baumwollspinnerei AG (presidency, one b.m.). The companies of the Knüpfteppich-Industrie System Banyai AG in Prague (two b.m.) and in Pottendorf (presidency, one b.m.) were also members of the Mautner group. The concern further included the Yugoslav Mautner AG (presidency, one b.m.) and a number of Hungarian companies. The bank also retained its strong influence in two other textile companies, the Czechoslovak Cosmanos company (presided by Sieghart, 5 b.m.) and the Austrian Hanf-, Jute- und Textil-Industrie AG (its general manager and its president of the board of directors were found on the board of the BCA) (Table 19.6).

Table 19.6   *Bank activities in the main industries of the BCA (selected number of companies) until 1928*

Industry and company name	1	2	3	4	5	6	7
Textile industry							
Cosmanos	C	48 Kč	6	1	F 1905	x	x
Textilwerke Mautner AG	C	100 Kč	3	1	F 1905	x	–
Vereinigte öst. Textil-Industrie AG	A	5	3	–	P 1912	–	–
Rosenberger Textilwerke Mautner AG	C	12 Kč	3	–	–	–	–
AG der Kleinmünchener Baumwollspinn.	A	6	3	1	–	x UB	–
Spinnerei M. Honig AG	A	2.5	3	–	T VB 1921	x VB	–
Hanf-, Jute- und Textilit-Ind. AG	A	11.72	3	2	–	x	–
Böhmische Glanzstoffabrik	C	50 Kč	3	–	P 1921	–	–
Bossi Hutfabrik AG	A	1.2	3	–	T 1926	–	–
Engineering and metal working							
Vereinigte Metallwerke AG	A	7.59	3	1	T,M 1927	–	–
Rottenmanner Eisenwerke AG Lapp	A	1	2	–	T,P 1928	–	–
Lapp-Finze AG	A	5.4	3	1	T VB 1912	x VB	x VB
Eisenwarenfabriks AG Sopron	H	1.2 P	2	–	–	–	x VB
Vereinigte Styria-Fahrrad- u. Dürkoppw.	A	2	2	1	–	x VB	x VB
Schoeller-Bleckmann Stahlwerke AG	A	6.84	3	1	F VB 1920	x VB	x VB
Wiener Lokomotivfabriks AG	A	4	2	1	–	x	–
Grazer Waggon- u. Maschinen-Fabr. AG	A	2.5	2	1	–	x BCA, VB	x VB
Ringhoffer Werke AG	C	42 Kč	2	–	T,P 1911 with CA	x	x
Nesselsdorfer Wagenbau Fabriks AG (since 1927 Tatra-Werke)	C	30 Kč	1	–	–	x	–
Steyr-Werke AG	A	15.12	4	1	–	x BCA, UB	–
Blech- und Eisenwerke Styria	A	2	1	–	T VB 1922	x VB	x VB
Wiener Automobilfabrik AG Gräf & Stift	A	2	1	–	F 1907 UB	x UB	x UB
C. Schember Brückenwaagen- und Maschinenfabrik AG	A	0.6	3	1	T 1917 VB	x VB	x VB

Industry and company name	1	2	3	4	5	6	7
Mining and metallurgy							
Berg- und Hüttenwerksgesellschaft	C	250 Kč	3	–	F 1905	x	–
Rossitzer Bergbau-Ges.	C	24 Kč	3	–	–	–	–
Veitscher Magnesitwerke AG	A	10	3	1	F UB 1899	–	x
Gebr. Böhler and Co. AG Stahlwerke	A	8	3	2	T 1924	x	–
Steirische Gußstahlwerke	A	1.76	1	1	–	–	–
Staatseisenbahngesellschaft	A	25.17	5	1	–	–	–
Ver. Metallhüttenwerke							
'Titan, Nadrag, Calan'	R	30 L	2	–	–	–	–
Serbische Berg- u. Hüttenindustrie							
AG	Y	50 D	2	–	–	x	–

Notes:
1 Seat of the company.
2 Share capital in millions of respective currency (A.S. if not otherwise specified).
3 Number of interlockings with the BCA.
4 Leading positions (defined as in Table 19.4).
5, 6, 7 Bank activities of the BCA*.
5 Foundation (F), participation (P), transformation into a joint-stock company (T) or merger (M).
6 Increase of capital or purchase of shares.
7 Issue of shares or introduction at the stock exchange.
Abbreviations:
   A – Austria
   C – Czechoslovakia
   H – Hungary
   R – Romania
   Y – Yugoslavia
   Kč – Czech Crowns
   P – Pengös
   D – Dinar
   L – Leva
*Bank activities of the UB and the VB, to whose concerns some of the companies had formerly belonged to, were also included. If the business was shared with another bank, the name of the bank is mentioned.

Source: Database, Peter Eigner; all *Compass* volumes, 1929.

Engineering and metal working was one of the main sources of interlocks for nearly all Viennese commercial banks. With regard to the number of inter-lockings of the BCA, it held second position (45 interlockings). The most important component of the bank's concern has been the Steyr-Werke AG which was also not free from foreign capital influence. In 1923 J.P. Morgan & Co., New York, and J. Henry Schroeder & Co., London, had acquired a con-siderable part of its equity. The advancing banking and industry concentration also led to consequences with regard to vertical and horizontal integration. The following shows this process developed in the producer goods sector. In order to be independent in its demand for steel the Steyr-Werke AG had acquired all shares of the Steirische Gußstahlwerke AG. In 1923 the Steyr Works purchased all shares of the 'Wemag' which had bought the works of a former BCA company, the Erste österreichische Zünder- und Metallwarenfabrik F. Keller AG in Hirtenberg. In 1924/25 the company was reorganized by the Steyr Works with the help of the German Kronprinz AG and was given a new name, 'Kromag' (presided over by Günther; 50 per cent of the shares belonged to the Steyr Works, the other half belonged to the German Kronprinz AG). Another subsidiary company, the Zündhütchenfabrik vorm. Sellier & Bellot (the Steyr Works had acquired the majority of its equity in 1915), was sold in 1925. In 1928 the Steyr Works purchased 70 per cent of the equity of the Styria-Fahrrad- und Dürkopp-Werke. A pooling agreement was arranged, its purpose being the rationalization of the Styrian company. Indirect links led to the Lapp-Finze AG which had shareholdings in the Eisenwarenfabriks AG Sopron (a majority) and in the Styria-Fahrrad- und Dürkopp-Werke. The Staatseisenbahn-Gesellschaft was also active with regard to vertical and horizontal integration. It had its own industrial group of coal, iron and steel works like the Romanian 'Titan, Nadrag, Calan' Works, the Serbian Mining and Metallurgic Company as well as engineering companies. Its Romanian works had been given to the newly founded Aciéries et Domaines de Resita SA against shareholding. The BCA also obtained a parcel of shares and put three representatives on to the board. The Ringhoffer Works took over the whole capital of the Nesselsdorfer AG (which changed its name to Tatra Works) in a barter transaction. Both boards were presided over by Ringhoffer, a Czechoslovak industrialist. The Iron Works Sandau AG, where Mautner, a member of the board of directors of the BCA, held the presidency and two other BCA directors were found to be on the board, produced textile machinery. It was a subsidiary company within the Mautner concern.

Mining and metallurgy was another of BCA's main industries. The number of interlockings increased from 17 to 40 during the period investigated. Western capital groups had soon realized that the bank was connected with some of the biggest and thus most influential industrial groups. In 1920 the Union Européenne Industrielle et Financière controlled 24 per cent of the capital of the former Austrian Mining and Metallurgy Co. (now Báňska a hutní společnost) and 48.4 per cent consisting of a decisive shareholders' syndicate including the BCA, Huta bankowa and the American group Equitable Trust Co. Nevertheless, the BCA continued to be the principal bank of the enterprise. The capital participation of the French group was increased so that in 1928 about half of the shares were controlled by the holding of Schneider–Creusot and its president, Schneider, held the presidency of the mining giant which had a number of subsidiary companies. The Schneider group had thus gained another key position in Czechoslovakia. The former general manager of the Mining and Metallurgy Co., Günther, an Austrian, had been replaced by a Czechoslovak general manager. A minority was in the hands of the BCA and the Živnostenská Banka. This development was caused by the Nostrification Act at the end of 1919. Together with other legislation the power of the Viennese banks was undermined and this was particularly true of the Boden-Credit-Anstalt, which had most of its shares in industrial companies on Czechoslovak territory.[32] The takeover of the Union-Bank had given the BCA 3 500 shares of another giant, the Veitscher Magnesitwerke-AG. The majority of the Veitscher Magnesitwerke-AG stock was originally held by a syndicate under the leadership of the BCA. But the participation of a group of French steel manufacturers, led by the Union Européenne, had gradually developed from a minority holding in 1919/20 to a majority one, so that the BCA lost its influence. The Veitscher Magnesitwerke also controlled 70 per cent of the Magnezitový priemysel účastinná společnost of Bratislava (Magnesite Industry Co.) which owned three further magnesia plants.[33] The Falknovská akciová společnost pro dolování uhlí, a coal-mining company, had already belonged to the mining industrial group of the BCA in 1917 (it had been founded by the bank in 1916). Though the managing board member of the BCA, Herzfeld, presided over the company, it had come under the control of the Czechoslovak Association for Chemical and Metallurgical Production (now Spolek pro chemickou a hutní výrobu). The merger of these two companies, while agreed, had not been realized in 1928. Eight of fourteen leading positions the BCA had in mining and metallurgy companies were held by one board member, the general manager and president of the Steel Works Gebr. Böhler AG, Friedländer. He was in a leading position in all other national Böhler companies which had been united in the holding company Vereinigte Böhlerstahlwerke AG in Zurich, controlling the whole equity of all these companies as well as that of the subsidiary company St Egyder Eisen- und Stahlindustrie. Though Friedländer was the chairman of the holding company too, the Böhler factories were under the influence of foreign capital. This had already been the case in 1917 when *Compass* mentions the company as a foreign undertaking. Friedländer acted as confidant of the Böhler family whose influence on the business policy of the company had survived, although the third of the equity which Hugo Stinnes had acquired in the 1920s had passed to the German Stahlverein GesmbH.[24] Another link to the mining and metallurgy companies was formed by board member Günther, who was president of the Österreichische Bundesbahnen and of the Steyr-Werke AG. He had eight interlockings with mining and metallurgy companies.

With regard to the electrical industry, Western capital groups (mainly German) had even before the First World War participated in the equity of Austrian companies. After its merger with Schuckert, Siemens had taken over the plants in Austria and Hungary and founded the Österreichische Siemens-Schuckert-Werke and likewise a Hungarian company. In 1902 and 1904 the Allgemeine Elektrizitäts-Gesellschaft (AEG) had acquired the Union Elektrizitätsgesellschaft and thus created the AEG-Union. What was left of the German multinationals' foreign investments after the war was mainly situated in Central and South-East Europe, especially in Austria. With these 'stepping stones' AEG and Siemens managed to build up their predominance again in this area of Europe.[35] It was Sieghart himself who in 1928 was president of the multinational board of the biggest electro-technical company of the former monarchy, the Österreich-ische Siemens-Schuckert-Werke. The managing director of the BCA, Steiner, was the president of the AEG-Union. But both electricity companies were in the hands of German capital.

Compared with other Viennese commercial banks the involvement of the BCA in the paper industry was of eminent importance. The Neusiedler AG had a number of subsidiary companies where the BCA was represented with one board member each. These were the nationalized Prager Neusiedler AG, the AG der Papierfabrik Schlöglmühl, the Lenzinger Papierfabrik AG (four board members) and the Theresienthaler Papierfabrik AG. Though the majority of the stock was in the hands of the Czechoslovak company Petschek & Co. the BCA was able to maintain its former influence. A participation of the Steyrermühl (which was presided by a board member of the bank) was the Hungarian Vaterländische Papierfabriks AG, where the BCA was represented with two board members. Through its strong involvement in the paper industry the Boden-Credit-Anstalt had secured a far-reaching influence upon Viennese newspapers. The *Neues Wiener Tag*- resp. *Abendblatt*, for example, were owned by Steyrermühl AG. The Österreichische Journal AG, on whose board Stein acted as vice-president, edited the *Neue Freie Presse*. As Sieghart was associated with the Christian Social Party the strong bank interest in the paper industry secured him political influence, too.[36]

The Association for Chemical and Metallurgical Production (Spolek pro chemickou a hutní výrobu) in Ústí nad Labem was one of the biggest chemical combines in Europe before the war.[37] Foreign capital influence was already found in 1917. As early as 1920 the Solvay group had taken over a parcel of shares and increased its influence during the 1920s. Solvay's head office for Central and South-East Europe was in Vienna and the Solvay combine enlarged its subsidiaries enormously during the 1920s. The Czech Živnostenská Banka was the second substantial shareholder in the Ústí works. This concern provides a good example of the fact that the Viennese banks – like the BCA with its five members on the board of the Ústí company and with Sieghart still acting as president until 1929 – were instrumental in helping Western capital to acquire access to the most important Central and South-East European industrial groups. How much of their former influence remained is a question that cannot be answered without studying the minutes of the banks. The same was true of the important petrol holdings of the BCA. The Fanto concern comprised almost 40 companies. The Swiss holding company Vereinigte Fanto AG (Consolidated Fanto Petroleum Company Ltd) bought all the shares that had belonged to the

Fanto group. For this reason a syndicate led by the BCA and consisting of the banking houses Schröder, London, and J.P. Morgan, New York, the Mutuelle Mobilière et Immobilière, Brussels, the Swiss Bankgesellschaft and the Živnostenská Banka, Prague, had been formed in 1923.[38] The BCA had three interlocking directorates with the AG für Mineralölindustrie vorm. D. Fanto (the vice-president of the BCA, Herzfeld, was the president of the company) and two interlockings with the Hungarian and Czechoslovak Fanto works respectively. With regard to the sugar industry the Schoeller group of companies had already belonged to the BCA's sphere of interest in 1917. After the war the business had to be shared with the Živnostenská Banka. In 1928 Schoeller & Co. sold their shares to the Czechoslovak bank which now held the majority of the stock. The influence of the BCA had considerably shrunk. A strong link to sugar companies was formed through board member Skene, who was the president of five sugar factories. The board member Bloch-Bauer presided over the Czechoslovak company AG für Zuckerindustrie. With regard to transport companies the most important was the Donau-Dampfschiffahrtsgesellschaft, on whose board the BCA was represented with five board members. Two insurance companies should also be mentioned: the 'Heimat', which was founded in 1921 by the BCA and other insurance companies, and the Erste Allgemeine Unfall-Versicherungs-Gesellschaft (former UB-company).

The banking network of the Niederösterreichische Escompte-Gesellschaft
The NEG did not dispose of a network of branches but it participated in a number of banks and thus created a network of affiliated banks in Austria and in the successor states. It was closely connected with the Steiermärkische Escompte-Bank, Graz (1928: four representatives of the NEG on the board). To its Austrian sphere of interest belonged the banking house Carl Spängler & Co., Salzburg, and the Tiroler Landesbank AG, Innsbruck (the NEG held the vice-presidency).

The sister institution of the NEG in 1917 was the Böhmische Escomptebank (Bohemian Discount Bank). As a result of the nostrification process in Czechoslovakia its head office was transferred to Prague after 1918. In 1920 the Credit-Anstalt transferred all its Czech branches to the Bohemian Discount Bank which changed its name to Česká eskomptní banka a úverní ústav (Czech Escompte Bank and Credit Institution, Böhmische Escompte-Bank und Credit-Anstalt or BEBKA). The NEG was able to maintain part of its former influence, although its participation in the share capital decreased.[39] In 1928 three directors of the NEG were on the board of the Czech bank (Wilhelm Kux, Felix Stransky and Heinrich Friedländer), while the board members Paul Lechner, Ludwig Neurath and Otto Deutsch came from the Credit-Anstalt. The composition of the board of the Czech bank resembled that of the NEG and emphasizes the fact of the existence of a multinational bank network.[40] In 1918 the NEG participated in the foundation of the Bosnische Industrie- und Handelsbank AG, Sarajevo (1928: one board member). The Polish Commerzbank (Bank Handłowy), Warsaw, joined its network of subsidiaries in 1927 (two members of the NEG on the board) as well as the Romanian Banque Chrissoveloni SAR, Bucharest (1928: two members on the board). The takeover of the Bank Handłowy in 1927 illustrated international bank cooperation. In this case it was the Italian Banca Commerciale Italiana which led a group consisting of W.A. Harriman & Co., the Banque de Bruxelles and the NEG. A close and long-standing connection of the Viennese bank (through its interest in the electrical industry) led to the Berliner Handels-Gesellschaft, the 'Hausbank' of the huge AEG concern. The bank's owner, Carl Fürstenberg, was the chairman of the AEG and a board member of the BCA.

In 1921 the Banque de Bruxelles together with the Crédit Liègeois acquired shares with a nominal value of 50 million crowns and could therefore provide four representatives on the NEG board. Shares of the same nominal value were bought by the Comptoir d'Escompte de Genève (1928: two members on the NEG board). In 1923 the Schneider–Creusot holding Union Européenne Industrielle et Financière (UEIF) in Paris bought shares with a nominal value of 40 million crowns (1928: one member on the board). The UEIF tried to get a foothold directly in the NEG in order to exert a stronger influence over the Alpine Montan Co. but also over the Czechoslovak mining interests of the NEG. In November 1923 Lloyds Bank Limited, London, and the Hambros Bank Limited, London, acquired a bigger parcel of shares of the NEG. In 1926 the banking house W.A. Harriman & Co., Inc., New York (1928: William A. Harriman on the board), completed the list of Western capital groups which had taken an interest in the NEG in the 1920s.[41] See Table 19.7 for the interlocking directorships of the NEG in 1928.

In comparing the composition of the bank board and the distribution of interlocking directorships of the BCA with the NEG, results were similar. Nine persons were identified as forming the top management of the NEG, and six had been in post since at least 1917. On the board of directors, however, only three out of 26 members had already been represented in 1917. There was a concentration of the majority of interlockings on the leading positions of the bank board, and the leading positions in the main industrial companies connected with the NEG were normally given to members of the managing board, too. Maxime Krassny-Krassien, for example, was the president of the board of directors of three electricity companies, among them the Vereinigte Elektrizitäts-AG, and of the most important engineering and metalworking companies. Siegwart Ketschendorf held this position in the AG der Vöslauer Kammgarnfabrik and the AG der Papierfabrik Schlöglmühl (he held six out of eight interlocking directorships with the paper industry). Stransky was the bank's 'multifunctionary' with no less than 37 industrial interlockings. He was at the head of the boards of the Inwald group of glass companies where the NEG could keep its dominant position in spite of nationalization. Kux was the president of the Alpine Montan Co. whose general manager, Anton Apold, was also represented on the board of the NEG. The general manager of the Vereinigte Elektrizitäts-AG, Ernst Egger, served as electricity expert of the bank. Other prominent Austrian industrialists or bankers were Wilhelm Schrantz, the president of both Hofherr-Schrantz-Clayton-Shuttleworth companies, Felix Pollack-Parnegg, Wilhelm Ofenheim-Ponteuxin, Georg Mautner-Markhof and Oskar Inwald-Waldtreu. Besides the group of 'multifunctionaries' there was also a group of 'veterans' in respect of the duration of their board membership. For example, Krassny-Krassien and Kux had started their bank board careers before the turn of the century.

Table 19.7   The board members of the NEG and their interlocking directorships, 1928

	1	2	3	4	5
Managing board					
Chairman: Krassny-Krassien, Maxime	A	26	9	5	–
Vice-Chairman: Kux, Wilhelm	A	12	3	4	–
Freund, Hermann	A	16	2	–	–
Friedländer, Heinrich	A	1	–	2	–
Kubie, Arthur	A	14	–	4	–
Oppenheim, Hermann	A	12	1	4	–
Stransky, Felix	A	37	6	2	–
Total		118	21	21	–
Board of directors					
President: Ketschendorf, Siegwart	A	14	2	–	–
Vice-President: Krassny-Krassien, Maxime	see managing board				
Vice-President: Kux, Wilhelm	see managing board				
Vice-President: Meran, Johann	A	–	–	2	–
Apold, Anton	A	5	3	–	–
Bäckström, Heinrich	A	–	–	–	–
Bendixson, H.	W	–	–	–	–
Blaschczik, Johann	A	4	2	–	–
Cheysson, Pierre	W	8	–	5	–
Coppée, Evence	W	23	8	6	2
Despret, Maurice	W	13	2	5	2
Egger, Ernst	A	23	4	–	–

	1	2	3	4	5
Feilchenfeld, Otto	C	27	1	2	–
Fürstenberg, Carl	W	30	5	6	3
Goffinet, Robert	W	–	–	–	–
Guastalla, Oscar	W	5	–	5	–
Harriman, William A.	W	–	–	–	–
Hentsch, René	W	1	–	–	–
Holden, Norman E.	W	2	–	–	–
Inwald-Waldtreu, Oskar	A	6	3	–	–
Julliard, Robert	W	9	2	3	1
Kann, Sigmund	C	–	–	2	–
Keller, Jacques	W	3	–	4	1
Mautner-Markhof, Georg	A	3	–	–	–
Ofenheim-Ponteuxin, Wilhelm	A	1	1	1	–
Pollack-Parnegg, Felix	A	2	2	3	–
Schrantz, Wilhelm	A	3	2	–	–
Terestchenko, Michael	W	–	–	–	–
Thys, William	W	8	–	35	9
Urban, Johannes	A	2	–	–	–
Total		192	37	79	18
Whole board*		310	58	100	18

Notes:
1 Origin.
2 Number of industrial interlockings.
3 Leading positions in industrial companies (defined as in Table 19.4).
4 Number of interlockings with other banks.
5 Leading positions in banks.
Abbreviations:
  A – Austrian representative
  C – Czechoslovak representative
  W – Representative of Western capital group
*There were also ten 'entitled directors' included in the database.
Together they held 11 seats in industrial joint-stock companies.
Six vice-directors mentioned in *Compass 1929* had no interlocking directorships.

Source: *Compass 1929*, vol. *Österreich*, list of the board members of the Niederösterreichische Escompte-Gesellschaft on p. 378; vol. *Personenverzeichnis* (*Verwaltungsräte und Direktoren*).

The NEG board of directors had a strong multinational character. Of the 26 members of the board of directors fourteen were representatives of Western capital groups. H. Bendixson and Norman E. Holden (Haes & Sons) came from London, Pierre Cheysson and Michael Terestchenko from Paris. Cheysson represented the Schneider–Creusot group. Five members came from Brussels, four of them, Maurice Despret, Oscar Guastalla, William Thys and Evence Coppée, from the Banque de Bruxelles. Baron Coppée and Despret were experts in the mining industry. Thys had 35 interlocking directorships with other, mainly Belgian banks. One of the most prominent members of the board of directors was Carl Fürstenberg, the owner of the Berliner Handels-Gesellschaft. Besides being the chairman of the AEG in Berlin he had a further 30 industrial interlockings. Fürstenberg also built the link to the Vereinigte Stahlwerke AG, which had taken over the majority of the Alpine shares. René Hentsch represented the Swiss banking house Hentsch & Cie. The Swiss Comptoir d'Escompte de Genève placed its general manager, Jacques Keller, and its president, Robert Julliard, on the board. Two members came from the Czech Escompte Bank in Prague: Otto Feilchenfeld was a member of its managing board, Sigmund Kann a member of its board of directors.

The industrial combine of the NEG in 1928
There were 189 interlocking directorships (about 58 per cent of all interlockings of the NEG board members included in the data base) which connected the Austrian board members with 113 industrial companies (see Table 19.8) According to the regional distribution of these companies more than 60 per cent were Austrian (69 companies) which underlined the efforts of the NEG to concentrate its business relations on domestic industry. Of the companies 22 were situated in Czechoslovakia, eight undertakings were Hungarian, six Yugoslavian. In 36 undertakings the positions were defined as leading. Forty-one companies had already belonged to the concern of the bank in 1917. A sample of 59 companies served as the basis for a detailed investigation of the activities of the NEG: fourteen had been founded by the bank; five had been transformed into joint-stock companies by the NEG. In two other cases *Compass* mentions a participation in the equity. In 35 companies the increase of capital and the purchase of shares were the result of bank activity. There were fourteen companies whose shares had been issued or had been introduced to the stock exchange by the NEG. With regard to distribution – by industry engineering and metalworking had lost its leading position to the electrical industry. The NEG concentrated its business policy on the 'new' industries, which was also underlined by the rapid expansion of the chemical industry (mainly under foreign capital influence) which had outstripped the mining and metallurgy companies according to the number of interlocking directorships (see Table 19.8). The disintegrational effects of the dissolution of the Habsburg Monarchy on the concern of the bank will now be investigated in detail.

Table 19.8   Distribution of the interlocking directorships[1] of the NEG by industry, 1917 and 1928

Industry[2]	1917			1928		
	NoI	NoC	NoLP	NoI	NoC	NoLP
Hotels	3	1	1	–	–	–
Building (materials) industry	9	5	3	14	8	5
Glass industry	6	3	2	10	5	4
Mining and metallurgy	24	10	6	16	8	2
Engineering and metal working	37	22	5	31	15	8
Spirit and brewing industry	11	8	1	9	5	–
Chemical and gas industry	14	9	4	24	15	2
Mineral oil, petrol industry	3	2	–	8	6	2
Food industry	1	1	1	1	1	–
Electrical industry	15	7	4	39	20	5
Wood industry	4	2	–	3	2	1
Leather and shoe industry	–	–	–	1	1	–
Paper industry	8	6	1	8	7	1
Textile industry	10	8	3	17	13	5
Sugar industry	1	1	–	5	4	1
Miscellaneous	1	1	1	3	3	–
Total	147	86	32	189	113	36

Notes:
NoI Number of interlockings.
NoC Number of companies.
NoLP Number of leading positions (defined as in Table 19.4).
[1] Omitting those of Czechoslovak citizens and representatives of Western capital groups.
[2] Branch differentiation according to *Compass*.

Source: As for Table 19.5.

Compared with the BCA the number of interlockings of the NEG with mining and metallurgy companies was not as impressive though this branch was considered to be one of the main industries of the bank in 1917. One-third of the interlockings had disappeared by 1928. Nevertheless, the listed companies included some of the most influential industrial groups in that industry. At the end of the war the Alpine Montan Co. belonged to the NEG concern as well as the Prague Iron Co. and the Poldi Works. There were indications, as already mentioned, that it was the Prague company which exerted the dominant influence. During 1919 the ownership of the Alpine Co. changed rapidly as the Austrian banker Richard Kola on behalf of the Italian Fiat concern acquired a large parcel of shares. In 1921 200 000 of the Fiat concern's shares were purchased by the Stinnes group through Camillo Castiglioni who, in conjunction with the Milan Banca Commerciale, had acquired 50 000 Alpine shares in 1919. After the collapse of the Stinnes concern the majority of the Alpine shares (56 per cent) finally went to the German steel trust (Vereinigte Stahlwerke AG; Düsseldorf).[42] Nevertheless, the personal connections between the NEG and the Alpine Co. remained close. Kux, the vice-president of the NEG, was president of the Alpine Montangesellschaft. The Alpine Co.'s general manager, Apold, was a member of the NEG board. With a capital participation of 13.6 per cent the Escompte-Gesellschaft was still the second strongest partner in the Alpine Co. which had a near monopolistic position in Austrian iron and steel production. The Montan-Union AG served as sole distributors of the coal production of the Alpine Montan and the Graz-Köflacher Eisenbahn- und Bergbau-Gesellschaft. Apold was also president of the Steirische Magnesit-Industrie AG. In 1927 a financial group led by the Vereinigte Elektrizitäts AG (its general manager Egger was a board member of the NEG) bought the majority of the stock of the Silesia Bergbau AG which was founded by the Depositenbank in 1918. In addition to Egger (vice-president of Silesia) two other interlockings led to the company. With regard to the now Czechoslovak companies the industry was a source of heavy losses for the NEG. The bank's influence had considerably shrunk in the 1920s. This was the case with the Prague Iron Co.,[43] a giant among the mining and metallurgy companies. The Prague Iron Co. had together with the Mining and Metallurgy Co. and the Vítkovice Mining and Foundry Works (these three companies were called the 'Big Three'), formed a mighty cartel, the Prodejna sdružených československých železáren (Selling Agency of the United Czechoslovak Iron Works), of which it had a quota of 25 per cent. Business relations had, after the Nostrification Act, to be shared with the Živnostenská Banka and with the Czech Escompte Bank and Credit Institution. Besides, the Mannesmann-Röhrenwerke AG in Düsseldorf had acquired shares in the company in 1921. The shrinking influence of the Viennese bank is stressed by another company which had belonged to the concern of the NEG in 1917, the Poldina hut̆. The NEG still held shares but the controlling shareholder was the Czech Escompte Bank and Credit Institute. Financial groups from Belgium, the UK and the USA have also to be regarded as indirect investors in the Poldina hut̆, because of their direct participation in the joint-stock capital of the Prague and Viennese banks.[44] One personal link to the Czech mining and metallurgy companies was built by Otto Feilchenfeld. He was chairman of the Poldina hut̆, vice-president of the Prague Iron Co., member of the managing board of the Czech Escompte Bank and a member of the NEG board.

The engineering and metal working companies still were one of the main sources of NEG interlockings, though the number of directorships had shrunk since 1917. In 1920 the NEG, Schoeller & Co., the Grazer and the Simmeringer

Maschinenfabrik had reached an agreement according to which the two engineering companies were connected. The former Brünn-Königsfelder Maschinen- und Waggonfabrik (now Brno-Královopolská továrna na stroje a vagony a. sp.) took over the Czechoslovakian works of the Simmeringer Maschinenfabrik in 1925. In both companies the chairman of the NEG's managing board, Krassny-Krassien, was president. This function he held in two further companies, Hutter & Schrantz and Ditmar. Another important link was formed by the industrialist Schrantz, the president of both Hofherr-Schrantz-Clayton-Shuttleworth companies, who was on the board of directors of the NEG. All these companies had been linked with the bank eleven years before. Figures for bank activities are given in Table 19.9.

Table 19.9 Bank activities in the main industries of the NEG until 1928 (selected number of companies)

	1	2	3	4	5	6	7
Mining and metallurgy							
Alpine Montangesellschaft	A	60	5	2	–	x	x
Bleiberger Bergwerks-Union	A	7.5	–	–	–	–	–
Sierszaer Montanwerke	P	1.5 Z	–	–	F 1907	–	x
Prager Eisen-Industrie-Ges.	C	72 Kč	2	–	–	x	–
Poldihütte	C	125 Kč	2	–	–	x with WBV	–
Engineering and metalworking							
Grazer Waggon- u. Maschinen-Fabr. AG	A	2.5	–	–	–	x with VB	–
Simmeringer Maschinenfabrik	A	6.4	3	1	–	x with VB	–
Brünn-Královo-Pole'er (Königsfelder) Maschinen- und Waggonbau-Fabriks AG	C	15 Kč	2	1	–	–	–
Hofherr-Schrantz-Clayton-Shuttleworth	A	3	4	1	F 1908	x with LB	x
Hofherr-Schrantz-Clayton Shuttleworth	H	5 P	3	1	F 1908	x with LB	x
Hutter & Schrantz AG**	A	12	5	1	F 1905	x	x
Kurz AG	A	0.75	2	1	F 1919	–	–
Ernst Krause & Co.	A	1.5	1	–	–	–	–
Lampen- u. Metallwarenfabriken Ditmar	A	7.5	3	1	F 1907	x	x
Maschinenfabrik Dolainski	A	0.33	–	–	F 1921	–	–
Gaswerksbau- u. Maschinenf. Manoschek	A	1.03	–	–	F 1907	x	x
Ungarische Stahlwarenfabriks AG	H	2.4 P	1	–	–	x	–
Electrical industry							
Vereinigte Elektrizitäts AG	A	15.75	4	2	F 1899	x	x
Mährisch-Ostrauer Elektrizitäts AG	C	5.5 Kč	2	–	–	–	–
Ver. Glühlampen- und Elektrizitäts AG	H	16.5 P	3	–	–	x	–
Glühlampenfabrik Watt AG	A	1	2	1	–	x	–
Oesterreichische Brown-Boveri-Werke	A	4	3	1	F 1910	x with DB	–
Felten & Guilleaume AG	A	10.125	2	–	–	x	x
Felten & Guilleaume AG	H	3.75 P	2	–	–	x	x
Elektrizitätswerk Wels	A	4	2	–	–	–	–

Notes:
1 Seat of the company*.
2 Share capital (see note to Table 19.6).
3 Number of interlockings with the NEG.
4 Leading positions (defined as in Table 19.4).
5, 6, 7 Bank activities of the NEG*.
5 Foundation (F).
6 Increase of capital or purchase of shares.
7 Issue of shares or introduction at the stock exchange.
Abbreviations:
   A – Austria
   C – Czechoslovakia
   H – Hungary
   P – Poland
   Kč – Czech crowns
   P – Pengos
   Z – Zloty
*If the business was shared with another bank, the bank was mentioned, too.
**The Hutter & Schrantz AG had two daughter-companies in Niemes (C) and in Budapest. The Czechoslovak government had disclaimed the transformation of the Czechoslovak company into a new joint-stock company because the two firms, considering their production line, belonged together and one complemented the other. Cf. *Compass* 1929, vol. *Österreich*, p. 778.

Source: Database Peter Eigner; all *Compass* vols, 1929.

The electrical industry was one of the branches which was traditionally closely connected with the NEG. During the interwar period the development of hydro-electric power was one of the main tasks of the banks. The Austrian water-power companies thus were foundations of nearly all the big Austrian banks. The NEG participated in nearly all foundations and organized several increases of capital.[45] Together with French and Belgian partners the NEG participated in the foundation of the Hydrofina, Compagnie Financière d'Exploitation Hydro-Electriques, Brussels, for the enlargement of water-power in Romania. The importance of the electrical industry for the NEG was stressed by its board member Egger, the general manager of the Vereinigte Elektrizitäts AG (VEAG), who was found on the boards of fifteen other electricity and electro-technical companies. The chairman of the managing board of the NEG, Krassny-Krassien, was the president of the Vereinigte Elektrizitäts AG, the Österreichische Brown-Boveri Werke and the Glühlampenfabrik Watt and the vice-president of four other companies. Another member of the managing board, Stransky, had eleven interlocking directorships with electricity or electro-technical companies. With the banker Carl Fürstenberg of the Berliner Handels-Gesellschaft the chairman of the AEG of Berlin was represented on the NEG board.

The biggest industrial group which was connected with the NEG was that of the VEAG. In addition to the above-mentioned Brown-Boveri works, the Mährisch-Ostrauer Elektrizitätswerke (in 1928 the VEAG held 22.5 per cent), the Vereinigte Glühlampen Ujpest and the power station Wels it consisted of the Elektrische Überlandzentralen AG in Sierska-Wodna (one board member) and a couple of electricity and tram or railway companies such as the Brüxer, Bielitz-Bialaer, Mährisch-Ostrauer, Teplitzer and Grazer companies. The industrial concern of the VEAG also possessed shares in the Central-Gas und Elektrizitäts AG in Budapest, the Austrian Gasbeleuchtungst AG and since 1927 the Silesia Bergbau AG. In 1927 the Vereinigte Elektrizitäts AG merged with the Wiener Gasindustrie-Gesellschaft. The NEG was also represented by two members on the board of the Standard Elektrizitäts AG in Budapest, which belonged to the industrial group of the Hungarian Vereinigte Glühlampen und Elektrizitäts AG. Through this connection the NEG was also represented in the Watt AG, whose shares had been bought by the Hungarian company. The industrial group of the Brown Boveri works also included a Hungarian (two board members) and a Yugoslav (one board member) company. The stock majority of the Austrian Felten & Guilleaume company which controlled 60 per cent of the stock of the Hungarian firm was held by the German Felten & Guilleaume Carlswerk AG.

The NEG holdings in the petrol industry had come under the influence of Western capital groups.[46] In the building industry, the glass industry and in the textile industry the NEG kept most of its holdings. The bank had a strong influence on the insurance company Donau AG on whose board the managing director Kux was president. Hermann Oppenheim was the president of the Internationale Transport-Gesellschaft AG, a forwarding agency, on whose board Hermann Freund was also delegated.

Conclusion
The collapse of the Habsburg Empire and the establishment of the successor states had far-reaching consequences for the Austrian banking system, though the Austrian banks facing the alternatives of either 'Austrification' or 'multi-nationalization' of their industrial networks decided in favour of upholding their former sphere of interest. The disintegrational effects were investigated in the light of the development of two Viennese commercial banks in the 1920s. The disruption of former economic links was not necessarily caused by the nostrification movement in the successor states.[47] The nostrification did not in all cases mean the total abandonment of the former influence of the Viennese banks but did nevertheless in many cases lead to a considerable reduction. Former monopolistic business relations had now to be shared with Czechoslovak banks. Equally important was the fact that the dominant position of the Viennese banks was considered by West European capital groups as a starting point for enlarging their influence in the most important industries of the successor states. Foreign banks and multinationals (such as the Solvay group, Schneider–Creusot or the German electro-technical companies) therefore participated in the equity of the Viennese banks whose boards became multinational.

This policy, combined with direct participation, enabled foreign capital to obtain influence in the largest concerns of the Czechoslovak economy such as the Škoda Works, the Prague Iron Co. and the Mining and Metallurgy Co. which had been controlled by the Viennese banks before the war. So substantial Western investment took place both in the banking system and the industrial concern and the dominant position of the Viennese banks was replaced by foreign capital. The impressive numbers of interlocking directorships and leading positions which still built a strong link between the Viennese banks and industry did not mean that the banks exerted decisive influence on these companies because Western capital groups often used the Viennese commercial banks as intermediaries. The network must also be considered as a mixture of direct and indirect connections. The banks assembled prominent industrialists on their boards to secure their influence but in the same way the industrialists have influenced the banks' policy towards their industries. The effects of postwar inflation had finally led to the destruction of finance capital. Long-standing credit connections and as a hypothesis personal relations and friendships (in the case of the BCA to the Mautner textile concern, in the case of the NEG to the now Czechoslovak mining and metallurgy giants personified by Feilchenfeld) survived the political turning point and the economic chaos. The continuing need to enlarge the equity bases of the banks resulted, if we think of the Boden-Credit-Anstalt, in what may be called 'disaster' banking. The bank could not get rid of its highly indebted companies. Excessive dividends were paid to secure an 'appearance of prosperity' but the huge industrial combine of the BCA soon turned out to stand on feet of clay. In October 1929 the Boden-Credit-Anstalt collapsed. The bank was highly illiquid with three concerns: the Erste Donau-Dampfschiffahrtsgesellschaft, the textile concern of Mautner, and the Steyr-Werke, Austria's greatest automobile producer, whose 'indebtedness vis-à-vis its patron bank, the BCA, surmounted even the latter's share capital in 1929'. This no longer had anything to do with sound banking principles.[48] Almost as impressive at first sight was the industrial combine of the Niederösterreichische Escompte-Gesellschaft. The NEG, however, seems to have pursued a more cautious business policy after 1918. Its activities were more directed towards Austrian companies and the bank could thus compensate for some of the heavy losses caused by the establishment of the successor states.

Notes
1. The role of the banks was normally not that of the founder of industrial joint-stock companies because the strategy was to intervene only after an enterprise had reached a certain size. More often the banks helped to transform the enterprises into joint-stock companies. The banks then introduced the shares on the stock exchange and/or took over part of the equity themselves – not always voluntarily as the market for industrial securities was not sufficient for the absorption of all the new joint-stock companies. See Richard L. Rudolph, *Banking and Industrialization in Austria-Hungary. The Role of the Banks in the Industrialization of the Czech Crownlands, 1873–1914*, Cambridge: Cambridge University Press, 1976, pp. 102–121; Dieter Stiefel, 'Die

österreichischen Banken am Höhepunkt von Macht und Einfluß. System und Problematik des österreichischen Finanzkapitals von den neunziger Jahren des 19. Jahrhunderts bis zur Weltwirtschaftskrise' in *Bankhistorisches Archiv* 1, 1984, pp. 18–34.

2. Even if the banks did not normally hold the majority of shares in the companies, the possession of 20 or 30 per cent was, in some cases, enough to dominate a joint-stock company. For the reasons see Walter Reik, *Die Beziehungen der österreichischen Großbanken zur Industrie*, Wien, 1932, p. 47.

3. Only occasionally has the accumulation of industrial co-directorships of directors of the major Viennese commercial banks been used to support the theory of predominance of the Austrian banks upon industry. See Jurij Křižek, *Die Frage des Finanzkapitals in der Österreichisch-Ungarischen Monarchie, 1900–1918*, Bucharest, 1965; Karl Ausch, *Als die Banken fielen. Zur Soziologie der politischen Korruption*. Wien-Frankfurt/M. Zürich, Europa, 1968; Eduard März, *Österreichische Bankpolitik in der Zeit der großen Wende 1913-1923. Am Beispiel der Creditanstalt für Handel und Gewerbe*. Wien, Verlag für Geschichte und Politik, 1981. März uses the fact of interlocking directorships in spite of restrictive remarks as an indication of a far-reaching sphere of bank influence, cf. pp. 75–98; Hans Kernbauer and Fritz Weber, 'Die Wiener Großbanken in der Zeit der Kriegs- und Nachkriegsinflation (1914–1922)', in *Die Erfahrung der Inflation im internationalen Zusammenhang und Vergleich*, ed. by Gerald D. Feldman et al., Berlin New/York, 1984, pp. 142–87.

4. The Swedish example was investigated by Jan Ottosson, to whom I am also indebted for valuable methodical suggestions with regard to the implication of the phenomenon of interlocking directorships. For a survey of the different lines of research see Jan Ottosson, *Network Analysis and Interlocking Directors in Interwar Sweden*. Paper presented at the London School of Economics, Business History Unit, London, 1989, esp. pp. 4–8.

5. John Sonquist and Thomas Koenig, 'Examining Corporate Interconnections through Interlocking Directorates' in *Power and Control*, ed. by T.R. Burns and W. Buckley, Beverly Hills, 1976, pp. 53–83.

6. Reik mentions merger tendencies in the field of locomotive engineering, the brewing and the rubber industry. See Reik, op. cit., note 2, p. 89. See also Alois Mosser and Alice Teichova, 'Investment Behaviour of Industrial Joint-Stock Companies and Industrial Shareholding by the Österreichische Credit-Anstalt: Inducement or Obstacle to Renewal and Change in Industry in Interwar Austria', in *The Role of Banks in the Interwar Economy*, ed. Harold James, Håkan Lindgren and Alice Teichova, Cambridge, Cambridge University Press, 1991, pp. 122–57. The influence of the phenomenon of interlocking directorships on business policy, on the production line and on marketing will be one of the main questions to be analysed in further studies.

7. It is important to mention that this number could be misleading because all board members of the Viennese banks were included and the representatives of Western capital were connected with a number of companies which had nothing to do with the industrial holdings of the Viennese banks.

8. See Peter Eigner and Andreas Weigl, *The Network of Directors – Interlocking Directorates of the 10 Major Viennese Banks and Industry in the Interwar-Period*, Paper for the Banks & Customers Conference, London School of Economics (Business History Unit), vol. 6, 1991, pp. 6–10.

9. See Alice Teichova and P.L. Cottrell, 'Industrial Structures in West and East Central Europe during the Inter-war Period', in *International Business and Central Europe 1918–1939*, ed. by Alice Teichova and P.L. Cottrell, Leicester, Leicester University Press, 1983, pp. 33–5.

10. Nevertheless, considerable differences between the banks were found as the example of the Credit-Anstalt shows. In 1913 out of 23 board members seven had been working for the bank since – at least – 1894, in 1919 out of 21 only two. A fundamental change took place after the 'Anschluß'. Out of eighteen board members in 1939 fifteen had entered the board only the year before.

11. See *Compass 1918*, vol. I, p. 277.

12. See Rudolf Sieghart, *Die letzten Jahrzehnte einer Großmacht*, Berlin, Ullstein, 1932, p.182.

13. To avoid misunderstandings in terminology a differentiation between three different levels of bank board hierarchy was made: the board of directors (Verwaltungs- or Administrationsrat), the executive board (Direktion) and at the top of the banks the managing board (Vorstand).

14. See Stiefel, op. cit., note 1.
15. Leading positions defined as: President of the board of directors, chairman, general manager or owner.
16. The governor had to be accepted by the monarch. Baron Chlumecky was a former minister. Baron Giannelia was the secretary and the administrator of property of Archduke Rainer.
17. Fritz Weber, 'Die österreichischen Großbanken in der Zwischenkriegszeit', in *Christliche Demokratie*, 4, 1985, pp. 323–57.
18. Alice Teichova 'Versailles and the Expansion of the Bank of England into Central Europe', in *Recht und Entwicklung der Großunternehmen im 19. und frühen 20. Jahrhundert*, ed. by Norbert Horn and Jürgen Kocka, Göttingen, 1979, p. 367.
19. See P.L. Cottrell 'Aspects of Western Equity Investment in the Banking Systems of East Central Europe', in *International Business*, 1983, p. 327.
20. Ibid., list on pp. 335–6.
21. Ibid., pp. 324–5; Karl Gendelin-Gendelmann, *Die Kreditlage in Österreich mit besonderer Berücksichtigung der Kreditbeziehungen der Banken zur Industrie*, (thesis) Heidelberg, 1929, p. 41; *Compass 1930*, vol. *Österreich*, pp. 256–7.
22. Cf. Cottrell, op. cit., note 19, p. 325.
23. Cf. *Compass 1929*, vol. *Österreich*, p. 281. There was no detailed information on the Neue Wiener Sparkasse, but its board of directors consisted of twelve members, all of whom, with one exception, were found on the board of the BCA.
24. Cf. Gendelin-Gendelmann, op. cit., note 21, p. 93.
25. Some members lived in Vienna but had summer residencies in Czechoslovakia (e.g. Ferdinand Bloch-Bauer). They were treated as Austrians.
26. Names that recur many times on bank and industrial boards indicate that there was a more or less hidden network of fathers, sons and uncles. The reputation of the board members in the Austrian economy was also stressed through their leading positions in some economic associations. Julius Stern was president of the Chamber of the Viennese stock exchange, Leopold Langer held this position in the committee of the Viennese Merchants and Traders. Emanuel Weissenstein was president of the Association of the Austrian Textile Industry.
27. Cf. Claude Ph. Beaud, 'The Interests of the Union Européenne in Central Europe', in *International Business*, 1983, p. 375; Eric Bussière, 'The Interests of the Banque de l'Union parisienne in Czechoslovakia, Hungary and the Balkans, 1919–1930', *International Business*, 1983, pp. 400–401; Cottrell, op. cit., note 19, p. 324.
28. Ibid., p. 322.
29. The sources of most importance were the above-mentioned thesis of Gendelin-Gendelmann (Note 21): industrial combine of the BCA: pp. 93–5; industrial combine of the NEG: pp. 96–8, and Egon Scheffer, *Der Siegeszug des Leihkapitals*, Wien, Burgverlag, list of the industrial combines, 1924, pp 389–98. See also Reik, op. cit., note 2, pp. 43–5. In the book *10 Jahre Nachfolgestaaten*, ed. by Walther Federn, Wien, 1928, I took the information given by the advertisements of the Boden-Credit Anstalt (p. 235) and of the Niederösterreichische Escompte-Gesellschaft (p. 236).
30. With regard to foundations, participations, transformations into joint-stock companies, mergers, reorganizations, syndicates, increases of capital, purchase of shares, issue of shares and introductions at the stock exchange. Share capital, headquarters and further information on the companies were taken from the *Compass* volumes for Austria and the successor states of the year 1929. I only considered the number of interlockings of the Austrian members. The same procedure was carried out for the NEG. Some corrections had to be made because the information given by the *Personenverzeichnis* of the *Compass* was sometimes inconsistent with the other *Compass* volumes. For more detailed information on single companies see Peter Eigner, *Industrial Combines and the Network of Bank-Relations of the Allgemeine Österreichische Boden-Credit-Anstalt and the Niederösterreichische Escompte-Gesellschaft in 1928*, paper presented at the conference on '20th Century Universal Banking: International Comparisons', vol. II, Budapest, 1992.
31. See *Compass 1929*, vol. *Čechoslovakei*, pp. 1141–2.
32. See Alice Teichova, *An Economic Background to Munich. International Business and Czechoslovakia 1918–1938*, Cambridge, Cambridge University Press, 1974, pp. 92–107; Beaud, op cit.,

note 27, figure 14.1, pp 382, 385–6; see also Beaud, 'Investments and Profits of the Multinational Schneider Group 1894–1943', in *Multinational Enterprise in Historical Perspective*, ed. by Alice Teichova, Maurice Lévy-Leboyer and Helga Nussbaum, Cambridge, Cambridge University Press, 1986, pp. 98–9.

33. See Beaud, op. cit., note 27, figure 14.1, p. 382.
34. See Franz Mathis, *Big Business in Österreich. Österreichische Großunternehmen in Kurzdarstellungen*, vol. I, Wien, Verlag für Geschichte und Politik, 1987, pp. 57–62.
35. Thus Siemens was soon represented in Czechoslovakia, Yugoslavia, Romania and Bulgaria. The same was true of the AEG. A new contract between the German and the Austrian company was signed in 1921. The Austrian company served as the headquarters for the Czechoslovak and the Hungarian enterprises and held 75 per cent of their equity in its portfolio. The decisive influence was exerted by the German headquarters though it only held a minority of the equity of the Austrian company. See Peter Hertner, 'Financial Strategies and Adaptation to Foreign Markets: the German Electro-technical Industry and its Multinational Activities: 1890s, to 1939', p. 152; Harm Schröter, 'A Typical Factor of German International Market Strategy: Agreements between the US and German Electrotechnical Industries up to 1939', p. 161, both in *Multinational Enterprise*, 1986; cf. also *Compass 1929*, vol. *Österreich*, 1091–3; Mathis, op. cit., note 34, vol. I, pp. 17–19.
36. See Ausch, op. cit., note 3, pp. 307–34.
37. See Teichova, op. cit., note 32, pp. 279–84; *Compass 1930*, vol. *Čechoslovakei*, pp. 980–84.
38. See *Compass 1929*, vol. *Österreich*, p. 998, pp. 1023–5.
39. See Herbert Matis, 'Disintegration and Multi-National Enterprises in Central Europe during the Post-war Years (1918-23)', in *International Business*, 1983, pp. 88–90.
40. The Czechoslovaks Feilchenfeld and Kann held positions in both banks. Thys and Guastalla, who were also found on the board of the NEG, came from the Banque de Bruxelles, Warburg represented the banking house M.M. Warburg, Hamburg, and Kleinwort acted for Kleinwort, Sons & Co., London. Cf. Advertisement of the BEBKA in *10 Jahre Nachfolgestaaten*, pp. 240.
41. Cf. *Compass 1929*, vol. *Österreich*, pp. 379–80; Advertisement of the NEG in *10 Jahre Nachfolgestaaten*, p. 236; Cottrell, op. cit., note 19, list on p. 337.
42. See Gendelin-Gendelmann, op. cit., note 21, p. 96; see also P.G. Fischer, 'The Österreichisch-Alpine Montangesellschaft, 1918-38', in *International Business*, 1983, pp. 253–67.
43. See Teichova, op. cit., note 32, pp. 119–24; *Compass 1929*, vol. *Čechoslovakei*, p. 741. The source material as above mentioned sometimes differs. Thus F. Stransky is mentioned in the *Personencompass* as a member of the board of directors of the Prague Iron Co. but is not in the above-mentioned *Compass* volume.
44. See Teichova, op. cit., note 32, pp. 134–5.
45. This group of companies consisted of the Wasserkraftwerke AG, the Tiroler Wasserkraft AG (the NEG held the position of the vice-president and had another banker on the board), the Niederösterreichische Wasserkraft AG, the Steirische Wasserkraft und Elektrizitäts AG (one board member), the Oberösterreichische (one board member), the Kärntner Wasserkraft AG and the Zillertaler Kraftwerke AG (the majority of the shares was held by the NEG, the BCA and the CA).
46. Cf. *Compass 1929*, vol. *Österreich*, pp. 1022–3.
47. Nostrification could either mean the transfer of a company's headquarters to one of the successor states or the splitting up of a company into two companies in two different countries.
48. Sieghart also considered the Fanto petrol concern as a main 'problem child'; cf. Sieghart, op. cit., note 12, p. 198; 'Appearance of prosperity' see: *Der Österreichische Volkswirt*, 12 October 1929, p. 42; Fritz Weber, Universal Banking in Interwar Central Europe', in *The Role of Banks*, 1991, p. 22.

Index

franchise system 120
General Commercial Code 1963 116
gold balances 122
  law on 121, 122
gold standard 179
guarantee fund, establishment of 118
interwar financing 208–14
  liquidity 209–14
  working capital 209–14
joint-stock companies 120, 122, 125,
    202, 209, 210, 212, 213
  control of 116–17
  law 116
Konzessionssystem 120
Länderbank Act 118
Lausanne Protocol 125
leather and shoe industry 200, 201
  interlocking directorships 263, 273,
    285
liability of banks, law on 120–21
licensing law 121
mining and metallurgy, interlocking
    directorships 262, 263, 264, 265,
    266, 267, 271, 273, 276, 277–8,
    285, 287
nostrification 267
order to relieve banks 125
paper industry 200
  interlocking directorships 263, 265,
    273, 279, 281, 285
petrol industry, interlocking
    directorships 263
Postal Savings Bank Act 1926 118
savings bank regulations 116
spirits and brewing industry,
    interlocking directorships 263,
    273, 285
stock market 156, 159
sugar industry 199, 200, 201
  interlocking directorships 263, 264,
    265, 267, 273, 280, 285
sugar production 199
textile industry 199, 200, 201
  interlocking directorships 263, 264,
    265, 267, 271, 273, 274, 275,
    285
trade regulations 116
Trades Inspectorate 116
wood industry 200, 201
  interlocking directorships 263, 273,
    285

Austro-Hungarian Bank 26, 40,
    100–101, 103
  Czechoslovakia and 99, 100–101, 103

Bäckström, Heinrich 282
Bagehot, Walter 59, 60, 74
Baltensperger, Ernst 59
Banco Adriatico 49
Banco Commerciale 51, 281
Banco di Roma 51
Banco Triestina 51
Bank of Athens 230, 233
Bank for Commerce and Industry 133,
    135
Bank of Crete 230
Bank of the Czechoslovak Legions 29,
    134, 135, 148, 151
Bank of England 59, 96
  Anglo-Austrian Bank and 96–111
Bank für Oberösterreich und Salzburg
    126, 268
Bank für Tirol und Vorarlberg 268
Bank Handlowy 281
Bank Małopolski 164, 269, 272
Bank of Norway 12, 13, 14, 17, 19–20,
    77, 78, 79, 80, 84, 85
Bank for Public Enterprise and Works
    121
Bank for Trade and Industry 29
Banka československých legií 29, 134,
    135, 148, 151
Banka pro obchod a průmysl 29, 133,
    135
Banka pro průmysl pivovarský 24
Banka stavebních živností a průmyslu
    24
Banque de Bruxelles 281
Banque de France 230
Banque de Paris et de Pay-Bas 133
Banque Générale de Bulgarie 269
Baring Bros. 109
Bark, Pierre 108, 109
Bauernbank 121
Bearle, A. 183
Bendixson, H. 282, 283
Beneš, Dr Edward 107, 108–9
Bergens Privatbank 78
Bergmann, Adalbert 266
Beverages production 200, 201
  Austria 199, 200, 201
Blackett, Sir Basil 102, 103